The Eighty Years' Crisis:
International Relations 1919–1999

The Eighty Years' Crisis:
International Relations 1919–1999

Edited by

Tim Dunne, Michael Cox and Ken Booth

CAMBRIDGE
UNIVERSITY PRESS

Published by the Press Syndicate of the University of Cambridge
The Edinburgh Building, Cambridge CB2 2RU, United Kingdom
40 West 20th Street, New York, NY 10011-4211, USA
10 Stamford Road, Oakleigh, Melbourne 3166, Australia

First published 1998

Printed in the United Kingdom by Henry Ling Ltd at the
Dorset Press, Dorchester, Dorset

ISBN 0 521 66783 6

The Eighty Years' Crisis: International Relations 1919–1999

CONTENTS

Law and Change

Prospects for a New World Order

NOTES ON CONTRIBUTORS

Emanuel Adler is Professor in the Department of International Relations at The Hebrew University of Jerusalem.

Ken Booth is Professor in the Department of International Politics at the University of Wales, Aberystwyth.

Michael Cox is Professor in the Department of International Politics at the University of Wales, Aberystwyth.

Tim Dunne is lecturer in the Department of International Politics at the University of Wales, Aberystwyth.

Roger Epp is Professor in the Department of Political Studies at Augustana College, Alberta, Canada.

Mervyn Frost is Professor at Rutherford College, The University of Kent at Canterbury.

David Held is Professor of Politics and Sociology at The Open University.

Paul Hirst is Professor in the Department of Politics and Sociology at Birkbeck College, University of London.

Kal Holsti is University Killam Professor in the Department of Political Science at the University of British Columbia.

Friedrich V. Kratochwil holds the chair of International Politics in the Geschwister-Scholl-Institut für Politische Wissenschaft at the Ludwig-Maximilians-Universität, München.

Anthony McGrew is Senior Lecturer in International Relations at The Open University.

Michael Nicholson is Professor of International Relations in the School of Social Sciences at the University of Sussex.

Jan Jindy Petman is Director of the Centre for Women's Studies at the Australian National University, Canberra.

Georg Sørensen is Professor in the Department of Political Science at the University of Aarhus.

Alexander Wendt is Associate Professor in the Department of Government at Dartmouth College, New Hampshire.

Peter Wilson is lecturer in the Department of International Relations at the London School of Economics and Political Science.

ACKNOWLEDGEMENTS

It would not have been possible to have produced this book, and the associated first Special Issue of the *Review of International Studies*, in such a short time after taking over as the editorial team, without considerable help and advice. In the first place, the support of BISA, and especially the Editorial Committee, was essential. The backing and expertise of Cambridge University Press has been constant and vital, and we would particularly like to acknowledge Patrick McCartan and Gwenda Edwards for their work on this book and the Special Issue. At the University of Wales Aberystwyth we want to thank Howard Adair for designing the cover (and also the new cover of the *Review*), and Steve Smith for providing the editors with more resources than we could reasonably expect. Most of all, however, we want to record our deep and daily respect and appreciation for the work done in the production of this book and the running of the *Review* office by our Editorial Assistant, Fiona Stephen: without her commitment and skills all our activities would be more stressed, take longer and would not meet the same standards.

Tim Dunne, Michael Cox, Ken Booth

FOREWORD

Over the past twenty-four years, under a series of outstanding editors, the *Review of International Studies* – the official journal of the British International Studies Association – has built up a reputation as one of the key journals in our field. In the early days, when the journal was published under the title *British Journal of International Studies*, high quality was established somewhat at the expense of quantity and the majority of authors published were British – Volume I, No. 1 was just 76 pages long and all seven contributors were British scholars at British Universities. Today the same high standard is maintained, but regular issues now reach around twice that length, and although the *Review* remains a British journal the authors it publishes are drawn from a much wider range of nationalities. As the journal of a professional association, the *Review* is obliged to eschew niche marketing and to publish important work drawn from all fields of international studies; as more and more journals become overspecialized and devoted to a narrow body of material, the principled eclecticism of the *Review* has been a source of strength not weakness.

Pace this eclecticism, it is clear that there is a strong case to be made for occasionally clustering articles on particular themes, and this also has become a feature of the *Review*. Now, in a logical extension of this latter practice, we are pleased to present the first of what will be a series of Special Issues published by the *Review* – The Eighty Years' Crisis: International Relations 1919–1999. Here are exhibited all the virtues referred to above: twelve strong essays by leading authorities, the majority British but with six other nationalities represented, and covering a wide range of material from a variety of perspectives. The essays collected here reflect the British base of the *Review*, but they also demonstrate the links between that base and the wider world of international relations scholarship. It is safe to say that this collection will become an important reference point for the future development of international studies as well as finding wide use in the classroom as a teaching text.

The British International Studies Association is proud to be associated with this new venture and offers its congratulations to Michael Cox and his colleagues, Ken Booth, Tim Dunne and Fiona Stephen at the University of Wales, Aberystwyth. Our thanks to them and to Patrick McCartan, Gwenda Edwards and their colleagues at Cambridge University Press. We look forward to future Special Issues and, of course, to the regular issues of 1999, the twenty-fifth anniversay volume of the *Review*.

Chris Brown
Chair, British International Studies Association
September, 1998

Introduction:
The Eighty Years' Crisis

TIM DUNNE, MICHAEL COX, KEN BOOTH

It is fitting that Carr's *The Twenty Years' Crisis* should be the point of departure for this collection of essays on the state of the discipline.[1] Many of the arguments and dilemmas in Carr's *The Twenty Years' Crisis* are relevant to the theory and practice of international politics today. One obvious parallel is that Carr wrote the book against the backdrop of a transition in the organisation and conduct of world politics. In his view, the crisis at the end of the 1930s was brought about by a collapse in the whole edifice of liberal-idealist thinking which had permeated theory and practice in the inter-war period.[2] Sixty years on, another sense of crisis pervades the discipline. The Cold War is over yet there is no consensus on what has replaced it. The best we can do it seems is to define our 'post'-Cold War era only in terms of what it is not. And like Carr's analysis of the 1930s, the uncertainty evident in our thinking about world politics today needs to be situated in the context of a broader intellectual transformation. One possible explanation for the lack of consensus runs deeper than merely acknowledging that the certainties of the past have gone, rather, it questions whether we can even know the world at all. Thus at the same time as we are trying to come to terms with a 'turbulent world', the epistemic foundations of truth and reason are also coming under siege from different intellectual quarters.

To underline the point that E. H. Carr provides the inspiration behind the volume, we have not only exploited the title of his best-known book in international relations, we have also borrowed his chapter titles and section headings in what follows. The fact that this was easily possible, offers clear testimony to the continuing relevance of Carr's questions—and indeed some of his answers. Carr has occasionally been criticised for his elastic use of the word 'crisis' in the title of his book, on the grounds that it should only be used to refer to very short periods of intense danger: we have stretched it further still, and we think with good cause. The years since 1919 have witnessed the two most destructive wars in history and the possibility of nuclear Armageddon for over 50 of them; there have been hundreds of inter-state wars and even more civil strife. States have collapsed and come into being, sometimes violently. The technological threat to humanity posed by military innovation has expanded alarmingly, and now includes the danger of biological weaponry. The threat to the global environment has become increasingly apparent over these years; sustainability remains out of reach for the majority of the world's growing population. Inequalities in the global economy and hierarchies of political

---

[1] First published in the *Review of International Studies* 24.5 (1998).
[2] E.H. Carr, *The Twenty Years' Crisis: An Introduction to the Study of International Relations* (London: Macmillan, 1939), p. 62.

power have resulted in the silent genocide of the poor and malnourished. Casualties of the global political economy, from wasted individual lives to collapsing economies in Russia and parts of Asia, bring up to date Carr's critique of liberal illusions—this time those of the triumphalists of 1989. Against this backdrop, who would not call these eight decades a 'crisis' on a world historical scale? We think Carr would have done.[3]

Within a few years of publishing *The Twenty Years' Crisis*, Carr himself admitted to being rather reticent about the work. It was merely, in his words, 'a study of the period' which 'must be treated on its merits as such'.[4] Judging by the subsequent importance of the book in the historiography of international relations, it would be fair to say that Carr's assessment has not been shared widely within the discipline. Successive generations of scholars have read it as an introductory text only to return to it and discover new meanings and overlooked phrases in later years. It has sold a remarkably high number of copies for an academic text.[5] In our judgement, *The Twenty Years' Crisis* is one of the few books in 80 years of the discipline which leave us nowhere to hide.

One reason for making this claim concerns the intimate connection between the text and the so-called great debates which conventionally define the historiography of the field.[6] Until the 1980s, few writers challenged the rather heroic interpretation of *The Twenty Years' Crisis* as the winner in the struggle for mastery between realism and idealism. The pivotal part played by *The Twenty Years' Crisis* in the development of the discipline was partly the result of the fact that it represented a moment of unity between British and American perspectives. After the book, realism became the dominant theory in both communities, and very quickly framed the world-views of politicians and other key decision-makers. However, in Britain, the academic study of international relations was institutionally underdeveloped by comparison, and for the most part those who defined themselves as 'thinkers' remained staunchly independent from the policy centred world of the 'doers'. More significantly, most of the key figures in British international relations theory resisted the polarity of realism and idealism that had structured the first debate. In this sense, British and American perspectives began to part long before the 'new great debate' between traditionalists and social scientists in the 1960s.[7] *The Twenty Years' Crisis* is therefore unique in that it is the only great text in the 80 years crisis of international relations which has been equally highly regarded by both major constituencies of our fragmented discipline. Such an achievement has not been

---

[3] For a detailed treatment of Carr's analysis of international politics from the late 1930s to the 1940s, see Charles Jones, *Carr on International Relations* (Cambridge: Cambridge University Press, 1998).

[4] Carr, *The Twenty Years' Crisis*, preface to the second edition (1946).

[5] According to Tim Farmiloe, the Publishing Director at Macmillan, the book has sold 30,660 copies in the second edition alone.

[6] For a powerful critique of the tendency to view the historiography of the discipline through the prisms of 'great debates', see Brian Schmidt, *The Political Discourse of Anarchy: A Disciplinary History of International Relations* (New York: NY State University Press, 1998).

[7] Hedley Bull, 'International Theory: The Case for a Classical Approach', in K. Knorr and J.N. Rosenau (eds), *Contending Approaches to International Politics* (Princeton: Princeton University Press, 1969), pp. 21–38. See M. Kaplan, 'The New Great Debate: Traditionalism vs Science in International Relations', in Knorr and Rosenau (eds), *Contending Approaches*, pp. 39–61.

repeated. Four decades later Kenneth Waltz's *Theory of International Politics* and Hedley Bull's *The Anarchical Society* resonated far more loudly in their own academic back yards than beyond them.

Another indication that *The Twenty Years' Crisis* leaves the discipline nowhere to hide is evident from its appeal to conservatives and radicals alike. Robert Gilpin, an example of the former, argued on the basis of *The Twenty Years' Crisis* that E. H. Carr was one of the all time 'three great realist writers'.[8] At the same time, a leading voice in the emergence of 'critical theory', Robert Cox, cites Carr as being one of his three most important influences (along with Vico and Marx).[9] A similar pattern can be discerned from diverging interpretations of *The Twenty Years' Crisis*. Although it has become fashionable to open texts to multiple interpretations, few have been as controversial and contested. Among contemporary scholars, standard realist readings of the book co-exist alongside rationalist and critical theoretical interpretations.

The contributors to this collection were asked to use a Carr theme or title as their point of departure, but it is a testimony to his work that a number of them developed their arguments with close reference to his ideas. In the opening essay, for example, Peter Wilson revisits the first 'great debate' between realism and utopianism, and shows how utopianism was a 'convenient rhetorical device' which Carr used to label 'a whole range of things he happened to disagree with'. However in so doing he unwittingly provided ammunition to a later generation of realists who wanted to discredit liberal internationalist lines of enquiry—such as the study of peaceful change, global governance and the impact of public opinion on the actions of decision-makers. Wilson also questions the tendency to read the history of the discipline through the prism of 'great debates'. In the case of the first debate he points out that there was never a genuine *debate* as such, since Carr did not respond to his critics, and no realist thinker of any repute rushed to his defence. Moreover (and more importantly) the idea of a great debate not only simplifies and distorts 'the richness and the complexity of the responses and exchanges that actually took place', but has also had a deleterious impact upon the subsequent evolution of the discipline.

While Wilson wonders whether there was ever a 'great debate' between idealists and realists in the inter-war period, Holsti questions how much the Cold War actually impacted upon the subject. As he shows, in the 'era of anxiety' many of the issues explored by scholars were not much different to those which had preoccupied previous writers: war and peace, the conditions of order, and the possibility of justice. Moreover, though realism may have predominated in the United States in particular, international relations during the Cold War was never an intellectual monolith, and different normative concerns drove competing research programmes. Morgenthau might have put the analysis of inter-state conflict at the centre of his agenda whilst Waltz celebrated the virtues of bipolarity. But the subject was far

[8] Robert Gilpin, 'The Richness of the Tradition of Political Realism', in R.Keohane (ed.), *Neorealism and its Critics* (New York: Columbia Univeristy Press, 1986), p. 306.

[9] Robert W. Cox with Timothy J. Sinclair, *Approaches to World Order*, (Cambridge: Cambridge University Press, 1996), p. 27.

more diverse and rich with critical inputs coming from liberal institutionalists, functional integrationists, and Marxists keen to explore the dynamics of dependency and underdevelopment in the newly emergent Third World. Yet there was no escaping the fact that in the Cold War, Americans dominated the discipline. This not only led to certain types of answers being provided, but also determined the sort of questions likely to be asked. That said, the study of international relations according to Holsti still managed to retain a degree of intellectual independence from American national interests. To this extent, while the Cold War may have affected scholarship in different ways, it did not dominate it to the exclusion of other perspectives.

Roger Epp focuses on another approach which remained resistant to both the demands of policy relevance and to the behavioural revolution. In his defence of the English School, Epp turns to Hans-Georg Gadamar's philosophical hermeneutics to tease out its interpretative method. In contrast to the empiricism which infused realism in the United States, the 'data' for Martin Wight and Hedley Bull was the diplomatic dialogue conducted by representatives of sovereign states in the wider society of states. Epp recognises the limits of this approach in that it can only deal with moves being made *on* the diplomatic chess board so to speak. What is left untouched is the wider question of how certain practices are normalised (like sovereignty) and others, marginalised (like the rights of stateless peoples). But it would be wrong, Epp argues, to pronounce the English School as being bereft of critical potential given that new voices have sometimes been able to make themselves heard even in the society of states.

At the start of Part 2, Michael Nicholson revisits the 'realism–utopianism' debate. According to Nicholson, because of the colonisation of *The Twenty Years' Crisis* by the realists, little attention until recently has been paid to the interplay between 'realism' and 'utopianism' in the text, and he seeks to overcome this by way of what has been called a 'utopian realist' synthesis. This position puts values at the centre of our enquiries into the social world, but recognises that there is no alternative to building theories from the floor up rather than from the ceiling down. For example, it is futile to work towards utopian goals such as the renunciation of the use of force or an end to sovereignty if the conditions for their realisation do not exist. As Nicholson and Wilson both note, it is hard to fix a meaning to Carr's political realism. Unlike other leading realists in the twentieth century, he did not prescribe realism as a foreign policy for maintaining and extending the power and influence of the state. Instead, realism was a tool; it was a 'weapon' to be wielded against all claims to a universal morality in order to reveal the partial interests that underlie those claims.

In one of the most famous passages in *The Twenty Years' Crisis*, Carr revealed the interests of the particular lurking beneath the profession of the universal: 'What matters is that these supposedly absolute and universal principles were not principles at all, but the *unconscious* reflections of *national interest* at a particular time.'[10] This thorough-going critique of the possibility of a true universalism is one which many

---

[10] Carr, *The Twenty Years' Crisis* (1939), p. 83. Emphasis added.

contemporary theorists endorse. Critical theorists use it to unmask the special interests of capitalist elites or hegemonic powers in maintaining the distribution of power and resources in the contemporary international order. For post-structuralists, epistemology does not provide a warrant for making the liberal claims about the virtues of sovereignty, self-determination, market liberalisation, and so on.

For some time now, various critical voices in international relations have been grouped under the umbrella term of 'post-positivism'. The contributions by Georg Sørensen and Alexander Wendt consider whether the so-called 'third debate', between positivists and their critics, amounts to theoretical innovation or obfuscation. The discipline, they both contend, has become divided over meta-theoretical rather than substantive issues. Sørensen believes that the positivism versus post-positivism dichotomy is unhelpful; in his view we should reject both positions. In their place, the discipline needs to cultivate a middle ground which recognises the inter-subjective nature of knowledge but at the same time holds fast to a loosely scientific goal of theory being driven by the need to find the best explanation. Not only is Sørensen sceptical about the coherence of these two extremes, he believes that 'the metatheoretical debate in itself tells us next to nothing about substance'. He then proceeds to analyse the traditional 'big questions of war and peace, conflict and cooperation, wealth and poverty' which, in his view, necessitates bringing the state back in.

Alexander Wendt returns to the question Sørensen started out with, namely, what is at stake in the metatheoretical 'third debate'? Wendt examines in depth two texts which have framed the way we think about the third debate. His choice of *Explaining and Understanding International Relations* serves to remind us all of the impact that the late Martin Hollis had on a discipline that was not his own.[11] Whilst acknowledging the importance of the 'rich' distinction between explaining and understanding, Wendt argues that it has privileged epistemological questions (How do we *know* what the world is like?) over ontological ones (How does the world work?). He would prefer to leave the former to philosophy, and concentrate on the kind of 'first-order issues of substance' which dominated the so-called first great debate between realism and idealism. Wendt is critical of the leading American text on social scientific methodology by Gary King, Robert Keohane, and Sidney Verba for different reasons. In their book *Designing Social Inquiry*,[12] they argue that only causal theories can provide explanations for how the social world works. This move, associating causal theories with science and constitutive theory with history, is problematic because it contributes to the 'naturalization' of certain social structures and a concomitant downplaying of the role that human agents can play in transforming these structures.

Taking the injunction to get on with the real business of international relations seriously, Mervyn Frost applies constitutive theory to international ethics. The

---

[11] Martin Hollis and Steve Smith, *Explaining and Understanding International Relations* (Oxford: Clarendon, 1990).

[12] Gary King, Robert Keohane, and Sidney Verba, *Designing Social Inquiry* (Princeton: Princeton University Press, 1994).

positivist distinction between facts and values must, according to Frost, be over-come. In its place, he maintains that our ethical beliefs are in part constitutive of the social world (and therefore cannot be treated as being independent from it). Once this has been granted, the task for normative theorists is 'to reveal our global international social order to be a human construct within which are embedded certain values chosen by us and to show how this construct benefits some and oppresses others'. To date, even those who have made this constitutive move have been unable to do much more than point to the silences and injustices of the prevailing order. What is needed, according to Frost, is normative visions about alternative forms of community and how they envisage human practices developing within and between communities.

The problem with normative visions, argued Carr, is that they are knocked off course by the intrusion of power. Paul Hirst argues that power is a slippery concept, but is not one we can easily avoid; we are driven back to it 'for want of an alterna-tive'. The question he then addresses is how far has power altered since *The Twenty Years' Crisis* and explores this by looking at the same three dimensions of power which Carr considered 50 years earlier: military power, economic power, and the power of opinion. Military power he concludes has diminished in importance, and while war continues to take place within states, the possibility of great power conflict occurring has greatly diminished. Economic power, on the other hand, continues to grow in importance; and though sceptical of the claims made by some of the more extreme 'globalists', Hirst believes that there are very real differences between the present international political economy and that of the laissez faire era before 1914. The same can be said of public opinion. Indeed, Hirst is emphatic: the era of enforced national mass culture is over in the advanced countries as the state no longer enjoys the control it once had. This leads into the much larger question of where power really lies in the modern world. If power—like the economy—has now escaped from the confines of the state, can we any longer talk of power in the classical sense? Here, Hirst takes issue with those who argue that the state, and with it the notion of state power, are things of the past.

Carr was one of the first thinkers to put the dilemma of the modern state into sharp relief. In the conclusion of *The Twenty Years' Crisis* he is keenly aware that the boundaries of the state are inadequate to deal with contervailing economic and social forces. Many of these ideas are developed further in his short book entitled *Nationalism and After*. Taking up this theme, Jan Jindy Pettman argues that the discipline of international relations has been unreflective 'about different political identities, including nationalism'. The reasons for the disengagement are put down to the assumption that political identities are bound up with state sovereignty; as Pettman argues, this of course overlooks the fact that there are frequent conflicts between communities inside states. In her words: 'What makes nationalist politics so powerful and potentially destructive is the way in which the boundaries of belonging can become the limits of the moral community.' The juggernaut of the global political economy is serving, as Carr predicted, to re-configure the relationship between nation and state. With mass migration, diasporic assertions of identity, and transnational identifications, there are signs, Pettman concludes—contra Hirst—that 'we may now be living in post nation-state times'.

The problem of how to effect necessary and desirable changes without war was a prevalent theme in international relations literature in the 1930s. Emanuel Adler argues that the condition (or state) of peace is a practice constituted through collective understandings—mainly collective identities—and that these are best identified in terms of the concept of 'security community'. He claims that a security community transcends both realist ('negative') and utopian ('positive') conceptions of peace by giving us a condition of peace that has positive meaning, is ontologically real, and epistemologically meaningful. Adler argues that, in the context of today, Carr would probably have defined peace very much like a security community, linking moral purpose, multiple identities, and loyalties, and collective institution building. By his identification of the reality of peace with the construction of moral purpose, Adler—in common with several other authors in this volume—reclaims Carr from the realist tradition. The chapter puts empirical flesh on the argument by identifying and illustrating the conditions of peace—the factors promoting the development of security communities in different regions.

One consequence of Carr's work for the development of international relations was his role in broadening the discipline away from its legal institutionalist origins. International relations after Carr could no longer be accused of being a surrogate of international law or international history. But Friedrich V.Kratochwil argues that a heavy price was paid for this retreat from institutionalism in that it made way for an unrealistic understanding of politics. By the time Waltz had remoulded realism into a systemic theory, traditional *political* concerns 'based on common notions of the good and the just' were no longer part of the realist discourse. In other words, in the journey from Carr to Waltz, the discipline of international relation took a wrong turn. Kratochwil attempts to put our understandings of norms and institutions back on course by reuniting politics with law and history. He compares *The Twenty Years' Crisis* and its evolution into the embedded liberalism of the post-1945 period with the 'move' to globalisation. We are, he admits, 'again facing a crisis of momentous proportions'. Much literature on globalisation assumes that the changes brought about by globalisation are compatible with—or even enhance—liberal democratic institutions. On the contrary, Kratochwil argues, 'the increasing disembeddedness of economic processes from its political and social moorings creates distinct dangers for our domestic and international order'.

In the final chapter David Held and Anthony McGrew take up the theme of the relationship between globalisation and the prospects for a new international order. They find in Carr a number of prescient passages in support of the view that the international system is undergoing a fundamental transformation. For example, towards the end of *The Twenty Years' Crisis*, Carr noted that 'few things are permanent in history; and it would be rash to assume that the territorial unit of power is one of them'. Held and McGrew point to a diversity of 'global flows'—in the economic, military and political spheres—to show that we no longer inhabit 'a world of "discrete civilizations"', or simply a society of independent states. At the same time, the globalisation of world politics should not be taken to signal an erosion in the capacity of states to govern or provide goods and services. Instead of thinking about states and global flows as though they were part of an either/or power political relationship, a more mature way to think about the dynamic is to understand how globalisation is transforming the context within which state power is exercised. By way of example, Held and McGrew point to the rise of 'transborder' political issues which blur the boundaries between domestic and foreign politics. They argue that globalisation offers a new context and new possibilities for various political traditions: 'neo-liberalism, liberal reformism, radicalism and cosmopolitanism'. In the coming decades, international relations has an important part to play in illuminating these possibilities.

The myth of the 'First Great Debate'

PETER WILSON

The story of international relations (IR) is conventionally told in terms of a series of 'great debates'. The first 'great debate' was the so-called idealist- or utopian-realist debate which took place in the late 1930s and the early 1940s. It was triggered by a number of 'real-world' events—Manchuria, Abyssinia, the failure of the League, Munich, the slide into war—but most importantly by the publication of E. H. Carr's *The Twenty Years' Crisis*. This book, it is said, had a devastating impact on the discipline. Idealism, the predominant mode of thinking about international relations, was revealed as 'bankrupt', 'sterile', 'glib', 'gullible', a 'hollow and intolerable sham'.[1] The rout, indeed, was so complete that some authors have contended that it led to a Kuhnian-style paradigm shift: idealism, the normal mode of enquiry, was thrown into a state of 'scientific crisis', particularly by the 'anomaly' of World War Two, the occurrence of which it was utterly unable to explain; realism, Carr's alternative scientific standpoint, offered not only a cogent explanation, but also the prospect of accurate prediction and effective policy prescription. It soon replaced idealism as the 'normal science' of the field.[2]

The argument of this paper is twofold. Firstly, it contends that, in the sense of a series of exchanges between interlocutors holding opposing 'idealist' and 'realist' points of view, the first great debate never actually occurred. As a pedagogic device for bringing order to a bewildering array of theories and approaches—'the menu for choice'—that IR has on offer, the notion of a 'first great debate' is not without merit. But as a statement of historical fact it is highly misleading. Secondly, it contends that in the sense of a cohesive, and certainly self-conscious, school of thought, an 'idealist' or 'utopian' paradigm never actually existed. 'Idealism'/'utopianism' turns out, on analysis, to be Carr's clever device for discrediting a whole range of things he happened to disagree with. It is a realist category of abuse. Its subsequent popularity—for reasons of both ideological and intellectual convenience—has had a inhibiting effect on disciplinary development. In brief, a rich variety of progressivist ideas have been consigned to oblivion as a result of an uncritical acceptance—and, indeed, a less than subtle reading—of Carr's rhetorically powerful text.

---

[1] E. H. Carr, *The Twenty Years' Crisis 1919–1939: An Introduction to the Study of International Relations* (London: Macmillan, 1939), pp. 49, 52, 80, 93, 110–11, 118.
[2] John Vasquez, *The Power of Power Politics: A Critique* (London: Frances Pinter, 1983), pp. 13–19.

Responses to Carr

The publication of Carr's book was a literary event of no small importance. It received reviews in all the main newspapers and journals. It produced a flurry of correspondence. It even provoked the writing of several books. There were many references to Carr's wit, intellectual vigour, and the brilliance of his achievement. The economist, Friedrich Hayek, newly ensconced at the London School of Economics, described Carr as a man of 'considerable intellectual distinction', a 'sincere', 'gifted', and 'disinterested' scholar.[3] Arnold Toynbee, one of Carr's chief utopian targets, described him as 'a man of very great ability, with a powerful and trenchant mind'.[4] The Fabian writer and resident of Bloomsbury, Leonard Woolf, agreed: Carr was an 'acute' and 'trenchant' thinker with an 'unusual capacity for historical impartiality'.[5] Fellow man of the Left and future Labour Minister, Richard Crossman, considered Carr's analysis of the utopians a 'brilliant success'. 'With admirable dexterity,' he said, 'he picks up Professors Zimmern and Toynbee as though they were delicate butterflies, and pins them on his board. And there, when his task is finished, is a perfect collection of the fauna of English international thought in the first quarter of the twentieth century.'[6] A *Times Literary Supplement* reviewer considered the book one of 'capital importance . . . as profound as it is provocative . . . Few can be unaware of the need for the fresh and fearless thinking which Professor Carr brings to an urgent task.'[7] The praise of the American political scientist, William Maddox, was even higher: it was, he extolled, a 'monument to the human power of sane and detached analysis . . . utterly devoid of national bias . . . a compound of much human wisdom . . . one of the most significant contributions to the systematic study of the theory of international politics . . . in years'.[8] Even Carr's *bête noir*, Norman Angell, conceded that 'Professor Carr does a public service in compelling those whom he terms the Utopians to take stock of their beliefs.' Indeed, he praised Carr's chapter 'on the relation of law to peaceful change' as a 'brilliant and most useful piece of work'.[9]

Such praise, however, formed only the preface to the far-reaching criticisms, doubts, and disagreements which almost invariably followed. Angell berated the book as 'completely mischievous a piece of sophisticated moral nihilism'. It was an attempt to justify 'do-nothingism' and 'over-caution'. Carr's theory that law, order, and peace were not general interests but merely the particular interests of the rich and the powerful gave 'aid and comfort in about equal degree to the followers of Marx and the followers of Hitler'. Moreover, if true it provided a 'veritable gold mine' for Dr Goebbels. His disparagement of reason, law, liberty, and other ideals for which Britain fought amounted to pessimism and defeatism.[10]

[3] F. A. Hayek, *The Road to Serfdom* (London: Ark, 1986 [1944]), pp. 137–8.
[4] Toynbee to Angell, 23 January 1940, Ball State University, Angell MS, Correspondence.
[5] Leonard Woolf, 'Utopia and Reality', *Political Quarterly*, 11 (2) (April-June, 1940), p. 171.
[6] R. H. S. Crossman, 'The Illusions of Power' (review of Carr, *Twenty Years' Crisis*), *New Statesman*, 18, 457 (25 November, 1939), pp. 761–2.
[7] Review of Carr, *Twenty Years' Crisis*, *Times Literary Supplement* (11 November 1939), p. 650.
[8] William P. Maddox, review of Carr, *Twenty Years' Crisis*, *American Political Science Review*, 34 (3) (1940), pp. 587–8.
[9] Norman Angell, *Why Freedom Matters* (Harmondsworth: Penguin, 1940), p. 47.
[10] Angell to Noel-Baker, 12 December 1939. Ball State University, Angell MS, Correspondence; Angell to Zimmern, October 1939. Bodleian Library, Zimmern MS, 45; Angell, 'Who are the Utopians? And who the Realists?', *Headway* (January 1940), 5; Angell, *Why Freedom Matters*, pp. 37–65.

Angell was not alone in finding Carr's moral stance disturbing. Zimmern felt that the many good things that Carr had to say were ultimately undermined by his 'thorough-going relativism'. The strength of the attack on absolute values, Zimmern contended, had always resided in demonstrating that values 'drawn from a deeper realm' had been misapplied, *not* in denying their existence. But if it was true that no such values existed—'if justice and liberty, courage and self-sacrifice, mercy and decency, right and wrong [were] only matters of ephemeral convention'—then the student of international relations was left in a state of 'blank frustration'. How could he find the necessary courage and determination to build something that was 'no more than a temporarily plausible conclusion'? The values required to promote the good life as it could be lived under twentieth-century conditions could not be evoked, he insisted, 'by running away from the notion of good because it is liable to misuse by the ignorant, the muddle-headed and the ill-intentioned or by refusing to admit that one foreign policy or one national tradition or one political cause can "better" than another'.[11]

Toynbee expressed a similar view. Carr, he said, was 'a consummate debunker', and if debunking were all that one needed his book would have been a 'very important contribution to the study of recent international affairs'. But debunking, however necessary and salutary, was only the preface to the real job, not the job itself. Carr left one 'in a moral vacuum and at a political dead point'. Debunking was barren unless it lead 'to a clearer view of what is morally right and wrong and what is politically destructive or disastrous'.[12]

R. W. Seton-Watson concurred, if not quite with his fellow historian's *sang-froid*. It was, he exclaimed, 'incredible' that in Carr's 'long and brilliantly reasoned' chapter on morality, the Church and the issue of religion did not arise once. Carr's assertion that, whatever the moral issue, the clash between the satisfied and the dissatisfied Powers was one in which power politics were equally predominant on both sides, was one that amounted to 'pagan negation'. It was just this negative attitude coupled with his rejection of permanent values which dominated the whole book. Not surprisingly, when it came putting forward a 'constructive programme', Carr had no foundations on which to build. World federation and 'a more perfect League of Nations' were dismissed as 'elegant superstructures'. The movement for an international union of democracies was dismissed in a single sentence. The cause of small states was implicitly abandoned as hopeless. And all Carr offered in their place was vague assertions about 'digging foundations', 'economic reconstruction', and 'the frank acceptance of [the subordination of] economic advantage to social ends'.[13]

Richard Crossman strongly commended Carr's exposure of the 'liberal or utopian fallacy' of the sovereignty of law, morality, and the popular will, and their 'airy neglect' of the significance of power. He similarly praised Carr's account of the enervating effect of utopian ideology on the will of the victorious Powers, who instead of using their power in defence of the *status quo*, or for the accomplishment of peaceful change, engaged in 'unilateral psychological disarmament'. But *The Twenty Years' Crisis*, as with that other masterpiece of power analysis, *The Leviathan*, led to practical conclusions that were already out of date by the time they

---

[11] Alfred Zimmern, 'A Realist in Search of Utopia' (review of Carr, *Twenty Years' Crisis*), *Spectator* (24 November 1939) p. 750.

[12] Toynbee to Angell, 23 January 1940. Ball State University, Angell MS, Correspondence.

[13] R. W. Seton-Watson, 'Politics and Power', *Listener*, 7 December 1939, Supplement 48.

were made. Carr's exposure of utopianism had led him to 'whole-hearted' support of appeasement, and the 'realistic' admission that since the balance of power had shifted, way must be made for Hitler. But this was to assume that Nazi Germany and Soviet Russia were nation-states on the nineteenth-century model, and that Hitler was simply a 'modern Bismarck'. Such an assumption, however, was an 'illusion as profound as that of Professors Zimmern and Toynbee'. In Crossman's view, the paramount fact of the age was the transformation, not only of nineteenth-century ideologies, but of nineteenth-century power. Nazi Germany and Soviet Russia were not simply new versions of the old model, but 'new forms of political and economic organisation which threaten to supersede the old order of national sovereignty'.[14]

Several commentators took particular umbrage at Carr's scientific pretensions. Woolf argued that Carr's principal concepts were ambiguous, and that no enquiry could be considered scientific if it rested on such insecure conceptual foundations. His whole argument rested on the distinction between 'utopia' and 'reality'. But Carr failed to make the distinction clear. In particular, he consistently used the term 'utopia' in two very different senses. On the one hand, he used it in opposition to 'realism', i.e., to describe a hope or an ideal or a policy 'incapable of fulfilment'. On the other hand, he used it in opposition to 'reality', i.e., to describe ideas and beliefs that were 'unreal' or 'false'. Thus, when Carr described the liberals of the nineteenth century and the supporters of the League of Nations as utopian, it was not clear whether he meant that their beliefs were false, or that their policies were impossible of attainment. Carr had a good deal to say about the falseness of their beliefs, 'but he never clearly demonstrates . . . why their objectives and policies were impossible of attainment'.[15]

In particular, Carr often implied that the failure of the League to maintain peace was 'inevitable' simply because it had failed. 'The first and most obvious tragedy of this utopia', Carr asserted, 'was its ignominious collapse.' Woolf angrily denounced this view as 'vulgar' and 'false'. Failure was not *ipso facto* ignominious. Nor was it true that just because the League failed, it was bound to fail. There was a striking inconsistency in Carr's logic: after all, Chamberlain's policy of appeasement had failed but this did not lead Carr to the conclusion that it was utopian; nor indeed that its failure was 'ignominious'. Similarly, Hitler's policy of creating a new European order based on German supremacy would fail, but neither did Carr view this as utopian.

In one of the most trenchant contemporary critiques of Carr's thesis, philosopher Susan Stebbing, of the University of London, also took issue with the way Carr used his principal words. 'Morality', for example, was a key term in Carr's vocabulary. Yet he never stipulated precisely what he meant by it. He sharply opposed it to 'power'. Pairs of opposites were then utilised throughout the text as corresponding synonyms of morality and power: conscience, coercion; goodwill, enmity; self-subordination, self-assertion; altruism, self-seeking; utopia, reality. These pairs of opposites clearly illustrated the nature of the confusion into which Carr had fallen. Morality sometimes meant 'a system of moral rules', sometimes 'conscience', sometimes 'altruism', sometimes 'benevolence'. But its meaning was never definite.

---

[14] Crossman, 'Illusions of Power', pp. 761–2.
[15] Leonard Woolf, 'Utopia and Reality', *Political Quarterly*, 11, 2 (April–June, 1940), p. 172.

Furthermore, by equating morality, conscience, goodwill, *etc.*, with utopia, and power, coercion, enmity, *etc.*, with reality, Carr created the impression that whereas the latter were significantly 'real', the former were importantly 'unreal'.

This in Stebbing's view was manifestly incorrect. Power was not the only reality. Men's ideals and values were also factors in determining social change. Indeed, Carr recognised this in the latter part of his book. He claimed, *inter alia*, that morality and power, utopia and reality, altruism and self-seeking, were 'dual elements present in every political society':

> The state [Carr said] is built up out of these two conflicting aspects of human nature. Utopia and reality, the ideal and the institution, morality and power, are from the outset inextricably blended in it . . . The utopian who dreams that it is possible to eliminate self-assertion from politics and to base a political system on morality alone is just as wide of the mark as the realist who believes that altruism is an illusion and that all political action is based on self-seeking . . . The attempt to keep God and Caesar in water-tight compartments runs too much athwart the deep-seated desire of the human mind to reduce its view of the world to some sort of moral order. We are not in the long run satisfied to believe that what is politically good is morally bad; and since we can neither moralize power nor expel power from politics, we are faced with a dilemma that cannot be completely resolved. The planes of Utopia and reality never coincide. The ideal cannot be institutionalized, nor the institution idealized.

For Stebbing this was an extraordinary conclusion to what was offered as a 'scientific' analysis. Since Carr presented power and morality as contradictions it followed that power could no more be moralised, nor morality made powerful, than black whitened and white blackened. This was no 'iron necessity' of history, or the nature of states, but a direct consequence of the way Carr used his words. The statement 'the ideal cannot be institutionalized' was a parallel truism. Since 'ideal' was equated with 'utopia', and 'utopia' meant 'imaginary, impracticable, ideal', it followed that the ideal could not be institutionalised *by definition*. The assertion concerning the utopian 'dream' of a political system based on 'morality alone' was problematic for the same reason. It was, moreover, difficult to believe that any scientifically minded professor could deliberately use 'morality' and 'imaginary ideals' as synonyms.[16]

Some of the strongest criticism, however, came from Hayek. Carr was one of Hayek's chief 'totalitarians in our midst': benign and well-intentioned on the outside, but on the inside, totalitarian to the core. Perhaps more than anyone else, in Hayek's view, Carr illustrated the extent to which the disparagement of the individual and the ideal of liberty—in the name of 'maximum efficiency', the 'big state', the 'national plan', and 'scientific organisation'—had gone in formerly liberal England. Following the German 'historical school' of realists, Carr asserted that morality was a function of politics, that the only standard of value was that of fact, that the individualist faith in human conscience as the final court of appeal was utopian, and that the 'old morality' of abstract general principles must 'disappear' with the arrival of a new empiricism which treated concrete cases on their individual merits. In Carr's world nothing but expediency mattered. Even the rule *pacta sunt servanda* was a matter not of principle but of convenience. That without such abstract general principles, merit became a matter of arbitrary opinion, and without

---

[16] L. Susan Stebbing, *Ideals and Illusions* (London: Watts and Co., 1941) pp. 12–16; Carr, *Twenty Years' Crisis*, pp. 124–5, 129–30.

a rule making them morally binding, treaties became meaningless, did not seem to worry him.

Indeed, Carr sometimes gave the impression that Britain had fought the last war on the wrong side. 'Anyone who re-reads the statements of British war aims twenty-five years ago and compares them with Professor Carr's present views', Hayek asserted, 'will readily see that what were then believed to be the German views are now those of Professor Carr who would presumably argue that the different views then professed in this country were merely a product of British hypocrisy.' How little difference Carr was able to see between the ideals held in Britain and those practised in present-day Germany was illustrated by his assertion that

[i]t is true that when a prominent National Socialist asserts that 'anything that benefits the German people is right, anything that harms them is wrong' he is merely propounding the same identification of national interest with universal right which has already been established for English-speaking countries by [President] Wilson, Professor Toynbee, Lord Cecil, and many others.

In addition, did Carr realise, Hayek asked, that his assertion that 'we can no longer find much meaning in the distinction familiar to nineteenth century thought between "society" and "state"', was precisely the doctrine of Carl Schmitt, the leading Nazi theoretician of totalitarianism, and the essence of the definition of that term that Schmitt himself had invented? Similarly, did he realise that the view that 'the mass production of opinion is the corollary of the mass-production of goods', and that 'the prejudice which the word propaganda still exerts in many minds to-day is closely parallel to the prejudice against control of industry and trade', was really 'an apology for a regimentation of opinion of the kind practised by the Nazis'?[17]

A 'First Great Debate'?

This brief account of the many responses to the publication of *The Twenty Years' Crisis* shows that although the work is generally considered to have had a devastating effect on the 'utopian' thinking of the inter-war period, the 'utopians' themselves did not feel particularly devastated by it. The general view, from 'utopians' and non-'utopians' alike, was that Carr was a brilliant and clever fellow, but that he had used his cleverness for certain disreputable, perhaps even diabolical, purposes. Questions were raised about the moral implications of the text, its prescriptive value, its claim to scientific status, and its likely effect on practical politics. The answers given were almost entirely negative.[18]

To my knowledge Carr never issued a rejoinder. Nor did any other 'realists' (on the identity of whom Carr was remarkably silent). Indeed, those later associated with political realism who themselves responded to Carr's book, shared many of the same doubts as the 'idealists'. Hans Morgenthau, it is true, considered Carr's work 'a contribution to political thought of the first order'. It provided 'a most lucid and brilliant exposure of the faults of contemporary political thought in the Western

---

[17] Hayek, *Road to Serfdom*, p. 139; Carr, *Twenty Years' Crisis*, p. 100.
[18] For a fuller account see my 'Carr and his Critics: Responses to *The Twenty Years' Crisis*', in Michael Cox (ed.), *E. H. Carr: A Critical Reappraisal* (London: Macmillan, forthcoming).

world'. But in exposing the defects of this thought, he felt, it also exposed its own share in them. The fundamental problem in Carr's work was a philosophical one. He set out to discover a new morality in the political world. But he was equipped with only the vaguest notion of what morality meant. The 'philosophically untenable equation of utopia, theory, and morality', which lay at the foundation of *The Twenty Years' Crisis*, lead 'of necessity to a relativistic, instrumentalist conception of morality'. Morality merely became 'an escape from the logical consequences of realism, which, once it is achieved, must once more be attacked with instruments of realism'.[19] Consequently, Carr had 'no transcendent point of view from which to survey the political scene and appraise the phenomenon of power'. The 'political moralist' thus transformed himself into a 'utopian of power'. Whoever held superiority of power of necessity became the repository of superior morality as well. Power thus corrupted not only the actor on the political scene, 'but even the observer, unfortified by a transcendent standard of ethics'.[20]

Martin Wight expressed similar concerns. Carr had sought to build his science of international relations around the antithesis of what he called utopia and reality. 'Every political situation', Carr had claimed, 'contains mutually incompatible elements of utopia and reality, of morality and power.' But the balance, Wight felt, was not maintained, and the book lacked the 'fruitful tension' of Reinhold Niebuhr's *Moral Man and Immoral Society*. Carr, indeed, was 'at his weakest' when dealing with the principles of political obligation, and the very choice of the word 'utopia' to describe the ethical side of politics 'itself shows the questions that the argument is going to beg'. Carr's book was thus 'brilliant', 'provocative', but also 'unsatisfying'. 'The student could have no better introduction to the fundamental problems of politics,' he concluded, 'provided always that he reads it side by side with Mr. Leonard Woolf's deadly reply in *The War for Peace*'.[21]

To the extent, therefore, that Carr set a debate in motion, it was not exclusively an idealist–realist debate, but also a realist–realist debate. Furthermore, to the extent that the radical proposals for change set out in the final chapter of *The Twenty Years' Crisis* can be regarded as 'utopian' (on which, more in a moment) it was also a utopian-utopian debate. The notion of a 'first great debate' between an idealist–utopian camp and a realist camp does little to convey, therefore, the richness and the complexity of the responses and the exchanges that actually took place (the hyperbole of the adjectives only heightening the magnitude of the distortion).

It is also worthy of note that although Carr did not issue a formal rejoinder, his subsequent work, *Conditions of Peace* especially, can be seen as a reply to his critics in its eagerness to begin the work of construction following the demolition-job of *The Twenty Years' Crisis*. There are, indeed, plenty of indications that Carr took his critics, or at least some of them, seriously. His remarkably sudden abandonment of the twin conceptual pillars of his science of international relations—'utopia' and 'reality'—in all his subsequent works, can be seen as a response, at least in part, to those critics who skilfully revealed the fragility of such a structure. His emphasis in *Conditions of Peace* on the 'great social revolution' of the twentieth century—a

---

[19] The words are Carr's.

[20] Hans Morgenthau, 'The Political Science of E. H. Carr', *World Politics*, 1 (1) (1948–9), pp. 127–34.

[21] Martin Wight, 'The Realist's Utopia' (review of *Twenty Years' Crisis*, 2nd edn), *Observer* (21 July 1946), p. 3. See also C. A. W. Manning's typically barbed review of Carr's *Conditions of Peace* in *International Affairs*, 19 (8) (June 1942), pp. 443–4.

revolution, essentially, of large-scale social and economic organisation of which totalitarianism, Bolshevism, the Nazi revolution, and the two world wars were symptoms—can be seen as a response to Crossman's attack on his static, largely state-centric, concept of power in *The Twenty Years' Crisis*.[22] The final chapter of Carr's *The New Society* entitled 'The Road to Freedom', with its emphasis on positive 'social and economic' freedoms as oppsed to negative political freedoms, can be seen as a direct response to Hayek's fierce assault on him in *The Road to Serfdom*.[23]

The manufacture of idealism

Disciplinary self-consciousness began in 1972. There are few intimations of such consciousness in Waltz's *Man, the State, and War* or Butterfield and Wight's *Diplomatic Investigations*. A veritable explosion of interest in the growth of the discipline—its schools, debates, 'defining moments', and trends—occurred in the 1980s.

The heuristic and pedagogic value of this development is undeniable. It has not only enabled students and scholars of the subject to get their intellectual bearings in an expanding and increasingly complex field, it has also provided an important means of self-criticism. One less agreeable feature, however, is that it has led to the ossification of a category of thought that until that time had been treated by many with a degree of caution, even scepticism. Idealism, which all now agree constituted the first, somewhat disreputable, phase of the subject, has been taken out of the inverted commas given to it by the author of 'The Theory of International Politics, 1919–1969', the first important article on its history,[24] and has become a normal, unproblematic, term of art alongside realism, behaviouralism, pluralism, structuralism, and other widely accepted categories. The problem with this, as Bull was aware, is that idealism is a negatively loaded term *par excellence*: it suggests unworldliness, impracticality, perhaps even woolly mindedness and untruth (the positively loaded term realism, on the other hand, suggesting worldliness, practicality, strong-mindedness, and truth). In addition, it is not a term that those supposedly offending from such traits themselves accepted. But rather a term, like impressionism in the art world or mercantilism in the world of political economy, imposed on a group of supposedly like-minded individuals by opponents bent on discrediting them.

The caution with which a so-called idealist 'school', 'paradigm', 'phase', or 'stage' has to be treated is betrayed by the astonishing array of characteristics that have been imputed to it in the aforementioned historiographical literature. Idealists, it is said, believed in progress, free will, reason, the primacy of ideas, and the malleability

---

[22] E. H. Carr, *Conditions of Peace* (London: Macmillan, 1942). See also Hidemi Suganami, *The Domestic Analogy and World Order Proposals* (Cambridge: Cambridge University Press, 1989), pp. 101–5; and Peter Wilson, 'The New Europe Debate in Wartime Britain', in Philomena Murray and Paul Rich (eds.), *Visions of European Unity* (Boulder CO: Westview, 1996), pp. 41–52.

[23] E. H. Carr, *The New Society* (London: Macmillan, 1951), pp. 100–19.

[24] Hedley Bull, 'The Theory of International Politics, 1919–1969', in Brian Porter (ed.), *The Aberystwyth Papers: International Politics 1919–1969* (London: Oxford University Press, 1972), pp. 30–55.

(perhaps even the perfectibility) of human nature. They believed that morality was absolute and universal, and that politics could be made to conform to an ethical standard. They asserted that in modern society war had become obsolescent, and that growing interdependence would render it obsolete. They believed in a harmony of interests between nations, actual or potential, the foundations of which being variously attributed to capitalism, socialism, free trade, self-determination, and the discovery that in modern societies self-interest lies in cooperation. They argued that war was a product of imperfect institutions, the balance of power, the international anarchy, nationalism, prejudice, ill-will, ignorance, miscalculation, and the machinations of sinister interests; that its elimination was practicable, perhaps immanent; that this achievement would be hastened by the spread of democracy and the growth of international law and organisation; and that the duty of the scholar was to educate the masses in peace and internationalism. They also advocated, as a means to peace, disarmament, collective security, world government, open diplomacy, freedom of the seas, the abolition of alliances, arbitration, mediation, 'peaceful change', decolonisation, self-determination, social and technical cooperation, and the creation of an international police force. They have been held guilty of innocence, moralism, superficiality, parochialism, legalism, optimism, pessimism, manichaeism, and eclecticism. They have also been charged with being the unwitting exponents of the special ideology of the satisfied Powers.[25]

This inventory of characteristics is far from exhaustive. It is sufficient to show, however, that if there is such a thing as an idealist paradigm or school of thought it is an exceedingly broad one. Indeed, if there is anything which binds these views and beliefs together into what remotely might be called a paradigm or a school of thought it is the assumption that conscious, progressive change is possible in international relations. Idealism becomes voluntarism plus progressivism in the international field. Indeed, as I have pointed out elsewhere,[26] this is the definition implicitly given to idealism by one of its foremost students. In an influential article J. H. Herz equated idealism with a breathtaking array of other 'isms': universalism; cosmopolitanism; humanism; optimism; liberalism; socialism; pacifism; anarchism; internationalism; 'idealist nationalism'; and chiliasm.[27]

[25] Bull, 'Theory of International Politics', 33–6; J. E. Dougherty and R. L. Pfaltzgraff, Jr., *Contending Theories of International Relations: A Comprehensive Survey*, 2nd edn (New York: Harper Row, 1981), pp. 4–6, 84–5; Vasquez, *Power of Power Politics: A Critique*, pp. 13–19; Michael Banks, 'The Evolution of International Relations Theory', in Michael Banks (ed.), *Conflict in World Society: A New Perspective on International Relations* (Brighton: Harvester Wheatsheaf, 1985), pp. 2–21; Trevor Taylor, 'Utopianism', in Steve Smith (ed.), *International Relations: British and American Approaches* (London: Basil Blackwell, 1985), pp. 92–107; Michael Joseph Smith, *Realist Thought from Weber to Kissinger* (Baton Rouge: Louisiana University Press, 1986), pp. 54–67; Charles W. Kegley, Jr, and Eugene R. Wittkopf, *World Politics: Trend and Transformation* (New York: St. Martins Press, 1989), pp. 12–15; Martin Hollis and Steve Smith, *Explaining and Understanding International Relations* (Oxford: Clarendon Press, 1990), pp. 10–22; Ken Booth, 'Security in Anarchy: Utopian Realism in Theory and Practice', *International Affairs*, 67 (3) (1991), pp. 527–545; William Olson and A. J. R. Groom, *International Relations Then and Now: Origins and Trends in Interpretation* (London: Harper Collins, 1991), pp. 46–134; Torbjörn L. Knutsen, *A History of International Relations Theory: An Introduction* (Manchester: Manchester University Press, 1992), pp. 184–207, 268–70.
[26] 'The Twenty Years' Crisis and the Category of "Idealism" in International Relations', in David Long and Peter Wilson (eds.), *Thinkers of the Twenty Years' Crisis: Inter-War Idealism Reassessed* (Oxford: Clarendon Press, 1995), pp. 13–14.
[27] J. H. Herz, 'Idealist Internationalism and the Security Dilemma', *World Politics*, 2, 2, (1950), pp. 157–80.

As well as the palpable absurdity of lumping together such disparate doctrines as socialism, anarchism, and chiliasm in the same category,[28] there are two connected problems with this formulation. Firstly, 'realism', the generally accepted (and in many accounts *definitional*) opposite of 'idealism', becomes an exceptionally bleak and deterministic doctrine. It becomes the doctrine that progress never has occurred and never can in international relations, and that the application of reason, except in a day to day, narrowly instrumental, managerial sense, is pointless. International relations become the realm of recurrence and repetition and international theory becomes the theory of survival. There are in fact few 'realists' who uphold this view. Perhaps only the Martin Wight of 'Why is there no International Theory?' and the Kenneth Waltz of *Theory of International Politics*. Secondly, because of the loaded nature of the terms 'idealism' and 'realism', purposeful, progressive, change automatically becomes associated with unworldliness, impracticality, and untruth (and fatalism, international *stasis*, human impotence, with worldliness, practicality, and truth). In a century which has seen the rapid growth of international organisation, the emergence of a complex network of international regimes governing trade, finance, and the environment, the establishment a universal code for the promotion and protection of human rights, the delegitimisation of empire as a mode of political organisation, and the forging of a new kind of pacific international union in a formerly war-torn part of the world, this is a remarkable state of conceptual affairs.

If we take the recent historiographical literature as our guide, therefore, we are forced to the conclusion that the distinguishing feature of 'inter-war idealism' is the belief or assumption that conscious, progressive change is possible in international relations: that 'the world does not have to look like the one we are familiar with' and that through reason, courage, imagination, and determination it may be possible 'to arrive at a better way of being and living'.[29] What explains this remarkable sweeping away of such a wide variety of ideas and beliefs into a single category pejoratively labelled idealism?

A large part of the answer lies in the influence of E. H. Carr. *The Twenty Years' Crisis* is a brilliant essay in criticism, and a work of considerable literary merit. But it is also a polemical work, as Carr himself came close to admitting in the preface to the second edition.[30] After all, Carr did not set out coolly and dispassionately the central tenets of the utopian school, and then proceed, equally coolly and dispassionately, to demonstrate their shortcomings. Rather he built up a picture impressionistically, sometimes by explicit assertion but often by inference and insinuation. In addition, it is difficult to separate Carr's explication of utopianism from his critique of it: there is a sense in which utopianism is a doctrine defined by its defects.

The list of assumptions, ideas, and beliefs condemned by Carr as utopian is in some ways more extensive than the one given above. According to Carr, utopians believed that the purpose of the study of international relations was to find a cure for war (p. 11); that the task of the student of international relations was to convert everyone to his desires (p. 13); that reality could be radically transformed by an act

---

[28] This is not to say that disparate doctrines can never have anything in common. But that is different to saying that such doctrines are themselves part of a broader one.

[29] The phrases are from Booth, 'Security in Anarchy', p. 535.

[30] '. . . some passages of *The Twenty Years' Crisis* state their argument with a rather one-sided emphasis which no longer seems as necessary or appropriate to-day as it did in 1939.'

of will (pp. 16–17); that political theory is a norm to which political practice ought to conform (p. 17); that enlightenment and progress could be achieved through reason (p. 34); that human conscience is the final court of appeal (p. 32); and that the same code of morality is applicable to states as to individuals (p. 194). They believed that war was largely due to the control of foreign affairs by diplomats (p. 24); that public opinion, if allowed to make itself effective, would in itself be sufficient to prevent war (pp. 34–5); that war results from a failure of understanding and that the spread of eduction would therefore lead to peace (pp. 35–6); that there was no necessary incompatibility between nationalism and internationalism (p. 60); that national self-determination was the key to world peace (p. 60); that there was no necessary incompatibility between the economic good of individual nations and the economic good of humanity as a whole (pp. 56–61); that every nation had an identical interest in peace (p. 67); that war had become useless as proven by the experience of 1914–1918 (p. 67); that the creation of the League would lead to 'the elimination of power from international relations and substitution of discussion for armies and navies' (p. 132); and that the League was the expression of 'the organised opinion of mankind' (p. 177). They also recommended, as a means to peace, collective security, world government, disarmament, free trade, the legal prohibition of war, 'all-in arbitration', world federation, a United States of Europe, a 'more perfect League of Nations', and the creation of an international police force.

Again, this list is not exhaustive, but it is sufficient to show the inclusive nature of Carr's concept of utopia. It is not so much a carefully defined scientific concept, as a highly convenient rhetorical device. This is nowhere better illustrated than the in range of actual persons, the thinkers and statesmen, that Carr condemns as utopian. Those he explicitly so condemns are actually few in number, and fairly homogeneous: President Wilson; Norman Angell; Alfred Zimmern; Arnold Toynbee; Robert Cecil; Nicholas Murray Butler; John Dewey; and the international lawyers, Hersch Lauterpact and Leon Duguit. But those he *implicitly* so condemns are much more numerous, and remarkably heterogeneous: Presidents Taft and Roosevelt, and Secretaries of State Stimson and Hull (for believing that public opinion will always prevail and can be trusted to come down on the right side); David Lloyd George (for believing the same with respect to the issue of disarmament); Anthony Eden (for echoing the Mazzinian doctrine of a pre-ordained division of a labour between nations, each with its special contribution to make to the welfare of humanity); Winston Churchill (for failing to recognise the interested character of his denunciations of, first, the Bolsheviks and, later, the Nazis); the *Times*, Cecil Rhodes, W. T. Stead, Arthur Balfour, Presidents McKinley and Theodore Roosevelt (for assuming that the national interests of their countries were synonymous with the universal good); Bernard Bosanquet (for separating politics from economics); Frederick Schuman (for doing the same); Karl Marx (usually quoted approvingly for his realism but in one instance (pp. 148–9) quoted disapprovingly for being dominated by the nineteenth-century presupposition that economics and politics were separate domains); Gilbert Murray (for harbouring the 'illusion' that certain disputes are *ipso facto* judiciable and others *ipso facto* non-justiciable); Hans Kelsen (for entertaining the 'dream' of a tribunal 'exercising not only the judicial function of interpreting the rights of states, but the legislative function of changing them'); Lord Davies (for entertaining the same).

The ideological and rhetorical nature (and, indeed, utility) of one of Carr's two key concepts could hardly be clearer: utopia is a weapon framed for the furtherance of Carr's preferences; an ingenious device for belabouring those who failed to assail the *status quo*.[31]

The influence of Carr on later accounts of inter-war 'idealism'/'utopianism' is unmistakable, both in terms of the nature of this putative doctrine and the attitude generally displayed towards it. But in one key respect later accounts have departed from Carr's account, and it is this difference which explains the emergence of an implicit definition of idealism as general as 'belief that conscious, progressive change is possible in international relations' (and the bleak corollary that realism means conscious, progressive change is impossible).

Carr did not believe that such change was impossible. The author who affirmed that 'the clash of interests is real and inevitable' (p. 77), that 'politics is not a function of ethics, but ethics of politics' (p. 82), and that 'there can be no reality outside the historical process' (p. 85), was also the author who advocated 'free housing, free motor cars, and free clothing' as part of a social programme of 'economically unremunerative expenditure' (pp. 304–5), who called for the extension of such a social programme beyond the national frontier (pp. 306–7), and who advocated 'practical international co-operation'—involving 'far-reaching schemes of international public works'—as a 'psychological substitute for war'.[32] The author who condemned a United States of Europe as a 'purely utopian project' (p. 39) was also the author who proposed the creation of a whole range of European institutions including a European Relief Commission, a European Transport Corporation, a 'Bank of Europe', and, overseeing them all, a European Planning Authority (the 'master-key to the problem of post-war settlement').[33] The author who branded utopianism as 'bankrupt', 'sterile', 'glib', 'a hollow and intolerable sham', was also the author who declared that 'any sound political thought must be based on elements of both utopia and reality' (p. 118), that realism which ignores the element of morality in international relations is an 'unreal kind of realism' (p. 302), and that peaceful change (surely not an exclusively 'utopian' concept?) 'can only be achieved through a compromise between the utopian conception of a common feeling of right and the realist conception of a mechanical adjustment to a changed equilibrium of forces' (p. 284).

There is a radical agenda in *The Twenty Years' Crisis* (and transparently in later works) which many of Carr's critics at the time, wilfully or not, failed to detect, and which has gone almost wholly unnoticed in post-war accounts of his contribution to the discipline. As David Long has observed, Carr's realism was a product of his radicalism:[34] a product of his broadly Marxist, certainly dialectical materialist, conception of the historical process. The slayer of utopianism and champion of

---

[31] It will be remembered that, in two of the most important passages in *The Twenty Years' Crisis*, Carr said: 'the intellectual theories and ethical standards of utopianism, far from being the expression of absolute and *a priori* principles, are historically conditioned, being both products of circumstances and weapons framed for the furtherance of interests' (p. 87); and that '[i]nternational morality, as expounded by most contemporary Anglo-Saxon writers, is now little more than a convenient weapon for belabouring those who assail the *status quo*' (p. 187).

[32] E. H. Carr, *Conditions of Peace* (London: Macmillan, 1942), pp. 236–75.

[33] Carr, *Conditions of Peace*, pp. 242–70.

[34] David Long, 'Inter-war Idealism, Liberal Internationalism, and Contemporary International Theory', in Long and Wilson, *Thinkers*, p. 310.

realpolitik was certainly no conservative. It was not change *per se* which he branded utopian; nor conscious, progressive change; but large-scale constitutional blue-prints for change: the drawing up of covenants and charters and the signing of pacts. In Carr's view, peace could not be achieved by states simply avowing not to resort to war. Rather, the social and economic conditions needed to be right: hence the title of his largely ignored, but in many ways most accomplished work, *Conditions of Peace*. Change, in Carr's view, needed to be substructural rather than superstructural, social and economic before legal and political.

This is the key point of departure between Carr's account of 'utopianism' and later accounts, and along with the general failure to appreciate the radicalism in Carr, the cause of this departure resides in widespread misunderstanding of his position on what he called the 'doctrine of the harmony of interests'. Belief in such a harmony has often been advanced as a key characteristic of utopianism. But this was not Carr's view. Carr did not object to the notion of a harmony of interests *per se*, but to the nineteenth-century liberal assumption of a *natural* harmony of interests: the assumption of a hidden hand which, if allowed to operate freely, would not only ensure the greatest possible freedom, welfare and peace for the strongest and fittest, but would also conjure up the greatest possible freedom, welfare and peace for humanity as a whole. Carr's critique of this doctrine—or more particularly the attempt to apply it in the very changed conditions of the twentieth-century world—was withering.[35] But he did not rule out the possibility of *consciously creating* such a harmony; of 'creating a new harmony by artificial means'. Indeed, the achievement of such a harmony, however temporary in broad historical time, is not only the thrust of his final chapter on the prospects for a new international order; it also receives explicit endorsement in the main body of the text.[36] In his belief in the possibility of creating some kind of technocratic, collectivist, and functionalist New Jerusalem—and not only on English soil—Carr was just as 'utopian', according to more recent definitions, as the 'utopians' themselves.

Conclusion: The dangers of misinterpretation

In conclusion I would like to briefly address two questions and make one clarification. The first question is: if inter-war 'idealism' never existed as a school of thought properly so-called—if it is merely a rhetorical device invented by Carr to discredit a wide range of things he happened to disagree with—then what did exist? The answer is: a wide variety of things: certainly a greater variety of ideas, opinions, and theories than is conventionally appreciated. Writings in the inter-war period ranged from the class-based analyses of the states-system of Brailsford, Palme-Dutt, and Laski, to the power-political analyses of Spykman and Schuman; from the Christian pessimism of Niebuhr and Voigt, to the humanistic pacifism of Russell and Huxley; from the 'peace through law' approach of Noel-Baker and Lauterpacht, to the 'peace through prosperity' approach of Keynes and Hobson. It is true that the great majority of writers on international issues during the inter-war period worked

[35] Carr, *Twenty Years' Crisis*, pp. 102–7.
[36] Carr, *Twenty Years' Crisis*, pp. 65–7, 103, 287–307.

within the tradition of what might be broadly called liberal internationalism, but even here it is important to separate three quite distinct strands of liberal thought: Hobbesianism (advocating a strong international authority to lay down the law); Cobdenism (advocating non-interventionism and *laissez faire*); and New Liberal Internationalism (advocating the construction of a wide range of functional, welfare-orientated, bodies operating between and across states).[37] To the extent that Carr's critique of 'utopianism' was essentially a critique of liberalism, it was a critique of the first two strands, but emphatically not the third.

The second question is: in what ways has the implicit association of progressivism with utopianism inhibited disciplinary development? The answer is that a number of potentially important lines of enquiry were effectively abandoned in the wake of Carr's critique: more specifically, Carr gave ammunition to those, predominantly of a more conservative cast of mind, who wanted to discredit and nullify the entire liberal internationalist agenda (even though there were certain, 'New Liberal', aspects of that agenda that Carr himself supported). Examples of such lines include: the study, normative and empirical, of peaceful change (begun so promisingly by Carr, Manning, and Dunn);[38] research into the economic bases of peace (begun equally promisingly by Hobson, Keynes, and Robbins but largely neglected since);[39] analysis of the development, function, and efficacy of the network of rules, regulations, and agreements which Leonard Woolf, as long ago as 1916, gave the name international government (and which has only recently been recommenced under the names 'governance' and 'regimes');[40] analysis of the effects of what Angell called 'modern economic civilisation' on the authority of states and the traditional means and goals of foreign policy (largely stifled during the Cold War but recently revived in studies of 'globalisation');[41] and the study of the role of public opinion in world politics, and its impact, in particular, on the development of an international social conscience (on which Carr and Zimmern made notable contributions).[42]

The clarification I would like to make is that it has not been my intention to suggest that the 'realists' were wrong and the 'idealists' were right. Many of the

---

[37] See David Long, 'J. A. Hobson and Idealism in International Relations', *Review of International Studies*, 17, 3 (1991), pp. 285–304.

[38] See Carr, *Twenty Years' Crisis*, Part IV; C. A. W. Manning (ed.), *Peaceful Change: An International Problem* (New York: Garland, 1972 [1937]); Frederick Sherwood Dunn, *Peaceful Change: A Study of International Procedures* (New York: Harper, 1937); Maurice Bourquin (ed.), *Peaceful Change* (Paris: International Institute for Intellectual Cooperation, 1937).

[39] See David Long, *Towards a New Liberal Internationalism: The International Theory of J. A. Hobson* (Cambridge: Cambridge University Press, 1996); D. J. Markwell, 'J. M. Keynes and the Economic Bases of Peace', in Long and Wilson, *Thinkers*, pp. 189–213; Lionel Robbins, *The Economic Causes of War* (London: Cape, 1939).

[40] See Paul S. Reinsch, *Public International Unions* (Boston: Ginn, 1911); Leonard Woolf, *International Government* (London: George Allen and Unwin, 1916); Pitman B. Potter, *An Introduction to the Study of International Organization* (New York: Appelton-Century, 1922); David Mitrany, *The Progress of International Government* (London: George Allen and Unwin, 1933); Peter Wilson, 'Leonard Woolf and International Government', in Long and Wilson, *Thinkers*, pp. 122–60.

[41] See Norman Angell, *The Great Illusion: A Study of the Relation of Military Power to National Advantage* (London: Heinemann, 1912); J. D. B. Miller, *Norman Angell and the Futility of War* (London: Macmillan, 1986); Cornelia Navari, 'The Great Illusion Revisited: The International Theory of Norman Angell', *Review of International Studies*, 15 (1989), pp. 341–58; David Mitrany, *A Working Peace System* (London: Oxford University Press, 1943); Lionel Robbins, *Economic Planning and International Order* (London: Cape, 1937).

[42] E. H. Carr, 'Public Opinion as a Safeguard of Peace', *International Affairs*, 15 (1936), pp. 846–862; Alfred Zimmern, *Public Opinion and International Affairs* (Manchester: CWS, 1931).

criticisms levelled by Carr, and others since, at the liberal internationalist thinkers of the inter-war period were valid, particularly with regard to their lack of rigour. Nor has it been my intention to suggest that the 'realists' were involved in some kind of conspiracy against the 'idealists'. On the contrary, the 'realists' have, on balance, displayed greater sensitivity and intellectual integrity, even sympathy, in dealing with ideas they have disagreed with than the 'idealists' (though both have indulged in more than the occasional misrepresentation). Rather, my object has been to show that certain regrettable consequences have flowed from characterising the thought and debates of the time in this bifurcated and prejudicial way. To paraphrase Stebbing, an idealist, someone with ideals, need not be impractical and foolish, nor a realist someone without ideals, or with ideals but without moral compunction. Yet this presumption has held sway in so much modern IR.

Scholarship in an era of anxiety: the study of international politics during the Cold War*

K. J. HOLSTI

To analyse an academic field of study in a particular era assumes two things: (1) that a particular era has properties that distinguish it clearly from predecessors and successors, and (2) that a field of study necessarily reflects or takes on a colouration of actual social conditions. Both assumptions are arguable, but the first is less contentious than the second. The Cold War was in many ways a distinct era, an era of anxiety caused by nuclear weapons, and an era in which diplomatic and military ideas, practices, and norms differed in significant ways from those prior to 1945 and after 1989. There were significant continuities, of course, but one would have little difficulty drawing compelling contrasts between the major characteristics of international politics in the 1920s and those of the 1950s.

The second assumption raises the question whether a field of inquiry does or can rise above current diplomatic, military, and economic contexts to uncover underlying 'logics' and patterns that transcend time, place, and personality; or whether it is condemned to be little more than a shorthand characterization of an age or an apologia for state policies or the status quo. The answer is probably both. E. H. Carr's classic, *The Twenty Years' Crisis*, suggests this. It was an effort stimulated by failures of both policy and of analysis. The book sought to get it right in the sense of a reasonable isomorphism between the observer and the world of diplomacy, security, and war, *and* policy prescription. But what Carr wrote was not confined to the analysis of diplomatic currents in the late 1930s. His book was at once a polemic, an intellectual history, a chronicle of the underlying diplomatic problems of his era, and a prescription for better theory and better policy.

The study of international politics during the Cold War years—roughly the late 1940s until the late 1980s—reflected national priorities and troubling security problems, but except in its explicit policy guise, it was not subordinate to daily headlines. There was a disciplinary dialogue that went on in academe that was fuelled by debates over the adequacy of concepts, methodology, and intellectual purpose.[1]

---

* I gratefully acknowledge the help and comments on an early draft of this paper by Mark Zacher and Daniel Wolfish.

[1] The primacy of intellectual discourse over context as explanation for the development of a field is argued by Brian C. Schmidt, 'The Historiography of Academic International Relations', *Review of International Studies*, 20 (October 1994), pp. 349–67. For the argument that theoretical renderings in the field are formed by both ideology and diplomatic context, see Torbjørn L. Knutsen, *A History of International Relations Theory*, 2nd edn (Manchester: University of Manchester Press, 1997), esp. ch. 9.

The comments that follow necessarily 'lift' a period of systematic thinking about international politics from the much longer context of a disciplinary history.[2] However, the questions we ask about a field at any given time are generic. Typical questions might be: how do we identify continuities and changes from what preceded? After identifying criteria, what are the main patterns of thought or discourses in a period? Which explanatory locations ('levels of analysis') predominate? And if a field of study is a social–academic construction, who defines it, who establishes the orthodoxies, which discourses predominate, and what is left out?

Several of these questions have been raised and analysed in a variety of publications dealing with the development of the field.[3] There is no need to repeat that material, particularly by identification of schools of thought. Instead, the approach here will ask a number of questions about the field during the era of anxiety and provide brief answers. These are *W* questions: what to study, where to study, study by whom, why study, how to study, what not to study, and what was left out?

What should we study?

Theoretical renderings of international politics have always been animated by normative concerns. Historically, analysts have concentrated on the sources of war, the prerequisites of peace, and the conditions necessary for stability, order, and justice. Hobbes, Rousseau, Kant, Bentham, Wilson, or Carr, were all ultimately concerned with understanding the sources of fear, insecurity, and conflict and explicitly or implicitly showing necessary changes to ameliorate those problems. No matter what their methodological proclivities or the structure of their analyses, thinkers have

---

[2] Schmidt criticizes many recent renditions of disciplinary history for legitimizing contemporary intellectual positions ('presentism'). I employ Hobbes, Rousseau, and others not to establish, as Schmidt suggests, a 'false sense of coherence and continuity' (p. 356) but to show that Cold War era normative concerns in IR theory were similar to those that preoccupied certain historical figures. Rousseau and Kant read Hobbes (and each other) and were engaged in a 'discourse' on the sources of war and the conditions of peace—just as Morgenthau and Waltz were. Morgenthau invoked Hobbes (via Niebuhr) in the first chapter of his famous text. Waltz' *Theory of International Politics* probably would have been very different had the author not fully studied Rousseau's writings on war. Stanley Hoffmann acknowledged that the works of Rousseau and Kant inspired his own scholarship—and thus constitute part of the history of the field. See Stanley Hoffmann, 'A Retrospective', in Joseph Kruzel and James N. Rosenau (eds.), *Journeys through World Politics: Autobiographical Reflections of Thirty-four Academic Travelers* (Lexington, MA: Lexington Books, 1989), p. 275. For an analysis of the continuity of analytical themes, see Jürgen Martin Gabriel, *Worldviews and Theories of International Relations* (London: Macmillan, 1994). The view that there is no continuity or discourse between generations separated by two or more centuries does not agree with the evidence. There is a 'classical tradition' that is continuous in the normative problem to diagnose, the perceived images of the world, the nature of actors, and other matters.

[3] K.J. Holsti, *The Dividing Discipline: Hegemony and Diversity in International Theory* (London and Boston: Allen & Unwin, 1985); William C. Olson and A. J. R. Groom, *International Relations Then and Now: Origins and Trends in Interpretation* (London: HarperCollins Academic, 1991); Yale H. Ferguson and Richard W. Mansbach, *The Elusive Quest: Theory and International Politics* (Columbia, SC: University of South Carolina Press, 1988); Torbjørn Knutson, *A History of International Relations Theory*; Steve Smith, Ken Booth, and Marysia Zalewski (eds.), *International Theory: Positivism and Beyond* (Cambridge: Cambridge University Press, 1996); Miles Kahler, 'Inventing International Relations: International Relations Theory after 1945', in Michael W. Doyle and G. John Ikenberry (eds.), *New Thinking in International Relations* (Boulder, CO: Westview Press, 1997), pp. 20–53; Peter J. Katzenstein, Robert O. Keohane, and Stephen D. Krasner, *Tombstones and Milestones: International Organization and International Relations Theory, 1968–1998* (forthcoming).

engaged in a common form of inquiry. It is, first, *diagnostic*—locating the sources of constructed social problems—and, second, *prescriptive*—outlining solutions to the problems that have been identified and explained in terms of etiologies.

International politics scholarship during the Cold War did not alter these intellectual practices and priorities. The problem of international conflict and the search for security provided a significant portion of the intellectual agenda for the field, just as war and fear had suggested the problems for Hobbes, Rousseau, and Kant. The core of the field did not change, although perhaps the sense of urgency and insecurity wrought by the possibility of nuclear annihilation was more profound than had been the case in other eras. One result was the development of a new subfield, variously named strategic studies, security studies, conflict resolution, or defence studies. Questions of security, weapons development and deployment, and strategy became the preserve of scholars and the denizens of government-funded think tanks. In these areas, the nexus between scholar and military officials, and between the university and the government became firmly established. Although the story has not yet been told fully, probably the relationship helped to modify government policies toward caution, for the traditional proclivity of military planners is to win wars. The essential requirement of deterrence theory, as spelled out by academic specialists, was, in contrast, to prevent wars. The subfield was thus an applied science, where the connection between diagnosis and prescription was clear, firm, and explicit.

For the broader field of international politics, the 'what to study?' question was answered in several ways. At the most abstract level, theorists needed to develop a conception of the entire international arena. Three major conceptualizations resulted: systems, societies of states, and transnational relations.

The systems concept was a metaphor borrowed from both plumbing and 'general systems theory', where actors and agents are interconnected in complicated ways, but also in which there are various regulatory mechanisms that bring stability or homeostasis. Morton Kaplan[4] provided the most abstract formulation of a system as relationships between variables. Charles McClelland, Herbert Spiro, and Richard Rosecrance[5] developed the idea in more concrete historical forms. They searched for similarities and differences in the actions of agents that had system-wide repercussions. The main thrust of this type of theoretical endeavour was to locate the sources of system stability and instability ('disturbance'), or chronic war.

Innovations in these works were not only the levels of abstraction, the technical vocabulary they employed, or the relevance of metaphors, but also the attempt to portray a totality made up of numerous parts. In the 1930s, the study of international politics had been foreign-policy oriented.[6] The purpose was to locate generic sources of government behaviour. These included nationalism, geographic location, population, ideologies, and the like. The system perspective, in contrast, aggregated the actions of at least the major powers, assuming that they produced system-wide consequences. In Kenneth Waltz' terms,[7] these studies were reductionist

---

[4] Morton Kaplan, *System and Process in International Politics* (New York: Wiley, 1957).

[5] Charles A. McClelland, *Theory and the International System* (New York: Macmillan, 1966); Herbert J. Spiro, *World Politics: The Global System* (Homewood, Ill.: Dorsey Press, 1966); Richard Rosecrance, *Action and Reaction in International Politics* (Boston: Little, Brown, 1963).

[6] Frank Simonds and Brooks Emeny, *The Great Powers in World Politics* (New York: American Book Co., 1935).

[7] Kenneth Waltz, *Theory of International Politics* (Reading, MA: Addison Wesley, 1979), ch. 3.

(system characteristics are defined by the actions of its components). But at least they acknowledged that outcomes, whether peace, war, stability, or order, are produced by the totality of foreign-policy actions. The turn from foreign policy to systems has withstood the test of time. Most contemporary renderings of international politics, or global politics, continue to see a whole made up of numerous interacting parts.

The conceptualization of international politics in terms of systems never delivered a general theory, however. Whether of the reductionist or structural versions, it left out too much. Reductionist versions ended up with a tautology: revolutionary (e.g. unstable) systems are caused by revolutionary states. Waltz' structural version, despite its powerful explanations about why the system reproduces itself, why wars and balances of power recur, and why states seek autonomy and are concerned with issues of relative gains, cannot explain more. Apparently—given the numerous criticisms of Waltz—most analysts want to know or understand more than just these questions, important as they are.

The influence of the Cold War was not revealed directly in conceptualizations of an international system, but rather in identifying key variables that explained variation in the incidence of crises and wars. The major debate was whether bipolar or multipolar power configurations were more likely to lead to war or peace.[8] There was no definitive, empirically based outcome of the numerous examinations, but the position that bipolarity is more conducive to stability was argued forcefully, though only on logical grounds, by Kenneth Waltz and John Mearsheimer.[9] Both of these analyses reflected a not very well concealed enthusiasm for American Cold War policies. On the other hand, these debates can also be seen as a continuation of an old discourse on the balance of power that goes back to the eighteenth century. As in other areas of 'what to study?' the Cold War gave an immediacy to the issue but did not originate the problem.

Within the systems literature there was also disagreement whether systemic characteristics such as the distribution of power or degrees of polarity mattered more than the domestic attributes of states. Adherents of the view that the nature of polities is critical to an understanding of war and peace outcomes—a position that generated considerable empirical research—eventually carried the day because they discovered strong correlations between war and democracy. The 'democratic peace' literature that emerged in the 1980s proved an effective challenge to the less robust findings of those who linked power distributions or polarity to variations in war incidence or system disturbance.

The second innovation was perhaps less intellectually innovative but richer in theoretical, historical, and policy implications. This is the concept of a society of states, that is, a collectivity whose members are related in more profound ways than mere propinquity or interaction, as systems theorists would have it. A society of states, according to Hedley Bull,[10] is held together by common aims (preservation of states), common institutions such as law and diplomacy, and a common fate. In the 1970s and 1980s the idea of a society of states spawned an interesting research

---

[8] Alan Ned Sabrosky (ed.), *Polarity and War* (Boulder, CO: Westview Press, 1985) and Daniel S. Geller and J. David Singer, *Nations at War: A Scientific Study of International Conflict* (Cambridge: Cambridge University Press, 1998), ch. 6.

[9] Waltz, *Theory of International Politics*, ch. 6; John Mearsheimer, 'Back to the Future: Instability in Europe after the Cold War', *International Security*, 15 (1990), pp. 5–56.

[10] Hedley Bull, *The Anarchical Society* (London: Macmillan, 1977).

agenda that, among other areas, explored how the European-based society of states expanded ultimately to encompass the world[11] and compared historical societies of states such as those of ancient China and Greece, with the European experience.[12]

For some, neither the concept of a system nor the concept of a society of states was sufficiently rich in detail and did not reflect the myriad of activities that tied not only states, but also societies, together. In today's parlance, both world images were state-centric. There is more to international politics than the practices, stratagems, and problems of states. Modern technology has made relations between societies or individuals as important as relations between governments. John Burton[13] developed a cobweb world model that placed heavy emphasis on the sociological aspects of international relations. His work was a foundational source, though not always acknowledged as such, of the efforts to expand the scope of the field to include 'transnational relations.'[14] This effort appeared mainly a narrative enterprise, where relations between non-state actors are described in great detail. In fact, that was its main shortcoming. The field was not ready to pile up an ever-increasing collection of descriptive studies that examined, for example, the relations between Canadian provinces and American states, between Scandinavian trade unions, or between cities in different countries. The proliferation of these studies seemed to be headed toward a theoretical void, and while mention of non-state actors began to appear in most international politics textbooks of the era, they did not displace the state-centrism of the systems and society of states conceptualizations of the world.

There were two other answers, during the Cold War, to the question of 'what should we study?' in international politics.

The 'forces' of nationalism, ideology, and geography that had been identified in the 1930s as the sources of foreign policy were obviously deficient from an explanatory point of view. Not all societies that were nationalist necessarily pursued predatory foreign policies, and not all ideologies were virulent. There was no necessary connection between sources and conduct. Classical figures in the field who put forward portraits of political personality were also unable to explain the great variations of foreign-policy behaviour. Hobbes' and Rousseau's political psychology were as insufficient as Hans Morgenthau's political man who ceaselessly seeks power, either to defend or to extend his domains. System-oriented theories simply ignored the personal sources of policy: the logic of the international system forces states-persons, whether saints, sinners, or bullies, to behave within strict limits imposed by the external environment.[15] The elements of free will and choice in these approaches were minimal In the 1950s, foreign-policy analysts therefore turned to the study of decision-making on the premise that it is not broad social 'forces' or some *a priori* definition of human nature that determine foreign-policy interests and actions, but the goals, values, 'images' and definition of state interests of those who make policy.

---

[11] Gerrit Gong, *The 'Standard of Civilization' in International Society* (Oxford: Clarendon Press, 1984); and Hedley Bull and Adam Watson (eds.), *The Expansion of International Society* (Oxford: Oxford University Press, 1984).

[12] Martin Wight, *Systems of States* (Leicester: University of Leicester Press, 1977); and Adam Watson, *The Evolution of International Society* (London: Routledge, 1992).

[13] John Burton, *World Society* (Cambridge: Cambridge University Press, 1972).

[14] Robert Keohane and Joseph S. Nye, Jr. (eds.), *World Politics and Transnational Relations* (Cambridge, MA: Harvard University Press, 1972).

[15] K.J. Holsti, 'Along the Road to International Theory', *International Journal*, 39, 2 (1984), p. 350.

Foreign-policy analysis thus took a phenomenological turn. This was a change toward a more explicitly scientific (formally causal) enterprise but the normative element never lurked far below the surface. The original theoretical thrust for this approach came from the work of the Sprouts [16] and the path-breaking essay by Richard Snyder and his colleagues.[17] Ole Holsti[18] wrote the first case study employing the approach. It became a classic and served as the prototype for succeeding efforts of the same genre. Robert Jervis' *Perception and Misperception in Internationl Politics*[19] demonstrated that a variety of psychological mechanisms could help to explain faulty policies, how they were rationalized, and how they led to deterrence failures, crises, and wars. Subsequent works[20] emphasized group and bureaucratic sources of misperception and faulty decision-making procedures. The message was clear: if you alter decision-making procedures to incorporate, for example, 'multiple advocacy'—an airing of all views and options—the probabilities of making poor decisions could be decreased.[21]

This area of study was influenced by the wish to prevent foreign-policy failures. In an era of nuclear weapons, when the fate of societies hung in the balance, the studies seemed to suggest that there was no room for the kinds of follies and errors that had typified European diplomacy in the nineteenth and early twentieth centuries. Instead of examining 1930s-style impersonal 'forces'—about which one can do little—or major abstractions such as systems or societies of states (which also cannot be manipulated) the study of decision-making has direct policy implications. We should explore decision-making because we can promote better policy.

The Cuban missile crisis of October 1962, one of the most dramatic confrontations of the Cold War, provided a major impetus for further development of decision-making studies; indeed, it promoted a sub-subfield of *crisis* decision-making. The original formulations of the Sprouts and Richard Snyder and his colleagues were designed to promote foreign-policy studies in general, but by the early 1960s the focus shifted to crisis decision-making, a study not of generic or comparative foreign policy, but of American foreign policy in high-threat situations. The literature on the Cuban missile crisis is extensive and fascinating for both conceptual and historical reasons, but it never generated a subsequent comparative field. More generic, comparative studies on crisis behaviour emerged in the late 1950s from the Stanford Studies on International Conflict and Integration under the leadership of Robert North. These culminated in the early 1970s with an explicitly comparative literature based not only on the Cuban

---

[16] Harold Sprout and Margaret Sprout, *The Ecological Perspective on Human Affairs* (Princeton: Princeton University Press, 1965).

[17] Richard C. Snyder, H.W. Bruck, and Burton Sapin, *Decision-Making as an Approach to the Study of International Politics*, Foreign Policy Analysis Project Series No. 3 (Princeton: Princeton University Press, 1954); and Richard C. Snyder, H.W. Bruck and Burton Sapin (eds.), *Decision-Making: An Approach to the Study of International Politics* (New York: The Free Press, 1962).

[18] Ole R. Holsti, 'The Belief-System and National Images: A Case Study', *Journal of Conflict Resolution*, 6 (1962), pp. 244–52.

[19] Robert Jervis, *Perception and Misperception in International Politics* (Princeton: Princeton University Press, 1976).

[20] Cf., Irving Janis, *Victims of Groupthink* (Boston: Houghton Mifflin, 1972).

[21] Alexander L. George, 'The Case for Multiple Advocacy in Making Foreign Policy', *American Political Science Review* (September 1972), pp. 751–85; and Alexander L. George, *Presidential Decisionmaking in Foreign Policy: The Effective Use of Information and Advice* (Boulder, CO: Westview Press, 1980).

episode, but also on the events of August 1914.[22] This literature raised questions about the assumption of rationality in realist thought; it demonstrated the relevance of social psychology to policy-making studies; it showed how decision-making styles and processes can both lead to and help prevent catastrophes; and it emphasized the capacity for learning and change, an important item in the liberal theoretical agenda of the 1970s and 1980s. The Stanford Studies also underlined the importance of examining foreign-policy-making in the context of bilateral and multilateral diplomatic relationships rather than as just the elaboration of a country's ends and means.

Foreign policy is ultimately a relationships with others, and in the absence of an authority which can arbitrate contending points of view, it is essentially a bargaining relationship. 'What to study?' thus should also include an understanding of how states bargain, particularly in conflict situations. The normative thrust of the very large literature on bargaining is not how to win, but how to avoid destructive outcomes or bargaining 'failures'. The relationship to deterrence is obvious, but how to make deterrence effective in real life is not so simple as theoretical cost/benefit/risk analyses might suggest.[23] This problem spawned an extensive literature that was given immediacy by the risks involved in the Cold War. Interest has not waned with the end of that protracted conflict because of the proximity of theoretical understanding to better (e.g. safer) policy for any government. It is as relevant today in the context of India–Pakistan or Greece-Turkey relations as it was during the Cold War.

While these answers to the question 'what to study?' differed substantially in their level of analysis, the conceptualization of actors, the degree of abstractness, or the methodologies they employed, they had in common the normative concern with war, conflict, instability, and disorder. They shared a view of international politics as a domain in which rivalry, competition, conflict, and violence are frequent if not the normal state of affairs. There was a common assumption that if we can better understand the dynamics of international politics through high quality diagnosis we may be in a position to do something about the risks of systems that go awry, of foreign policies that lead to wars, of decisions that lead to disasters, and of bargaining strategies that lead to escalation. We should study these matters, ultimately, to have a better world.

But while these problems informed the mainstream of international political studies during the Cold War, they did not monopolize the field. In 1748, Montesquieu wrote: 'The natural effect of commerce is to lead to peace ... Commerce has spread knowledge or the mores of all nations everywhere; they have been compared to each other, and good things have resulted from this.'[24] International politics is not only about conflict and war. Like Janus, it has another side,

---

[22] For the example of the Cuban crisis, see Graham Allison, *The Essence of Decision: Explaining the Cuban Missile Crisis* (Boston: Little, Brown, 1972); for a summary of the comparative study, see Ole R. Holsti, *Crisis, Escalation, War* (Montreal: McGill-Queens University Press, 1972). For general essays on crisis decision-making, see Charles F. Hermann, *Crises in Foreign Policy* (Indianapolis, IN: Bobbs-Merrill, 1969).

[23] For a comprehensive review of the development of this literature, see Richard Ned Lebow, 'Beyond Parsimony: Rethinking Theories of Coercive Bargaining', *European Journal of International Relations*, 4, 1 (March 1998), pp. 31–66.

[24] Montesquieu, *The Spirit of the Laws*, translated and edited by Anne M. Cohler, Basia Carolyn Miller, and Harold Samuel Stone (New York: Cambridge University Press, 1989), p. 339.

the side of cooperation, mutual benefit, and welfare opportunity. This aspect of the field is not to be confused with idealism, which remained alive in the World Order Models Project (WOMP) during even the darkest days of the Cold War, but it has a similar diagnostic and normative thrust: what are the conditions of peace, co-operation, and order?

David Mitrany[25] originally paved the way for an expansive research agenda that went under the name of 'integration'. The European Coal and Steel Community and, later, the European Economic Community, provided the impetus for numerous studies that tried to locate the sources of economic and, possibly, political integration. Researchers argued over appropriate methodologies and ultimately foundered over the problem of the dependent variable, that is, what is it that should be explained? Political integration, economic integration, cooperation, or peace? While there was no consensus on these matters, the work on integration solidified the place of the cooperative dimension of international politics in textbooks and in the theoretical approaches to the field. The pile of studies was an implicit reminder that the realist version of international politics that focused on security, conflict, and war was incomplete. Perhaps the most important theoretical contribution came from Karl Deutsch.[26] In his work on integration of communities (not necessarily states), he demolished one of the pillars of realist thought from Rousseau to Morgenthau: the idea that sovereignty (and when multiplied, anarchy) necessarily creates security dilemmas between states. In his concept of the 'pluralist security community' Deutsch outlined the conditions under which two or more states can coexist without facing security dilemmas. The consequence of sovereignty, in other words, is as likely to be cooperation as conflict.

Integration studies both in their reformist and in their theoretical guises went out of fashion in the early 1970s, but the cooperative aspect of international politics did not cease to command attention. The conditions for cooperation and peace took on new colours variously named interdependence, neo-liberal institutionalism, international regimes, or learning through epistemic communities.[27] While much of the theoretical debate during this time pitted realists against liberals of various persuasions, efforts were made—quite in the spirit of Carr—to synthesize the two approaches or at least to reconcile the primacy of national interest with cooperative outcomes. During the 1970s, liberals also became more interested in security issues and explicitly began to adopt realist concepts and vocabulary even to the analysis of non-security issues. The results were mixed and theoretically problematic.[28] It may be more fruitful to acknowledge that the assumptions and main concepts of the realist and liberal traditions in international thought represent two sides of international politics and that attempts to synthesize them only confuse the issue.

---

[25] David Mitrany, *A Working Peace System* (Chicago: Quadrangle, 1966).

[26] Karl W. Deutsch, *Political Community at the International Level: Problems of Definition and Measurement* (Garden City, NY: Doubleday, 1954); and Karl W. Deutsch, *et al.*, *Political Community and the North Atlantic Area: International Organization in the Light of Historical Experience* (Princeton: Princeton University Press, 1967).

[27] Edward L. Morse, *Modernization and the Transformation of International Relations* (New York: The Free Press, 1976); Robert O. Keohane, 'International Institutions: Two Approaches', *International Studies Quarterly*, 32, 4 (December 1988), pp. 379–96; and Peter Haas (ed.), *International Organization* (Special Issue on Epistemic Communities), 46 (1992).

[28] Robert M. A. Crawford, *Regime Theory in the Post-Cold War World: Rethinking Neoliberal Approaches to International Relations* (Aldershot, Hants.: Dartmouth, 1996).

The liberal side of the coin of international politics gained prominence during the later Cold War years and perhaps dominated the field in the 1980s.[29]

The concern with cooperation and international institutions was an important antidote to the pessimism of realism, not only because it sought to explain a happier side of the relations between states but also because it diverged from the crude material explanatory mechanisms of war/security theory. In realism, the interests of states were under-theorized. They emerged either from power capabilities or from responses to external threats. In Morgenthau's version, for example, state interests ranged from self-abnegation to drives for world domination. Aside from capabilities or responses to threats, however, nothing explained this wide variation.

In contrast, liberal approaches to the question introduced the importance of learning. Liberal theories challenged the static, repetitious characterization of international politics portrayed in realism. Explaining interests thus became a major theoretical problem to unravel. By emphasizing the possibilities of learning through interaction, liberal theories opened up the possibility of change. Toward the end of the Cold War period, this theoretical innovation led directly to the social constructivist approach to the field[30] which argued that state interests are highly variable and constructed through a combination of ideas, roles, and interaction patterns. This meant that states were not inevitably ensconced in perpetual security dilemmas, that there were ways to avoid the most dangerous consequences of anarchy and sovereignty, and that through learning and cooperation, new forms of international regulation and governance were possible. Liberal approaches to the field ultimately made four notable contributions to the study of international politics: the importance of commerce in generating habits of cooperation; the crucial role of interactions in defining interests; the link between democracy and peace; and the possibilities of progressive change.

The normative agenda of liberal approaches to international relations emphasized reciprocity, cooperation, peace, and order. But what was taking place within Western Europe during the Cold War was not a global phenomenon, much as integration and neo-liberal institutionalists liked to pose their puzzles and explanations in universal terms. By the late 1960s, many expectations about the developing countries were not being borne out by economic and other quality-of-life statistics. While, roughly speaking, realists were concerned with security and conflict and liberals examined the sources of cooperation, the question of equity and justice was not a prominent value underlying these analyses. From the perspectives of the Third World, the Cold War and its attending threats were not nearly so immediate as the problems of economic development. The figures pointed to a morally intolerable condition: the gap between living conditions in the industrialized countries, including the socialist states, and the developing countries was growing exponentially. Nostrums of 'nation-building,' foreign aid, foreign investment, and a host of United Nations-sponsored activities were not bringing anticipated results.

---

[29] A comprehensive survey of the various strands of liberalism in international relations theory is in Mark W. Zacher and Richard A. Matthew, 'Liberal International Theory: Common Threads, Divergent Strands', in Charles Kegley (ed.), *Controversies in International Relations Theory: Realism and the Neoliberal Challenge* (New York: St. Martin's Press, 1995), pp. 107–50.

[30] See Nicholas Onuf, *World of our Making: Rules and Rule in Social Theory and International Relations* (Columbus, SC: University of South Carolina Press, 1989).

Dependency theory provided yet another possibility to the question 'what to study?' The answer was the sources of underdevelopment and the conditions that perpetuate it. Both were located in the global capitalist system. The development of the West had underdeveloped the south,[31] and the economic structures built during the eras of colonialism and imperialism remained in place. These siphoned surplus value from the peripheries to the centres, and while formal colonialism had retired, the old structures of domination and exploitation, propped up by foreign aid, military assistance, advertising, and cultural imperialism, remained in place.[32] As with the studies on war/security and peace/cooperation, here was a clear diagnostic exercise motivated by normative concerns of equity. The diagnosis then led to prescriptions that seriously challenged liberal conventional wisdom about the supposedly mutual benefits of trade, interdependence, and transnational relations. Dependency theory introduced a number of novel perspectives on international politics. Like some versions of realism, it was systemic; behaviour in the components of the system was explained by the structural properties of the entire system. Second, it explicitly linked elements of Marxism and Leninism to the study of international politics. Third, it posited concerns of equity above those of security and conflict or peace and cooperation. It raised economics or the search for profit rather than fear as the prime motivator of political action and structures. Also in contrast to realism and liberalism, following Marx, it implicitly *praised* conflict since dependency structures could not be torn down through pacific means. Finally, dependency theory analytically downgraded the behaviour of states in favour of classes, transnational relations, and sectors.

During the heydays of the Cold War, then, the field was characterized by three distinct sets of normative concerns or discourses that answered the 'what to study'? question: (1) security, conflict, and war; (2) cooperation and the conditions for peace; and (3) equity, justice, and the sources of international inequality. While from an American-centred point of view, realism may have predominated,[33] a broader perspective suggests the prominence of the second and third normative discourses. International theory in these years was never an intellectual monolith or 'orthodoxy'. Even with the high risks and threats occasioned by the Cold War, other normative concerns drove competing research programmes.

Where to study?

By 'where', I do not mean the choice between the groves of academe. The 'where' refers to the implicit or explicit area of analytical concern, that is, geographic location. Theoretical statements about the quality, logic, or major characteristics of international politics usually have been couched in universal terms. For Hobbes and Rousseau, the universe of relations between states was, of course, European. This

---

[31] Andre Gunder Frank, 'The Development of Underdevelopment', in James Cockroft (ed.), *Dependence and Under-Development* (New York: Doubleday, 1972), pp. 3–17.
[32] Johan Galtung, 'A Structural Theory of Imperialism', *Journal of Peace Research*, 8 (1971), pp. 81–117.
[33] Domination of the field in the United States by realism is empirically supported in the important study by John A. Vasquez, *The Power of Power Politics: A Critique* (New Brunswick, NJ: Rutgers University Press, 1983).

focus did not change for the next two centuries. A few textbooks in the field prior to and after World War I offered chapters on colonial government or imperialism,[34] but the view of these phenomena was from the centres. The peripheries were objects of action, but seldom agents.

These intellectual habits did not change significantly during the Cold War. The universalism of Morgenthau, Bull, Wight, Waltz, and of integration and inter-dependence theorists, was notable. Since their characterizations of international politics focused almost exclusively on the activities of the great powers—indeed, Bull lifted them to the status of an international institution[35] and Waltz declared that a theory of international politics is a theory of great power behaviour[36]—other states were deliberately left out by virtue of not being great powers (China was, perhaps, a marginal exception). The field of security studies was particularly deficient in its concern with the security problems of Third World states. This field focused primarily on problems of deterrence and nuclear deployments, but in the late 1960s a literature on 'sage brush wars', 'low intensity conflicts', and 'guerrilla war' began to appear. The impetus here came from the perceived threats of communism. Hence, while Malaya, the Philippines, and Vietnam became the objects of study, wars in Burma, Sri Lanka, Nigeria, Sudan, and Eritrea—to mention just a few—were ignored. With the end of the Cold War, analysts suddenly and inappropriately discovered 'ethnic [sic] wars', as if they were a new phenomenon that had appeared on the landscape because of the end of the Soviet–American rivalry. Intellectual myopia or Eurocentrism had helped to lead to both policy disasters and a deficient security studies field. Theoretical approaches to international politics hardly fared better. The essential elements of realism, integration studies, interdependence, and liberal institutionalism were supposed to be universal, but in fact they described or diagnosed relations primarily within and between the OECD countries, and between the Cold War protagonists. Where were classical European-style arms races in Africa? Where were stag hunts and security dilemmas in the Caribbean or Central America? Where was balancing behaviour or bandwagoning in South America? Where were the harmonious consequences of interdependence in South Asia? Where was political integration in Southeast Asia?[37] Indeed, the essential actor in all theories of international politics during the Cold War—the state—was assumed rather than problematized, whereas in many areas of the world, it was and remains *the* problem. International politics as a theoretical study during the Cold War, as it had been in earlier decades, was a grounded in European history and relegated the rest of the world to a lower ontological status, indeed to one that was characterized by considerable over-generalization, if not ignorance. Dependency theory was in part a response to this problem.

---

[34] The most important English-language non-theoretical treatment of imperialism remains Parker T. Moon *Imperialism and World Politics* (New York: Macmillan, 1926).

[35] Hedley Bull, *Anarchical Society*, ch. 9.

[36] Kenneth Waltz, *Theory of International Politics*, pp. 72–3.

[37] K.J. Holsti, 'International Theory and War in the Third World', in Brian Job (ed.), *The Insecurity Dilemma: National Security of Third World States* (Boulder, CO: Lynne Rienner Publishers, 1992), pp. 37–62; and K.J. Holsti, 'International Relations Theory and Domestic Wars in the Third World: The Limits of Relevance', in Stephanie Neuman (ed.), *International Relations Theory and the Third World* (New York: St. Martin's Press, 1998), pp. 103–32.

Who studies?

Part of the explanation for the limited geographical scope of international politics lies in the people who performed the diagnoses, painted the portraits of the essential characteristics of international politics, and offered solutions to pressing problems. For the most part, international politics as an academic field, organized departmentally, existed primarily in English-speaking countries, and its theoretical aspects were developed exclusively in those domains. I have covered this problem elsewhere,[38] and Stanley Hoffmann has offered an incisive analysis of the reasons why the field flourished particularly in the United States.[39] A combination of policy-problems, the close relationship between academics and the government, the professionalization of the field, and American leadership during the Cold War help to explain American academic predominance.[40] Hoffmann was correct to chastise Americans for parochialism, but his dismissal of non-American contributions to the field needs to be queried. The commanding figures in the field during the era of anxiety included many non-Americans, and thus Hoffmann's characterization of it as an 'American social science' was not entirely accurate.[41] Aside from citing one major French contribution—by Raymond Aron—Hoffmann acknowledged only the works of Carr and Dahrendorf in his survey of the field. This was hardly an adequate or comprehensive review. He failed to mention major contributions from scholars in the United Kingdom, for example.

The 'where to study?' question was influenced by American government involvement in the world. Academic analysis focused heavily on Europe and on Asian and Middle Eastern centres of rivalry and conflict. Other areas of the world were left primarily to regional or country specialists. As suggested, regional dynamics and security problems were not incorporated into theoretical renderings of the field.

As for the rest of the world, international politics as a separate academic field either did not exist or, where it was reasonably well-developed, as in Japan or India, its practitioners focused on national problems and rarely sought to set those within larger theoretical contexts. Indians were preoccupied with non-alignment, Koreans with reunification, and Japanese with status, trade, and regional security issues. In a few other locales, however, there was considerable work of note. Many conflict resolution theories, as well as systematic empirical work, originated in Scandinavia and Israel. True, many of the underlying analytical models came from American sources, but there was a considerable amount of theoretical innovation as well. Johan Galtung's extensive corpus is one prominent example. Raymond Aron's *Peace and War* is another. If we look at the entire field during the Cold War era, however, the conclusion remains that the theoretical agenda was set primarily in American and British institutions, with prominent appendages appearing in Australia, Canada, and Scandinavia as well. But this conclusion does not tell the whole tale, for during the 1980s a major assault on the field emerged primarily from Continental intellectual sources. More on this below.

---

[38] K.J. Holsti, *The Dividing Discipline*.

[39] Stanley Hoffmann, 'An American Science: International Relations', *Daedelaus*, 106, 3 (1977), pp. 41–60.

[40] See a further elaboration in Miles Kahler, 'Inventing International Relations'.

[41] Hoffmann's argument is more accurate if it refers primarily to the extent and pattern of funding, the relationship between scholars and government, and the organization of academic departments and schools.

Why study international politics?

Here we enter the domain of theoretical functions. I have already alluded to the diagnostic function: theorists wish to understand the sources of socially constructed problems such as war, order, justice, equity, reciprocity, or quality-of-life issues. This should be sufficient justification for any major scholarly enterprise, but it is not complete.

A second function of theory is to make a vast field, characterized by innumerable facts, trends, anomalies, structures, agents, and behaviours, more intelligible. Or, as Torbjørn Knutsen suggests, theories *enlighten*.[42] Diverse data have to be made comprehensible in some way. This can be done by developing concepts, by locating, constructing, or establishing patterns that transcend time, location, and personality, and by generalization. Through these operations, detail and randomness get washed out (see below), but comprehension, often in a causal sense, increases. Understanding grows in rough proportion to abstraction. Thanks to monuments of scholarly work by Quincy Wright, Hedley Bull, Karl Deutsch, Hans Morgenthau, Harold and Margaret Sprout, or Kenneth Waltz—to name just several major contributors to the field during the Cold War years—we learned a good deal that did not come to mind simply by keeping up with the daily news. Each of the works contained major flaws—some indeed creating a growth industry of criticism—but all made readers and analysts think about things in ways they had not thought before. They were not only creative enterprises; they helped others to create.

Nevertheless, many were convinced that the theoretical efforts of the early Cold War years were deficient in many ways. They could not, in fact, make the world more *authoritatively* intelligible because many were logically or empirically slipshod. And indeed some were. Assumptions were often unexamined. Generalizations were offered without compelling evidence (certainly not an appropriate criticism of Karl Deutsch or Quincy Wright!). Some texts contained contradictory propositions; for example, that balances of power help create wars, while later claiming that they prevent them.[43] Some textbooks were unashamedly prescriptive, showing, for example, how best to fight the threat of communism. A particularly annoying habit, critics suggested, was the propensity to select evidence to support generalizations, without making any effort to systematize data so that the generalizations might be based on a reasonable empirical foundation. A third function of theory, then, is to *improve* the quality of knowledge, that is, to give it more authority. This could be done in part through traditional means of logical analysis, as Hedley Bull suggested: '. . . the [theoretical] enterprise is concerned . . . with theoretical construction: with establishing that certain assumptions are true while others are false, certain arguments valid while others are invalid, and so proceeding to erect a firm structure of knowledge'.[44] Here, Bull suggests another function of theory: criticism. Virtually all theoretical contributions during the Cold War were critiques of existing knowledge as well as creative enterprises.

---

[42] Torbjørn Knutsen, *A History of International Relations Theory*, p. 1.

[43] See the critiques of the balance of power concept by Ernst B. Haas, 'The Balance of Power: Prescription, Concept, or Propaganda?' *World Politics*, 5 (July 1953), pp. 442–77; and by A. F. K. Organski, *World Politics* (New York: Alfred A. Knopf, 1958).

[44] Hedley Bull, 'International Relations Theory 1919–1969', in Brian Porter (ed.), *International Politics 1919–1969* (London: Oxford University Press, 1972), p. 32.

Quality-of-knowledge concerns do not complete the list of theoretical functions. The scholarly enterprise is also based on curiosity, on the needs for more precise information, more isomorphic models of phenomena, more refined classifications (taxonomic work), enhanced conceptual clarity, and better appreciation and understanding of historical perspectives on the field. International politics does not differ in these regards, and a good deal of its theoretical development is derived from such concerns. Inis Claude Jr.'s *Power and International Relations* and Ernst B. Haas' analysis of the balance-of-power concept were classic efforts at conceptual clarification.[45] The intellectual history of our field—defined, refined, and often reinterpreted—offers other areas of development that highlight continuities, themes, and new departures. Ian Clark's *The Hierarchy of States: Reform and Resistance in the International Order* is just one of several examples.[46] Many important contributions have not been mentioned, but the purpose here is only to point out that intellectual curiosity, the search for more precise and authoritative knowledge, and providing intellectual roots for a discipline are important elements of an answer to the 'why study?' question.

In the early 1980s emancipation became a major answer to the 'why study?' question. Emancipation was both political and intellectual. Out of Europe came a number of figures, some refugees from Marxism, others major amenders of that faith, and still others prominent critics of what came to be known as the 'Enlightenment project.' If problems originally posed by Hobbes, Rousseau, Bentham, Kant, the Mills, Marx, and their twentieth-century descendants comprised the core of the field during the early years of the Cold War, toward the end of the period the advocates of critical theory, post-structuralism, and other posts-, anchored their criticisms of the field in the ideas of Habermas, Bourdieu, Foucault, Nietzsche, and Gadamer (to mention only the more prominent), most of whom wrote nothing about international politics, or of Gramsci, who did have an interest in the field.[47] Since this area has developed most fully in the period since the end of the Cold War, it is not appropriate to explore it at length. But in terms of our category, 'why study?', it is important to emphasize that this area of inquiry (with a few notable exceptions such as Robert Cox) has not been fundamentally concerned with understanding the world of diplomats, merchants, and warriors, but with attempting to question and/or destroy the foundations of positivist-based exercises. There are two main reasons for intellectual emancipation. The first is the conviction that conventional approaches to international theory are based on a positivist epistemology that implicitly validates existing conditions. Kenneth Waltz' *Theory of International Politics* stimulated the first systematic attack[48] on realism as essentially a political project that is not only intellectually flawed (as many others had argued previously) but normatively dangerous. To view and explain world

---

[45] Inis L. Jr. Claude, *Power and International Relations* (New York: Random House, 1962); and Ernst Haas, 'The Balance of Power', pp. 442–77.

[46] Ian Clark, *The Hierarchy of States: Reform and Resistance in the International Order* (Cambridge: Cambridge University Press, 1980); see also Torbjørn Knutsen, *A History of International Relations Theory*.

[47] For a review of the intellectual pedigree of various contemporary approaches to theories of international relations, see Vendulka Kubalkova, 'The Twenty Years' Catharsis: E. H. Carr and IR', in Vendulka Kubalkova, Nicholas Onuf, and Paul Kowert (eds.), *International Relations in a Constructed World* (Armonka, NY and London: E. M Sharpe, 1998), pp. 25–57.

[48] Richard Ashley, 'The Poverty of Neorealism', *International Organization*, 38(2) (1984), pp. 225–86.

politics in utilitarian, economist, mechanistic and structural terms, as Waltz did, leads the analyst implicitly to say that because the world is this way, this is the way it ought to be. The accusation against Waltz was multi-layered, but was really centred on the question of change. According to Waltz, in a system of anarchy the only significant change is between multipolar and bipolar power configurations, with the latter as the preferred layout because it reduces the probabilities of major war. Ashley and many subsequent critics charged that the purpose of inquiry should be to show how to escape all war-producing systems, not just how to fine-tune existing systems. We need to emancipate ourselves from Waltz-like projects because of the necessary connection between thought and practice. International theories are not just abstract playthings of academics. Their elaboration has political consequences and thus the answer to the question 'why study' is ultimately to demolish all intellectual projects that sustain the *status quo* and other evils in the world.

The second reason for emancipation is to rid ourselves of another pervasive danger, the idea that we can understand the world through general theories and 'meta-narratives' that in fact hide a world of flux, contradiction, paradox, and complexity under cloaks of generalization and disciplinary orthodoxy. To be truly liberated intellectually, and thus ultimately in a political sense, is to acknowledge uncertainty and to eschew all projects that reek of 'sovereign voices' and intellectual closure. Because of the close connection between knowledge and power, it is critical to question, query ('interrogate' is the preferred jargon), and unmask all knowledge claims no matter on what basis they are made. Scholarship *is* politics, and in the 1980s the critics were convinced that the positivist-based theoretical enterprise was, at heart, a political project.

Richard Ashley, James Der Derian, Jim George, Robert Cox, and R. B. J. Walker made major interventions along these lines. The main outlines of the debate these critiques engendered about the time of the deconstruction of the Berlin Wall are summarized in a useful synthetic exercise by Joseph Lapid.[49] This brief excursion into late Cold War developments in the field is placed in the 'why study?' category rather than 'what to study?' because it was oriented primarily toward an epistemological/political purpose rather than to shed light on the substance of the field. It was at once an intellectual demolition derby and a project of liberation, but only rarely devoted to helping us understand substantive issues such as those raised in more 'orthodox' versions of the field.

The full story of the migration of Continental philosophy to the study of international politics has not been told. Cold War context is an insufficient explanation because the first salvos of those who sought intellectual emancipation were fired during the contrasting eras of détente and the 'second Cold War.' The development of critical studies was more importantly fed by other disciplines, internal debates, novelty, and a broad pessimism deriving from disillusion with 'modernism'. Yet, it is difficult to envisage these currents of thought successfully migrating to the field in the 1950s or 1960s. The declining threat of nuclear war thus may be part of the explanation.

---

[49] In his 'The Third Debate: On the Prospects of International Theory in a Post-Positivist Era', *International Studies Quarterly*, 33(4) (September 1989), pp. 235–54.

How to study?

The question of the functions of theory is closely connected to the problem of how to approach the subject(s), that is, how to do research and how to develop knowledge. For example, one of the prime reasons knowledge should become more reliable, according to J. David Singer,[50] is to provide sound advice to those who are responsible for making and applying foreign and defence policies. But scholarship in general should have the goal of being 'sound', 'rigorous', and 'unbiased', no matter for what purposes it is designed. This is what sets it off from legal argumentation or journalism. Presumably few scholarly works will have any authority (e.g. they will not become part of the current wisdom, conventional or otherwise) unless they are grounded in evidence. In the West, at least, scholarship no longer can appeal to God, Marx, or some higher spirit for validation. These are replaced by logic and evidence.

But how one applies logic and evidence is not beyond dispute. Let me quote a passage that evaluates the quality of international politics scholarship in the 1940s and 1950s:

> The laws of international politics to which some 'realists' appealed in such a knowing way appeared on closer examination to rest on tautologies or shifting definitions of terms. The massive investigation of historical cases implied in their Delphic pronouncements about the experience of the past had not always, it seemed, actually been carried out. The extravagant claims made by some of them turned out to rest on assumed authority rather than on evidence or rigorous argument. Indeed, not even the best of the 'realist' writings can be said to have achieved a high standard of theoretical refinement: they were powerful polemical essays—brilliant and provocative in the case of Carr, systematic and comprehensive in the case of Morgenthau, learned and profound in the case of Wight—but the theory they employed was 'soft', not 'hard.'

One might think that the author of this methodological critique was an American enthusiast of the behavioural revolution. In fact, it was Hedley Bull.[51]

Those who considered themselves social scientists wanted to go further than Bull. They sought to create a science of international relations (or politics) that could meet a number of tests of reliability, including empirical verification, logical consistency, and reproducibility. This attempt to bring reliability to the field went under the poorly chosen name of 'behaviouralism', somehow implying that what predecessors of the field had been concerned with was not behaviour. The 'behavioural revolution' was primarily, if not exclusively, an attempt to improve the quality of knowledge and to correct some of the problems Bull listed above. As with most reform movements, there were sects, schisms, and censures. There was a special vocabulary that sought to demarcate the new fraternity from the old. 'Rigour', 'models', 'data', and 'laws' were in; judgement, history, impressions, and feelings were out. Values were data, not impulses that drove research. A true science of international politics was the great end which was to be achieved through collecting reliable data, replication, and cumulation. International politics was to become modelled upon physics and chemistry, not on history, philosophy, or jurisprudence.

---

[50] J. David Singer, 'The Responsibilities of Competence in the Global Village', *International Studies Quarterly*, 29 (September 1985), pp. 245–62.
[51] Hedley Bull, 'International Relations Theory 1919–1969', p. 39.

Much energy was expended in the repartee sparked by the behavioural revolution. Indeed, for much of the 1960s and 1970s, debate concentrated on matters of method rather than of substance. I have argued elsewhere[52] that the behavioural revolution did not inaugurate a new way of looking at the world, a new paradigm (to use later jargon), or a new set of normative problems. It revolved around the ways one generates knowledge. Positivist methodologies have theoretical implications—a standard position today—but the essential positions in contention during the Cold War involved questions of reliability rather than 'what to study?' issues or epistemology. The debates were largely exclusionist in the sense that few of the protagonists were prepared to acknowledge the contributions of the others. Among the casualties of the methodological Cold War was a whole generation of American graduate students excused from studying history, law, and foreign languages so that they could enter as experts into discussions of statistical method. Emphasis on honing research skills, including quantitative analysis, is to be applauded, but not necessarily when it replaces history, law, and languages.

Toward the end of the era of anxiety, the methodological wars largely dissipated. Search for the holy grail of a science of international politics had been abandoned, the promises of high-order causal explanations went largely unfulfilled, and it was clear that, despite some notable exceptions, the field was not built on an agenda of cumulation.[53] Scholars of international politics did not often duplicate the working patterns of chemists and physicists. Theoretical individualism, the reputational rewards accruing from novelty, the changing diplomatic agenda, lack of funding, faddism, and boredom with the canon, among other reasons, militated against science. The work pattern of scholars looked much more like informal groups or networks toiling in a common problem-area such as integration in the 1960s, dependency theory in the 1970s, and the democratic peace in the 1980s. There is theoretical debate, empirical exploration, methodological contestation, and eventually some pattern of increased understanding emerged. But this was seldom a general theory in the scientific sense. This understanding then became a general part of the overall field's lore, incorporated as reasonably common knowledge. For example, we do not have a formal theory of foreign-policy decision-making, but we do have a repertoire of insights and understanding about the sources of policy-making pathologies and individual misperceptions. Our students can read that in reasonably authoritative textbook accounts and use it as a foundation for further work.

Overall, the behavioural revolution heightened sensitivity to questions of research design, to the importance of systematic evidence to test propositions and hypothesized connections, to clearer recognition of the normative foundations of problem identification, and to the limits of formal causal explanation. And as Bull's quotation suggests, the traditionalists were not immune from these currents. While dismissing much of the formal scientific work as mediocre and regressive, Bull acknowledged areas of progress such as a 'decline of innocence' that marked the scholarship of the 1920s and 1930s, an awareness of much intellectually 'shoddy'

---

[52] K.J. Holsti, *The Dividing Discipline*, ch. 2; Schmidt disagrees strongly with this position. See Brian C. Schmidt, 'The Historiography of Academic International Relations', pp. 349–68.

[53] This is the argument in Yale Ferguson and Richard Mansbach, *The Elusive Quest*. Areas of notable cumulation included studies on crisis decision-making, alliances, international regimes, correlates of war, and the democratic peace literatures.

work, and a general concern for logical rigour and precision.[54] Whatever the ultimate evaluation, the great methodological debates of the Cold War years were necessary and of lasting significance.

But the search for greater rigour or a scientific version of the field was not just an abstract discussion of methodology. It was, more broadly, an attempt to free the field from the shadow of the Cold War. In the 1960s, in particular, there was a sense that too much writing that was passed off as scientific scholarship was really policy promotion. Too many scholars, as some textbooks of the era demonstrated, were advocates rather than students. Partisanship sometimes paraded as science. Perhaps these people even compounded the dangers of the Cold War. By adhering to certain standards of scholarship that emphasized data, comparison, and empirically based generalization, the practices of partisanship and demonization could be undermined and the study of the *real* sources of threat to the world could be uncovered wherever they were found. Actors, processes, systems, and variables suggested a clinical rather than partisan approach to the field. The Cold War thus helped to energize a formally scientific scholarly enterprise.

What not to study?

Several areas of inquiry were developed into research programmes, but were ultimately abandoned for lack of progress or declining interest. The study of political integration, a major theoretical preoccupation during the 1960s and 1970s, waned significantly after Ernst Haas declared it an intellectual dead-end.[55] There were methodological and conceptual problems, including lack of consensus on what exactly was to be explained, that is, 'what is integration?'. But the demise of integration was not essentially a technical problem. These studies, despite their universalist pretensions, were confined primarily to Europe. Yet, many of the characteristics associated with European integration were typical of all OECD countries. Moreover, since the theoretical study of European integration was primarily an American craft, the Americans were in a sense outsiders looking in. With the development of the concept of interdependence, and an accompanying argument that international relations were in the midst of a transformation,[56] a more generic subfield could be developed, one in which the United States played a leading role in driving the transformation. Interdependence studies colonized integration. The focus of research thus changed: the purpose was no longer to explain European integration processes, but to use those processes to test the explanatory capacities of rival realist and liberal/ interdependence theories. In the theoretical realm, then, Europe moved from being an object of study to being a test case of more generic theories of international politics.

The field of comparative foreign policy was also abandoned. The theoretical platform for comparative foreign-policy analyses was largely developed by Richard Snyder and his associates, and by James Rosenau.[57] There was much enthusiasm for

---

[54] Hedley Bull, 'International Relations Theory 1919–1969', pp. 50–2.

[55] Ernst Haas, 'The Obsolescence of Regional Integration Theory' (Berkeley: Institute of International Studies, University of California, 1975).

[56] Morse, *Modernization and the Transformation of International Relations*.

[57] James N. Rosenau, 'Pre-Theories and Theories of Foreign Policy', in R.B. Farrell (ed.), *Approaches to Comparative and International Politics* (Evanston, Ill: The Free Press, 1966), pp. 27–92.

the field, particularly in the area of data gathering. But early promise faded. Some genuinely comparative efforts did appear, including studies of foreign-policy change,[58] numerous inquiries into decision-making and leadership styles,[59] and perhaps most uniquely, Bahgat Korany's important comparative study of foreign-policy-making in the Middle East.[60] But these early comparative endeavours were not followed up. A major literature review incorporating an extensive bibliography provides clues that help explain the demise of the field.[61] The problem was that most of the work was not comparative, and most theoretically inspired efforts used the United States as the sole model or example for analysis. But the United States is hardly a modal country. Its policy-making procedures and problems are far too unique to serve as a basis for generalization. Of the 228 bibliography items in Hudson's list, I found only 24 (10.5%) to be explicitly comparative or focused on a country other than the United States. But few of these met even minimum criteria for the development of a comparative foreign policy field. These include:

- A consensus on critical questions to ask (the criterion of centrality);
- Examination of a sufficiently large number of cases, that is, countries' foreign policies (the criterion of representativeness);
- Agreement on major analytical categories and how to connect them (the criterion of conceptual consensus); and
- and, Using concepts, categories, and typologies that foster rather than hinder comparative analysis (the criterion of comparability)[62]

Lack of concern for these criteria and the ultimate abandonment of this subfield is unfortunate because comparative studies in domestic politics are moving ahead. An increasing number of country and area experts will probably take over the comparative foreign-policy field, but this is one area where collaboration rather than colonization would be a preferred route.

Finally, we have to acknowledge the abandonment of the great project of developing a 'grand' theory of international politics/relations. No matter what the criticisms against Morgenthau or Waltz, they were able to accomplish a great deal more than most analysts would even dream of doing. The scope of their theorizing was immense and the questions for which they sought answers were compelling. Morgenthau wanted to locate the sources of conflict, the typical forms of behaviour in systems of power politics, and the efficacy and difficulties of policies of prudence in a domain dominated by insecurity. Waltz was committed to answering big questions as well: why wars and balances of power recur, why states seek autonomy

---

[58] K.J. Holsti *et al.*, *Why Nations Realign: Foreign Policy Restructuring Since World War II* (London: Allen & Unwin, 1982); Kjell Goldmann, *Change and Stability in Foreign Policy* (Princeton: Princeton University Press, 1988). Declaring this subject obsolete may be premature. A major resuscitation effort is Jerel A. Rosati, Joe D. Hagan, and Martin W. Sampson III (eds.), *Foreign Policy Restructuring: How Governments Respond to Global Change* (Columbus, SC: University of South Carolina Press, 1994).

[59] Cf., Margaret G. Hermann, 'Explaining Foreign Policy Behavior Using Personal Characteristics of Political Leaders', *International Studies Quarterly*, 24 (1980), pp. 7–46.

[60] Bahgat Korany and Ali Hillal Dessouki (eds.), *The Foreign Policies of Arab States* (Boulder, CO: Westview Press, 1984); See also Bahgat Korany (ed.), *How Foreign Policy Decisions are Made in The Third World* (Boulder, CO: Westview Press, 1986).

[61] Valerie Hudson, 'Foreign Policy Analysis Yesterday, Today, and Tomorrow', *Mershon International Studies Review*, 39, supplement no. 2 (1995), pp. 238–309.

[62] K.J. Holsti, 'The Comparative Analysis of Foreign Policy: Some Notes on the Pitfalls and Paths to Theory', in David Wurfel and Bruce Burton (eds.), *The Political Economy of Foreign Policy in Southeast Asia* (London: Macmillan, 1990), pp. 9–10.

and relative gains, and why the states' system reproduces itself. There is nothing trivial about these issues, and while they reflected in part the normative concerns of an age which saw the systematic predation of Nazi Germany, Fascist Italy, Imperial Japan, and Soviet Russia during the 1930s, and the Cold War, they are of enduring significance. While most scholars have abandoned the single-theory scientific project, they continue to situate themselves within broad theoretical traditions that provide coherence and a record of cumulation and progressive problem-solving, that is, evidence of a *systematic* dimension to the field.

By the 1970s, détente was in the air, economic policy problems were commanding more attention, and publics were becoming more aware of environmental degradation. Although the nuclear arms race was still a menace, other causes, ideas, and areas of exploration became fashionable. The normative problems of war, peace, and security, or cooperation and interdependence could no longer monopolize the field. Competition from concerns of equity and the environment helped to expand the field in new directions. The dynamics and logic of stag hunt scenarios were no longer relevant to these new areas—or so it was claimed. Experimental and conceptual work demonstrated that insecurity, conflict, and defection (war) are not the only consequences of prisoners' dilemma situations.[63] And a precipitous decline in the incidence of interstate war rendered the fear and security problem less compelling. Finally, the search for a single, scientific theory of international politics was abandoned because the expectation of cumulative progress did not materialize across all subjects in the field. It was confined primarily to the study of crisis decision-making, deterrence, alliances, international regimes, the correlates of war, and a few other areas.

What was left out?

By contemporary standards, the study of international politics during the Cold War was not sufficiently self-reflective in the philosophical sense. Debates about theory and the scientific method did not go beyond technical issues, important as those might be. Epistemological and ontological issues were not engaged. The philosophers of the social sciences won the day and propelled the methodological outlines of research programmes. Those who did not wish to become formal modellers or quantitative wizards at least began to pay more attention to the requirements of sound evidence and inference. Abstract models, while not always up to empirical validation, nevertheless offered many insights. We use the analogies of prisoners' dilemma, stag hunt, and chicken in the field's everyday vocabulary, and they lurk suggestively behind the detailed narratives of international conflicts reported in the media. But positivism has its limits, and by adopting it as the main epistemological approach to the study, certain things were necessarily left out.

The relationship between ethics and politics was initially one of them. It did not disappear, but during the height of the Cold War it was a problem taken up mostly by scholars outside the field (e.g. Michael Walzer) and diverse individuals who examined the difficult problem of the ethics of nuclear war. Only in the 1980s did it

---

[63] Robert Axelrod, *The Evolution of Cooperation* (New York: Basic Books, 1984).

reappear as a major theme in the study of international politics in general. It did so in two ways. First, as suggested in the work of Andrew Linklater,[64] there was the problem of diverse and conflicting conception of the human community and, specifically, how individuals bear responsibilities and derive sustenance from them. Linklater's work was largely responsible for reintroducing to the international relations' literature important themes initially raised by sources as diverse as the Stoics and Karl Marx. It highlighted the fact that International Relations is not just a narrow, technical field converging upon issues made prominent by the Cold War— as important as these were—but raised a number of critical problems that link the individual to the larger philosophical issues of 'what is and should be the nature of political community?'. A similar theme, though handled differently, emerged in Nardin's[65] important analysis of the fundamental distinctions between the nature of community within a state and between states. This problem takes on increasing significance in the post-Cold War era as forces of both fragmentation—ethnic politics, for example—and integration (in the form of a growing 'international civil society') become more salient.

Second, the normative dimensions of all theories of international politics were brought out most explicitly—though only after the end of the Cold War—in Chris Brown's *International Theory: New Normative Approaches* (1992) and Nardin and Mapel's edited volume on the various traditions of ethical reasoning in IR theory.[66] Both volumes have helped to resuscitate a dimension of the field that had been discredited by the unsatisfactory realist–idealist debates of the 1930s and 1940s and discarded by the proponents of science in the 1950s and 1960s. It may be significant, however, that most of the authorship in this analytical tradition is English and the work is not yet incorporated among the field's major developments, as reported by contemporary American analysts. Yet, by the end of the Cold War, the idea that international politics, like all politics, is necessarily both a diagnostic and a prescriptive enterprise had been re-established to the point that in many graduate programmes, particularly in England, it was blended in with other approaches or became a distinct subfield.

International law was another casualty. It is not a field that lends itself to quantification and formal modelling, and yet it is an important institution of international politics. Indeed, it is so important that it distinguishes a society of states from a conglomeration of independent political units.[67] During the Cold War, international law experts—with some major exceptions such as Quincy Wright, Richard Falk, and Charles Kegley—became divorced from international politics. The separation was reflected administratively as well. Many political science depart-ments sloughed off their international law courses to faculties of law. Here, one suspects the spillover effect of the Cold War, for there seemed to be little law-like behaviour between the main Cold War protagonists, and thus academics assumed that it was of only marginal importance everywhere. Georg Schwartzenberger, an

---

[64] Andrew Linklater, *Men and Citizens in the Theory of International Relations* (London: Macmillan, 1982).

[65] Terry Nardin, *Law, Morality, and the Relations of States* (Princeton: Princeton University Press, 1983).

[66] Chris Brown, *International Theory: New Normative Approaches* (Hemel Hempstead: Harvester, 1992); Terry Nardin and David R. Mapel (eds.), *Traditions of International Ethics* (Cambridge: Cambridge University Press, 1992).

[67] Hedley Bull, *The Anarchical Society*, pp. 8–16.

international lawyer by training, penned an influential textbook of the early Cold War period in which he characterized law in essentially instrumental and expedient terms.[68] His analysis reflected concerns about aggression rampant in the 1930s and Soviet post-war behaviour. He had some difficulty reconciling his conception of a society of states with what he saw around him. The role of norms as sources of and constraints upon behaviour re-emerged as a focus of study only in the later years of the Cold War.[69] Up to that time, they tended to be viewed as epiphenomena.

From comparative foreign policy, through security studies, to international relations theory generally, the developing countries were left out as theoretical or ontological agents. Despite the universalism of grand theoretical projects, from realism to liberal institutionalism and others, researchers simply assumed that all states face similar problems in similar ways. Balances of power, arms races, alliances, security dilemmas, stag hunts, interdependence, cooperation, and wars were never portrayed as regional phenomena, or as phenomena that grew out of distinct histories and cultures. One would observe them in any anarchical system.

The foreign-policy behaviour of many states in non-Cold War locales did not always approximate, indeed often veered far from, those models. This was seldom recognized in international politics scholarship during the Cold War. Countries in the peripheries were portrayed primarily as arenas of great power competition. But if one had bothered to examine many of these areas in their own terms, they would have uncovered so many anomalies that the universalist pretensions of international politics theorists and security analysts would have come under serious question. Recognition of the problem began to appear in the 1980s[70] but received only systematic treatment after the end of the Cold War.[71] In an over-reaction to universalism, post-Cold War analysts now accept as conventional wisdom the 'tale of two worlds' thesis[72] that the industrial heartland of the world is increasingly a zone of peace and all the characteristics associated with interdependence, while the peripheries are zones of turmoil, violence, and instability—a characterization that is badly at odds with the evidence. As far as the developing countries are concerned, then, their academic treatment ran the gamut from systematic ignoring during the early years of the Cold war to over-generalization toward the end of the era.

Another omission in the field was the problem of change. One possible exception to the generalization was work by Robert Gilpin.[73] It developed a broad set of factors, including technology, that influenced the texture of international politics, but the outcomes were narrowly confined to system-wide wars in which great powers replaced each other in hegemonic positions. Overall lack of concern with the

[68] Georg Schwartzenberger, *Power Politics* (London: Jonathan Cape, 1941, New York: Praeger, 1951).

[69] Friedrich V. Kratochwill, *Rules, Norms, and Decisions: On The Conditions of Practical and Legal Reasoning in International and Domestic Affairs* (Cambridge: Cambridge University Press, 1989); and Onuf, *World of Our Making*.

[70] Cf., Bahgat Korany, 'Strategic Studies and the Third World: A Critical Evaluation', *International Social Science Journal*, 38 (1986), pp. 547–62.

[71] Robert Jackson, *Quasi-States: Sovereignty, International Relations and the Third World* (Cambridge: Cambridge University Press, 1990); Mohammed Ayoob, *The Third World Security Predicament: State Making, Regional Conflict, and the International System* (Boulder, CO: Lynne Rienner, 1995); and K.J. Holsti, *The State, War, and the State of War* (Cambridge: Cambridge University Press, 1996).

[72] James Goldgeier and Michael McFaul, 'A Tale of Two Worlds: Core and Periphery in Post-Cold War Era', *International Organization*, 46 (Spring 1992), pp. 467–92; and Max Singer and Aaron Wildawsky, *The Real World Order: Zones of Peace, Zones of Turmoil* (Chatham, NJ: Chatham House Publishers, 1993).

[73] Robert Gilpin, *War and Change in World Politics* (Princeton: Princeton University Press, 1981).

problem of change derived from the one-dimensional assumptions of realism, the idea that anarchy has only a limited range of consequences and that these will repeat themselves at least until the demise of the Westphalian states system. It may also have been a reflection of the glacial pace of movement that occurred in the diplomatic–strategic realms of the Cold War until the 1970s. It was, finally, a consequence of the constructs and data-generating activities of formal science. Scientists search for regularities, usually formulated as correlations. As Singer noted,[74] when scholarship moves from description to explanation and/or prediction, 'we become automatically involved in the search for correlation.' But as A. L Burns[75] pointed out in an effective critique, dynamic change is typically irregular and seldom appears as a trend. It can emerge in aggregate data as an anomaly, but anomalies are difficult to deal with in searching for correlations. For example, the projections at the turn of the last century, based on regularities and trends of trade, investment, increasing war casualties, tourism, education, and democratization, led Norman Angel in 1909 to predict the declining possibility of war.[76] August 1914 proved him wrong. Hitler represented a similar anomaly, one that raised even more fundamental problems about generalization in international politics. For his combination of will, racism, and long-range plans for a new world order blew away the theoretical significance of sociological trends. Theories that place systemic causes above individual actions—which is what all theories of international politics must do—insufficiently accept the freedom of human choice and the consequences of will. The search for regularities *necessarily* reduces individuals and the fundamental changes they can cause, to inferior causal status and in some versions, to no status at all. This is not a general condemnation of scientific method—it is a cost of generalization—but it does alert us to one of its most important limitations. Both realist and dependency approaches were essentially static. Dynamics occurred only within clearly defined structures and limits. Of the various theoretical traditions during the Cold War, only liberals were essentially concerned with the problem of change. Indeed, progressive change is a *leitmotif* that pervades all studies of international cooperation. Since the end of the Cold War, the study of change— often underspecified, however—has become ubiquitous. During the era of anxiety, it was not a prominent focus of the field.

The last omission is perhaps the most difficult to understand or account for. In an era sometimes called 'the age of ideologies', most of the major diagnostic strategies neglected to examine, as an empirical question, the role and functions of ideas in foreign policy and international politics. The reigning approaches to the field were ultimately materialist, defining actor interests in terms of power, security, economic welfare or, as in the case of dependency approaches, greed and profits. Realists, liberals, and dependency analysts offered different explanations of the origins of actor interests, but they commonly ignored the ideas around which interests are defined. The issue of purposes in neo-realism and systems approaches was solved simply by stating that they can range from self-abnegation to the search for world

[74] J. David Singer, *Quantitative International Politics: Insights and Evidence* (New York: The Free Press, 1968), pp. 1–2.

[75] Arthur Lee Burns, 'Scientific and Strategic-Political Theories of International Politics', in Brian Porter (ed.), *International Politics, 1919–1969*, pp. 60–1.

[76] Norman Angell, *The Great Illusion: A Study of the Relations of Military Power to National Advantage* (London: Heinemann, 1909).

domination. Comparative foreign-policy analysts never reached a consensus on what, aside from actions and strategies, foreign policies are. Liberals tended to emphasize economic gains. Lack of interest in ideas as major sources of behaviour was rather peculiar at a time when Sino-Soviet relations were in a critical state over major ideological issues, when the rhetoric of American foreign policy was imbued with, though not dominated by, Wilsonian formulae, and when many Third World governments were promoting their vision of a more equitable economic order. Remarkably, the first volume in the field to be explicitly focused on the role of ideas in international politics did not appear until 1993.[77]

Critical theorists and post-modernists who were highly critical of neo-realism's utilitarianism and materialism did not offer much in the way of alternatives. In some of their works of the late 1980s, identity replaced interest as a motive or goal for action. The question, they suggested, should no longer be 'what do we want', but 'who are we?'. This move may have reflected the identity politics that were rampant in some countries more than observed behaviour in the international realm. Identity concepts do not offer greater analytical precision than traditional notions such as 'national interest'. Nor is there much evidence to suggest that, for example, Brezhnev, Mao, Carter, Begin, DeGaulle, or Thatcher spent sleepless nights worrying about who they or their countries were. While a few have recently begun to take the role of ideas in international politics seriously, at the end of the Cold War era it remained significantly under-theorized.

Evaluation

Were there unique characteristics to the study of international politics during the Cold War? Was there progress in the field?

At least three unique characteristics are noteworthy. The first directly reflects the Cold War, particularly the problems raised by nuclear weapons. The others bear traces of the diplomatic–military environment, but are not directly related in a formal, causal sense. They arise from theoretical debates largely detached from political context.

Security studies as a subfield of international relations developed as an explicit response to the incorporation of nuclear weapons in the arsenals and strategic planning of the major powers. Prior to World War II strategic studies had been dominated by professional military figures, or by individuals whose primary careers had been in armed forces. After 1945 the field became dominated by political scientists/international relations scholars. But it also included a number of important disciplinary migrants from economics (Thomas Schelling and Kenneth Boulding) and from mathematics and the physical sciences (Oskar Morgenstern and George Rathjens). It was the problem rather than the discipline that mattered.

Security studies during the Cold War era differed in many ways from preceding efforts. The purpose of analysis changed from studying the dynamics of war and the role of weapons in overall strategy to specifying the necessary and sufficient conditions for effective deterrence. The theme changed from 'how do we win a war'

---

[77] Judith Goldstein and Robert O. Keohane (eds.), *Ideas and Foreign Policy: Beliefs, Institutions, and Political Change* (Ithaca, NY: Cornell University Press, 1993).

to 'how do we prevent a war?'. The diagnostic and prescriptive functions of theory were closely linked. The analytical approaches included logical analysis, analysis through metaphors such as the Prisoners' Dilemma, rational choice theory, studies of perception and misperception incorporating insights and evidence from social psychology, and bargaining theory.

This subfield reflected international relations' normative concerns with the problem of peace, conflict, and war. Crises over Berlin in 1948 and again in 1958 and 1961, and over Cuba in 1962, provided an immediacy to the normative problem that overshadowed all other concerns of the age. Any of those crises, and several others, might have ended in nuclear war. These problems gave rise to strategic and decision studies that buttressed the realist characterization of international politics as a realm of dangers and threats, and pointed out the need for constant vigilance against adversarial probes. There was little in Cold War crises, rivalry, diplomacy, and strategy to suggest that international politics were anything more than zero-sum bargaining relationships taking place within an environment of formal anarchy. The arms race sustained the security dilemma construct, much to the ire of peace movements which could not fathom why governments spent increasing sums on arms instead of peaceful pursuits. In brief, many of the behavioural patterns of the Cold War almost perfectly fit the realist image of international politics. If one did not understand the logic and practices of the Cold War, the texts by Hans Morgenthau and George Schwartzenberger, among others, certainly cleared up loose ends and gave a reasonably persuasive rendition of 'what was going on' between Moscow and Washington, or between NATO and the Warsaw Pact.

And what did international relations theory give to security studies? The subfield borrowed from many disciplines, including social psychology, economics, and history, but the entire theoretical substructure came from the classical tradition of international relations: the actors are states; they compete for power; there is no overarching authority that can compel states to promote some 'community interest' (as some early analysts of the United Nations contended); in a system of anarchy, security is a scarce commodity; in attempting to defend themselves, states necessarily create security threats for others; and national interest/security is a prime normative value that must be enhanced to provide the possibility for the political community to pursue the good life. Welfare and other values necessarily are subordinate to the protection of political independence, sovereignty, and security. Security studies, in brief, were concerned ultimately with a wide spectrum of normative problems that far transcended technical questions of weapons technology or deployment. It is no accident that some of the era's most prominent theorists of international politics were also analysts of international security issues. A few, like Hedley Bull and Joseph Nye, served in security-related government portfolios.

A second unique characteristic of the era, starting in the early 1970s, was the broadening of the theoretical agenda. In the 1920s and 1930s only two interrelated problems—the conditions of peace and the sources of war—oriented the field. This continued in the 1940s and 1950s, but already in the late 1960s traces of discontent over the predominance realist characterizations of international politics began to appear. The early forays of what later came to be known by some as the 'English School' began to appear, most notably in the work of Martin Wight.[78] The zero-sum

---

[78] Martin Wight, *Systems of States*.

and materialist assumptions of realism were scrutinized and found wanting in the institutional and legal aspects of international politics. Within common cultures, at least, norms and institutions (in the broad sense, not to be confused with organizations) temper power politics so that diplomatic relations begin to take on the characteristics of a society or at least a *Gesellschaft*. In Europe, the old universalist tradition never died with the formation of states. The community component of the *respublica Christiana* lived on in the thinking of Grotius, Vattel, Burke, and even Metternich. Europe was, alternatively, a 'family', a 'republic', a 'community of princes' and other organic metaphors. The idea that the decisions of the Concert of Europe became the 'law of Europe' (Metternich's term) implied that international politics on the continent were much richer in social and normative elements than was implied in realist lore. Martin Wight and Hedley Bull, among others, resurrected an older tradition of thinking that was more consistent with the totality of European diplomatic history and less influenced by the perversities and anomalies of the 1930s and 1940s which had served as the background for the works of Carr, Morgenthau, Schwartzenberger, and others. The general tenor of the 'English School' was more consistent with an era of détente than of repeated military crises and serial aggressions.

The theoretical agenda also broadened to include concern with the collaborative characteristics of international relations. This began with studies of European integration, expanded in the 1970s to include all aspects of 'interdependence' and international political economy. Liberal international theory, whose roots go back to Bentham, Mill, Cobden, and Woodrow Wilson, made a stunning comeback, perhaps also reflecting the lessening Cold War tensions associated with the era of détente. Though deriving from Marxist origins, dependency theory added the problem of equity and welfare to the purview of the field.

By the 1980s, quality-of-life issues emerged from environmental concerns, and the first claims from feminists began to appear. By the end of the Cold War, the normative claims of inclusion into the field of international relations had proliferated to such an extent that it was no longer possible to talk of an intellectual 'core' or set of coherent problems that gives the field its distinct character. The claim that the internal–external distinction was little more than a social construct with no ontological basis led inevitably to the claim that international relations no longer exists as a distinct field of inquiry,[79] much less a discipline.

During the Cold War era of anxiety, then, the field evolved from one which was theoretically and normatively concentrated on the peace and war problems to one which, by 1989, was either unravelling into a cacophony of competing normative and epistemological claims of exclusiveness—the pessimistic view—or liberating to include a whole range of new subjects reflected in a rapidly changing world. The functions of theory also proliferated from diagnosis, prescription, conceptual clarification, and concerns with the reliability of knowledge, to include emancipation.

The final element unique to the Cold War era can go under the general term 'professionalization'. This was particularly pronounced in the United States where the subfield became institutionalized in departments of political science, with even a few schools offering Ph.D. degrees in the field. A Master's degree in International

---

[79] Cf., Terry O'Callahan, 'The Real World of Normative Theory in International Relations', Department of Politics, University of Adelaide, South Australia (mimeo), 1996.

Relations was fairly common in graduate schools. The International Studies Association, appearing in the late 1950s in the west coast of the United States, by the 1970s was an organization of more than 2000 encompassing members from many countries, disciplines, and specializations.

In an age of relativism, exponential growth of normative problems, decline of immediate military threats (in the OECD world primarily), and epistemological preoccupations, it may seem quaint or irrelevant to raise the issue of progress. For many, such a stance reeks of the optimism of modernism, the faith of science, or the naiveté of liberalism. Already in the 1970s, Stanley Hoffmann[80] expressed pessimism about progress that has today become a conventional theme of contemporary critical studies: 'What was supposed to be a celebration of creativity [behaviouralism] seems to have degenerated into a series of complaints.' International politics' scholarship in the early years of the Cold War began with a sense of optimism and hope despite the state of the world. With professionalization, recognition of the field as a legitimate social science—at least in the United States—and new tools of research, the slipshod, current affairs, and partisan approaches of the 1930s through the 1960s would be replaced by theoretically-inspired and empirically validated 'hard' knowledge that could serve as the basis of both a general theory of international politics and sound policy advice. Ferguson and Mansbach[81] on the eve of the Berlin Wall's deconstruction declared both aspirations to have failed; few dissented from their judgement. Shortly after, a major assault on positivism began and epistemology replaced methodology as the prime area of non-substantive concern. For some, an escape from the substance of the field into the arcane terminology of post-modernism offered new hope—or was it the expression of despair? This was the ultimate put-down on the scholarly work of a generation: there is nothing intrinsically worth studying, generalization is intellectual totalitarianism, analyses are mere texts, emancipation takes precedence over knowledge, and the life-stories of African market women are more important to the field than all the ideas, actions, plans, and policies of governments.[82] Nietzsche and Foucault replaced Hobbes, Rousseau, Mill, and Marx as the founts of enlightenment about the ideas, practices, and norms of international politics.

But a stance of despair is not warranted as the ultimate evaluation of the field during the Cold War era. Abandoning the 'grand' theory project and recognizing the limitations of methodologies which place quantification as the ultimate fount of knowledge are not adequate indications of failure. Let me suggest a test for those today who share the pessimism of post-modernism, or any who question the notion of intellectual progress on whatever grounds. Examine one of the several textbooks

---

[80] Stanley Hoffmann, 'An American Social Science', pp. 59.

[81] Yale Ferguson and Richard Mansbach, *The Elusive Quest*.

[82] The claim that 'orthodox' theories of international politics 'marginalize' certain classes of people and their everyday experiences rests on the valid point that one of the costs of generalization is knowledge of the particular. It cannot be any other way. Ryszard Kapuscinski summarizes the dilemma well: 'The language of . . . political discourse forces out, from the mass media and, what is worse, from our memory, the vocabulary with which one can express his private problems, personal drama, individual pain . . . And yet it is impossible to avoid this abstract approach. One can present the enormous scale of . . . unfolding events only through language and concepts that are general, synthesizing—yes, abstract—all the while remaining aware that time and time again one will fall into the trap of simplification and statements easily undermined.' See Ryszard Kapuscinski, *Imperium*, translated by Klara Glowczewska (Toronto: Vintage Canada, 1995), pp. 308–9.

on international politics available in the 1930s or 1940s, then compare it with a contemporary one. Some of the differences, suggesting progress, include:

1. Greater theoretical awareness, that is, placing descriptive narratives in the context of theoretical questions rather than as ends in themselves.
2. More sensitivity to theoretical debates in the field and demonstrating how different theoretical positions highlight different aspects of international practices and institutions.
3. Greater reliance upon systematic rather than anecdotal evidence.
4. Employment of generic analytical devices, such as Prisoners' Dilemma, to show the underlying logics and similarities of, for example, conflict situations.
5. Deployment of a variety of concepts that expand the repertoire from just conflict or national interest. These include as typical examples, 'free-riders', 'chicken' games, the requirements for effective deterrence, the 'demographic transition', interdependence, dependence, international regimes, misperception, and many others that were not part of the field's lexicon in the 1930s.
6. Broader scope of the field to include the roles non-governmental organizations play in diplomacy and agenda-setting, the vast areas of international collaboration that eventuate in international regulation, regimes, or even 'governance', international environmental problems, and the like.
7. Firm empirical knowledge about major trends in war, conflict management activities of international organizations, trade, commerce, communications, and investment.
8. Development of the concept of power, away from its crude determinism in the 1930s, to complicated sets of bargaining relationships in which greater 'power resources' do not always predict to victory.

Would one choose a textbook of the 1930s as a suitable teaching vehicle today? The obvious choice is not based solely on the argument that the predecessors of the 1930s or 1940s were concerned solely with the headlines of the day. Some were, but most authors recognized that a field of study is more than factual reporting of the week's or year's events, and that there is a set of theoretical issues and problems that is generic to international politics and that distinguish it from other fields. A textbook, one decade after it was written, should be more than a historical curiosity. Yet, most of the efforts of the 1930s were dated within a decade. Many textbooks of the early 1980s, in contrast, can be read with considerable intellectual profit today. Theoretical offerings of the 1960s and 1970s serve many contemporary intellectual purposes and are foundations for all scholars who represent themselves as experts on international politics. Perhaps it is because of their success—the way their major ideas have become part of the ordinary vocabulary of international politics' discourse—that we tend to take their work for granted.

The field during the Cold War was not devoid of ethnocentrism, sectarian and intolerant in-fighting, geographical myopia, and a host of other shortcomings. There were intellectual dead-ends, and some areas were, perhaps prematurely, abandoned. Some of the efforts at quantification were regressive in the sense of trivializing important problems or excluding major areas of the field such as international law. The syndrome of doing things only one way (e.g. my way) is as much a characteristic of the field today as it was in the heyday of the 'behavioural' revolution. The confusion between international politics and international relations (or world politics) remains, although most undergraduate students seem to have no difficulty understanding the differences. There is no shortage of problems in the field.

A litany of shortcomings is not, however, a general indictment or an indicator of lack of progress. There is little compelling evidence that the body of Cold War era scholarship was simply an apology or justification for American national interests.[83] The behavioural revolution was an explicit attempt to divorce analysis from partisanship. There were in fact few critics of established policy as compelling as Hans Morgenthau, George Kennan, Hedley Bull, or David Singer, all major theorists of the era. The claim that positivism—or, more broadly, empiricism—was regressive also challenges the idea of progress, but aside from the renewed study of the normative and legal dimensions of international politics the alternatives to empiricism have not provided much enlightenment on the substantive problems of the field. Over the time period in question, scholars became more scholarly, though not necessarily more philosophical. They acknowledged the need for more reliable evidence, many coming to appreciate the classical traditions that set the main issues and problems in the field; and most welcomed new and novel ways of posing both old and new problems. Substantive studies in the areas of decision-making, state formation, bargaining, international regimes, the democratic peace, dependency relationships, among others, deepened the field in its historical, theoretical, and empirical dimensions. And all of this was not just 'for' some political or national programme, as Robert Cox[84] and numerous other critics have declared. The normative foundations of international relations' scholarship have been acknowledged above, but we also have to re-emphasize that scholarship derives from curiosity, a human drive to create better understanding of complexities, from the desire to solve puzzles, and from a critical attitude toward official policy. Seeking conceptual clarity, taxonomic work, examining the logic of situations and previous theoretical constructs, and scholarly criticism in general is not necessarily 'for' some political programme. Scholarship has its own standards, requirements, and goals. It does not need a political project to animate them.

The Cold War affected scholarship in many different ways, but it did not dominate it to the exclusion of other impulses. Realism as a philosophical and positivist rendering of the essential characteristics of international politics owes its origins as much to both a classical tradition of thinking and to the serial aggressions of the 1930s as it does to the diplomatic and strategic behaviour typical of the Cold War years. That realism became a predominant representation of international politics during part of this era should come as no surprise because much of what observers saw in the practices, ideas, and norms of Cold War rivalry and competition fit reasonably well with the texts of Carr, Morgenthau, Schwartzenberger, and others. The areas of crisis decision-making, bargaining theory and deterrence, and security studies in general demonstrated most explicitly the nexus between the Cold War and scholarship. The dangers and threats of Soviet and American behaviour lent an urgency to studies which had as their underlying purpose not only increasing knowledge but making the world a safer place. As these threats began to wane during the era of détente, and as the Western economies became increasingly integrated, the cooperative side of international politics began to assume more

---

[83] Hoffmann argued in 1977 that American policy-makers used scholarship *after* it was produced; thought preceded policy. Later, policy and scholarship, particularly in security studies, became entwined and blended, invigorating each other. Stanley Hoffmann, 'An American Social Science', pp. 47–8.

[84] Robert Cox, 'Social Forces, States, and World Orders: Beyond International Relations Theory', in Robert Keohane (ed.), *Neorealism and Its Critics* (New York: Columbia University Press, 1987), pp. 204–55, especially p. 207.

theoretical prominence, although it had never disappeared even during the height of the Cold War. By the 1980s, despite a resurrection of Cold War-type behaviour (e.g. the shooting down of KAL 007, the 'Star Wars' programme, Nicaragua, and the like) the field developed many new ideas, directions, and debates. Some were inspired by new normative concerns such as the environment; others derived from debates within the discipline, and the 'post' movement searched for inspiration in the works of Continental philosophers who had no interest in wars, cold or otherwise. Our excursion thus suggests that while context matters, seemingly in direct proportion to the perceived intensity of threat or fear, it is not a sufficient explanation for the development of the field. Scholarship has its own mores, demands, and foibles. Academics do not need major international trends to animate their debates and to search for more reliable knowledge. Scholarship is a part of the world, but is also a world of its own.

The English school on the frontiers of international society: a hermeneutic recollection

ROGER EPP

> . . . it is, contrary to what one would expect, the future which drives us back into the past.
>
> Hannah Arendt

It is almost two decades ago that the *Review* published Roy Jones' famous 'case for closure' against what he christened the English school of international relations. While that case was couched in an anxious foreboding that the school was 'still in its prime', that its bonds 'are proving much too strong', and that 'young recruits are constantly coming forward', it arguably registered a growing sense at the time that its target was a safe one, a spent force—one whose attraction defied explanation. For the work of the English school was a 'sterile regime'. It lacked intellectual coherence, rigour, passion, and acquaintance with such important social–scientific fields as economics.[1] Whether Jones had cast his polemical net too widely over a heterodox group, or missed the mark with his criticisms, the absence of any spirited, sustained reply along these lines seems, in retrospect, to reinforce the impression that the approach identified most closely with Martin Wight and Hedley Bull had run out of steam. It had made little impression in the United States.[2] In British circles it had become the faintly embarrassing traditionalism which scholars were obliged to overcome, a synonym for scholarly provincialism, one that engaged the world from such insular vantage points as the common room of the London School of Economics. It stood accused of inhibiting access to the fruits of American social science while inclining, at bottom, to the same political realism that had predominated in the U.S.[3] The mostly unspoken accusation of anachronism has never gone away.

Judged in hindsight, however, the case for closure has not succeeded. If anything, the theoretical orientation marked variously as the 'English' or 'classical' or

---

[1] Roy Jones, 'The English School in International Relations: a Case for Closure', *Review of International Studies*, 7 (1981), pp. 1–13, quotations at 1, 12.

[2] Only three non-American authors—Raymond Aron, E. H. Carr, and the mathematician Lewis Richardson—are listed among the first 50 in a citation count of major U.S. journals. Richard Finnegan and John Giles, 'A Citation Analysis of Patterns of Influence in International Relations Research', *International Studies Notes*, 1 (1975), pp. 11–21. While Hedley Bull's subsequent *The Anarchical Society: A Study of Order in World Politics* (London, 1977) may have achieved a slightly higher profile, Stanley Hoffmann's foreword to its 1996 reissue suggests that its impact was slight because 'its "Britishness" did not fit with the prevailing American approaches' (vii).

[3] A relatively modest protest was Stephen George, 'The Reconciliation of the "Classical" and "Scientific" Approaches to International Relations', *Millennium*, 5 (1976), pp. 28–40.

'international society' or 'rationalist' school has been reinvigorated in recent years, and put to purposes more critical—perhaps—than its central thinkers intended. Those whose names are associated with it are as likely to reside outside of England: in Wales, Australia, Canada, Norway, Germany, even the U.S.[4] Its trademark conception of international society is at least as prominent as ever in the literature of academic international relations. It has been grafted to regime theory; it has been retrieved around post-Cold War questions of multilateral intervention and self-determination; and it has been challenged afresh—in ways that still recognize its centrality—by critics who identify it with statist or communitarian assumptions of human belonging and moral obligation.[5] All the same, inclusion of the English school in this volume requires a stronger footing than home-side chauvinism or evidence of either piecemeal trans-Atlantic borrowing, reinvigoration in small circles, or mere academic survival into a generation that eschews tweed. What about it should command our notice? What is distinctive about it? What unexplored promise does it contain? As Tim Dunne argues in *Inventing International Society*, it remains necessary to rescue the English school from its 'marginal presence in the dominant self-images of the discipline' and, to that end, to clarify its commitment to interpretive modes of inquiry. Dunne shows in particular that a 'profound anti-positivism' and a deliberate 'move away from realism' have animated the school since it coalesced in the committee on international theory whose published work is framed by *Diplomatic Investigations* (1966) and *The Expansion of International Society* (1984).[6]

This article, too, is intended as a re-collection of the English school. My purpose is not to rehearse either its historical lineage or what are by now well-worn debates between its exponents and its critics.[7] Rather it is to draw out three neglected

[4] Tim Dunne, *Inventing International Society: A History of the English School* (London: Macmillan 1998), ch. 1, fn. 54. The fact that this article on the 'English school' has been entrusted to a Canadian suggests that the label now functions mainly to designate its historical origins and its ongoing intellectual centre, though Ole Waever complained as late as 1992 that 'the problem with the English school is that it has actually become—an English school'. 'International Society—Theoretical Promises Unfulfilled?' *Cooperation and Conflict*, 27 (1992), p. 107.

[5] See, e.g., examples of each of these uses in Rick Fawn and Jeremy Larkins (eds.), *International Society after the Cold War* (London, 1996). Another graft onto regime theory is Barry Buzan, 'From International System to International Society: Structural Realism and Regime Theory meet the English School,' *International Organization*, 47 (1993), pp. 327–52. See also Terry Nardin's general adoption of international society in *Law, Morality, and the Relations of States* (Princeton, 1983).

[6] Dunne, *Inventing International Society*, ch. 1. One example of this post-modern dismissal of the English school as traditionalist, unself-conscious empiricism is Jim George, *Discourses of Global Politics: A Critical (Re) Introduction to International Relations* (Boulder, CO, 1994), pp. 80–2. Cf. James der Derian's much rarer acknowledgement, in his editor's introduction to *International Theory: Critical Investigations* (New York, 1995), that Wight and Bull are important for the foundations in 'classical thinking' they provide but also for their 'speculative and self-reflexive attitudes which allow for supplementary readings' (pp. 6–7). The latter title is itself a statement of continuity with the British committee, as is the foreword by Adam Watson.

[7] I have followed Dunne in defining the English school primarily around a Wight–Bull–Vincent axis, leaving C. A. W. Manning to the side. To an unusual degree, the English school has been knitted together by collaborative volumes, introductory essays, *festschrifts*, and commemorative lectures. Key texts include: Herbert Butterfield and Martin Wight (eds.), *Diplomatic Investigations* (London, 1966); Wight, *Systems of States* (Leicester, 1977); Wight, *Power Politics* (Harmondsworth, 1978); Wight, *International Theory: The Three Traditions* (Leicester, 1991); Bull, *The Anarchical Society*; Bull, *Justice in International Relations* (Waterloo, 1984); Bull and Adam Watson (eds.), *The Expansion of International Society* (Oxford, 1984); Bull, Benedict Kingsbury, and Adam Roberts (eds.), *Hugo Grotius and International Relations* (Oxford, 1992); Watson, *The Evolution of International Society* (London, 1992); J. D. B. Miller and R. J. Vincent (eds.), *Order and Violence: Hedley Bull and International*

characteristics that help to distinguish the English school as a living tradition in the study of international relations. The three might be imagined as concentric circles. The first is a strong interest in the 'Third World', in decolonization and its consequences—this over against the Cold War fixation of much of the discipline whether in the 1950s or the 1980s. The second is an understanding of international relations that is less about structure or what Wight called 'mechanics' than it is about the diffuse, imprecise domain of culture. Hence an attentiveness, *inter alia*, to the history of ideas; to the presence (or absence) of a common diplomatic culture; to suzerain relations of deference in antiquity; to 'Western values' and the Third World 'revolt against the West'; to tectonic shifts in standards of international legitimacy; to the socialization of revolutionary states; indeed, to the modern states-system as an artefact, whose gradual universalization is marked by a series of ideological displacements and a homogenization of political forms. All this amounts to what has been called 'the only fully fledged research programme in the field outside the United States'[8]—one that is, in Dunne's words, 'subversive of the post-positivist claim that 'culture and identity' are making a 'dramatic comeback' in the post-Cold War era. Civilizations, cultures, values, rules, encounters, meaning and so on, never went away; at least not for thinkers working within the English School from the early 1950s onwards.'[9]

The third and most elemental characteristic is an interpretive orientation that bears strong resemblances to the practical philosophy of Hans-Georg Gadamer's hermeneutics. This claim will require the fullest demonstration, though in a certain sense, too, it may seem unsurprising. Even unwittingly, the English school's attentiveness to diplomatic practice—in which the interpreter is a key figure—pushes the hermeneutic elements of language and understanding to the fore where a great deal is at stake. Indeed, the connection has been drawn on rare occasions. Richard Shapcott has suggested that the conceptions of international society developed by Wight and Bull, as something resembling a 'dialogical experience' around the normative bases of coexistence, not a 'means of perpetuating separateness', are most amenable to Gadamer's position.[10] But this linkage is more a matter of promise than of inheritance. Andrew Linklater too has identified the English school insightfully with a practical–hermeneutic knowledge interest in international order.[11] But he

Relations (Oxford, 1990); Vincent, *Nonintervention and International Order* (Princeton, 1974); Vincent, *Human Rights and International Relations* (Cambridge, 1986); Gerrit Gong, *The Standard of Civilization in International Relations* (Oxford, 1984); James Mayall, *Nationalism and International Society* (Cambridge, 1990); Robert Jackson, *Quasi-States: Sovereignty, International Relations, and the Third World* (Cambridge, 1990); Jackson, 'The Political Theory of International Society', in Ken Booth and Steve Smith (eds.), *International Relations Theory Today* (London, 1995); David Armstrong, *Revolution and World Order: The Revolutionary State in International Society* (Oxford, 1993); Ian Clark and Iver Neumann (eds.), *Classical Theories of International Relations* (London, 1996).

[8] Iver Neumann, 'John Vincent and the English School of International Relations', in Iver Neumann and Ole Waever (eds.), *The Future of International Relations: Masters in the Making?* (London, 1997), p. 38. I owe to Mark Neufeld the point that there is a second such 'fully-fledged research programme outside the U.S.' in the Gramscian school formed around Robert Cox, and that there are unexplored points of convergence—unlikely but strong—between the two schools.

[9] Tim Dunne, 'Colonial Encounters in International Relations: Reading Wight, Writing Australia', *Australian Journal of International Affairs*, 51 (1997), pp. 309–23.

[10] Richard Shapcott, 'Conversation and Co-existence: Gadamer and the Interpretation of International Society', *Millennium*, 23 (1994), pp. 57–83, quotations at pp. 79–80.

[11] Andrew Linklater, *Beyond Realism and Marxism: Critical Theory and International Relations* (London, 1990), pp. 8–9. See also his 'Rationalism', in Scott Burchill *et al.* (eds.), *Theories of International Relations* (London, 1996).

does so in a way that subordinates it, in the cognitive hierarchy of an earlier Habermas, to a higher critical–emancipatory interest, which he articulates at length while leaving unexplored the significance of the former for the discipline. The hermeneutic conception of language as constitutive rather instrumental, that is, as bound up with practices and institutions, as not simply the rationalization or mystification of 'interest', is sufficient in itself to open a great gulf with mainstream realists, marxists, and, not least, E. H. Carr's hybrid sociology of knowledge. Something like a hermeneutic interest in the fusion of horizons also gives a certain colouration to the English school's account of the international relations of colonial and post-colonial encounters—in place of, say, political-economy considerations. Suffice to say that any identifiable intellectual orientation or school is known by the dilemmas it keeps. It can be understood as an extended answer to a set of questions which, in turn, shape it in ways that open up certain kinds of inquiry and preclude others. In the case of the English school the questions that framed Wight's influential lectures in the 1950s for students at the LSE still hold: What is international society? How far does it extend? What obligations does it create? And what about the barbarian outside it?[12] The hermeneutic work that follows from those questions, I argue, necessarily has moved in two directions: towards the frontier, the unfamiliar; but also—crucially—back towards the seemingly familiar, 'the West', which, on closer, self-reflexive scrutiny, stands in need of interpretation no less than that against which historically it has been defined.

A hermeneutic sensibility

While plenty of 'post-positivist' approaches now flourish in the global subcultures of academic international relations, almost all of them pegged to a continental luminary, hermeneutics has received scant attention.[13] Shapcott's worthy but lonely essay on Gadamer in the journal *Millennium* has prompted no ripple of citations. This marginalization, of course, is not peculiar to international relations; it prevails across the so-called human sciences. The ironic effect is that hermeneutics has been confined largely to rarefied philosophic development, despite its commitment to the universal, everyday nature of the problem of human understanding.

Hermeneutics developed in 19th-century German thought around the problem of interpreting biblical and classical texts, and then history at large. Its purpose was methodological: that is, to represent the 'true' meaning of a text or event as an author or historical actor intended or saw it. To do that, Dilthey among others posited a basic distinction between explanation and understanding—the former appropriate to the natural sciences, the latter required of any account of society, in which self-conscious subjects attached meanings to their actions. *Verstehen* sociology is one important trajectory emerging from this distinction.

---

[12] Wight, *International Theory*, chs. 3–4.

[13] The point is Steve Smith's in a very instructive essay, 'Positivism and Beyond', in Steve Smith, Ken Booth, and Marysia Zalewski (eds.), *International Theory: Positivism and Beyond* (Cambridge, 1996), pp. 25–7, 37. See also Mark Neufeld, 'Interpretation and the "Science" of International Relations', *Review of International Studies*, 19 (1993), pp. 39–61.

Gadamer's monumental reformulation of hermeneutics began with *Truth and Method*, published in 1960 and first translated into English only in 1975.[14] His argument, in short, is that all understanding is interpretation, and that all interpretation is expressed in, and bounded by, the medium of language. Language therefore acquires ontological significance, displacing the narrow methodological concern with intentions, which are intelligible only against the prior existence of a web of shared meaning. What also sets Gadamer apart is his retrieval of the ideas of prejudice and tradition from the wastebasket of the Enlightenment. Far from being a barrier to objective, replicable knowledge, his prejudices are embedded in the very act and possibility of understanding. They form a shared, socially formed 'historical reality' or finite horizon of meaning, for which tradition is the repository. As Richard Bernstein puts it: 'Gadamer reminds us that we belong to tradition, history, and language before they belong to us.'[15] Prejudices enable as well as limit. They are the 'biases of our openness to the world';[16] they are risked, called into question, and reconstituted dialogically in the encounter with what is at once unfamiliar and yet makes a claim on us. Thus understanding is an existential enterprise, an 'effective moment of one's own being.'[17] Employing the elements of language, prejudice, and tradition, Gadamer resists in a particular way the sharp subject–object dichotomy that is central to modern epistemology and to classical hermeneutics. His understanding of a text, an event, a practice, or a face-to-face interlocutor, is neither subjective (where meaning is idiosyncratic to the knower) nor objective (where meaning inheres in the known and remains only to be discovered by a detached knower). Instead, understanding is denoted metaphorically as a fusion of horizons that changes both knower and known. In this way, too, tradition is not static. As Gerald Bruns puts it: 'From a hermeneutic standpoint, tradition is more accurately not a structure of any sort, but just the historicality of open-ended, intersecting, competing narratives that cannot be mastered by any Great Code . . .'[18]

Gadamer's account of what it means to understand is essentially dialogical in character. His hermeneutic circle comprises to-and-fro movement between knower and known, between part and indeterminate whole, through the enabling and confining medium of language. This represents his attempt at a theoretical grounding that is neither foundationalist nor radically subjective. For all interpretation is tempered by an accountability to the 'thing itself'—literally so where 'it' is another person capable of response—and secondarily to a community of interpreters working within a tradition (who will surely decide whether my own interpretation 'rings true'). The correlate political–ethical posture for Gadamer's dialogical hermeneutics is an Aristotelian emphasis on practical judgement that is tested in argument and praxis. For this reason he argues that the 'chief task' of

---

[14] Hans-Georg Gadamer, *Truth and Method*, 2nd edn, trans. Joel Weinsheimer and Donald Marshall (London, 1975/1989); *Philosophical Hermeneutics*, trans. David Linge (Berkeley, CA, 1976); and, *Reason in the Age of Science*, trans. Frederick Lawrence (Cambridge, MA, 1981). For commentary see, e.g., Richard Bernstein, *Beyond Objectivism and Relativism: Science, Hermeneutics, and Praxis* (Philadelphia, 1983); Josef Bleicher, *Contemporary Hermeneutics* (London, 1980); and, Gerald Bruns, *Hermeneutics Ancient and Modern* (New Haven, 1992).

[15] Bernstein, *Beyond Objectivism*, p. 167.

[16] Gadamer, 'The Universality of the Hermeneutical Problem', in *Philosophical Hermeneutics*, p. 9; *Truth and Method*, Part III.1: 'Language as the Medium of Hermeneutic Expression', *passim*.

[17] Gadamer, Foreword to the Second Edition, *Truth and Method*, p. xxxv.

[18] Bruns, *Hermeneutics*, pp. 204–5.

philosophical hermeneutics is to 'defend practical and political reason against the domination of technology based on science'.[19]

My argument in this section is that a similar hermeneutic sensibility has been implicit all along in the work of the English school even in the absence of any self-conscious and sophisticated metatheoretical ambition. Put playfully, the English school might justifiably enlist a German if it requires the respectability of a contemporary continental luminary. The match is not so far-fetched. There are points of intellectual intersection, say, in the appreciative echoes of Edmund Burke and the more immediate thought of R. G. Collingwood. Collingwood's influence on Gadamer was considerable. Wight recommended *The Idea of History* ('powerful and exciting', though carried 'too far') as an 'obligatory book' for 'the student of international affairs who is ready to examine the foundations of his thinking'.[20] There are also striking similarities in critical characterizations of the two. Readers may be excused for thinking of Wight when it is said of Gadamer that he engages in mere descriptive phenomenology, not theory at all,[21] or that his writing 'at first might appear to be only a display of erudition'.[22]

The more substantial parallels have to do with the dialogical, practice-oriented nature of theory and the constitutive nature of language. The introduction to Wight's published lectures—presumably the same one that he gave students—proposes that to study politics is to enter into a 'conversation' or a 'tradition' stretching back to the ancient Greeks and animated by a range of questions about authority, obligation, and so on. While the same is true of international theory, here the tradition is obscure, scattered, and in need, one imagines, of precisely the sort of collection the lectures were meant to provide.[23] A great deal of commentary has challenged the inside/outside bifurcation of politics and international relations suggested in this position, which is made more famously and sharply in the deliberately provocative essay, 'Why is there no International Theory'—now a standard reference in refutations of the distinction, though it is not one that Wight held with any consistency, especially in his reflections on international legitimacy or revolution.[24]

Much less attention has fallen in other possible directions. There is, for example, the partial explanation that follows in both lectures and the essay for the paucity of

---

[19] Gadamer, 'Hermeneutics as a Theoretical and Practical Task', quoted in Bernstein, *Beyond Objectivity*, p. 150. One translation of the full essay is found in *Reason in the Age of Science*.

[20] Martin Wight, review of *The Idea of History*, *International Affairs*, 23 (1947), pp. 575–7. Above all, Wight praised the book for tracing, through Vico and Croce, the 'liberation of history from the bonds of natural science'. See also his BBC presentation of history as an analogue of literary criticism, involving a sense of imagination, architecture, and what is essentially hermeneutical reflection 'on the culture within which it is written'. 'What Makes a Good Historian?', *The Listener*, 53 (1955), pp. 283–4. In historiographical terms, Wight did not share Butterfield's Rankean position, which aimed to represent the 'past as it really was'. Gadamer's interest in Collingwood, meanwhile, was substantial enough that he translated his *Autobiography* into German. Bernstein speculates that if Collingwood's work had achieved more prominence in Anglo-American circles, hermeneutics too would have received a more generous hearing (*Beyond Objectivism*, p. 111).

[21] William Outhwaite, 'Hans-Georg Gadamer', in Quentin Skinner (ed.), *The Return of Grand Theory in the Human Sciences* (Cambridge, 1985), p. 28.

[22] Bernstein, *Beyond Objectivism*, p. 114.

[23] Wight, *International Theory*, p. 1.

[24] Wight, 'Why is there no International Theory' in *Diplomatic Investigations*. Two different kinds of critical commentary are Robert Jackson, 'Martin Wight, International Theory, and the Good Life', *Millennium*, 19 (1990), pp. 261–72; and R. B. J. Walker, *Inside/Outside: International Relations as Political Theory* (Cambridge, 1993), ch. 2.

the tradition in international thought: namely, the 'intellectual prejudice imposed by the sovereign state' on modern political thinkers.[25] The word 'prejudice' alone invites comment at this stage in the article. While Wight in his earlier writings was given to an almost-apocalyptic anti-statism, it is, I think, not unreasonable to formulate his usage here in a Gadamerian sense, that is, as part of an intellectual horizon. The more considerable oversight, however, has to do with the idea that the study of international relations be regarded as an entry into a conversation or a tradition of inquiry. The metaphor of conversation is fraught with associations of genteel clubbiness perhaps involving the same common room to which reference has been made. But there is more at stake here. In the first place, inquiry understood as conversation has as its objective something quite unlike the generation of causal, law-like explanations in the form of testable hypotheses. It was in the 1950s and early 1960s that practitioners of Wight's analogue, political theory, invoked a 'tradition' around what Sheldon Wolin called an inherited 'common language' and 'familiar landscape'—partly as a rearguard defence against the behavioural revolution.[26] Elsewhere in his lectures, indeed, Wight makes the intriguing suggestion that international theory is 'more akin to literary criticism' than to 'scientific analysis'; for it requires a 'sympathetic perception' of political actors, their principles, and their circumstances.[27] Theory in this sense is a kind of depth-reflection whose purpose is to disclose or put into perspective.[28]

In the second place, Wight's lectures flesh out the conversation dialogically with the positions denoted by the 'three Rs'—realist, rationalist, revolutionist—for which he is arguably best known. As a triadic architecture for the lecture-hall and the discipline, they were intended partly to displace a simple realist–idealist dichotomy. In subsequent usage the 'three Rs' have functioned rhetorically as a means of staking out a *via media* against the extremes, such as Bull's elaboration of a Grotian tradition. Again, the difficulties or ambiguities with the 'three Rs' or traditions have been widely noted, as have their possible insights.[29] On the one hand, it is unclear whence they come, why there should be only three, and whether they can be personified by historic flag-bearers such as Hobbes, Grotius, and Kant—a tactic from which Bull later distanced himself by tackling a more conventional history of Grotian ideas. At points in Wight's lectures there is an anachronistic, contrived insistence that each tradition has a distinct angle on a succession of subjects; in

---

[25] Wight, 'International Theory?', p. 26.

[26] Sheldon Wolin, *Politics and Vision* (Boston, 1960), pp. 22–3. John Gunnell gives a good account of the idea of tradition within the crisis in political theory in *Political Theory: Tradition and Interpretation* (Cambridge, MA, 1979), ch. 2.

[27] Wight, *International Theory*, p. 258. See also the allusions to literary criticism in 'What Makes a Good Historian', pp. 283–84.

[28] Wight's dialogical orientation can be found as early as a war-time essay that captured his struggle as a conscientious objector between Christian pacifist and just-war options. 'War and the Christian Conscience', *Haileyburian* c. 1940–41. A copy is in the possession of the author. On this and other aspects of his dialogical orientation see Roger Epp, 'Martin Wight: International Relations as Realm of Persuasion', in Francis Beer and Robert Hariman (eds.), *Post-Realism: The Rhetorical Turn in International Relations* (East Lansing, MI, 1996).

[29] Bull's reservations about Wight's use of traditions are found in 'Martin Wight and the Theory of International Relations' (1976), reprinted as an introduction to *International Theory*, p. xviii. For other treatments see Ian Clark, 'Traditions of Thought and Classical Theories of International Relations', in *Classical Theories of International Relations*; Steve Smith, 'The Self-Images of a Discipline', in *International Relations Theory Today*, pp. 11–13; and my review of Wight's lectures in *International Journal*, 48 (1993), pp. 561–6.

others, Wight's categories are drawn so tightly that they squeeze out individuals or movements that otherwise catch his interest. On the other hand, there is a creative insight in the 'three Rs'. Linklater does not have to stretch them far to reach the distinction between positivist, hermeneutic, and critical modes of inquiry.[30] Dunne reads them as a historically situated representation of plurality in international theory and as a 'medium for interrogating theory and practice'—not as paradigms, which would imply their incommensurability.[31]

Wight's own clarifications indicate his awareness of some of the difficulties. More than once he cautions that his traditions should not be read as 'railroad tracks running parallel into infinity' but rather as 'threads interwoven in the tapestry of Western civilization'[32]—one crossing another most often in the crucible of practical judgement. The affinity between this formulation and Bruns' hermeneutic account of tradition, quoted above, as the 'historicality of open-ended, intersecting, competing narratives' is worthy of mention. It carries over to Wight's concluding metaphor. His intention, he says, was to stake a circle for international theory—a horizon?—around which 'any reflective person will perhaps feel free to move . . . without settling' and around which, though his own 'prejudices' were rationalist, he found himself moving.[33] The purpose was a reflective and ultimately an ethical one. From this perspective a fresh light is shed on Wight's complaint against Carr that the past had no claim on his loyalty: 'He has no views on the irreducible values of his own civilization or the degree of breach with tradition that would be intolerable.'[34] Bull's key charge in his somewhat problematic 'Case for a Classical Approach' might be recalled in that same light. It was that would-be scientists—cut off from history, philosophy, and 'any sense of inquiry into international politics as a continuing tradition'—would therefore have a 'callow and brash view of their subject and its possibilities'; moreover, they would be unreflective both about their 'preoccupations and perspectives' and about the moral and political positions unacknowledged in their work.[35]

The commitment to theory in dialogical form rooted in Wight's lectures has two additional implications that bear mention. The first is the erasure of any sharp line between participant and observer, between the known and the knower in international theory. The ideas at play in the conversation are the property neither of academic specialists, nor political philosophers, nor jurists, nor state leaders, nor revolutionaries. They are interwoven into a single tapestry that is constituted by, and bounded by, the language of practice broadly defined, which might be said to act as the 'thing itself' to which all interpretation is tempered. This is equally true of R. J.

---

[30] Linklater, *Beyond Realism*, ch. 1.

[31] Dunne, *Inventing International Society*, ch. 3. See also his 'Mythology or Methodology? Traditions in International Theory', *Review of International Studies*, 19 (1993), pp. 305–18.

[32] Wight, *International Theory*, p. 266, and p. 259: 'Classification becomes valuable in the humane studies only at the point where it breaks down.' See also Wight, 'An Anatomy of International Thought', *Review of International Studies*, 13 (1987), pp. 221–7: 'when I scrutinize my own psyche I seem to find all these three ways of thought within me' (p. 227).

[33] Wight, *International Theory*, p. 268.

[34] Wight, 'Problems of Mass Democracy', review of *The New Society* by E. H. Carr, *The Observer*, 23 September 1951, p. 7.

[35] Bull, 'International Theory: The Case for a Classical Approach', in Klaus Knorr and James Rosenau (eds.), *Contending Approaches to International Politics* (Princeton, 1969), p. 37. Suffice to say that neither Bull's combativeness nor Wight's indifference demonstrated a hermeneutic 'openness' to the scientific/American 'other'.

Vincent's account of human rights in international relations, in which the metaphor of (disputatious) conversation—East–West, North–South—recurs prominently around a 'vocabulary' that extends seamlessly from the 'everyday language of diplomacy' and advocacy to the latest treatise from Ronald Dworkin.[36]

The second implication is to reinforce the centrality of language in any account of international relations. Wight's inquiries again set an example in this respect. Invariably they circle back to consider when and how the words that constitute the practice of international relations enter its vocabulary, are mediated historically in their meanings, and find institutional expression. Thus Herbert Butterfield treats the *idea* of *raison d'etat*; Robert Jackson, self-determination; Vincent, human rights and race; and, Bull, to some extent, order—though his approach is least philological.[37] Wight, for his part, marks the 'cultural chasm' that divides medieval Christendom from the modern states-system by a gradual transition from a language of legal right to one of temporal power.[38] His excavation of that states-system begins in an important sense with the appearance in print of the phrase *de systematibus civitatum*.[39] In the same way, the balance of power is an idea with a history rather than an abstract iron law of neo-realist anarchy. It is a way of understanding a situation, and at some points in history a matter of conscious policy and diplomatic design. As such it begs hermeneutic scrutiny: why did people come to think in such terms? Here, Wight's speculations range from the influence of renaissance art, astrology, and book-keeping, each of them preoccupied with balance, while Herbert Butterfield asks how the parallel emergence of Newtonian physics lent mechanistic associations to what was an 'elaborate artifice'.[40]

This general outlook undergirds the idea of international society, which presupposes for Wight an 'international social consciousness' manifested in the solidarities of language,[41] or, for Bull, a sense of common interests, rules, and values.[42] Like the balance of power, international society is a matter of inter-subjective meaning embedded in practice. It represents the 'handiwork of real people';[43] it is 'an imagined community with an existence in the life-worlds of statesmen';[44] and it is 'reproduced in the treaties they sign, friendships they form,

---

[36] Vincent, 'The Idea of Rights in International Ethics', in Terry Nardin and David Mapel (eds.), *Traditions of International Ethics* (Cambridge, 1992), *passim*: 'All this may be dismissed as merely language, but to some extent the conversation about human rights is setting out what is to be agreed upon as the content of civilized life within the states making up international society' (267).

[37] In order, Herbert Butterfield, *Raison d'Etat: The Relations between Morality and Government*, the First Martin Wight Memorial Lecture, University of Sussex, 23 April 1975; Robert Jackson, 'The Weight of Ideas in Decolonization: Normative Change in International Relations', in Judith Goldstein and Robert Keohane (eds.), *Ideas and Foreign Policy: Beliefs, Institutions, and Political Change* (Ithaca, NY, 1993); Vincent, *Human Rights*, chs. 1–2; 'The Idea of Rights'; 'Race in International Relations', in R. B. J. Walker (ed.), *Culture, Ideology, and World Order* (Boulder, CO, 1984).

[38] Wight, *Power Politics*, ch. 1. This point is clearer in the original version of *Power Politics* (London: Looking Forward Pamphlet, No. 8, 1946), p. 11.

[39] Wight, *Systems of States*, ch. 1.

[40] Wight, *Power Politics*, ch. 16; *International Theory*, pp. 18–19, and ch. 8; and 'The Balance of Power' in *Diplomatic Investigations*. In the latter Wight notes that the 'plasticity' of the balance of power as a metaphor has generated several distinct meanings, but he makes no attempt to resolve the confusion in the interest of distilling a scientifically operational concept. Butterfield's speculations are found in an essay in *Diplomatic Investigations* also entitled 'The Balance of Power'.

[41] Wight, 'Western Values in International Relations', in *Diplomatic Investigations*, pp. 96–97.

[42] Bull, *Anarchical Society*, p. 13.

[43] Jackson, 'The Political Theory of International Society', p. 113.

[44] Neumann, 'John Vincent', p. 40.

customs they observe, and laws they comply with'.[45] On this basis, Linklater ascribes to the English school, and rationalism in particular, an important shift in theoretical emphasis away from systemic forces towards systemic principles of international cohesion and legitimacy, which can be situated historically and which are subject to change.[46] That emphasis, in turn, has generated a considerable interest in the politics of decolonization and North–South dialogue. If Grotius could delineate the globe by two concentric circles—an inner one limited to the historical–cultural unity descended from Western Christendom, and an outer one including all humanity—the English school's preoccupations have been most vigorously and consequentially at issue in the latter circle, or perhaps in relations between the two.

The World and the West

As founding figure of the English school, Wight is conventionally regarded as a detached scholar, the polar opposite of a public intellectual. This reputation has been reinforced by Bull among others, and persists in the face of Wight's many public interventions in the late 1940s and 1950s in the form of radio talks and accompanying essays in *The Listener*, journalistic reportage, and regular book reviews in *The Observer*. Among the most striking was a spirited public defence in 1954 of Arnold Toynbee, whose BBC Reith Lectures, *The World and the West*, had been condemned in some quarters as nothing short of a betrayal of 'Christian civilization'. Wight contributed at least twice to the controversy that dominated the letters pages of the *Times Literary Supplement* from April to June, and took issue in several reviews with the published counter-case written by a conservative Catholic, arguing on theological grounds against any divine assurance that 'the West will win all its battles'. He proposed that to view history from non-European standpoints, as Toynbee had tried to do, was to see the West less as 'special agent of Providence,' more as 'aggressor' and 'exploiter'.[47]

The freshness of that public defence might help to account for the unusual ferocity that attends the preoccupation in Wight's lectures with 'the fit of world-conquering fanaticism' that describes 'the West since 1500'.[48] The preoccupation itself may have reflected his participation in a research study of colonial constitutions, and the salience of the post-war debate about the future of the Empire. For whatever reason, long before it could be intellectually fashionable, Wight's lectures put the problem of relations with the other, the outsider, the barbarian, at the moral-ontological centre of the study of international relations.[49] He makes the brilliant point that modern international law emerges for a world of multiple sovereigns out of the 16th-century Spanish debate about the status of the Indian, rather than out of any strictly intra-European requirements related to

---

[45] Dunne, *Inventing International Society*, ch. 5.

[46] Linklater, *Beyond Realism*, pp. 17–18.

[47] Wight, 'Written in Anger', review of *The Lie about the West*, by Douglas Jerrold, *The Observer*, 18 April 1954, p. 7; and *International Affairs*, 30 (1954), pp. 352–53.

[48] Wight, *International Theory*, p. 68.

[49] In a letter to the author, Gabriele Wight writes: 'Whenever anyone not really interested in or connected with IR or M. Wight asks me what to look at or begin with, I suggest this chapter. Its particular strength and message may seem to some somewhat subversive, though.'

restraint of war or respect of resident embassies amid the dissolution of Christendom. He suggests the importance of the Turk to European cohesion. He documents frontier atrocities and dubious resort to the legal fiction of *terra nullius*. He quotes Swiftian satire to mock the transformation of piracy into respectable civilization. He discerns in Western liberal rationalism—the tradition with which he is often identified—a paternalism from which emerges the tutelary 'humbug' of colonialism in its latter stages; for realist and rationalist modes of dispossession had much the same outcome. He is unsparingly sardonic about the way that, in white settler societies, one finds 'barbarians herded into reserves', renamed, and protected by a Department of Barbarian Affairs, which can then 'see that the brighter specimens get presented to the Queen if she comes around'.[50] In the period literature of the 1950s, there is nothing remotely comparable in substance or style to this interrogation.

In an important sense, the English school like the history of international society it excavates is founded on the problem of relations with the outsider. As the progression of Wight's organizing questions makes clear, it is impossible to think about international society without also thinking about its limits, whether geographic, ideological, or cultural. For this reason the post-colonial world has been central to the English school's account of contemporary international relations. It is neither a sideshow nor an academic after-thought. Bull in his 1983 *Hagey Lectures* was not abandoning one subject for another when he gave an account of the 'revolt against Western dominance', charted the development of the anti-colonial idea in United Nations conventions, and made a case for economic redistribution in respect of Third World demands, partly to preserve a fragile international order.[51] He had signalled many of the same interests in *The Anarchical Society*. Likewise, *The Expansion of International Society*, produced under the direction of Bull and Adam Watson, represented no radical departure from the sort of inquiry undertaken by founding members of the British committee. For all the criticisms that might be made of the volume, among them the near-teleological character of its narrative in which a Vattelian world exclusively of states unfolds over centuries, it is addressed to the same kinds of questions set out in Wight's lectures: 'Has the geographical expansion of international society led to a contraction of the consensus about common interests, rules, and institutions . . .? Or can we say that the framework of the old European international society has been modified, adapted, and developed in such a way that a genuinely universal and non-hegemonial structure of rules and institutions has taken root?'[52] The book's multifarious chapters trace, for example, the reciprocal diplomatic relations between African and European polities dating back to the first stirrings of the modern states-system; the European application of a 19th-century 'standard of civilization' and the imposition of unequal treaties in relations with Asia; the significance of race; and the reassertion of non-Western cultures over against colonialist presumption, but within the paradox of the post-colonial state that insists on the Westphalian norms of non-interference and sovereign equality. Again, there is nothing resembling it in the discipline. One recent

---

[50] Wight, *International Theory*, ch. 4, *passim*, quotation at pp. 52–3.
[51] Bull, *Justice, passim*.
[52] 'Introduction', *Expansion*, p. 8. See also Bull's, 'The West and South Africa', *Daedalus*, 111 (1982), pp. 255–70.

survey cites it as a rare instance when an international relations text has intersected the concerns of post-colonialist literature.[53]

At the same time, *The Expansion of International Society* was not a one-time effort. Numerous other examples can be cited in support of my general claim. Vincent, who is regarded often as a third central figure after Wight and Bull in the English school's lineage, is known primarily for two books: one on the idea of non-intervention, the other on the idea of human rights.[54] In each case, the post-colonial world is the principal terrain on which these ideas are shown to have the greatest vitality in contemporary practice. Robert Jackson came to the study of international relations via the comparative politics of development in Africa. His work has explored the way in which decolonization on that continent gave new territorial footholds to the idea of self-determination and continues to reshape standards of international legitimacy, creating both fragile 'quasi-states' and new pariahs in the process.[55] David Armstrong's study of revolutionary states, meanwhile, the nearer it comes to the present, deals of necessity with the post-colonial world—specifically Indonesia, Cuba, China, Iran, perhaps Libya—and with the ideological revolt against the West.[56] More recent inquiries have bridged Wight's work with the re-emergent international political status of indigenous peoples entrapped within white-settler states.[57] As Wight himself wryly remarked about the narrow, 'blue-water' definition of colonial possessions that became the norm with the support of both Cold War superpowers: 'In the field of international legitimacy, . . . land power has triumphed over sea power'.[58]

Two caveats are probably necessary at this stage of the argument. One is that even where English school texts are critical of Western policy and sympathetic to the post-colonial 'revolt'—there is some variation on this score—they typically also evince a more conservative concern for order in international society. In Bull's case, this latter concern had the effect of strengthening both an instrumental argument for partial Western accommodation of the South's demands and a dubious working assumption that post-colonial states spoke for their populations. The second caveat is that while the English school has made the post-colonial world integral to the study of international relations, that interest has not been reciprocated. The most notable exception may be the Chinese officials who quote Bull on the norm of non-intervention and in defence of international pluralism.[59] I am not aware that the work of the English school has been widely appropriated by scholars in Africa, Asia, Latin America, or the Middle East. There may be many reasons for this, including the predominance of American publishers and graduate training. Nonetheless the point should not go unnoticed.

[53] Philip Darby and A. J. Paolini, 'Bridging International Relations and Postcolonialism', *Alternatives*, 19 (1994), p. 380.

[54] Vincent, *Nonintervention*; *Human Rights*, esp. ch. 5.

[55] Jackson, *Quasi-States*; 'The Weight of Ideas'. The latter essay stands out against the standard instrumentalist and utilitarian treatment of ideas against interests in the Goldstein and Keohane volume.

[56] Armstrong, *Revolution*, esp. ch. 5.

[57] Dunne, 'Colonial Encounters'; and, with explicit hermeneutical purposes, Roger Epp, 'At the Wood's Edge: Towards a Theoretical Clearing for Indigenous Diplomacies in International Relations', in Darryl Jarvis and Robert Crawford (eds.), *International Relations: Still an American Social Science?* (Albany, NY, forthcoming).

[58] Wight, *Systems of States*, p. 171.

[59] See, e.g., Yi Ding, 'Opposing Interference in Other Countries' Internal Affairs through Human Rights', *Beijing Review*, 6 November 1989, pp. 14–16.

At the same time, judgements about the work of the English school should not rest inordinately on the matter of post-colonial appropriation or influence. In one respect, international society or Vincent's human rights narratives have been offered to account for the whole of the encounter; as such they operate like what Charles Taylor calls a 'language of perspicuous contrast'.[60] But they also represent a thinking-through of the encounter invariably from one side of it. The considerable interest in those narratives in the spread of, modification of, or resistance to, Western ideas, practices and political forms is more than evidence of ethnocentricity at work. From another angle it is an unsurprising hermeneutic outcome. As Taylor puts it, a language of perspicuous contrast 'also forces us to redescribe what we are doing',[61] to inquire into the horizons from within which originates the attempt to understand an encounter. The 'West' too needs to be understood and interrogated. One fine example of this kind of critical enterprise is an essay written by two of Vincent's students on how the 19th-century expansion of international society to include the Ottoman Empire—the traditional 'other'—affected the diplomatic culture of its European core.[62] In the same spirit one can cite Wight's recurrent, if suggestive, allusions to the peculiar 'missionary' element in Western culture that could produce a fit of world-conquering fanaticism, and Vincent's speculation that Western liberal conceptions about human rights had been modified in the North–South encounter, though not enough to produce a self-conscious critique of the causes of hunger or efforts to alleviate it.[63] To pursue such reflections was not to step outside the study of international relations, but rather to come to terms with what it meant to do so from within a particular horizon.

What's critical about the hermeneutics of the English school?

Perhaps the most persistent criticism of Gadamer's hermeneutics is that it hides a political conservatism, or that, at the least, it lacks any explicit critical dimension. Gadamer himself has understood his critics to say that his position amounts to a 'prejudice in favor of existing social relations'.[64] Certainly this was the thrust of Habermas' rejoinder, however admiring he was of *Truth and Method* in other respects. This essentially is Linklater's response to the English school even as he takes up 'official dissident' membership in its revolutionist branch: the practical interest of the rationalist mainstream lies in order and social consensus; the emphasis on culture and language cannot account for 'distorted thought and communication'.[65] To some extent this criticism echoes Marx's injunction for

---

[60] Charles Taylor, 'Understanding and Ethnocentricity', in *Philosophical Papers*, vol. 2: *Philosophy and the Human Sciences* (Cambridge, 1985), p. 125.

[61] Ibid., p. 129.

[62] Iver Neumann and Jennifer Welsh, 'The Other in European Self-Definition: An Addendum to the Literature on International Society', *Review of International Studies*, 17 (1991), pp. 327–48.

[63] Wight's comparison is with China. In *Systems of States,* he locates the roots of Western expansion partly in a 'pecular culture' shaped by universalist claims and a 'missionary dynamic' exemplified by crusaders and Franciscans well in advance of the Spanish conquistadores (p. 119). In the lectures he lists 'doctrinal extermination' in war as no less a distinctly Western invention than the steam engine or the orchestral symphony (*International Theory*, p. 229). Vincent's comments are from *Human Rights*, p. 147.

[64] Gadamer, *Truth and Method*, afterword, p. 566.

[65] Linklater, *Beyond Realism*, p. 9. The designation, 'official dissident', is from Neumann, 'John Vincent', p. 60.

philosophers to change the world, not merely interpret it. The underlying assumption is that the hermeneutical problem is not universal after all, that it is possible to engage in a critique of ideology or 'oppressive' webs of meaning from a reference-point beyond what are only the horizons of another tradition and the limits expressed in language. Put another way, the critical response has been to call philosophical hermeneutics to reflect on the limits of its understanding. Specifically, Gadamer is said to 'ontologize language' in a way that neglects both the role of language as a medium of domination (or psychanalytic repression) and the need to account for structural, non-linguistic forms of power in social relations.[66]

None of this is new in the currents of contemporary thought that now spill over academic disciplines, in which the Gadamer–Habermas and Gadamer–Derrida debates have clarified positions, and in which the limits of a neo-Kantian critique of ideology have themselves become apparent. My purpose in recalling it is not to offer a new resolution, but rather to reflect it back onto my recollection of the English school as a mode of interpretive inquiry that bears a strong resemblance to Gadamerian hermeneutics. Questions about the limits of hermeneutical understanding are relevant here. One broadbrush observation that is made unassailably, I think, about the international society literature is that a category such as power is undertheorized within it. English school scholars can document insightfully the exchange of positions, say, at the UN as they concern human rights or a new economic order, and thereby show with great subtlety how an idea is put on the diplomatic agenda and comes to frame a discussion, even while its meanings may be disputed and turned against those who first used it. This is the direction in which their horizons show a generous openness. But the reader is unlikely to find an account of debt structures that frame the exchange or even an account of the complementary ideological vocabulary of neo-liberalism. The same kinds of limitations may help to explain the English school's curiously superficial account of *pax americana* in the post-1945 period. To be sure, there are flashes of idiosyncratic insight that follow from the stock depiction of the U.S. as a latent revolutionary state, ambivalent about the 'old world' norms of international society—a depiction implied in Bull's jeremiad against both of the 'great irresponsibles' at the collapse of détente.[67] But those flashes leave a good deal of ground uncovered. Tellingly, there are chapters in *The Expansion of International Society* devoted to the 20th-century roles of several key states, but not to the U.S., even though American military intervention, political–economic leverage, and even civil-rights struggles are crucial pieces in the larger picture of change and contestation around systemic principles.

That said, it would be a mistake to pronounce the English school bereft of critical possibilities on the basis of an either/or distinction between hermeneutic interpretation and critique, between a hermeneutics of faith whose purpose is recollection and a hermeneutics of suspicion whose purpose is to unmask and emancipate. In a strong sense, any act of hermeneutic recollection is potentially

---

[66] The principal critics on this score were Habermas and Karl-Otto Apel. For an overview, see the relevant chapters in Bleicher, *Contemporary Hermeneutics*, which includes a translation of the former's most direct response, 'The hermeneutic claim to universality'.

[67] Armstrong, *Revolution*, ch. 2, draws a detailed and persuasive portrait of the U.S. as the first revolutionary state. Bull's scolding is found in 'The Great Irresponsibles? The United States, the Soviet Union, and World Order', *International Journal*, 35 (1980), pp. 437–47.

critical insofar as it treats the world as shaped rather than found. Rather than cast the purposes of recollection and criticism as opposites, Bruns argues that it is possible—and dialectically preferable—to 'abide within their opposition and interplay'.[68] This formulation provides a way of thinking about the tensions present within the English school as well. Vincent has put it as follows: 'if the modern history of Europe can be written in terms of the defence of the system against revolutionaries who broke its rules, . . . it is as important to pay attention to the attack on the system as to its defence'.[69] In other words, the English school recollects a tradition—'the historicality of open-ended, intersecting, competing narratives'—*within* which critical resources are already present. Its erudite, generous horizons contain what amount to enabling prejudices: the biases of openness to an indeterminate future.

One side of this critical potential lies in the richness of a historical memory in which 'other Wests'—revolutionary, pacifist, medieval-cosmopolitan—are subordinated but not forgotten alongside what Bull once conceded was the 'establishment' doctrine of international society. Wight's reflections on revolution again stand out in this respect. Beginning from the claim that revolution is necessarily an international event, and from the calculation that the history of the modern states-system divides roughly into equal periods of settled consensus and doctrinal rupture, so that the former cannot be assumed 'normal',[70] Wight's account widens to include a succession of revolutionary 'waves': Calvinist, Jacobin, Leninist. His lectures betray a fascination with revolutionary figures. Indeed, the lectures begin with revolutionism, because its universalist 'moral dynamism' and its conviction that the world can be changed are 'in a special way representative of Western civilization'.[71] Wight's interest extends similarly to the 'inverted revolutionist' or pacifist underside of a states-system built around the possibility, even necessity, of war. It is from a clue deposited in Wight's essay on 'Western values' that I was drawn to interrogate Grotius' first flight into international theory, *De Jure Praedae*, which prefigured much of the classic *De Jure Belli ac Pacis* in its argument. The earlier work was prompted not at all by the concern to rein in the destructive practice of *raison d'etat* or to present a counterweight to some timeless realism. Rather, it was directed with full rhetorical vehemence at a group of pacifist Mennonite shareholders of the East India Company, whose doctrinal renunciation of the 'natural law' of self-preservation and whose scruples about taking their share of prize seized from a Portugese ship threatened no less than the 'fellowship of mankind'.[72] The shareholders, too, like Gandhi, Tolstoy, and the Quakers, were part of the historical-dialogical circle of international theory shaped in relation to practice. Their exercise of a 'dramatic moral veto on political action', as Wight later called the pacifist option, was one that remained 'in reserve'.[73]

---

[68] Bruns, *Hermeneutics*, p. 62. See also Shapcott, 'Conversation'.

[69] Vincent, 'The Factor of Culture in the Global International Order', *Yearbook of World Affairs*, 34 (1980), quoted in Neumann, 'John Vincent', p. 259.

[70] Wight, *Power Politics*, ch. 7.

[71] Wight, *International Theory*, *passim*, esp. ch. 1, pp. 8–12, quotation at p. 9.

[72] Wight, 'Western Values', pp. 104–5. My account of this incident and its significance for interpreting Grotius is '"To Enlighten Artless Innocence . . .": Grotius, the Law of Prize, and the Idioms of Political Exclusion', *Conrad Grebel Review*, 12 (1994), pp. 63–78.

[73] Wight, 'Western Values', p. 128. Wight's argument nonetheless has the effect of identifying politics fundamentally with violence in a Weberian sense. To this extent he is a realist.

The other side of this critical potential arises from the fact that international society in the work of the English school is never the full story. This is true even for Bull, who was least 'solidarist' in his sympathies and most combative in his defence of states as 'order on a local scale', the sum of which was—'until recently'—the extent of world order.[74] In his *Hagey Lectures* he leaned in another direction: 'the mere existence of this moral concern with welfare on a world scale represents a major change in our sensibilities. . . What is ultimately important has to be reckoned in terms of the rights and interests of the individual persons of whom humanity is made, not the rights and interests of the states into which these persons are now divided.'[75] A year earlier, Bull, in an article that made South Africa a microcosm of world politics, identified the repudiation of white supremacism as the one principle on which the international community could be united, though the principle itself drew its strength from outside the limited confines of the society of states.[76] One of the distinguishing features of the English school generally is its formulation of an interplay, first, between pluralist and solidarist positions in international society, and, second, between international society and world society—the latter an old idea that, at least since Dante, is said to have 'haunted international thought'.[77] Another distinguishing feature in each case is a resistance to having to choose one against the other, or necessarily even to put the two in tension. Both ideas remain present and embedded, to some degree, in practice. Thus Vincent, with one eye looking back before the Westphalian settlement gave rights to sovereigns, aims to 're-open' the state and 'work human rights into the cracks of international society', but without also demanding against prudence that the states-system be dismantled and its norms be swept aside to achieve it.[78] Working in some of the same cracks, a self-described critical international society position has coalesced in the 1990s. Committed to the project of 'securing legitimacy for new practices of humanitarian intervention', this position challenges the members of international society to be 'guardian angels' not 'gangsters' by contributing to the development of a capacity to respond to genocide and other extreme instances of human suffering.[79]

---

[74] Bull, 'The state's positive role in world affairs', *Daedalus*, 108 (1979), p. 115. While the pluralist–solidarist distinction was introduced in Bull's essay in *Diplomatic Investigations* on the 'Grotian Conception of International Society', it is developed most notably in Nick Wheeler, 'Pluralist or Solidarist Conceptions of International Society: Bull and Vincent on Humanitarian Intervention', *Millennium*, 21 (1992), pp. 463–87.

[75] Bull, *Justice*, p. 13.

[76] Bull, 'South Africa', p. 266. This repudiation is the strongest contemporary example of what Wight called 'the idea of mankind as a great society whose majority vote can override individual nations' ('Anatomy', p. 226). His inquiries into international legitimacy were shaped, I would argue, partly by the concern to refute the South African Manning's conception of international society as based on an almost-unbreakable doctrine of non-interference in 'domestic' affairs. On this point, see also Dunne, *Inventing International Society*, ch. 3.

[77] Wight, 'Anatomy', p. 226.

[78] Vincent, *Human Rights*, p. 3.

[79] Nick Wheeler, 'Guardian Angel or Global Gangster: a Review of the Ethical Claims of International Society', *Political Studies*, 44 (1996), pp. 123–35, quotation at p. 134. Cf. Robert Jackson's more cautious 'Armed Humanitarianism', *International Journal*, 48 (1993), pp. 581–606. Another example of critical international society writing is Linklater's 'What is a Good International Citizen?' in Paul Keal (ed.), *Ethics and Foreign Policy* (Canberra: Allen and Unwin, 1992). The Kantian influence follows Habermas and, arguably, mirrors the narrowing of Wight's revolutionism to Kant by the end of the lectures. The appellation 'critical', however problematic, retains a considerable currency in the IR literature. Its use as a modifier for international society in this case is Habermasian in inspiration, and to that extent—in the implicit claim to a vantage point outside the hermeneutic problem—it marks a

In the end, one reason why the case for closure has not succeeded is that the English school is not at all a sterile or even homogenous regime. Part of the reason why it has flourished of late is that, unlike some orientations in international relations, it has not been vulnerable either to the end of the Cold War or to interpretive challenges to positivism. Its view of the subject has been an expansive one in spatial, cultural, and chronological terms. Its hermeneutic orientation, as I have presented it here, is at its best the source of a distinctive attentiveness to language, an openness to the world, and a critical cultural and disciplinary reflexivity. If the effect of my argument is to nudge those who, like myself, identify in some way with the English school towards a firmer metatheoretical grounding, one in which Gadamer's work will be important, it is not meant to encourage either a reliance on imported gurus or a preoccupation with metatheoretical questions in international relations to the neglect of practice and life-worlds. Hermeneutics in particular lives when it is done, that is, when the unfamiliar but unavoidable is encountered with good will and rigorous thinking-through of horizons.[80] International relations by a broad definition is filled with such possibilities. In that respect the inheritance of the English school is a rich and complementary one, which ought not to be squandered, as has been suggested, in the role of intersubjectivist *via media* between the latest versions of neo-realist and neo-liberal explanations of international relations.[81] The tradition it recollects embraces both curatorial and critical elements within its horizons, and the conversational metaphor deployed within the tradition as a synonym for the whole of theory implies room for additional voices, the hearing—and not merely the toleration—of which is a matter of hermeneutic insistence.

---

departure from the Gadamerian position I have read into the English school's core theorists. Mark Neufeld distinguishes helpfully between varieties of 'critical' theory, hermeneutics and the critique of ideology, and traditional and critical forms of hermeneutics. See 'Interpretation' (fn. 13) and also 'What's Critical About Critical IR Theory?' in Richard Wyn Jones and Roger Tooze (eds.), *Critical Theory and World Politics* (Boulder: Lynne Rienner, 1998).

[80] See Epp, 'At the Wood's Edge' (fn. 57), in which, following Wight, I examine the formative but unacknowledged presence of indigenous peoples within the horizons of academic international relations, in order to think about their contemporary diplomatic activity.

[81] Waever, 'International Society', pp. 106–7.

Realism and utopianism revisited

MICHAEL NICHOLSON

Realists and utopians*

For Carr, the contrast between utopians and realists was between 'those who regard politics as a function of ethics and those who regard ethics as a function of politics'.[1] In other words, can we direct society in benevolent directions, perhaps to a utopia, or do we take what we are given and try to rationalize this into some form of moral acceptability? In the context of International Relations, the utopian aspires to a world without war and where power is not the primary determinant of relationships. The realist is more sceptical. Broadly, the realist stresses the constraints in life; the utopian stresses the opportunities. At this level, they are not social theories but temperamental attitudes.

Writing originally in 1939, Carr regarded the realists as those who understood the significance of power in the international scene and whose voices had been neglected in the interwar years. The utopians espoused a set of disparate views prevalent at that time linked by their neglect of power. Carr held these utopian positions to be impractical and dangerous. My aim in this article is to look at some versions of realism and some of utopianism, to see how they have developed today into modern variants. I ask how relevant are these traditions, if traditions they be, to the present world.

'Realism' in International Relations is used in a broad sense and a narrow sense. In the broad sense it is the view that human beings are fundamentally selfish. In political contexts, as with Bertrand Russell, this might centre on power but power conceived of rather widely. This can lead to pessimism about human improvement, notoriously in International Relations with Martin Wight. It need not lead to pessimism. A realist can argue that change can come and be directed but only by working with the grain of self-interest and not against it. Utopians believe there is greater scope for persuading people to be virtuous.[2]

Realism in the narrow sense used in International Relations is a special case of broad realism as applied to the world of states. States are held to be the dominant

---

* I am grateful to Ken Booth, Stephanie Hoopes, Georg Sørensen and an anonymous referee for their helpful comments on an earlier draft. They are not responsible for the uses and abuses I have made of them.
[1] E.H.Carr, *The Twenty Years' Crisis: An Introduction to the Study of International Relations* 1946 (2nd edn.) (London and Basingstoke: Macmillan (Papermac editions. 1981)), p. 42.
[2] Relations between political realism in general and that in International Relations are discussed by Martin Griffiths, *Realism, Idealism and International Politics: A Reinterpretation* (London: Routledge, 1992).

and, perhaps, the exclusive actors in an anarchic system, while power is seen as the central feature of interstate relationships. Realists in this narrow sense, by adopting the name, have cleverly implied that they are the true representatives of the broad realist view in International Relations. Inasmuch as realism and realistic is contrasted with 'unrealistic' meaning impractical, which may be personally endearing but not very useful, particularly in International Relations, they have won a public relations battle. Of course, this implied claim is not true. It is perfectly possible to be a realist in the sense of looking at the world, warts and all, without subscribing to the tenets of one particular approach to International Relations which many hold to be an empirically flawed account.[3]

There is a clear realist tradition, or set of traditions, in International Relations linking the realism of Carr and others such as Morgenthau to Waltz and to many writing today. It is common to add the familiar list of Thucydides, Machiavelli, Hobbes, Clausewitz, and others. Ideas have developed and the world has changed, but within the context of an identifiable intellectual programme.

Utopianism is not a true parallel or opposite to realism. It does not form a coherent theoretical tradition except in the very general sense that some people are more optimistic about the improvability of the international scene than others. There is no utopian theory in the sense in which we can talk, loosely at least, of a realist theory. Idealism, often used in International Relations literature as a synonym for utopianism, was one of the parties to the 'first great debate' in International Relations (if a debate of which only a few thousand people were aware can properly be referred to as 'great': our profession does not suffer from modesty). However, the parties were false opposites except within the rather particular context of the interwar years. Then utopianism spanned from a belief that the League of Nations would provide the umbrella for collective security to a belief that World Government would come about soon and be the answer to the problem of war. The most utopian of all were the pacifists. Now those we might call utopians consider very different things.

If we do not have a utopian theory to parallel the realist theory we must take some rather more general attribute of utopianism in order to identify the descendants of those in the 1930s of whom Carr disapproved. I shall regard utopianism as any view that radical change can be brought about in the international system by sets of political choices, and we are not simply under the control of forces which we can only influence only tangentially by manipulating power balances and the like. On this definition, there are clearly many versions of utopianism today. Some, stressing the interrelationships between economics and politics, look to a radically restructured form of the international political economy. Environmentalists require some degree of global governance to control the environment. Feminists want a social restructuring to empower gender relations, normally as part of a general emancipatory move. All these movements embody ranges of radicalism from moderate moves to fundamental change. However, World Government, once thought highly of by some, is now deeply out of fashion. Perhaps one day it will return.

---

[3] A vigorous critique of realism as an appropriate framework for the analysis of International Relations on the grounds that it is empirically inadequate is by John A. Vasquez, *The Power of Power Politics: A Critique* (London: Frances Pinter, 1983). A set of empirical studies which are more sympathetic to realism is edited by Frank W. Wayman and Paul F. Diehl, *Reconstructing Realpolitik* (Ann Arbor: Michigan University Press, 1994).

However, none of these movements has an obvious intellectual origin in the interwar period amongst the utopians. It is interesting that, with the exception of feminism, these were issues which people hardly recognized in the interwar years. One area with family links (sometimes literal ones) from the pre- to the post-war era is the peace movement. At least during the Cold War, organizations such as the Campaign for Nuclear Disarmament clearly descended from earlier peace movements. Peace research is an intellectual movement which in part links in with this. Peace researchers can be seen as modern utopians, but ones who have fully digested the objections raised by the realists.

Many modern utopians would argue that they were now realists in that they were looking at achievable utopias which allowed for the actual and not idealized characteristics of human beings. They might well adopt Ken Booth's happy phrase of 'utopian realists'[4] and avoid the slightly pejorative, or at least condescending, sense in which utopianism has been, and sometimes still is, used in International Relations.

Realism in International Relations

Realism as a conceptual framework

There are many versions of realism in International Relations, but they all share a few basic principles.[5] First, the main actors in International Relations are states who seek to maintain their existence and general security. Secondly, the system of states is anarchic: no government or quasi-government exists to control states. Thirdly, and following from these, the 'power–security' principle is the dominant mode of interaction. Fourthly, while for some states purely defensive security is all that matters, if a state's power position warrants it, it will become a predator and force concessions from a weaker power. Finally, but rather more cautiously, internal politics and external politics are largely separate. Thus, the behaviour of one state *vis-à-vis* other states can be explained largely in terms of the behaviour of these other states. The primary exogenous influence of the internal political system on the external is power. Anything else is secondary. Security is a dominant goal of a state. Thus, if there is the possibility that at least one other state will be a predator, then it follows that all internal matters will be subordinated to external matters. This is a

---

[4] Ken Booth 'Security in Anarchy: Utopian Realism in Theory and Practice', *International Affairs*, 67 (1991), pp. 527–45.

[5] The various modifiers of realism are numerous and not used consistently. Waltz prefers 'structural realism' for his version of realism. Buzan, Little and Jones refer to this as 'neorealism', leaving 'structural realism' for later developments. Spegele uses 'concessional realism' for Waltz's version of realism on the grounds that it makes concessions to the 'positivist–empiricist' position and in so doing marks some decline from the faith of the true believer. His version of realism he calls 'evaluative political realism', a relative of 'commonsense realism'. However, as Michael Donelan puts in a surprise appearance in Spegele's work as a 'positivist–empiricist', the whole system is rather confusing. I shall use 'realism' as a generic term, 'classical realism' for anything before Waltz, and, with apologies to Waltz for not following his terminology, 'neorealism' for Waltz and after. See Barry Buzan, Richard Little, and Charles Jones, *The Logic of Anarchy: Neorealism to Structural Realism* (New York and Chichester: Columbia University Press, 1993). Roger D. Spegele, *Political Realism and International Relations* (Cambridge: Cambridge University Press, 1996).

stark statement of the principles, which many would want to modify in detail. In broad outline, however, they define realism.

In very general terms and for some historical periods, this realist picture of the international system provided a set of concepts which explained some of its aspects, particularly those connected with war and peace. Even here we have to be careful. As Rosenberg points out, what are called 'states' are very different things at different times.[6] As an explanatory mode for the contemporary international system, realism is developing problems though it still has many enthusiastic followers. Certainly there are those who toil industriously to interpret the world in terms of what Barry Buzan perhaps rashly called 'The Timeless Wisdom of Realism?'.[7] Similarly, Alan James' attempt to show that realism is still not only a viable but the best way of interpreting the international system is either penetrating or forlorn according to one's approach to realism.

There are nevertheless serious philosophical fissures amongst realists. The mainly United States realists saw themselves as social scientists, Waltz being prominent.[8] The classical realists such as Morgenthau[9] and particularly the so-called English School did not. For the most part, the classical realists were unmoved by the serious problems in the philosophy of social sciences and never tackled those particular philosophical issues which scholars like Waltz took very seriously.[10] Charles Reynolds was the exception who attacked the social scientific school from a philosophically sophisticated position.[11] Interestingly, Tim Dunne does not mention him as a member of the English School in his fascinating book on the English School.[12] In his introduction to *Theories of International Politics,* Waltz thanks effusively the London School of Economics for the help he received there—but from the Department of Philosophy. The English School's disdain for the philosophy of science is no longer the case. Its members are now as involved in philosophical issues, including those in the philosophy of the social sciences, as anyone.[13]

In its classical form, and as presented by people like Morgenthau, realism is a tautological system. This has often gone unnoticed but, like any other theory, there is the constant temptation to bolster it up to face the inconveniences of comparison with the real world. One of Karl Popper's insights was to recognize that the danger

---

[6] Justin Rosenberg, *The Empire of Civil Society: A Critique of the Realist Theory of International Relations* (London and New York: Verso, 1994).

[7] Barry Buzan, 'The Timeless Wisdom of Realism', in Steve Smith, Ken Booth, and Marysia Zalewski (eds.), *International Theory: Positivism and Beyond* (Cambridge: Cambridge University Press, 1996), pp. 47–65.

[8] Kenneth N. Waltz, *Theory of International Politics* (Reading: Addison-Wesley, 1979).

[9] Hans J. Morgenthau, *Politics Among Nations: The Struggle for Power and Peace,* 6th edn, revised by Kenneth W. Thompson (London and New York: McGraw-Hill, 1985).

[10] Hedley Bull's famous attack on the social scientists interestingly made no reference to the debates in the philosophy of the social sciences. Hedley Bull, 'International Theory: The Case for a Classical Approach', in K. Knorr and J.N.Rosenau (eds.), *Contending Approaches to International Politics* (Princeton: Princeton University Press, 1969). See also David Singer's response to Bull in the same volume 'The Incomplete Theorist: Insight Without Evidence'.

[11] For example, Charles Reynolds, *The Politics of War: A Study of the Rationality of Violence in Inter-State Relations* (Hemel Hempstead: Harvester-Wheatsheaf, 1989) and *The World of States.*

[12] Tim Dunne, *The English School* (Oxford University Press, 1998).

[13] See Barry Buzan, Richard Little, and Charles Jones, *The Logic of Anarchy: Neorealism to Structural Realism* (New York and Chichester: Columbia University Press, 1993). See also Roger D. Spegele, *Political Realism and International Relations* (Cambridge: Cambridge University Press, 1996). Spegele, as an American resident in Australia demonstrates the geographical weakness of the term 'English School'.

of explaining everything in the terms of a theory is that one ends up by explaining nothing.[14] Enmeshed in a tautological system, all things are true, because all things are defined as true, though possibly in rather convoluted ways so that the definitional aspect to the problem is not readily visible. Just as, for the Marxists, the concept of 'false consciousness' can be used to 'explain' any failures of the working class, or anyone else for that matter, to believe what they are supposed to believe, so 'power' is sufficiently versatile to outwit most objections to a realist scheme. If all else fails, any deviation from the realist portrait can be explained as a temporary lapse due to the system not reacting quickly enough to the change in circumstances. Mearsheimer uses this stratagem in explaining away the European Union, which he sees as explicable in the context of the Cold War, but slow in fading away.[15] In all these things we are dealing with long historical periods. We can be safely dead before the facts posthumously inconvenience us. Popper's ire was directed particularly against Marxism and psychoanalysis. They are irrefutable, at least in the ways in which they were proposed by their founders and their immediate successors. Realism in International Relations is in the same class. We can always provide some device so that it appears to explain the world whereas in fact it provides only a tautological covering of concepts.

It is odd that realism was not mentioned by Popper as another example of tautological theories which were subject to the same objections as Marxism and psychoanalysis. Popper worked in the London School of Economics in the post-war period when this also housed one of the leading schools of International Relations in the world. He seems not to have noticed. The International Relations scholars, who must have noticed Popper, seemed oblivious to the pressingly relevant problems in the philosophy of science being discussed on their doorstep. Further, Popper did not trawl the social sciences to look for other examples of tautological systems. He was content to attack these two doctrines which were of course very conspicuous and which he disliked for other than academic reasons. International Relations was something of a specialist area. Probably few people had heard of (or hear of today) realism as understood in International Relations compared with the many who had heard of Marxism and psychoanalysis. Also, the conservative implications of realism would be more likely to appeal to Popper than the more disturbing radical implications of both Marxism and psychoanalysis with their emphasis on change. This might have made him less enthusiastic about 'outing' it as tautological.

More charitably we can see realism as a 'Scientific Research Programme' in the sense of Lakatos.[16] Though Lakatos was a dedicated Popperian, he elaborated the Popperian principles, in a way he argued was implicit in Popper, to make it less sensitive to 'naive falsificationalism'. Lakatos argued that a scientific research programme consisted of a 'hard core' of central hypotheses which were regarded as given. These defined the family of theories which constitute the programme. These are surrounded by a protective belt of auxiliary hypotheses which, if they are found

---

[14] Karl R. Popper, *The Logic of Scientific Discovery* (New York: Harper and Collins, 1959) and *Conjectures and Refutations: The Growth of Scientific Knowledge* (London: Routledge and Kegan Paul, 1963).

[15] John J. Mearsheimer, 'The False Promise of International Institutions', *International Security*, 19, 3 (winter 1994/95), pp. 5–59.

[16] Imre Lakatos, 'Falsification and the Methodology of Scientific Research Programmes', in Imre Lakatos and Alan Musgrave (eds.), *Criticism and the Growth of Knowledge* (Cambridge: Cambridge University Press, 1970).

to conflict with the evidence, are rejected and replaced with other hypotheses which continue to protect the hard core. In any field there are likely to be several competing research programmes all pursuing partially inconsistent courses. The problem comes in how to choose between them. Lakatos argues that, as auxiliary hypotheses are developed and change, the theory itself changes either in a degenerative or in a progressive way. If they are progressive, the auxiliary hypotheses will expand the range of explanatory theory. Further implications and predictions of the theory will be found which were not apparent with the initial formulation of the hard core hypotheses. However, in degenerative research programmes, the auxiliary hypotheses do what they were designed to do—protect the hard core—but nothing else. The programme becomes weighed down by a cumbersome set of hypotheses necessary to protect the hard core from inconvenient confrontations with facts. A progressive programme will explain more and more events parsimoniously. Lakatos does not provide a criterion for deciding when a degenerative research programme is finally defeated. Apparently it just fades away. People do not reject theories at the first whiff of counter-evidence. On the contrary, they preserve and try to incorporate or outflank the apparently discordant facts.

On this view, the hard core consists of the principles mentioned at the beginning of this section, notably the centrality of the state and the centrality of power. It now becomes a virtue for the realists to work to accommodate the programme to make it fit the facts of the real world.[17] Stubbornness in the face of awkwardness now becomes a virtue, not a vice.

Lakatos' methodology was developed in the context of the natural sciences and in particular physics. Lakatos himself paid little attention to the social sciences. There is a major difference between research programmes as conceived in the natural sciences and the social sciences. The natural sciences involve stable relationships. Thus, while the planet earth may be evolving and changing, it is doing so according to the stable laws of physics, chemistry and so on. In the physical world, a scientific research programme alters not because the world alters but because our knowledge of the world alters. This is only partly true of the social sciences. A research programme in the social sciences alters for two reasons. First because our knowledge alters but secondly because the world itself alters. This is not an issue for the natural sciences. There may be some very basic laws of human behaviour which are invariant with circumstance. If so, we do not know what they are. If they exist it is not relevant to the present task as it is improbable (Barry Buzan notwithstanding) that these apply to International Relations.

I am sure that many realists, particularly of the English School, would be outraged to think of themselves as participants in a 'scientific' research programme as they are eager to dissociate themselves from such an American fad. However, in a broader sense of the phrase 'research programme' inspired by, rather than strictly following Lakatosian principles, they might grudgingly consent.

However, work such as Bueno de Mesquita's analysis of war initiation fits rather naturally into Lakatos' methodology of scientific research programmes.[18] His analysis is clearly within the realist programme or tradition in that he assumes that the state is the primary actor and for all practical purposes is a unitary actor.

---

[17] Michael Nicholson, *Causes and Consequences in International Relations: A Conceptual Study* (London: Frances Pinter, 1996).

[18] Bueno de Mesquita, *The War Trap* (New Haven: Yale University Press, 1981).

However, he brings in uncertainty. Probability and the value of winning a war are traded off against each other; this is the essence of the expected utility hypothesis. Though Bueno de Mesquita contrasts his view with realism, this is only if realism is viewed as a static set of hypotheses. It is definitely different from realism as Morgenthau understood it (and even more so in its methodology). Nevertheless it is within the broad realist framework and can be quite reasonably be regarded as part of the same scientific research programme.

Waltz's version of realism can be seen as a modification, albeit a major one, around the central realist core. The core is undoubtedly still there but reinterpreted in the rather different conceptual framework where the system, rather than the individual actors, is the dominant feature. In Waltz's version the behaviour of the actors can be interpreted only in terms of the system rather than seeing them as autonomous, if constrained, elements themselves. This can be seen as introducing a set of auxiliary hypotheses but to do so is rather clumsy. It is more natural to see the development as one of devising another set of concepts which can quite reasonably be regarded as 'auxiliary concepts' and also is better seen in a broadened sense of the Lakatosian system.

Some weaknesses of realism

There are two classes of problem with the realist programme as a tool of analysis for today's world. First, its hard core requires more and more convoluted arguments to defend it even for what it is supposed to be good at, namely the analysis of interstate behaviour. Parsimony, which all theorists long for, stands sadly by. Secondly, while realism does not deny them, nor does it confront some major problems which are properly those of International Relations. Thus, interstate war is the realist's forte but nonstate wars, genocides and so on are now the major forms of political violence and death. Similarly, globalization goes unexplained within its rubric.

Consider three problems which involve realism's hard core. In realism, the state is the dominant actor. Other actors are hierarchically inferior to them. Thus, the international state system determines the economic actors but not vice versa. States may give economic actors a lot of latitude, but, in the end, states write the rules. However, looking at the world today, it seems hard to see actors such as multinational corporations acting purely by the consent of states. It is a much more plausible interpretation of the world that we have a political/economic system in which they are endogenous variables and not subordinate to the security variables. That is, they are all part of a common system.

Secondly, states may still be ardent in their defence against military invasion but they are nevertheless relaxed about giving up sovereignty in more peaceful contexts. In many cases, sovereignty is not the primary motive, as the development of the EU demonstrates. This major development of the post second world war period has no parsimonious explanation in the realist framework.[19]

[19] The ingenious attempts of Grieco to defend neorealism on this difficult ground do not properly address the question of sovereignty. 'State Interests and Institutional Rule Trajectories: A Neorealist Interpretation of the Maastricht Treaty and European Economic and Monetary Union' in Benjamin Frankel, *Realism*, pp. 261–306.

Thirdly, states are clearly willing to take great risks with security when certain sorts of economic issues are at stake. The growth of military exports means that internal and external politics, at least internal economic matters, are important determinants of foreign policy and the behaviour of states. A great deal of international behaviour is parsimoniously explained by the assumption that a state wishes to do well by its economy in both employment and profits and only awkwardly by security considerations. Britain's arms exports and its enthusiasm for some very distasteful regimes cannot plausibly be seen in terms of security but quite readily in terms of short-period economic advantage. The distastefulness of a regime is, of course, not a relevant issue for the hard-line realist, but the possibility that a regime such as that of Iraq might become an enemy should be a feature. The readiness to put short-term economic interests before long-term interests of world security is not consistent with the classic realist position viewed as the pursuit of enlightened self-interest by states.

Now let us turn to some aspects of the international scene which are not explained in the realist context though they are not inconsistent with it. Realism deals with interstate wars. However, though wars and political violence are still a major feature of our age, wars are less often between states, though they are often with the aim of setting up a state. The massacres in Rwanda and of the Pol Pot regime are horrific but relate very little to realism. Similarly the Vietnam war was not a realist war conducted by settled states with settled armies as happened the nineteenth century. Interstate violence continues to exist. The wars in the Gulf are perhaps cases of wars which are sufficiently close to the old realist ways to make it worth while analysing in such a context. However, internal factors are still very much an issue in these cases. In the Falklands/Malvinas war, the internal insecurities of Argentinians and to some extent Britain were major factors. The perennial India/Pakistan conflict is fuelled as much by internal factors as external. The recent nuclearization of that dispute (never far from the surface since 1974) was largely caused by internal factors. On most definitions, the two countries are less secure now than they were. Further, this reduction in security was clearly a very likely consequence of India's action in detonating a nuclear bomb and must have been recognized as such by the Indian government.

Finally, globalization is a factor which is not explained within the realist context. There is legitimate controversy about the significance of globalisation and how far it is continuing, but the realist research programme has little to say about it either in its causes or in its consequences. What seems to be happening now is rather surprising and was not foreseen. The state system is not so much working differently as being bypassed. The relative significance of states has decreased. Economic actors have always been more significant than has been allowed in realist theory but now they are much more important. States, or more properly governments, are often willing to give in to economic actors rather than the other way round. The current dogma is that markets should be globalized and not nationally based. This inevitably means the weakening of the state, a factor not always realized by nationalist free marketeers of the 1980s new right.

Realism may be declining in effectiveness as a description of the international system, not because we have found a better theory to explain the same events, but because the structure of the international system is altering to make it less relevant. It is called upon to explain events which do not correspond to the basic postulates of the theory.

One can try to evade this by adopting the stratagem of Alan James, which is to restrict the definition of International Relations to that which can be explained by the realist programme.[20] That is, even though the range of the programme is narrower than it was, that there are still some aspects of the world which are explained according to the hard core of the realist programme. The question comes down to how interested we are in these features of it. As a tool for analysing many interesting things of the present era it seems to be sadly wanting. The classical notion of sovereignty seems to be dwindling in Europe where age-old enemies are adopting a common currency. If we define International Relations as that which can be explained in a realist manner, we are going to miss out a great deal which is important. The power–security approach to state behaviour explains some things, but on its own it is insufficient.

If we use realism to explain some of the behaviour of small subsets of states, we have moved a long way from Waltzian versions of realism based on the centrality of the system rather than of the actors. This is not a systemic view, at least in Waltz's sense. Even contemporary issues of violence are far removed from the classical portrait of realism where the warring and potentially warring parties were states. This was not regarded as problematic, though perhaps it ought to have been. However, now the problem is to find who the parties are who might go to violence. Why the Hutus and the Tutsis for instance? Who are the parties in Algeria and why have they formed in the ways they do? Why do people identify with the groups they do? These are the problems which concern the contemporary analyst of violence. Civil wars have always existed but they now seem to dominate, but in a context where state boundaries are of no great importance.

Though realism is meant to be realistic, it leaves a number of issues inadequately addressed even at the conceptual level. Thus, self-interest and the concept of the group (in the case of International Relations, the state) as an actor are both seriously problematic issues.

Gilpin argues that human beings act together in groups and that groups must be seen as actors.[21] He acknowledges some problems, but I wish to extend the list. I shall consider three. First, while rationality in the context of an individual choice can be defined straightforwardly, its extension to groups is less clear. We can assume that a government acts more or less like a collective individual, but this is an assumption. Such characteristics as stable preferences which underlie a lot of choice theory cannot be assumed about a group which consists of changing individuals. This is a problem which attends all group decision-making theories and is not particular to realism. Secondly, the motivation of the individual human beings in a supposedly selfish state system becomes very problematic. The use of military power requires that the individuals involved must be willing to behave in very unselfish ways for the system to work at all. Specifically, people have to be willing to get killed and maimed in order to contribute towards the greater good of the community. This is not obviously consistent with the hypothesis of self-interest much less of selfishness. It is certainly a problem which needs addressing. Thirdly, why people are willing to make states (or perhaps nations) the basis of their primary identity?

[20] Alan James, 'The Realism of "Realism": the State and the Study of International Relations', *Review of International Studies*, 15 (1989), pp. 215–29.
[21] Robert G. Gilpin, 'No One Loves a Political Realist', in Benjamin Frankel (ed.), *Realism: Restatements and Renewal* (London and Portland: Frank Cass, 1996), pp. 3–26.

Joseph Grieco's interpretation of the European Union in neorealist terms depends on the states of France, Germany, and so on remaining constant and unproblematic actors.[22] Will the French and the Germans and their governments see themselves as promoting the interests of their own citizens for which the EU has just been a manoeuvre, or will they see Europe as the basic collective, or even at some stage, something non-territorially based? A crucial question, however, is whether the actors themselves remain stable or break up, amalgamate, or re-form. There are a thousand ways in which a mass of people can divide.

This argument merely strengthens my earlier argument about the tautological dangers of realism. The concepts used purportedly to explain the world are so flexible that they can be interpreted in almost any way.

Realism and its relatives

The classical realists, and particularly the English School, see history as a parent discipline for International Relations. Most neorealists explicitly view International Relations as a social science and relate it to other social scientific approaches to social behaviour. Following this latter tradition, I shall discuss realism in its relationship to two aspects of social science, theories of the market system in economics, used as analogy and stressed by Waltz, and the rational choice approach to social behaviour.

In both the market system and the Waltzian picture of the international system, we have actors operating in anarchy. The system consists of the totality of actors. The system constrains the actors, but the constraints are endogenous to the system and are not provided exogenously by an authority. Providing some firms maximize profits, and providing some firms are predators, then a firm has no option but to maximize profits if it is not to become bankrupt or be taken over. Choice boils down to a question of survival. It is similar in the realist version of the international system. If a state does not pay attention to security, a predator will strike.

It is objected that the market system is not anarchical. It might be subordinate to the state. In many cases it obviously is, though the degree of this in the case of the global economy is becoming increasingly in doubt. This causes Charles Jones to worry that the analogy of market and international system may be a flawed one.[23] However, the question is posed improperly. It is not a dichotomy between anarchic and hierarchic systems. It is a question of how much anarchy and how much hierarchy or authority. Almost all relationships between groups or individuals within a social system have some degree of flexibility and choice and some degree of constraint which is imposed from the outside constraining the set of choices available. Only rarely is the set of choices totally imposed. Perhaps in some very strict nunneries and monasteries this is so, but these are rarities. Even in prisons, except in solitary confinement, there is a wide range of choices in social interactions, making issues of cooperation, strategy and altruism relevant considerations. Free market economic systems have some externally imposed constraints, but actors have

---

[22] Joseph Grieco, 'State Interests and Institutional Rule Trajectories', in Benjamin Frankel, *Realism*, pp. 261–306.

[23] Charles Jones, in Buzan, Little, and Jones, *The Logic of Anarchy.*

a wide degree of choice. The international system is a different case, but only because it is a limiting case, not a totally different sort of entity. Manifestly there are major differences between the market system and the international system. There is no analogue in the international system. However, the same model[24] can still describe important features of both of them.

Many realists overtly write in a rational choice tradition which also originates in economics. Indeed, some interesting developments in rational choice theory and its sibling game theory have come in the context of International Relations.[25] Even those who avoid rational choice are accused of being closet or, more plausibly, unwitting rational choice theorists. This leads to the incorrect supposition that rational choice theorists are necessarily realists.

Broadly, rational choice theory, which originated in micro-economics, relates the choices of actors to the goals they pursue.[26] Sometimes this leads to a plausible description of what the actor will choose and do: often it demonstrates the ambiguities of the situation and the difficulties of choice as is the case in the prisoners' dilemma. Despite its name, rational choice theory purportedly is about actual behaviour (a positive theory) and is not a normative theory of what ought to be the case. The preferences of the actors are assumed given. They pursue them in an 'instrumentally rational' manner. All rationality means here is that the preferences are consistent, and in particular are transitive and that, in situations of risk, the rules of probability are followed. We have to remember that this is used as a model rather than a theory. For many practical applications, the actors are regarded as unitary actors. Similarly the goals are regarded as unproblematic whether they are those of an organization or of an individual. Just as the state is a unitary actor in many versions of neorealism, so the firm is in neo-classical economics. This is useful only for answering a limited range of questions and it normally leaves open many others. It is dangerous only if we believe that it embodies some final truth. Waltz, understandably, is rather pained at this misunderstanding.[27] Handled with appropriate caution, it can yield useful results within its domain. Like realism,

---

[24] I use 'model' to mean a set of concepts, a calculus, or whatever, which is used to describe a simplified world. I use 'theory' to be the same, but with the intention of describing the actual world. Thus, it can therefore be tested (or refuted). The same model in formal terms can be applied to very different processes. For example, similar differential equation models can describe the movement of cannon balls, the growth of plants, and arms races. See R.B.Braithwaite, *Scientific Explanation* (Cambridge: Cambridge University Press, 1953) and Michael Nicholson, *The Scientific Analysis of Social Behaviour: A Defence of Empiricism in Social Science* (London: Pinter, 1983)

[25] There are many examples, but the relative gains/absolute gains controversy is a good example. See Robert Powell, 'Absolute Gains and Relative Gains in International Relations Theory', *American Political Science Review*, 85(4) (1991), pp. 1303–20; Duncan Snidal, 'Relative Gains and the Pattern of International Cooperation', *American Political Science Review*, 85(3) (1991), pp. 701–26; Duncan Snidal, 'International Cooperation and Relative Gains Maximisers', *International Studies Quarterly*, 35(4) (1991), pp. 387–402. The problem is discussed in a more general rational choice context by Michael Taylor, *The Possibility of Cooperation* (Cambridge: Cambridge University Press, 1987) and in a non-realist International Relations context by Michael Nicholson, 'Interdependent Utility Functions', in Pierre Allan and Christian Schmidt, *Game Theory and International Relations: Preferences, Information and Empirical Evidence* (Aldershot and Brookfield Vermont: Edward Elgar, 1994). Other important developments relating to International Relations have been made by Steven Brams, for example *The Theory of Moves* (Cambridge: Cambridge University Press, 1995).

[26] See Michael Nicholson, *Rationality and the Analysis of International Conflict* (Cambridge: Cambridge University Press, 1992).

[27] Kenneth Waltz, 'Reflections on *Theory of International Politics*, A Response to my Critics', in Robert O. Keohane (ed.), *Neorealism and its Critics* (New York: Columbia University Press, 1986), pp. 322–45.

rational choice theory can be seen as a Lakatosian scientific research programme. Many of its adherents seek to develop it while remaining critical of its more simplistic manifestations. Amartya Sen, a prominent scholar in this tradition, analysed some of its limitations in a paper called 'The Theory of Rational Fools' which indicates a healthy scepticism.[28]

It is obvious why rational choice analysis should appeal to the realists, particularly the neorealists, who are interested in models of actors in systems. However, it is relevant for any analysis where choice is central no matter who the relevant actors may be. A pluralist who includes other actors besides states as endogenous actors in the system can do so from a rational choice perspective. Any social theory involving actors pursuing goals can come under its rubric.

The rational choice programme has given some interesting insights, perhaps particularly about cooperation and conflict. The analysis of the repeated prisoners' dilemma has suggested that cooperation in an anarchic system is more likely to come about than intuition suggests. Axelrod (1984) is the best known work, but Taylor (1987) and, much earlier, Howard (1971) have shown this in the context of models in different but consistent ways.[29] These analyses suggest that self-interested actors are not as red in tooth and claw as some of the more pessimistic of the realists seem to think. They are, of course, models. The gap between them and 'real life' can be a big one. This does not stop them being very suggestive, though, even if their policy application is necessarily weak.

Utopian realism

Peace research: the utopian realists

Both Morgenthau and Carr characterize utopians as people who believe in a fundamental harmony of interests amongst human beings. This may be true of some, but not of all. There are many who are clearly of utopian temparament who have taken to heart the view that one must work with human beings as they are and not how one would wish them to be. This led to the view of many that, while conflicts are inevitable, violence as a way of solving them is not. It was not conflicts as such which were damaging such as the appalling way in which they were carried out such as by war. Thus 'peace research' in one way or another has characterized at least one form of practical or realistic utopianism since the second world war.

Peace research comes in even more variants than realism or utopianism in its more traditional sense. However, I shall concentrate on empiricist peace research. This I identify as the intellectual movement originating with the work of people like L.F. Richardson and Quincy Wright and taken up by scholars in the 1950s such as

[28] Amartya Sen, 'The Theory of Rational Fools: A Critique of the Behavioral Foundations of Economic Theory', *Philosophy and Public Affairs*, 6 (1977), pp. 317–44.
[29] Robert Axelrod, *The Evolution of Cooperation* (New York: Basic Book, 1984); Michael Taylor, *The Possibility of Cooperation* (Cambridge: Cambridge University Press, 1987); Nigel Howard, *The Paradoxes of Rationality* (London and Cambridge, MA: MIT Press, 1971).

Boulding, Rapoport, Singer and Deutsch.[30] Like the earlier generation of utopians, they were shocked at the idea of war which was now made all the more horrific by the threat of nuclear war. Also, like their predecessors, they were reluctant to accept that this was the only possible way of running the world; they thought it possible to create something better in which war became a redundant institution. The traditional realists, who were prominent at the end of the second world war, seemed marooned in pessimism and more intent on describing a future of uninterrupted international gloom than in exploring the possibilities of change. Unlike their predecessors and unlike many realists of the time (and now) the peace researchers were unsure how to do it. Further, they argued that the international system and all the systems of political violence are systems about which we know very little. It is not just what sort of change is necessary, it is how even to set about it. The goal, then, became to find out how the present international system works as a basis for working out how to alter things. The medical analogy was often appealed to. If we want to cure a disease, we need to know how the human body works both when it is healthy and when it is not. This did not mean that, in a state of ignorance, one postpones action until the completion of the necessary research, but it does mean that one acknowledges one's ignorance. They pointed out that confident assertions about the balance of power by the realists, or the efficacy of international organizations by the utopians, were based on examples (or sometimes hopes) but rarely on systematic observation. David Singer famously remarked at the lack of 'reproducible results'.[31]

At first there seemed to be a great deal of hope for the new utopians. The empiricist tradition in the philosophy of the social sciences was dominant and in some of the social sciences such as economics was hegemonic. We can have hypotheses, testable by observation, which will be the basis for a happier and more stable society. If we can do so in economics, why not in international affairs? Further, the complexity of social systems had at one time made people pessimistic about the possibility of analysing them. This seemed to have been overcome by the computer which, even in the 1960s, had an enormous capacity for dealing with masses of information and for simulating the behaviour of complex systems. Complexity itself became a phenomenon to be analysed and less of a fearful barrier to the acquisition of knowledge.[32] Everything seemed set for a development of a social science of war and peace.

Hopes were perhaps higher than achievement here as in all the social sciences. The optimism of the earlier peace researchers perhaps made this inevitable. However, the frequent claims, usually from people who never liked it much in the first place, that positivism, empiricism, and so on has produced nothing in

---

[30] L.F. Richardson, *Arms and Insecurity* and *Statistics of Deadly Quarrels* (both Pittsburgh: The Boxwood Press, 1960); Quincy Wright, *A Study of War* (2 vols.) (Chicago: University of Chicago Press, 1942); Kenneth Boulding, *Conflict and Defense: A General Theory* (New York: University Press of America, 1988) (1st edn, 1962); Anatol Rapoport, *Fights, Games and Debates* (Ann Arbor, Michigan: University of Michigan Press, 1974); Karl Deutsch, *Nationalism and Social Communication* (Cambridge, MA: MIT Press, 1963).

[31] J. David Singer, *A Peace Research Odyssey* (Ann Arbor, Michigan: University of Michigan Press, 1990).

[32] Herbert A. Simon, 'The Architecture of Complexity', *Proceeding of the American Philosophical Society* 1960. A recent work in International Relations stressing complexity is by Lars-Erik Cederman, *Emergent Actors in World Politics: How States and Nations Develop and Dissolve* (Princeton: Princeton University Press, 1997), significantly published in the series *Princeton Studies in Complexity.*

International Relations and is in any case philosophically dead, seems to be based on an unusual capacity to ignore what has gone on.[33]

Arguments for utopia

The true utopian has a vision of some perfect world which will come about at some point in the future. It quickly becomes clear that not only are these utopias far away but that what is utopia for one is dystopia for another. Utopianism now is what is a contradiction for the true utopian. The modern utopian or, again to use Ken Booth's terminology a 'process utopian', aims at improvement rather than perfection. Commonly the aim is to eliminate violence as a political tool and in particular the use of war, though poverty is often added to the list.

While the pessimists have plenty to reflect on in justification of their pessimism, the utopians also have some reflections of a more consoling nature. These are three. First human behaviour varies radically in different circumstances. This is very clear at the individual level. On the negative side, we know that normal human beings can behave in very wicked ways. Concentration camp guards were ordinary people. As Hannah Arendt pointed out, evil is banal.[34] A host of psychological experiments testify to the capacity of human beings to be crudely authoritarian, cruel and heartless (and, of course, submissive and weak) when put in the appropriate roles.[35] If this is coupled with an ideological justification, then normal human beings can do horrific things.

However, if circumstances can produce malevolent behaviour, then they can also produce benevolent behaviour. Furthermore, we should be able to construct such circumstances. There are two problems. First, what are these circumstances and secondly, if we know them, how do we persuade people to adopt them? As far as the international system is concerned, there is still a great deal of ignorance about what these conditions are. This was the point of peace research. The interwar utopians thought they knew what to do (as, indeed, do many present-day utopians and radicals of right and left). Modern utopians are much more modest. We are often ignorant of the conditions for peace, which is why we think it appropriate to research these conditions and find out what may work. The 'democratic peace' thesis[36] is one which gives us a certain amount of hope in this respect.

The second factor giving some solace to the utopian is that there are some features of the world which suggest some sort of improvement. Clearly the vast increase in technology and resultant wealth has not improved the moral capacities of human beings. However, the alteration of some social structures may have achieved what morality failed to provide. Thus, slavery has declined as a human institution. While there may still be more than we would wish in various disguised forms, nevertheless it is almost universally condemned. The cynic might argue that this is

---

[33] I consider the philosophical issues in Michael Nicholson, *Causes and Consequences in International Relations: A Conceptual Study* (London and New York: Cassell 1996).

[34] Hannah Arendt, *The Trial of Eichman: An Essay on the Banality of Evil.*

[35] A classic is the Milgram experiment. See Stanley Milgram, *Obedience to Authority: An Experimental Approach* (London: Tavistock, 1974).

[36] There is a vast and rapidly growing literature. A clear statement is by Bruce Russett, *Grasping the Democratic Peace: Principles for Post-Cold War World* (Princeton: Princeton University Press, 1993).

not because of an increase in moral awareness but because the economic structures have altered such that slavery is no longer a profitable institution. This may be why it was possible to get rid of slavery in the United States after the Civil War. It would have become obsolete anyway.[37] However, at least for some utopians this is not a matter of concern. If the structures alter such as to cause superior forms of social organization, this is all to the good. Mueller[38] makes this argument suggesting from the case of slavery that progress, even moral progress, is possible.

Change and flexible utopias

All social systems are changing very rapidly at the moment and not least the international system. We can confidently expect it to carry on changing, though in ways in which it is hard to predict.

In general, it is easier to influence the direction of a changing social system than it is to induce change in a static social system. The problem is often to induce change in the first place. Many social systems resist change because those who benefit from the system, either in economic or in power terms, want to keep it that way. Thus there are often powerful coalitions of interests wishing to retain the status quo or something like it.[39] If change is coming already, this obstacle is diminished. Nevertheless, the problem is still not wholly solved. Change can come about because it is in the interests of powerful people in the original system. They expect to gain even more power in the new system. However, a fluid and dynamic system is much less controllable by the powers that be than a static system. Take the present communications system. While it would be foolish to deny that powerful actors in the scene can strongly influence the direction of change, it is also foolish to suppose that this is totally under their control. Thus, the Internet is made to the measure of a few powerful actors but its use is not easily controllable. The whole nature of the printed word is becoming less and less under the control of publishers in the traditional sense. As a group they are unable to control things even though, by building vast conglomerates, they are doing their best. Having large resources is a great help in directing change but it is not the only issue concerned. Those with few resources, like the original environmental movement, can have a significant impact. (I am assuming that normally utopians have few resources.)

One problem about change is the high degree of unpredictability about the future of the international system. If we go back to the 1930s, even some of the major developments in the physical sciences which directly affect International Relations could not have been predicted. In 1930 we might have predicted that aeroplanes would develop rapidly, but it would have required remarkable prescience to foresee the Intercontinental Ballistic Missile. It would have been totally impossible to

---

[37] There is a large literature, but see Peter Temin, *Causal Factors in American Economic Growth in the Nineteenth Century* (London and Basingstoke: Macmillan, 1975).

[38] John Mueller, *Quiet Cataclysm: Reflections on the Recent Transformation of World Politics* (New York: HarperCollins, 1995).

[39] Mancur Olson, *The Rise and Decline of Nations: Economic Growth, Stagflation and Social Rigidities* (New Haven: Yale University Press, 1982).

predict nuclear weapons[40] or computers.[41] Both have had enormous impact on International Relations. In the case of computers, they have influenced practically every aspect of life. It is quite possible that the next eighty years may provide us with equally big developments which at the moment are quite impossible to foresee. Social affairs would have been equally hard to predict. The holocaust must have seemed incredible. That at the end of the century primitive forms of religious fundamentalism would be major factors in domestic and international politics would seem to be beyond belief. Even if the social sciences develop dramatically, forecasts about, say, the year 2100 are unlikely to be much better.

Hence, our utopias must be flexible utopias. They must concentrate on desirable inclusions such as happy personal relationships and on desirable exclusions such as war. Thus, utopians, of whatever breed, cannot say what will be the ideal international system but they can hope to influence the world in benevolent directions. This hope is possible because of the permanent flux the world is in.

The social world must have some stable characteristics for it to be possible to influence it. If the world is random, we can say nothing about the future. To influence it is impossible. Likewise, at the other extreme, if the world is deterministic in which everything is preordained, there is nothing we can do either. The world in which we can do something is what I shall call 'structured'. For much of the time, social systems follow reasonably deterministic courses but the directions can be influenced, possible given frequent but gentle nudges. There are also points where major change is possible such as the end of war, 'revolutionary moments', the collapse of a regime such as with the USSR, or other 'switch points', when social systems can be set on different paths. In principle, we can know when intervention is possible as well as what its effects will be. The utopian must believe social systems are like this as the utopian must believe in the possibility of influencing change.

Some Conclusions

Referring to *The Twenty Years' Crisis* in 1980, Carr said that by 1945 it was already a period piece.[42] It was a harsh judgement on a book which has been so influential since then. Nevertheless, he was partly right. Realists and utopians have altered a great deal since the interwar period. They still worry about war, but other factors such as the international political economy and the continuation of acute poverty are seen by all as major and interdependent factors. Above all, the utopians, or some of them at least, took to heart the criticism that, to bring about benevolent change, we must understand how the existing systems work. Also we must work with the grain of human behaviour.[43] Human beings are not infinitely malleable.

[40] Famously, Lord Rutherford, having split the atom, denied as late as 1933 that there was any possibility of a practical use for nuclear energy. C.P. Snow, *Variety of Men* (London: Macmillan, 1967).
[41] The mathematics behind the development of 'computable numbers' was not developed until the late 1930s. See Andrew Hodges, *Alan Turing: the Enigma* (London: Vintage Books, 1992), 1st edn. 1983.
[42] Preface to the 1981 printing. Russell Hardin uses exactly the same phrase about Bertrand Russell's book in 'Russell's Power', *Philosophy of the Social Sciences*, 26, 3 (September 1996), pp. 322–47.
[43] A recent vigorous statement of this point of view is by Peter Singer, 'Darwin for the Left', *Prospect*, 31 (June 1998), pp. 26–30.

The issues facing utopians and realists, whether separate or in tandem, are now much broader than they were. Non-state political violence has increased in proportion to interstate violence. While it is a mistake to forget the interstate aspects of it and forget the interstate quarrels which are potentially violent, a great deal of political violence is not interstate violence. Further poverty, famines and other negative aspects of the economic system are aspects of the same problem. Realism here would seem to be the recognition that the political system is not isolated from the economic system but is part of a single system. States may not have withered away but they have been shaken in their primacy.

A weakness of the realist analysis of the international system even in its heyday was its neglect of irrational factors in human behaviour. Nazi Germany was not just an exercise in power politics but an exercise also in human irrationality. Iraq, a potentially wealthy country, is poor and insecure because of its government's fascination with violence. Current events seem to show that the human capacity for cruelty, particularly in its racist forms, is unabated. All the major religions seem to be indulging in spasms of irrational fundamentalism. A realist, a utopian, or a utopian realist have to recognize these, as well as simple power, as being the reality of the present world. Human beings have very complex motivations, and the societies they construct are correspondingly complex.

Moving on from the narrow definitions of realism and utopianism, I suggest that we can identify a realist temperament and a utopian temperament. These differ along three dimensions, which need not be closely related. First, they differ in their optimism about guiding change. The realist stresses our limitations and sees only modest intervention as possible (or even none at all): the utopian believes in the possibility of greater control. The debate over globalization is instructive in this respect. Many people ('realists') appear to regard it as inevitable. Others ('utopians') regard its more malevolent aspects as alterable. However, any attempts to alter it must be based on a thorough understanding of its processes. We must understand the power structures within both the political system and the economic system and work in the recognition of these. Secondly, they differ on their views of human nature. Realists stress selfishness, which they argue will appear under most situations. Utopians stress that human beings are both good and bad and that the circumstances influence heavily (though not necessarily dictate) which predominates. These are general aspects of realism and utopianism and are not particular to the field of International Relations. The third aspect relates to realism in International Relations and the realist theories (in the plural) about its subject matter. Seduced by Carr's categories, we are apt to think that the opposite of the realist theories must be utopian theories, but on reflection that seems a very odd use of the word 'utopian'. The opposites are simply all those theories which do not accept the realist hard core discussed above. There may be a correlation amongst scholars of those who fall into the realist or the utopian camp on all three criteria, but there is certainly no logical requirement that they should do so. We are faced with a false dichotomy. Ultimately the welfare of the realist theories and their research programmes depend on them demonstrating that they can account for the condition of the international system better than any alternatives. To a sceptic like myself, the programme looks frayed at the edges, but as a good Lakatosian, I think it is still worth pursuing. In the end, I shall be persuaded or not by rational argument (or so I like to think). The other conditions are matters of degree. Whether human beings are the creatures of circumstance or not is a matter of degree. Realism and utopianism represent the ends of a spectrum on which we can take up many intermediate positions. Our views on the degree of control we can exercise over social systems likewise fall on a spectrum. This is so whether we are dealing with the international system or any other. Facts are clearly relevant to both those. They are not purely acts of faith. However, while facts may shift us one way or another along these spectra, it is possibly our temperament which dictates the starting point and how far we move.

IR theory after the Cold War

GEORG SØRENSEN

The end of the Cold War has prompted a good deal of soul-searching in the academic discipline of International Relations (IR).* Some results of this process are already apparent; the dominant version of realism, neorealism, is developing in new directions in an attempt to address major areas where the theory has been shown to contain weaknesses (e.g. domestic politics, international cooperation, the analysis of change).[1] Liberal IR-theory is becoming less focused on international institutions and has devoted more attention to the larger issues of democracy and democratization, sovereignty, and change in the context of modernization and globalization.[2] Some bodies of established theory are receiving fresh attention, including the International Society (or English) School,[3] and there is a renewed interest in the field of international political economy.[4]

Yet all these theoretical traditions (realism, liberalism, International Society, international political economy) can be seen as enduring perspectives in IR; they build on a long intellectual tradition concerning problems of relations between

---

* Many thanks to Kenneth Glarbo, Knud Erik Jørgensen, Michael Nicholson, Steve Smith, and Alexander Wendt for very helpful comments on earlier drafts.

[1] See, for example, Joseph M. Grieco, 'Realist International Theory and the Study of World Politics', in M.W. Doyle and G.J. Ikenberry (eds.), *New Thinking in International Relations Theory* (Boulder, 1997), pp. 163–202; Michael E. Brown *et al.* (eds.), *The Perils of Anarchy. Contemporary Realism and International Security* (Cambridge, MA, 1995); John A. Vasquez, 'The Realist Paradigm and Degenerative versus Progressive Research Programs: An Appraisal of Neotraditional Research on Waltz's Balancing Proposition', and the responses by Kenneth Waltz, Thomas Christensen, and Jack Snyder, Colin and Miriam Fendius Elman, Randall Schweller and Stephen Walt, *American Political Science Review*, 4 (1997), pp. 899–935.

[2] Bruce Russett, *Grasping the Democratic Peace. Principles for a Post-Cold War World* (Princeton, 1993); Michael W. Doyle, *Ways of War and Peace* (New York/London, 1997); Henry R. Nau, 'Democracy and the National Interest: An American Foreign Policy for the Twenty-First Century', paper for SSRC Conference on U.S. Promotion of Democracy, Washington 1997; Joseph S. Nye, *Bound to Lead: The Changing Nature of American Power* (New York, 1990); Robert O. Keohane, 'Hobbes's Dilemma and Institutional Change in World Politics: Sovereignty in International Society', in H-H. Holm and G. Sørensen (eds.), *Whose World Order? Uneven Globalization and the End of the Cold War* (Boulder, 1995), pp. 165–87.

[3] Robert H. Jackson, 'International Community beyond the Cold War', in G.M. Lyons and M. Mastanduno (eds.), *Beyond Westphalia? State Sovereignty and International Intervention* (Baltimore/London, 1995), pp. 59–87; Robert H. Jackson, 'The Political Theory of International Society', in K. Booth and S. Smith (eds.), *International Relations Theory Today* (University Park, PA, 1995), pp. 110–29; Tim Dunne, 'The Social Construction of International Society', *European Journal of International Relations*, 3 (1995).

[4] Richard Stubbs and Geoffrey D. Underhill (eds.), *Political Economy and the Changing Global Order* (London, 1994); Susan Strange, *The Retreat of the State. The Diffusion of Power in the World Economy* (Cambridge, 1996); Philip G. Cerny, 'Plurilateralism: Structural Differentiation and Functional Conflict in the Post-Cold War World Order', *Millennium*, 1 (1993), pp. 27–51.

communities and states including classical literatures from Thucydides and onwards.[5] A major debate in IR after the end of the Cold War involves various critiques of all these established traditions by alternative approaches, sometimes identified as post-positivism.[6] There have always been 'dissident voices' in the discipline of IR: i.e. philosophers and scholars who rejected established views and tried to replace them with alternatives. But in recent years these voices have increased in strength and number. Two factors help explain that development. First, the end of the Cold War changed the international agenda in some fundamental ways. In place of a clear-cut East/West-conflict dominated by two contending superpowers a number of diverse issues emerged in world politics, including, for example: state partition and disintegration; civil war; democratization; national minorities; mass migration and refugee problems, environmental issues; and so forth. Second, an increasing number of IR scholars expressed dissatisfaction with the dominant Cold War approach to IR: the neorealism of Kenneth Waltz. Many scholars now take issue with Waltz's claim that the complex world of international relations can be squeezed into a few law-like statements about the structure of the international system and the balance of power. They consequently reinforce and qualitatively expand the anti-behaviouralist critique first put forward by International Society theorists such as Hedley Bull.[7] Many IR scholars also criticize Waltzian neorealism for its conservative political outlook. There is not much in neorealism which can point to qualitative change and the creation of a better world.

The vague label of 'post-positivism' contains a variety of different approaches. I am going to deal with the metatheoretical (in the broadest sense) debate first. Two main points will be argued. First that it is indeed that—a metatheoretical debate— which is helpful in a number of respects but which contains very little about the real issues in IR, the meat of the discipline. Second that the most extreme metatheoretical positions in both positivist and post-positivist directions are less useful for our analytical purposes than those which try to find a middle ground. As will become clear, that middle ground can be found with respect both to epistemology and to ontology.

Hoping to have clarified at least some of the metatheoretical questions, I move on to the substantial debate about the core issues in the discipline after the end of the Cold War. A survey of the major substantial debates combined with my own predilections leads to the identification of three main issue areas. They are: (a) globalization; (b) sovereign statehood; and (c) world order. The core content of each of these issue areas is set forth briefly. In conclusion, I argue that IR is again as close as we are able to get to a state of pursuing 'normal science' in our part of the scientific universe. My attempt to cover both metatheoretical and substantive issues has one obvious downside: there is insufficient space to cover all the important issues and literatures that characterize the period since 1989. So what follows is by no means a comprehensive in-depth treatment; it is rather an introduction of some, but not all, of the most important issues.

---

[5] See, for example, Robert H. Jackson and Georg Sørensen, *International Relations: Introduction to a Discipline* (Oxford, forthcoming 1999).
[6] E.g., Steve Smith, Ken Booth, and Marysia Zalewski (eds.), *International Theory: Positivism & Beyond* (Cambridge, 1996).
[7] Hedley Bull, 'International Theory: The Case for a Classical Approach', in K. Knorr and J. Rosenau (eds.), *Contending Approaches to International Politics* (Princeton, 1969).

Metatheoretical Issues

It should be noted right away that there are many different ways of presenting the debates between established traditions and post-positivist currents in IR. What follows is no complete account; no attempt has been made to single out all relevant issues and questions. But I do claim to address some of the most important items in the metatheoretical debate. A proper place to begin is in one of the most radical (in philosophy of science terms) and outspoken parts of the post-positivist camp, namely the post-modernists. Post-modernism can aptly be defined as 'incredulity towards metanarratives'[8] even if Lyotard emphasizes that this definition involves 'simplifying to the extreme'. Metanarratives are accounts that claim to have discovered the truth about the social world. In Steve Smith's helpful terminology, metanarratives are theories based on a foundational epistemology, that is, a position according to which 'all truth claims (i.e. about some feature of the world) can be judged true or false'.[9] An anti-foundational epistemology, by contrast, argues that truth claims 'cannot be so judged since there are never neutral grounds for so doing; instead each theory will define what counts as the facts and so there will be no neutral position available to determine between rival claims'.

The metanarratives attacked by post-modernists are also most often explanatory as opposed to constitutive. Explanatory theories 'sees the world as something external to our theories of it; in contrast a constitutive theory is one that thinks our theories actually help construct the world'.[10]

The IR-theory or metanarrative most strongly attacked by post-modernists is neorealism,[11] in part because of its perceived dominance in the discipline, and in part because of its structuralist parsimony. After all, here is a theory which claims that only a few elements of information about sovereign states in an anarchical international system can tell us most of the big and important things we need to know about international relations. And the theory even claims to reflect the reality of international politics 'through all the centuries that we can contemplate'.[12]

Post-modernist critiques of neorealism emphasize the structuralist quality of the theory. The anarchical structure of the international system confronts individual actors as a given material reality which they cannot change; adaptation is their only option.[13] The theory is ahistorical and that in turn leads to reification, the move whereby historically produced structures are presented as unchangeable constraints given by nature. Individual actors are 'reduced in the last analysis to mere objects who must participate in reproducing the whole or . . . fall by the wayside of

---

[8] J.-F. Lyotard, *The Postmodern Condition: A Report on Knowledge* (Manchester, 1984), p. xxiv.

[9] Steve Smith, 'New Approaches to International Theory', in J. Baylis and S. Smith (eds.), *The Globalization of World Politics. An Introduction to International Relations* (Oxford, 1997), p. 67.

[10] Ibid.

[11] E.g., Richard K. Ashley, 'The Poverty of Neorealism', in R.O. Keohane (ed.), *Neorealism and Its Critics* (New York, 1986), pp. 255–301; R.B.J. Walker, *Inside/Outside: International Relations as Political Theory* (Cambridge, 1993); R.B.J. Walker, 'International Relations and the Concept of the Political', in Booth and Smith, *International Relations Today*, pp. 306–28. There are other positivist positions than neorealism, of course, and Kenneth Waltz is not the sole standard bearer of neorealism. But for lack of space, I focus on the critique of Waltz.

[12] Kenneth N. Waltz, 'The Emerging Structure of International Politics', in Brown, Lynn-Jones, and Miller, *The Perils of Anarchy*, p. 75.

[13] See for example, Ashley, 'The Poverty of Neorealism', p. 289, and Walker, *Inside/Outside*, p. 123.

history'.[14] It follows that neorealism has big difficulties in confronting change in international relations. Emphasis is on 'structural continuity and repetition',[15] the anarchical structure of international relations remains in place. This leads to poverty of imagination; any thinking about alternative futures remains stuck in forced choice between sovereign statehood and anarchy or the (unlikely) abolition of sovereign statehood and the creation of some world government. 'This certainly provides a powerful and familiar ground on which to argue that because universal human community is not in sight, the world remains more or less the same'.[16]

In Foucauldian terms, post-modernists see neorealism as a 'regime of truth'; 'statements about the social world are only "true" within specific discourses . . . It is for this reason that post-modernists are opposed to any metanarratives, since they imply that there are conditions for establishing the truth or falsity of knowledge-claims that are not the product of any discourse, and thereby not the products of power'.[17] In that way, the severe problems and shortcomings of neorealist theory can be explained primarily through the metatheoretical stance adopted by the theory. In the terms introduced above, it is an explanatory theory based on a foundational epistemology. These are the basic metatheoretical characteristics of positivism.

According to this analysis then, there is a gulf between positivist (foundational and explanatory) IR-theory on the one hand and post-positivist (anti-foundational and constitutive) IR-theory on the other. And the preferable metatheoretical way ahead is the post-positivist one, because it promises to deconstruct any meta-narrative claiming to represent some universally valid truth. For post-positivists, there is no 'truth' outside of power.

Positivism versus post-positivism

I believe that this is a core metatheoretical debate in IR after the Cold War. Many post-positivists of various colours have contributed to this debate, but it is the work of Steve Smith[18] which has been most helpful in clarifying the points of contention and drawing up the front-lines of the debate. Steve Smith is firmly on the post-positivist side in the debate. His position is premised on the notion of an insurmountable gulf between positivist and post-positivist methodology. The two 'cannot be combined together because they have mutually exclusive assumptions'.[19] I am going to question this position in two ways. First I argue that even if there are problems with positivism, the post-positivist position is also in several respects

---

[14] Ashley, 'The Poverty of Neorealism', p. 291.
[15] Walker, 'International Relations and the Concept of the Political', p. 309. It is fair to add that reflections on change are not strange to all positivist, systemic theory. See, for example, Ole R. Holsti, Randolph M. Siverson, and Alexander George (eds.), *Change in the International System* (Boulder, 1980).
[16] Walker, *Inside/Outside*, p. 120.
[17] Smith, 'New Approaches to International Theory', p. 181.
[18] Martin Hollis and Steve Smith, *Explaining and Understanding International Relations* (Oxford, 1990); Steve Smith, 'Positivism and Beyond', in Smith, Booth, and Zalewski, *International Theory: Positivism & Beyond*, pp. 11–47; Smith, 'New Approaches to International Theory'; Steve Smith, 'Epistemology, Postmodernism and International Relations Theory', *Journal of Peace Research*, 3 (1997), pp. 330–37.
[19] Smith, 'New Approaches to International Theory', p. 186.

problematical if taken to the extreme, as is the case in some post-modernist con-tributions.[20] Second, I argue that the notion of an insurmountable gulf between positivist and post-positivist methodology is incorrect. This is true both in the epistemological sense and in the ontological sense, as will be clarified below. Fortunately, both epistemological and ontological middle-roads are possible and it is those middle-positions which promise the most fruitful roads ahead for IR. What follows is certainly not any sweeping attack on post-positivism; I rather believe that most of those positions associated with positivism (realism, liberalism, some versions of Marxism) as well as with post-positivism (critical theory, historical sociology, normative theory, and several version of post-modernism and feminist theory) can be placed in the productive middle ground between the positivist and the post-positivist extremes. It is the extremes of which I am critical and, by implication, I question the utility of casting this whole metatheoretical debate in terms of (extreme) positivism versus (extreme) post-positivism. That is, if and when there is room for almost everybody in the middle ground, the basic lines of battle should be drawn somewhere else.

Before moving on with these issues it is relevant to note the constructive side of deconstructivism. The 'incredulity towards metanarratives' seems to me to be a relevant element in dealing critically with any theory. In other words, deconstructing any theory can produce helpful insights. The problem only comes in when this is taken to the extreme where everything in the criticized theory is rejected and the possibility of any cross-fertilization between theoretical traditions is denied.

What, then, are the more general problems with the extreme versions of the post-positivist position? The first problem is that they tend to overlook, or downplay, the actual insights produced by non-post-positivists, such as, for example, neorealism. It is entirely true that anarchy is no given, ahistorical, natural condition to which the only possible reaction is adaptation. But the fact that anarchy is a historically specific, socially constructed product of human practice does not make it less real. In a world of sovereign states, anarchy is in fact out there in the real world in some form. In other words, it is not the acceptance of the real existence of social phenomena which produces objectivist reification. Reification is produced by the transformation of historically specific social phenomena into given, ahistorical, natural conditions.[21] Despite their shortcomings, neorealism and other positivist theories have produced valuable insights about anarchy, including the factors in play in balance-of-power dynamics and in patterns of cooperation and conflict. Such insights are downplayed and even sometimes dismissed in adopting the notion of 'regimes of truth'. It is, of course, possible to appreciate the shortcomings of neorealism while also recognizing that it has merits. One way of doing so is set forth by Robert Cox. He considers neorealism to be a 'problem-solving theory' which 'takes the world as it finds it, with the prevailing social and power relationships . . . as the given framework for action . . . The strength of the problem-solving approach lies in its ability to fix limits or parameters to a problem area and to reduce the

---

[20] Tendencies in that direction can be found, for example, in Jim George, *Discourses of Global Politics: A Critical (Re)Introduction to International Relations* (Boulder, 1994); Roland Bleiker, 'Forget 'IR' Theory', paper for the Second Pan-European Conference on International Relations, Paris, 13–16 September 1995; Roger D. Spegele, 'Political Realism and the Remembrance of Relativism', *Review of International Studies*, 21 (1995), pp. 211–36.

[21] As explained in Curt Sørensen, *Marxismen og den Sociale Orden* (Marxism and the Social Order) (Kongerslev, 1976), p. 62.

statement of a particular problem to a limited number of variables which are amenable to relatively close and precise examination'.[22] At the same time, this 'assumption of fixity' is 'also an ideological bias . . . Problem-solving theories (serve) . . . particular national, sectional or class interests, which are comfortable within the given order'.[23] In sum, objectivist theory such as neorealism contains a bias, but that does not mean that it is without merit in analysing particular aspects of international relations from a particular point of view.

The second problem with post-positivism is the danger of extreme relativism which it contains. If there are no neutral grounds for deciding about truth claims so that each theory will define what counts as the facts, then the door is, at least in principle, open to anything goes. Steve Smith has confronted this problem in an exchange with Øyvind Østerud. Smith notes that he has never 'met a postmodernist who would accept that "the earth is flat if you say so". Nor has any postmodernist I have read argued or implied that "any narrative is as good as any other"'.[24] But the problem remains that if we cannot find a minimum of common standards for deciding about truth claims a post-modernist position appears unable to come up with a metatheoretically substantiated critique of the claim that the earth is flat. In the absence of at least some common standards it appears difficult to reject that any narrative is as good as any other.[25]

The final problem with extreme post-positivism I wish to address here concerns change. We noted the post-modern critique of neorealism's difficulties with embracing change; their emphasis is on 'continuity and repetition'. But extreme post-positivists have their own problem with change, which follows from their metatheoretical position. In short, how can post-positivist ideas and projects of change be distinguished from pure utopianism and wishful thinking? Post-positivist radical subjectivism leaves no common ground for choosing between different change projects. A brief comparison with a classical Marxist idea of change will demonstrate the point I am trying to make. In Marxism, social change (e.g. revolution) is, of course, possible. But that possibility is tied in with the historically specific social structures (material and non-material) of the world. Revolution is possible under certain social conditions but not under any conditions. Humans can change the world, but they are enabled and constrained by the social structures in which they live. There is a dialectic between social structure and human behaviour.[26] The understanding of 'change' in the Marxist tradition is thus closely related to an appreciation of the historically specific social conditions under which people live; any change project is not possible at any time. Robert Cox makes a similar point in writing about critical theory: 'Critical theory allows for a normative choice in favor of a social and political order different from the prevailing order, but it limits the range of choice to alternative orders which are feasible transformations of the existing world . . . Critical theory thus contains an element

[22] Robert W. Cox, 'Social Forces, States, and World Orders: Beyond International Relations Theory', in R.W. Cox with T.J. Sinclair, *Approaches to World Order* (London, 1996), pp. 85–124, quote from p. 88.
[23] Ibid., p. 89.
[24] Smith, 'Epistemology, Postmodernism and International Relations Theory', p. 332.
[25] The difficult part is, of course, establishing precisely what those common standards shall be, and post-positivists often complain that the other side wants them to 'do more of the moving' on the continuum between positivism and post-positivism. The quote is from J. Ann Tickner, 'Continuing the Conversation ...', *International Studies Quarterly*, 42 (1998), p. 209.
[26] Sørensen, *Marxismen og den Sociale Orden*, pp. 68–73.

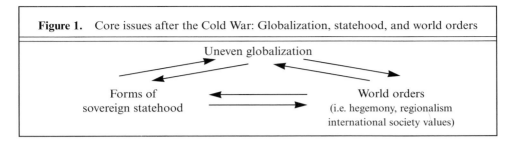

Figure 1. Core issues after the Cold War: Globalization, statehood, and world orders

their citizens; they even sometimes put their people in danger including mortal danger. People that are stateless or people that live in weak or failed states[47] are in serious jeopardy compared to people that live in well-functioning states which provide for these basic values. Given the importance of the sovereign state, a measure of statism, i.e. analytical focus on the sovereign state, is thus warranted in the study of basic problems of international relations. This is true even when our main concern is the life and well-being of individuals.

The question, then, is what can we say about the big issues of war and peace, conflict and cooperation, and wealth and poverty after the end of the Cold War? Figure 1 presents a suitable entry point for discussing this question.

This approach is inspired by (but not identical to) the work of Robert Cox.[48] The idea is that the core issues of war and peace, conflict and cooperation, wealth and poverty can be suitably approached in their post-Cold War format through the study of the entities and relationships expressed in Figure 1. It will appear from what follows that this approach builds on the metatheoretical middle ground identified above; in particular it stresses the need to analyse material as well as non-material aspects of social reality.

Uneven globalization

Globalization increasingly defines the context for economic and social development in the world. It is therefore a core issue in the analysis of wealth and poverty. The content of globalization can be clarified through two major distinctions. The first is between globalization as a primarily *economic* process involving, e.g., production, distribution, management, and finance,[49] and globalization as a broader *sociological* process involving all aspects of social activity, including, e.g., culture, reproduction, communication, ideology, etc.[50] The second major distinction is between 'Globaliz-

---

[47] Robert H. Jackson, *Quasi-states: Sovereignty, International Relations and the Third World* (Cambridge, 1993); Georg Sørensen, 'Individual Security and National Security'.

[48] Robert W. Cox, 'Social Forces, States, and World Orders: Beyond International Relations Theory'.

[49] Paul Hirst and Grahame Thompson, *Globalisation in Question: The International Economy and the Possibilities of Governance* (Cambridge, 1996); Robert W. Cox, *Production, Power and World Order: Social Forces in the Making of History* (New York, 1987); Robert Boyer and Daniel Drache, *States Against Markets. The Limits of Globalisation* (London/New York, 1996); Jeremy Howell and Michelle Wood (1993), *The Globalisation of Production and Technology* (London/New York, 1993).

[50] Ulrich Beck, *Risk Society: Towards a New Modernity* (London, 1992); Anthony Giddens, *The Consequences of Modernity* (Cambridge, 1990); Martin Albrow, *The Global Age* (Cambridge, 1996).

Figure 2.   Dimensions of globalization

Type of globalization	Consequences of globalization	
	'Globalization sceptics'	'Globalization believers'
Narrow: economic	Economic interdependence; nothing new	Globalized economic system. Qualitative shift
Broad: comprehensive social change	Interconnectedness increases; nothing new	Globalized societies redefine conditions of life for individuals and groups

---

ation Believers' and 'Globalization Sceptics'. According to the former, globalization is changing or has already changed both the economic and the social world in fundamental ways.[51] On this view, we are entering a qualitatively new reality where national economies are subsumed by a globalized economic system, and where individuals and groups face radically different conditions of existence in a globalized world where sovereign states have lost most of the power they used to have.

According to 'Globalization Sceptics', nothing much is new.[52] The processes under the globalization label have been at work for many decades. There was a high level of economic interdependence between countries already before the First World War; and in broader terms, the increasing interconnectedness between societies at social, cultural, and political levels began a very long time ago. In short, globalization is not new; it has been around for a long time. The two distinctions can be summarized as shown in Figure 2.

I find it misleading to make a clear choice between these four positions in the globalization debate. The point is that all four aspects of globalization can be found in the real world. Furthermore, the distinction between a narrow and a broad concept of globalization is analytical, meaning that the choice between them depends on what one wants to analyse. As far as the debate between 'believers' and 'sceptics' is concerned, this is yet another version of the discussion about whether the glass is half full or half empty. The real world is an uneven mixture of traditional interdependence and interconnectedness on the one hand, and new elements of globalized economic systems and societies on the other. The interesting question is to find out about the concrete substance of that mixture in different specific countries and regions.

Uneven globalization redefines the context for economic development and thus for the welfare of people. It presents new opportunities for dynamic development

---

[51] Robert Reich, *The Work of Nations. Preparing Ourselves for 21st Century Capitalism* (New York, 1992); Kenichi Ohmae, *The Borderless World* (London, 1990); Kenichi Ohmae, *The End of the Nation-state: The Rise of Regional Economies* (London, 1995); John Stopford and Susan Strange with John S. Henley, *Rival States, Rival Firms: Competition for World Market Shares* (Cambridge, 1991).

[52] E.g. several contributions in Boyer and Drache, *States Against Markets;* Paul Hirst, 'The Global Economy—Myths and Realities', *International Affairs*, 3 (1997), pp. 409–25; Robert H. Jackson, 'Continuity and Change in the States System', in R.H. Jackson and A. James (eds.), *States in a Changing World. A Contemporary Analysis* (London, 1993).

but also new obstacles. The greatest problem may be that the weak states in the periphery of the world economy are losing out in the globalization race. Such states face two kind of problems. On the one hand, access to the world economy is increasingly difficult, not primarily because of trade barriers but due to lack of demand. Industrialized countries have a decreasing need for the weak states, be it as sources of raw materials, as markets, or as cheap labour.[53] On the other hand, in order to reap maximum benefits of any world market integration, domestic political and economic reform is needed in many countries, and it may not be forthcoming, not even as a result of fragile democratization.[54] Several scholars have demonstrated the decisive importance of domestic preconditions for successfully facing external challenges and for seizing opportunities.[55] In an increasingly globalized world, such lessons are acutely relevant.

In sum, what I foresee as a result of uneven globalization is a world tied closer together in the sense that autarchic development (e.g. North Korea) is less and less feasible. But it is also a more fragmented and hierarchical world in the sense that a number of weak states will be unable to reap the potential benefits of uneven globalization. A complete answer to the question about the effects of globalization requires an analysis of the reciprocal relationships in Figure 1 as they are played out in the present historical conjuncture. Let me turn to the next major item, forms of sovereign statehood.

Forms of sovereign statehood

It is relevant to begin with an outline of the two major analytical positions in the debate about sovereign statehood. The dominant theoretical position in IR theory, realism, considers the state an unproblematic given. The state is seen as a sovereign, territorially based unit run by a government which enjoys a high level of autonomy in both domestic and foreign affairs.[56] On this view, that is really all we need to know about the state; we do not need to analyse statehood as such, because all states are basically 'like units', i.e. they have to perform similar functions of government and they all enjoy sovereignty. The only interesting difference between states is their power capabilities; some are strong, some are weak.

This 'fixed' view of the state is most often combined with a 'sceptic' view of the consequences of globalization. Globalization does not challenge the sovereign state in basic ways. Statehood is not in decline: the institution of sovereignty is more popular than ever and the new challenges to the state, such as an increasingly globalized economy, must be seen in the context of the state's increased capacities

[53] Kari Levitt, 'Debt, Adjustment and Development: Looking to the 1990s', *Economic and Political Weekly*, July 21 (1990). Oil and a few strategic raw materials are exceptions from this trend.

[54] Georg Sørensen, *Democracy and Democratization. Processes and Prospects in a Changing World* (Boulder, 1998).

[55] Dieter Senghaas, *The European Experience: A Historical Critique of Development Theory* (Leamington Spa/Dover, 1985).

[56] Kenneth N. Waltz, '*Theory of International Politics*' (Reading, MA, 1979); see also Mark V. Zacher, 'The decaying pillars of the Westphalian Temple: Implications for International Order and Governance', in J.N. Rosenau and Ernst-Otto Czempiel (eds.), *Governance Without Government: Order and Change in World Politics* (Cambridge, 1992), pp. 58–102.

for response. In terms of domestic extraction of surplus and regulation, the state is stronger than ever; in terms of the external environment, the long-term trend has been toward more, not less autonomy.[57]

Against this mainstream view of the state in IR-theory stands a growing number of analysts who argue that the state is basically in decline, not least due to the forces of globalization. The 'declinists'[58] first and foremost argue that globalization is challenging the state in fundamental ways. Economic and ecological interdependence decrease state autonomy. Democratization erodes the domestic autonomy of state elites. The information revolution has made communication much less bound by time and place.[59] Together with increasing individual skills this challenges the state from below.[60] The argument of the 'declinists' is that all these developments seriously weaken the sovereign state.

Yet it is clear that neither the 'declinists' nor the 'strong state' adherents can win this debate for the simple reason that both have a valid point. Sovereign states have been both strengthened and weakened in complex ways since the end of World War II. What we need, then, is an approach that can accommodate both 'declinist' and 'strong state' elements. Such an approach focuses on *changes* in statehood that can lead to both stronger and weaker states. A suitable way of initiating this analysis is through the identification of main types of state in the present international system.

In more concrete terms, I would argue that processes of uneven globalization under the conditions of the post-World War II world order has led to the creation of three main types (i.e. Weberian ideal types) of state.[61] They are: (a) the modern 'Westphalian' state, a consolidated nation-state with its own structural dynamic and relative autonomy; (b) the post-colonial state, that is, the weak and unconsolidated state on the periphery, often in an ongoing state of entropy; and (c) the 'postmodern' state, a complex, transnationallly interpenetrated entity immersed in globalization and multi-level governance. The EU-members are the major examples of this last-mentioned type of state.

Space does not allow a full elaboration of these main types of state here. Figure 3 provides a summary of the major characteristics of the three types. The point worth stressing here is that the state typology provides a preliminary answer to the crucial question about how globalization in the present world order affects the state. This discussion has hitherto been dominated by the unfruitful dead-end debate of 'decline of state' versus 'continued strength of state'. By focusing on change of statehood (in the direction of both stronger and weaker states) and combining this with the notion of different main types of state, this debate can move forward in a much more fruitful way.

---

[57] Janice Thompson and Stephen D. Krasner, 'Global Transactions and the Consolidation of Sovereignty', in E-O. Czempiel and J.N. Rosenau (eds.), *Global Changes and Theoretical Challenges: Approaches to World Politics for the 1990s* (Lexington, MA, 1989), pp. 195–221.

[58] James N. Rosenau, *Turbulence in World Politics: A Theory of Change and Continuity* (Princeton, 1990); Ohmae, *The End of the Nation-state: The Rise of Regional Economies;* Susan Strange, 'Wake up, Krasner! The World *has* Changed', *Review of International Political Economy*, 2 (1994), pp. 209–19; Zacher, 'The Decaying Pillars of the Westphalian Temple'.

[59] E.g., William H. McNeill, 'Winds of Change', *Foreign Affairs*, 69 (1990), pp. 162–72.

[60] See Rosenau, *Turbulence in World Politics: A Theory of Change and Continuity.*

[61] Georg Sørensen, 'An Analysis of Contemporary Statehood: Consequences for Conflict and Cooperation', *Review of International Studies*, 3 (1997), pp. 253–69.

Figure 3.   States in the present international system: Three ideal types

	'Post-Colonial'	'Westphalian'	'Post-Modern'
Sovereignty	Juridical, negative, formal	Substantial, internal and external state autonomy	Operational, shared with supra-national institutions
Economy	Dependent, structural heterogeneity	Self-sustained, no specialization, a coherent national economy	Globalized, some specialization, part of larger welfare community
Polity	Personal rule, weak institutions	Polyarchy, strong institutions	Plurilateral: emerging transnational policy network
Nationhood?	No	Yes	Yes, but challenged by competing identities

Furthermore, the state typology provides a framework for analysing future prospects for conflict and cooperation, peace and war. The standard security problem in IR concerns the external threat of violent conflict between sovereign states in an anarchic international system. The security problem in post-colonial states is qualitatively different. The most significant difference is that the serious threat to security in terms of large-scale violent conflict is internal, not external. Lack of developed statehood presents many post-colonial states with a perennial problem of domestic security. Such states are not internally pacified. In the post-Cold War world, the large majority of violent conflicts are domestic conflicts in post-colonial states.

In globalized post-modern states, on the other hand, economic and social integration has led to the formation of a tightly knit security community. In other words, violent conflict between consolidated liberal states in the North is no longer on the cards. The security community is based on four liberal elements: the republican element, stressing peaceful cooperation between democracies; the commercial element, emphasizing networks of economic interdependence; the sociological element, underscoring the intense transnational linkages between countries; and the institutional element which emphasizes the importance of common institutions facilitating cooperation. There is a mutually reinforcing synergy between these different aspects of liberalism.[62]

The liberal issues of democracy and democratization and of international institutions have been the subject of large debates after the end of the Cold War,

---

[62] Robert O. Keohane *et al.*, *After the Cold War. International Institutions and State Strategies in Europe 1989–91* (Cambridge, MA, 1993); Georg Sørensen, 'Det Liberale Fredsperspektiv i Teori of Praksis', *GRUS*, 53 (1997), pp. 7–27.

especially in North American IR.[63] The position taken here is that these issues should be tied in with the larger subject of the development and change of sovereign statehood. Democratization is not likely to bring peace to weak states in the Third World; it will frequently spark more intense conflict. The involvement in international institutions will hardly have far-reaching consequences in countries where domestic institutions are extremely weak and fragile. At the same time, institutional development and democratic governance is developing in new ways in the context of globalized, highly integrated, post-modern states.

In sum, violent conflict between post-modern states is highly unlikely. But there are large zones of conflict in the Third World where domestic conflict in weak, post-colonial states is prevalent. And in consolidated liberal states, new forms of (non-violent) threat appear to be on the rise, due to the 'risk-society' created by globalization. Further exploration of these patterns of conflict and threat is an important element on the post-Cold War IR-agenda.

World order

The third and final leg in the analytical framework in Figure 1 is 'world order'. Defined as the configuration of forces which define the systemic context for any concrete ensemble of states,[64] I conceive of world order as containing the following main elements: (a) hegemony; (b) regionalism; and (c) international society values. Space only allows brief comments on each of these items.

Re. (a): Hegemony concerns the distribution of power. The end of the Cold War has started a comprehensive debate about the relative distribution of power in the international system following the decline of the Soviet Union. Neorealists characterize the present system as 'bipolarity in an altered state'.[65] Bipolarity continues because militarily Russia can take care of herself and because no other great powers have emerged. Yet with the waning of Soviet power, the United States is no longer held in check by any other country or combination of countries; the system leans towards unipolarity with the U.S. as the unipolar power. Against neorealism liberals argue that a qualitative change is under way, towards an international system characterised by interdependence, democracy, and liberal institutions.[66] They argue that in such a world, power is more diffuse, less tangible, and the non-material 'soft power' is of increasing importance.[67]

My starting point on this issue is the Coxian notion of hegemony which contains material as well as non-material aspects of power. Hegemony is a 'fit between a configuration of material power, the prevalent collective image of world order (including certain norms) and a set of institutions which administer the order . . .'.[68]

---

[63] As evidenced in leading North American journals, such as *International Security, World Politics, International Organization* and *American Political Science Review.*

[64] The definition is a modified version of the one appearing in Cox, 'Social Forces, States, and World Orders: Beyond International Relations Theory'.

[65] Waltz, 'The Emerging Structure of International Politics'.

[66] An overview of the liberal arguments appears in Sørensen, 'Det Liberale Fredsperspektiv i Teori of Praksis'.

[67] See Nye, *Bound to Lead: The Changing Nature of American Power.*

[68] Cox, 'Social Forces, States, and World Orders: Beyond International Relations Theory', p. 103.

The undisputed U.S. hegemony of the post-World War II era is a thing of the past, but a new hegemony has not been established. There is international governance in the form of various regimes and institutions, but there is no apparatus to deal comprehensively with either global economic crisis (as it threatens, for example, due to the present downturn in Asian economies) or global security problems (e.g. state failure in Africa and elsewhere). There is no clear hegemony in the present period. Cox speculates that we may be entering a 'post-hegemonic' world because the forces of globalization have led to a transformation of statehood which mitigates against a new hegemony.[69] Yet a more likely prospect appears to be an order based on an alliance between the three regional clusters led by the EU in Europe, the United States in America, and Japan/China in East Asia.

Re. (b): Regionalism. There has been a proliferation of regional cooperation in recent years, from NAFTA and MERCOSUR in America, ASEAN in East Asia, and the EU in Europe. Several analysts argue that we are well on the way towards a regionalized world.[70] It appears that regional cooperation is in important respects the answer given by states to the challenges of globalization. Economic globalization has increasingly restricted the national autonomy of many states. Increased supranational cooperation is thus partly an attempt to regain some of the regulatory influence lost in the national political space owing to the very success of the modern state in organizing transnational economic development during the post-World War II era.

Yet it is crucially important to emphasize that the type of regional cooperation is not uniform. There is qualitative variation: only the EU has moved towards forms of cooperation with clear consequences for the sovereignty of member states. Both the United States and Japan appear to respond to the challenges to states with more conventional forms of regional cooperation. Therefore, while regionalism is on the increase, we are in important respects *not* moving towards a world of regions.[71] Most forms of regional cooperation are of a rather loose and open kind. It will be an important issue on the IR-agenda to further analyse regional cooperation in comparative perspective.

Re. (c): International society values. The end of the Cold War also meant the end of the Communist challenge to liberalism. There is now an extensive debate about new possible cultural and ideological challengers to modern, liberal society. It is becoming clear that the popular notion of a coming 'clash of civilizations' is a misleading approach.[72] A more appropriate point of departure is the English School notion of an 'international society', that is, the society of sovereign states with common institutions and common rules and norms. Following Jackson,[73] there can be varying degrees of society between states, from very limited contact and interaction at one extreme, to comprehensive interaction in a highly institutionalized setting at the other extreme, sustained by common norms and rules. Against this background, it can be argued that there is 'more society' in the post-Cold War

---

[69] Robert W. Cox, 'Global Restructuring. Making Sense of the Changing International Political Economy', in Stubbs and Underhill (eds.), *Political Economy and the Changing Global Order*, pp. 45–60.

[70] For an overview, see B. Hettne and A. Inotai, *The New Regionalism* (Helsinki, 1994).

[71] For a similar view, see Miles Kahler, 'A World of Blocs: Facts and Factoids', *World Policy Journal*, 1 (1995), pp. 19–28.

[72] Samuel Huntington, 'The Clash of Civilizations', *Foreign Affairs*, 3 (1993), pp. 22–50.

[73] Jackson, 'The Political Theory of International Society'.

international system. There is more agreement about liberal values, including human rights, and there is more preparedness to act in coalition when the basic values of international society are violated (e.g. the Gulf War, humanitarian intervention in failed states). At the same time, processes of globalization can lead to confrontation between modern and traditional values,[74] but even if it is a fragile and stepwise process, I would argue that the accent is presently on integration and stronger common values, instead of fragmentation and clashes between different values.

Conclusion

The IR community has reason to be pleased with the metatheoretical and the substantial debate triggered by the end of the Cold War. The metatheoretical tools have been sharpened; there is much more clarity about the ontological and the epistemological bases for the various theoretical approaches. That service has, in the main, been provided by post-positivists. Even if it is true that the debate recapitulates many elements from earlier debates, including the debates between behaviouralists and traditionalists[75] and the debates between Marxists and non-Marxists,[76] every discipline needs a metatheoretical inventory and house-cleaning from time to time, because it always produces a number of fresh insights.

As for the substantial issues, there has been a healthy shake-up as well. I have argued that the core issues of the discipline: peace and war; wealth and poverty, conflict and cooperation, involve a certain amount of statism, i.e. focus on sovereign states. But this does not exclude issues based on other identities, including gender, class or culture. In sum, there is more clarity about what we know and about what we don't know. And there is more sound humility towards the magnitude of the task we face, both methodologically and substantially. Combined with a healthy pluralism in both areas, that is all for the best. There is also a constructive trend towards opening up the discipline of IR to other areas of human and social science, including comparative politics, sociology, economics, and the humanities. Both in substantive and in methodological terms there should be much to gain from living less isolated. Getting thus far has involved a number of battles and controversies, some of them more productive than others. This is all business as usual. Social science cannot and should not attempt to achieve the paradigmatic 'normal science' of the natural sciences, where there is much more agreement about basic assumptions concerning metatheoretical premises and scientific habits.[77] But we do have a common ground of intersubjectively transmissible knowledge.

---

[74] See Albrow, *The Global Age*.

[75] Bull, 'International Theory: The Case for a Classical Approach'.

[76] E.g., Georg Sørensen, 'A Revised Paradigm for International Relations', *Cooperation and Conflict* (1991), pp. 85–116.

[77] See, for example, Arend Lijphart, 'The Structure of the Theoretical Revolution in International Relations', *International Studies Quarterly*, 1 (1964), pp. 41–75.

On constitution and causation in International Relations

ALEXANDER WENDT*

Within the community of academic students of international politics today there is a deep epistemological rift over the extent to and ways in which we can know our subject. Speaking very broadly, on one side stand what have become known as 'positivists', who think we can get closer to the truth about international politics, but only if we follow the methods which have proven so successful in the natural sciences. And on the other side stand 'post-positivists',[1] who think we do not have privileged access to the truth about international politics, and least of all through the methods of natural science. Although it can seem far removed, this epistemological disagreement actually matters quite a lot to our collective efforts to make sense of the real world, since we cannot avoid taking some position on it, and those positions affect the questions we ask, the methods we use to answer those questions, and ultimately the kinds of knowledge that we produce. Perhaps for this reason what may seem more a dispute for philosophers than political scientists has become one of the 'Great Debates' (the Third) in the discipline of International Relations (IR), and, indeed, it arguably underlay the 'Second' Debate between behaviouralists and traditionalists in the 1960s as well.[2]

There are many issues in this debate, most of which I will not take up here.[3] What I am interested in is just one, albeit particularly common, way of framing the debate, perhaps best exemplified by Martin Hollis and Steve Smith's rich and thought-provoking book, *Explaining and Understanding International Relations*.[4] Drawing on

---

* The author thanks Mlada Bukovansky for helpful comments on a draft of this paper, and Jennifer Mitzen for conversations that helped clarify some key points.

[1] These labels are far from ideal, since in the strict 'logical' sense 'positivism' has been dead in the philosophy of science for decades, and as such *all* contemporary epistemologies are 'post'-positivist. However, they are the terms in which the current debate in International Relations about the epistemological status of social science is being carried out and as such I reluctantly adopt them here.

[2] For a good overview of the Third Debate, see Yosef Lapid, 'The Third Debate: On the Prospects of International Theory in a Post-positivist Era', *International Studies Quarterly*, 33 (1989), pp. 235–54, and the subsequent commentaries in the same journal. On the Second Debate see, for example, Hedley Bull, 'International theory: The Case for a Classical Approach', in K. Knorr and J. Rosenau (eds.), *Contending Approaches to International Politics* (Princeton, NJ: 1969), and Morton Kaplan, 'The New Great Debate: Traditionalism vs. Science in International Relations', Ibid.

[3] For a broader exploration, see 'Scientific Realism and Social Kinds', ch. 2 in Wendt, *Social Theory of International Politics* (Cambridge, 1999).

[4] Martin Hollis and Steve Smith, *Explaining and Understanding International Relations* (Oxford, 1990). The author addressed the ontological aspects of this book in 'Bridging the Theory/Metatheory Gap in International Relations', *Review of International Studies*, 17 (1991), pp. 383–92, which was followed by a reply from Hollis and Smith, 'Beware of Gurus: Structure and Action in International Relations', Ibid., pp. 393–410, and a further exchange in 1992. Here I take up its epistemological aspects, which I had set aside in my 1991 review.

a long tradition in the philosophy of social science, Hollis and Smith argue that social scientists face a basic choice between two approaches to or 'stories' about their subject matter. 'One story is an outsider's, told in the manner of a natural scientist seeking to explain the workings of nature and treating the human realm as part of nature.'[5] The goal of this story is to find causal mechanisms and social laws. This has become known as 'Explaining', and is usually identified with a positivist approach to IR. The other story 'is an insider's, told so as to make us understand what the events mean, in a sense distinct from any meaning found in unearthing the laws of nature'.[6] The goal of this story is to recover the individual and shared meanings that motivated actors to do what they did. Known as 'Understanding', this is usually identified with post-positivism.

Hollis and Smith's intent is pluralistic, since they emphasize that neither story can be reduced to the other and that both are valuable. 'There are always two stories to tell' about international politics. Yet contained within the 'Explanation and Understanding' frame are the seeds of a more conflictual, zero-sum view, which has gripped at least a significant part of the Third Debate. The seeds of conflict lie in Hollis and Smith's assumption, shared with many positivists and post-positivists alike, that natural science is characterized by the outsider's focus on causal explanation, and does *not* include the kind of intellectual activity associated with the insider's focus on actors' understandings. Since the natural sciences constitute our model for 'science', this assumption suggests that the choice facing social scientists is not between two ways of knowing, both seen as part of the scientific enterprise, but between science (as outsider story) and non-science. Given the interest of positivist IR scholars in establishing the epistemic authority of their work as Science, this choice leads them to emphasize that the overriding goal of IR must be Explanation and only Explanation. And given the interest of post-positivist IR scholars in Understanding, this leads them to reject characterizations of their work as science, and some even to reject the possibility as well of Explanation in social inquiry. The belief that the distinction between Explanation and Understanding is one between science and non-science, in other words, is a recipe for the kind of epistemological 'paradigm wars' that have riven the field in the past decade.

On the surface the assumption that natural scientists do not engage in Understanding seems to make sense, since the objects of natural science are not intentional beings and as such not capable of having 'understandings' in the first place. However, in this article I suggest that despite this important ontological difference between the objects of natural and social inquiry, there is no fundamental epistemological difference between the natural and social sciences. The intellectual activities associated with Explanation and Understanding *both*, are, and should be, practised in *both* domains. To the extent that 'Explanation and Understanding' is equated with 'science and non-science', therefore, it is misleading and encourages unnecessarily zero-sum arguments about epistemology. These arguments can only lead to the impoverishment of our collective efforts to make sense of international politics and, given the disciplinary dominance in IR of Explainers, to the professional marginalization of Understanders.

---

[5] *Explaining and Understanding International Relations*, p. 1.
[6] Ibid.

In my view, the essence of the insider's story is not a focus on actors' under-standings, but an interest in a particular kind of *question*. That question, speaking broadly for the moment, is 'how are things in the world put together so that they have the properties that they do?'. This question transcends the natural/social science divide; it is routinely asked by researchers in both domains. But the ways in which they answer it must differ because the objects of their respective inquiries are made of different kinds of stuff. Things in the social world (what philosophers call 'social kinds'), like money, the state, and international society, are made largely of ideas. This means that if we are interested in the question of how social kinds are put together we will have to engage in an interpretive recovery of actors' private and shared beliefs, just as proponents of Understanding have long argued. However, the same question can be asked, and routinely *is* asked, of 'natural kinds' like dogs, elm trees, and DNA. Natural kinds are made of physical substances, not ideas, which means that if we want to know how *they* are put together we will have to study their genetic, chemical, or other material structure. This shows that an interest in actors' beliefs is not intrinsic to the insider's search for Understanding, but contingent on the nature of the properties by which the objects of this activity in social science are constituted. Put another way, the Third Debate has tended to conflate two distinct issues—what things are made of (ontology) and what questions we should ask (part of epistemology). Disentangling these issues enables us to see that Explanation and Understanding are not only not mutually exclusive, but mutually implicating.

If Explanation and Understanding are distinguished not by science vs. non-science but by the kinds of questions that they are asking, then we need some way of characterizing those questions. There are different ways to do this, but I shall take Explainers to be asking 'causal' questions, and following David Sylvan, to whom much of my thinking on this score is indebted,[7] Understanders to be asking 'constitutive' ones. The differences between these two kinds of question are not well understood, and they are often conflated; it is increasingly common in IR scholar-ship, for example, to see the phrase 'mutually constitutive' used to describe relation-ships that are in fact causal, and relationships that are in fact mutually constitutive described in the causal language of 'interaction'. In the first half of this article I explore the differences between causal and constitutive questions, with particular reference to the latter since causal questions are relatively well understood.

A question-oriented approach to the Third Debate in one sense leaves us in a position similar to that advocated by Gary King, Robert Keohane, and Sidney Verba in *Designing Social Inquiry*, which has rapidly become a canonical 'positivist' text on social scientific method.[8] King, Keohane, and Verba interpret the distinction

---

[7] First as a student of his in graduate school and then through several unpublished manuscripts on the logic of constitutive inquiry which he co-authored with Stephen Majeski, most recently 'Modeling Theories of Constitutive Relations in Politics' (1998); for an earlier approach, see David Sylvan and Barry Glassner, *A Rationalist Methodology for the Social Sciences* (Oxford: Oxford University Press, 1985). Two other key sources for thinking about constitutive theory are Friedrich Kratochwil, *Rules, Norms and Decisions* (Cambridge, 1989) and Nicholas Onuf, *World of Our Making* (Columbia, SC, 1989). And although using other terminology, much the same kind of argument has long been advanced by Hayward Alker; see *Rediscoveries and Reformulations* (Cambridge, 1996). Use of the term 'constitutive' to describe this kind of theory seems to be gaining ground, as evidenced by Steve Smith's 'The Self-images of a Discipline: A Genealogy of International Relations Theory', in K. Booth and S. Smith (eds.), *International Relations Theory Today* (Cambridge, 1995), pp. 26–8.

[8] Gary King, Robert Keohane, and Sidney Verba, *Designing Social Inquiry* (Princeton, 1994).

between Explanation and Understanding as one between 'causal inference' and 'descriptive inference', which although not put in these terms seems equivalent to saying that the two kinds of inference answer different questions. An important virtue of their book is its emphasis on the fact that descriptive inference is a crucial part of science, both natural and social, which traditional positivists often neglect, and as such like Hollis and Smith, their view attempts to be methodologically inclusive and pluralist. But they specifically reject as 'confusing' the idea that the non-causal inquiries associated with Understanding might be 'explanatory', which means that for them, as for Hollis and Smith, Explanation equals causal inference.[9] This I think understates the contribution of the 'insider' approach to knowledge, and—albeit unintentionally—both reinforces its second-class status in social science and contributes to the reification of the social world. The distinction between Explanation and Understanding is not one between explanation and description, but between explanations that answer different kinds of question, causal and constitutive. In the second half of this article I attempt to dispel King, Keohane, and Verba's confusion by clarifying the explanatory role of constitutive theory and showing that this matters for how we think about international politics.

Causal and Constitutive Theories

In the philosophy of science a common way to characterize the differences between kinds of explanations is in terms of the kinds of questions which they answer.[10] It seems useful to apply this approach to the distinction between causal and constitutive explanations.

Causal theories answer questions of the form 'why?' and, in some cases, 'how?'. 'Why did the Protestant Reformation occur?', 'why did Gorbachev move to end the Cold War?', 'why does the sun rise in the east?', and 'why does salt corrode metal?' are all questions about the causes of things. Certain how-questions are also inquiries into causes: 'how did the Germans conquer France in 1940?', 'how did Christianity displace paganism?', 'how are babies made?', and 'how does the AIDS virus work?'. Causal researchers disagree among themselves about the importance or distinctiveness of how-questions, which may to some extent reflect competing conceptions of causality. Those who subscribe to the logical empiricist view that we have explained something causally only when we have subsumed it deductively under a law tend to concentrate on why-questions, while those who subscribe to the scientific realist view that we have explained something causally only when we have described the mechanisms or process by which it is generated tend to attach more importance to how-questions.[11] These disagreements are important, but for present purposes they can be downplayed because they are within the family of requests for causal explanations, and so I shall not pursue them further here.

---

[9] Ibid., p. 75, footnote 1.

[10] See, for example, Charles Cross, 'Explanation and the Theory of Questions', *Erkenntnis*, 34 (1991), pp. 237–60.

[11] For discussion of these competing views of causal explanation, see Russell Keat and John Urry, *Social Theory as Science*, 2nd edn (London, 1982), and Ernan McMullin, 'Two Ideals of Explanation in Natural Science', in P. French, *et al.* (eds.), *Midwest Studies in Philosophy*, vol. 9 (Minneapolis, MN, 1984), pp. 205–20.

In providing answers to causal questions, in saying that 'X causes Y', we assume three things: 1) that X and Y exist independent of each other, 2) that X precedes Y in time, and 3) that but for X, Y would not have occurred. The first two conditions should not pose anything more than a conceptual problem for the causal researcher and as such do not generally receive much attention. It is essential that the effort to establish causal connections make sure that X and Y are independently existing and temporally separated, but having done so the causal researcher's main problem is to satisfy the third, counterfactual condition, which involves distinguishing causation from mere correlation, or necessary from accidental association. This is no easy task, since our inability to experience causation directly means that 'we can never hope to know a causal effect for certain',[12] and as a result much methodological advice has been devoted to improving the quality of the inferences that we inevitably have to make. But in thinking about the difference between causal and constitutive questions it is the first two assumptions which are crucial, since constitutive stories do not make them. These assumptions reflect the central objective of causal stories, which is to explain *changes* in the state of some variable or system. To highlight this objective, Robert Cummins refers to causal theories as 'transition' theories.[13] In order to explain transitions it is necessary that the factors to which we appeal be independent of and temporally prior to the transitions themselves; hence the terminology of 'independent' and 'dependent' variables that is often used in causal theorizing.

Constitutive theories have a different objective, which is to account for the properties of things by reference to the structures in virtue of which they exist. Cummins calls such theories 'property' theories.[14] Unlike transition theories, which explain events through time, property theories are static. Their goal is to show how the properties of a system are constituted. The systems whose properties they explain may be dynamic, and indeed *all* systems, natural and social, are always in process, continually being reproduced through time even if they do not change. But constitutive theories abstract away from these processes and take 'snapshots' instead, in an effort to explain how systems are constituted.

As such, constitutive questions usually take the form of 'how-possible?' or 'what?'. 'How was it possible for Stalin, a single individual, to exercise so much power over the Soviet people?' 'How is it possible for Luxembourg to survive in an anarchic world next door to Great Powers like France and Germany?' 'How is it possible for a gas to have a temperature?'[15] And 'how is it possible for the Earth to keep the moon in its orbit?' are all requests for information about the conditions of possibility for natural and social kinds. A related logic underlies what-questions: 'What kind of political system is the European Union?'. 'Was Serbian behaviour during the Bosnian Civil War "genocide"?'. 'What are comets made of?'. And 'what is ball lightning?'. What we seek in asking these questions is insight into what it is that instantiates some phenomenon, not why that phenomenon comes about.

Adequate answers to how-possible and what-questions must satisfy different truth conditions than answers to causal questions. As with the latter, the answers to constitutive questions must support a counterfactual claim of necessity, namely that

---

[12] King, Keohane, and Verba, *Designing Social Inquiry*, p. 79.
[13] Robert Cummins, *The Nature of Psychological Explanation* (Cambridge, MA, 1983).
[14] Ibid., pp. 14–22.
[15] The example is Cummins', ibid., p. 15.

in the absence of the structures to which we are appealing the properties in question would not exist. But the kind of necessity required here is conceptual or logical, not causal or natural. The relationship between the factors constituting the social kind 'Cold War' and a Cold War is one of *identity*, in the sense that those factors define what a Cold War *is*, not one of causal determination. And this in turn means that the answers to constitutive questions will necessarily violate the first two assumptions of causal explanations, independent existence and temporal asymmetry. The factors constituting a Cold War do not exist apart from a Cold War, nor do they precede it in time; when they come into being, a Cold War comes into being with them, by definition and at the same time. This means that the 'independent variable/dependent variable' language that characterizes causal inquiries makes no sense, or at least must be interpreted very differently, in constitutive inquiries.[16] The effects of constitutive structures might be said to 'vary' with their constituting conditions, but the dependency reflected in this variation is conceptual rather than causal. When constituting conditions vary, then so do their constitutive effects, *by definition*.

However, although they have different truth conditions, this does not mean that causal and constitutive theories imply different 'epistemologies'. Both kinds of theory are true or false in virtue of how well they correspond to states of the world. This is perhaps more obvious in the case of causal theories: a theory of what caused the Cold War which made no mention of competing ideologies, mutual distrust, and rough material parity is unlikely to be true. But correspondence to states of the world is also an important goal for constitutive theories: a theory of how the state is constituted that made no mention of sovereignty, territoriality, or a monopoly on the legitimate use of organized violence would not reflect what are in fact the conditions of possibility for that social kind, no matter how satisfying such a theory might be on other grounds (internal coherence, parsimony, political correctness, or whatever). Not all constitutive theories are true any more than all causal theories are true, and the test for both is ultimately their relationship to how the world works.

Post-positivists might object that a correspondence test of truth for constitutive theories is problematic because human beings do not have direct access to how the world is constituted. What we see in the world is always and necessarily mediated by the background understandings we bring to bear on our inquiries. I agree that all observation is theory-laden, and this means that we can never test our theories directly against the world, but only indirectly via other, competing theories. But this is equally true of causal and constitutive theories (and, note, it also compatible with what is today called 'positivism' in IR). Moreover, for both kinds of theory the 'scientific' solution to the problem is the same, namely to rely on publicly available, albeit always theory-laden, evidence from the world, which critics of our theoretical claims can assess for relevance, accuracy, and so on. The importance of such evidence is not lost even on the most hardened post-positivists who, while perhaps overtly rejecting the correspondence theory of truth, in their empirical work routinely try to find accurate and relevant evidence from the world to support their claims. Why limit themselves in this way if the external world does not somehow set the truth conditions for their theories? Why not be creative and choose arbitrary 'evidence'? One answer may be that post-positivists at least implicitly realize that

---

[16] For a good discussion of how behavioural methods and language relate to constitutive theorizing, see David Sylvan and Barry Glassner, 'Is Statistical Inference Appropriate to Structuralism?', *Quality and Quantity*, 17 (1983), pp. 69–86.

they would not be saying anything interesting about the external world, even if they might still be saying interesting things in the form of art, poetry, or revelation. At the end of the day, in other words, most post-positivists are 'tacit realists' (a form of positivism) in their empirical research, which is to say that they are guided by the desire to make their theories correspond to how the world works.[17]

Doubting that the truth of constitutive theories depends on correspondence to the world is one road that post-positivists take to get to the conclusion that their work requires a different epistemology than causal theorizing. However, there is another pathway to this conclusion as well. This road starts out by highlighting the ontological differences in what the natural and social worlds are made of—physical substances and ideas respectively—and then associates materialist ontologies (and thus natural science) with causal theories and idealist ontologies (social science) with constitutive theories. If this association makes sense then that might imply different epistemologies for the natural and social sciences, because the ways in which we would 'know' whether causal and constitutive theories are true would be radically different in the two domains, observing physical facts on the one hand and interpreting meanings on the other.

It is certainly the case that the natural and social worlds are at least in part made of different kinds of stuff, and that these ontological differences require different methods and data for their study. We simply can't study ideas in exactly the same way that we study physical facts because ideas are not the kinds of phenomena that are even indirectly observable. However, this does not imply different epistemologies for the natural and social sciences, since it is wrong to think that material conditions imply causal theorizing and ideas imply constitutive theorizing. Both kinds of stuff have both causal and constitutive effects. Ideas have constitutive effects insofar as they make social kinds possible; masters and slaves do not exist apart from the shared understandings that constitute their identities as such. But those shared understandings also have causal effects on masters and slaves, functioning as independently existing and temporally prior mechanisms motivating and generating their behaviour.[18] The same dual role is found in the case of physical substances. The human brain is a causal mechanism generating intelligent behaviour, but it is also a condition of possibility for being human. Indeed, some of the most important theories in the natural sciences are constitutive rather than causal: the double-helix model of DNA, the kinetic theory of heat, and so on.[19]

The paired examples provided above of causal and constitutive questions from the natural and social sciences show that the differences between those questions cannot be reduced to the differences between physical substances and ideas. Both

---

[17] The phrase 'tacit realism' is Mario Bunge's in 'Realism and Antirealism in Social Science', *Theory and Decision*, 35 (1993), pp. 207–35. A similar argument is made by Linda Alcoff about Foucault's work in 'Foucault as Epistemologist', *The Philosophical Forum*, 25 (1993), pp. 95–124.

[18] For perhaps the definitive statement of how ideas, in the form of reasons, can have causal effects on behaviour see Donald Davidson, 'Actions, Reasons, and Causes', *Journal of Philosophy*, 60 (1963), pp. 685–700. In saying that reasons can be causes I am taking one side in a debate about what remains a controversial issue; for an opposing, Wittgensteinian, view see David Rubenstein, 'The Concept of Action in the Social Sciences', *Journal for the Theory of Social Behaviour*, 7 (1977), pp. 209–36. On the causal role of ideas in international politics, see especially Judith Goldstein and Robert Keohane (eds.), *Ideas and Foreign Policy* (Ithaca, NY, 1993).

[19] See John Haugeland, 'The Nature and Plausibility of Cognitivism', *The Behavioral and Brain Sciences*, 2 (1978), p. 216, and Cummins, 1983, p. 15.

kinds of question get asked in both domains. Although the kinds of evidence that we need to answer these questions in the two domains may be different, there is no essential difference in the questions themselves; they are isomorphic. Things get caused in society just as much as things get constituted in nature.

Constitutive Theory as Explanation

In *Designing Social Inquiry,* King, Keohane, and Verba accept that Understanding or constitutive theory is a distinct intellectual activity, but consider that activity to be descriptive inference. Thinking about constitutive theory in this way is in some respects attractive, since constitutive analyses do have a substantial descriptive component. Also, by emphasizing inference, King, Keohane, and Verba highlight the fact that description is not just a matter of reporting observations, but requires theory to unite and make sense of them. In the end, however, I think this interpretation of constitutive theory falls short. Constitutive theories provide *explanations*. These explanations are not causal, but they are explanations just the same. The burden of this argument, therefore, must be to dispel the 'confusion' that King, Keohane, and Verba feel attends the idea of non-causal explanation. Before trying to do so, however, it may be useful to say something about why we should care about what seems to be merely an issue of semantics.

At least two things are at stake. One is rhetorical but has real consequences for the sociology of knowledge. Despite King, Keohane, and Verba's call to social scientists to treat descriptive inference as an important end in itself, in disciplines worried about their epistemic status as 'science' the incentive to distinguish one's work as explanatory, and to distinguish it in particular from history—often seen by social scientists as being 'mere' description—will be a powerful force. As long as such worries exist, scholars, and perhaps especially younger ones, will face strong disciplinary pressures *not* to treat descriptive inference as an end in itself, but to go 'beyond' description to causal inference. The latter is also important, of course, and gives us insight into the world that description does not. But in the social sciences today the connotations of having one's work characterized as 'descriptive' are so negative that almost all scholars want to be seen as engaging in 'explanation', as even a cursory survey of most dissertations and our leading journals will attest. Even if coupled with an effort to change these perceptions, therefore, at least in the short run treating constitutive theory as descriptive inference will inevitably have the effect of reinforcing the prejudice that it is second-best, inferior, and not fully 'science'.

That the rhetoric of descriptive inference might contribute to the marginalization of constitutive theory may be unfortunate, but that doesn't necessarily mean it is misleading with respect to our substantive inquiries. The other issue at stake here centres on that possibility, and specifically the kind of knowledge that constitutive theory generates and thus the uses to which it can be put. Treating constitutive theory as descriptive rather than explanatory contributes to the 'reification' or 'naturalization' of social kinds, in the sense that it obscures the extent to which they are ongoing social constructions and encourages us instead to see them as if they were like natural kinds, the character of which is independent of what human beings think and do.[20] The language of descriptive inference does this by the way in which it implicitly characterizes the relationship between intersubjective understandings—shared ideas—and the social kinds they constitute: in saying that ideas 'describe' the Cold War we do not get a sense that they generated or produced the Cold War, that but for certain shared ideas the Cold War would not have existed, in short, that they 'explained' the Cold War.

Consider the effects of such an assumption. If shared ideas do not explain the Cold War, then policymakers could not end the Cold War by changing their ideas. The Cold War becomes seen as something external to how they think, in the same way that rocks and trees are external, and as such can only be dealt with in the manner in which we deal with nature, i.e. through the manipulation and control of objects for whose dispositions we are not ourselves responsible. Such reification in fact characterized the Cold War for many years; each side thought the conflict was caused by the intrinsically aggressive, implacably hostile nature of the Other, not by the behaviour of the Self. Their own ideas about the conflict were therefore nothing more than necessary reflections of an externally existing fact, not constitutive of that fact in the first place. Social science and specifically the language of descriptive inference were of course not responsible for this situation, but to the extent that social scientists took the existence of the shared ideas constituting the Cold War as given, failing to problematize the role of those ideas in generating the conflict, social scientists participated in the naturalization of the Cold War and by extension were not helping to empower policymakers to end it, just to manage it. It took the 'New Thinking' of the Gorbachev regime, with its realization—prompted, to be sure, by changing material conditions—that the Soviets' own behaviour helped sustain the Cold War, to get the two sides out from under the seemingly inexorable, externally imposed logic of their situation. Such a realization, embodying an attitude of 'reflexivity' rather than reification toward social kinds, is more likely if constitutive theory is seen as explanatory than merely descriptive.

This example gives us a sense of what is at stake in how we interpret constitutive theory, and also a suggestion of how constitutive theory might be seen as explanatory, but more needs to be said about the nature of this kind of explanation, and especially about its non-causal character. To do so I shall deal separately with the two characteristic questions of constitutive inquiries—what? and how-possible?—since their answers explain in somewhat different ways.

What-questions seem on the surface to be wholly concerned with description. When a small child asks her parent, 'what's that?', she might be satisfied with the response, 'a dog'. That answer doesn't seem to involve much in the way of 'explanation'. If the child persists and asks 'what's a dog?', the parent may say 'man's best friend'. This too seems descriptive, since it doesn't seem to do more than point to the role that dogs play in human society, although it also sends the implicit message to the child that dogs are not dangerous. Yet, the English language permits an explanatory interpretation of the parent's answer as well: it would be equally valid to say that the parent was 'explaining' the role of dogs in society, and 'explain-

---

[20] On this conception of reification, see Douglas Maynard and Thomas Wilson, 'On the Reification of Social Structure', in S. McNall and G. Howe (eds.), *Current Perspectives in Social Theory*, vol. 1 (Greenwich, CT, 1980), pp. 287–322, and also Peter Berger and Thomas Luckmann, *The Social Construction of Reality* (New York, 1966), p. 89.

ing' the fact that dogs are not dangerous by reference to their being our friends. Neither of these explanations is causal. Semantics perhaps, but it suggests that already at this very simple level the answers to what-questions might not be purely or unambiguously descriptive, but have varying degrees of explanatory content.

The explanatory potential of what-questions becomes clearer when dealing with unobservables. If we ask an astronomer, 'what's that dark spot in the telescope around which stars swirl in a downward spiral?', she might say 'a black hole'. In addition to its descriptive qualities, this answer explains in the sense that it accounts for certain capacities (to absorb light, suck in stars, etc.) by positing a structure in virtue of which those capacities exist. Once we have classified the dark spot as a black hole, in other words, we have made an *inference* that makes sense of phenomena. An emphasis on the inferential quality of some descriptions is one of the important contributions of *Designing Social Inquiry*. Yet, inferences are always based on *theories*, and one of the essential features of theories seems to be that they 'explain'. Granted, it does not violate any grammatical rules to say that 'theories describe', but this is not how we normally use the term; normally we say that theories 'explain'. Again, perhaps only semantics, but I am trying to build a case here that, at least on an intuitive level, non-causal explanation may not be as confusing as King, Keohane, and Verba think.

These examples could be multiplied indefinitely with social kinds. 'What was the mass of disparate interactions between the U.S. and Soviet Union between 1947 and 1989?' Answer: 'an instance of the social kind known as Cold War'. 'What are the behaviours of the individuals at the border crossing who are going through my luggage?' Answer: 'the legitimate actions of the state'. 'What was the downturn in Western economic activity from 1929 to 1933?' Answer: 'the Great Depression'. In each case the answer to our question is in part descriptive, since our disparate observations are subsumed within it, but it is also explanatory, since it *classifies* those observations as a such-and-such and *unifies* them as parts within some coherent whole.

This combination of classification and unification is characteristic of what William Dray, a philosopher of history, called 'explanations-what'.[21] Explanations-what explain by subsuming observations under a *concept*—as opposed to a law, as in the logical empiricist model of causal explanation—and as such they are also sometimes and perhaps less awkwardly called 'explanations by concept'. In a recent review and extension of Dray's idea, Steven Rappaport points out that unification is increasingly seen as a key, distinguishing feature of scientific explanation more generally.[22] He quotes Wesley Salmon's discussion of the Newtonian synthesis in physics, which Salmon thinks is explanatory in part precisely because it unified a variety of otherwise discrete laws and regularities under more general laws.[23]

---

[21] William Dray, '"Explaining what" in history', in P. Gardiner (ed.), *Theories of History* (Glencoe, IL, 1959), and *Philosophy of History* (Englewood Cliffs, NJ, 1964). For a contemporary critique of Dray's position, see Richard Reiner, 'Necessary conditions and explaining how-possibly', *The Philosophical Quarterly*, 43 (1993), pp. 58–69.

[22] Steven Rappaport, 'Economic Models and Historical Explanation', *Philosophy of the Social Sciences*, 25 (1995), pp. 421–41. For a good overview of the role of unification in scientific explanation more generally see Philip Kitcher, 'Explanatory Unification and the Causal Structure of the World', in P. Kitcher and W. Salmon (eds.), *Minnesota Studies in the Philosophy of Science*, vol. 13 (Minneapolis, MN, 1989), pp. 410–505.

[23] Ibid., pp. 430–1.

Although Salmon is talking about causal explanations, Rappaport argues that the same principle of achieving explanatory power through unification applies by analogy to explanations by concept.

An interesting illustration of how this principle functions in IR concerns the current debate about 'what is the European Union?'. Is it an emerging federation? An international state? A post-modern state? A confederal consociation? An international regime? Governance without government? Neo-Medievalism? Each of these proposals is an attempt to classify and unify a diverse and complex set of phenomena under a single concept. The concepts are partly descriptive, but they seek to be explanatory as well; indeed it is hard to imagine that people would care so much about what the EU is if the answer to the question were *not* explanatory. Yet the kinds of explanations which these concepts offer are constitutive, not causal. Each tries to make sense of the properties of the EU and in so doing provide insight into its dispositions. Dispositions are propensities to behave in certain ways under certain conditions. If the EU is an emerging federation then it will have a disposition to centralize authority; if it is an international regime then it will have a disposition to preserve the sovereignty of states; if it is a neo-Medieval structure then it will have a disposition to disperse and duplicate authority; and so on. These claims tell us something about the EU's 'laws of motion', but for our purposes here a key feature of dispositions is that if the relevant activating conditions are not present then they will not be actualized in behaviour. Salt has the disposition to dissolve in water, for example, but if it is not placed in water then it will not dissolve. When dispositions *are* actualized then we are in the domain of causal rather than constitutive theories, since then we are dealing with changes of state—'transitions' rather than 'properties'. Gaining explanatory leverage on transitions is of course often one of the main reasons that we try to explain properties, and it is here that causal and constitutive theories abut one another, but that does not mean that the two kinds of theory are equivalent. Explaining dispositions is one of the main objectives of explanations by concept, and is worth doing even if those dispositions have not been manifested in a given case.[24]

Explanations by concept pervade the social sciences. Dray argues that they, rather than causal explanations, are the dominant mode of explanation in history. Interestingly, given the positivist sensibilities of most economists, Rappaport argues that much of what economics offers is actually also explanations by concept, since much of economic theory—and by extension rational choice theory in IR—is concerned *not* with finding lawlike generalizations or testing hypotheses against data, the activities we normally associate with science, but with investigating the properties of *models*.[25] Those models are thought to 'explain' insofar as they capture the properties and dispositions of the systems they represent, even if they do not relate effects to independently existing causes. Turning to psychology, although he does not use Dray's terminology, Cummins argues that many of the theories in that discipline are best seen as property theories rather than transition theories. And as the examples above indicate, explanations by concept are also common in IR. 'Explanations-what' are not the *only* kinds of explanations found in these disciplines, nor am I arguing that they should replace causal explanations. The point, rather, is

---

[24] Cummins, p. 18.
[25] Rappaport, 'Economic Models and Historical Explanation'.

simply that answering what-questions should be recognized as a valuable and distinct kind of theorizing in its own right, and that, properly understood, it can have explanatory as well as descriptive pay-off.

Sometimes an answer to a what-question will offer a satisfactory constitutive explanation by itself. But other times we may want to know more about the structure in virtue of which a social or natural kind has certain properties or dispositions, to know how it is possible. Answers to how-possible questions explain not by telling us how or why a thing came about, or what it is, but by telling us how its elements are composed and organized so that it has the properties that it does. John Haugeland calls these 'morphological' explanations,[26] and they come in two forms, reflecting the two kinds of structures, internal and social, that can constitute kinds.

By an internal structure I mean the structure of a thing as such. Water is constituted internally by the atomic structure H_2O; human beings are constituted internally by their genetic structures; doctors are constituted internally by the self-understandings necessary for someone to play the role of 'doctor'; states are constituted internally by organizational structures that give them a territorial monopoly on organized violence. In each case, appeals to internal structures do not explain the properties associated with them in a causal sense, because structure and properties are not independently existing, and those appeals also contain a substantial descriptive element. But they are nevertheless more than descriptions, because the analyst is using one set of facts (the nature and organization of genes, the character of self-understandings, etc.) to account for another (being human, being a doctor, etc.). This something 'more' is the sense in which they are constitutive explanations.

When we account for a thing by referring to its internal morphology we are engaged in what might be called 'reductionism'[27] or 'essentialism'. We are hypothesizing an internal core or essence to which a thing's outward properties can in some sense be reduced. In the natural sciences this is the dominant, perhaps even sole, way to answer how-possible questions, since it is by internal structures that natural kinds are in fact constituted; few, if any, natural kinds are constituted by relationships to other entities. As such, it may be that constitutive explanations in the natural sciences are inevitably essentialist.[28]

Essentialism is more problematic in the social sciences. Some social scientists seek constitutive explanations in the essentialist, natural science manner by reducing the properties of social kinds to their internal structures. On this view, usually identified with the doctrine of methodological individualism, the properties of social kinds like gender or the state should be reducible to the attributes and interactions of independently existing agents. The properties of those agents, like identities and interests, might in turn be caused by their relationships with other agents (in a process of socialization for example), but they are not constituted by them. If that

---

[26] Haugeland, 'The Nature and Plausibility', pp. 215–26.

[27] This usage is different to Kenneth Waltz's in *Theory of International Politics*, but compatible with the idea of 'structural' explanation. See Ernan McMullin, 'Structural Explanation', *American Philosophical Quarterly*, 15 (1978), pp. 139–47.

[28] See Jarrett Leplin, 'Is Essentialism Unscientific?', *Philosophy of Science*, 55 (1988), pp. 493–510. For doubts about the claim that an essentialist strategy is necessary in the natural sciences see Paul Teller, 'Relational Holism and Quantum Mechanics', *British Journal for the Philosophy of Science*, 37 (1986), pp. 71–81, and for a thoughtful discussion of essentialism in the social sciences, see Andrew Sayer, 'Essentialism, Social Constructionism, and Beyond', *Sociological Review*, 45 (1997), 453–87.

were true then the *only* type of constitutive structure we would need to explicate to answer how-possible questions about a social kind would be its internal structure.

It is beyond the scope of this article to criticize methodological individualism.[29] Suffice it to say that there are theoretical reasons to doubt that social kinds can always be reduced to their internal structures, and political reasons to worry that the effort to do so will obscure the role, and therefore responsibility, of society in making social kinds what they are. Consider the social kind known as 'rogue state'. Part of what makes states rogues is their rejectionist attitude toward the norms of the international community; to that extent states are constituted as rogues by their internal structure. But rogue states are also constituted by social relations to other states in the form of the representational practices of the international community (and of the Great Powers in particular). This opens the door to the possibility that one state may violate the norms of the international community without being constituted as a rogue (Israel?), while another state doing so is (Syria?)—with all the differential consequences for the life chances of these states and their populations that follow. Some scholars might take this as evidence for the proposition that *any* essentialist answer to a how-possible question about social kinds is wrong or politically incorrect. However, we do not have to accept that radical conclusion to think that many social kinds are constituted not only by internal structures, but by social ones as well.

By a constituting social structure I mean the set of relationships with other actors that define a social kind as such. A familiar example is the master and the slave. Each is a social kind with certain properties and dispositions: ownership and the enforcement of obedience on the one hand, and chattel and wanting to escape on the other. Individuals acquire these properties through a causal process of accidents of birth, socialization, coercion, and so on. And they are constituted with them in part by their internal, self-understandings; it is hard to be a master (and perhaps even a proper slave) if one does not see oneself as such. But if we want to explain how a master can sell his slave then we need to invoke the structure of shared understandings existing between master and slave, and in the wider society, that make this ability to sell people possible. This social structure does not merely describe the rights of the master; it *explains* them, since without it those rights by definition could not exist. By way of contrast, even if a parent in the antebellum American South had the physical capability and desire to sell their child, they could not do so because the structure of that culture did not recognize such a right. These explanations are not causal. It's not as if the social structure of slavery exists independent of the master's right to sell his slave and causes that right to come into being. Rather, the master's right is conceptually or logically dependent on the structure of slavery, such that when the latter comes into being so does the former, by definition. Hegelians call this kind of relationship an 'internal relation', by which they mean that the properties of a relation's elements are internal to the relation itself, and so do not exist apart from it.[30] (Note that this is in effect the opposite of what I referred to as an 'internal structure' above). In the terminology of this essay, when Hegelians appeal to internal relations to explain the powers of masters and slaves they are offering a constitutive explanation.

---

[29] See Wendt, *Social Theory of International Politics*, ch. 4.
[30] For a systematic development of this idea, see Bertell Ollman, *Alienation* (Cambridge, 1971).

Although the social structure of international politics is thinner and simpler than that of domestic politics, there are many examples in that domain as well of the properties of social kinds being made possible by social structures. The case of rogue states has already been mentioned. I have argued elsewhere that the deep structure of anarchy varies as a function of whether states constitute each other in the role of enemy, rival, or friend.[31] The properties of an 'enemy', for example, are in part made possible by his self-understandings (internal structure), since he will not be able to properly fill that role unless he sees himself as your enemy. But being enemies is also about being in a particular social relationship with an Other, like master and slave, that defines who both of you are.

However, the most widely acknowledged example of how a state's properties can be explained, constitutively, by social relations is the property of state sovereignty. How is it possible for Luxembourg to survive in an anarchic world surrounded by states with thousands of times its military power? The answer is that other states recognize its sovereignty as a *right*—in effect, to 'life, liberty, and territory'—and therefore do not try to conquer it. In order to acquire such a right an entity must have the kind of internal structure that constitutes it with 'internal' sovereignty, namely exclusive political control and a territorial monopoly on the legitimate use of organized violence. Collectivities lacking this internal structure like football teams and churches don't get recognized as sovereign in today's international system. States that have a lot of military power may be able to survive in an anarchic world with nothing more than this internal structure, but in the modern international system, military power is in fact not crucial to state survival, since states recognize each other's internal sovereignty as a right (what is sometimes called 'external' sovereignty). This means that today sovereignty is not only an internal or essential property of states, but also an *institution* between states that constitutes them with social capacities—rights—that they would not otherwise enjoy. These rights make it possible for even very weak states like Luxembourg, or 'failed' states like Somalia, to survive in an anarchic world. To that extent the institution of sovereignty *explains* state survival even though it does not exist independent of or prior to the rights to life, liberty, and property which make that survival possible.

It is important to see this constitutive story as an 'explanation' in part just because that is what it in fact is; it is not merely a description, nor is it a causal explanation. As Charles Cross concludes after reviewing a variety of answers to how-questions (both causal and constitutive), 'explanations of these sorts are widely regarded by scientists as *explanatory* (and as scientific)'.[32] However, returning finally to the larger issue of what is at stake in this semantic battle, it is also important to see the story as explanatory because denaturalizing sovereignty increases the ability of international society to make progressive changes in it. In saying this, it should be emphasized that reification is sometimes good, even essential, to the maintenance of social order. As presently constituted the institution of sovereignty plays a vital role in reducing the incidence and severity of war and in helping weak states survive. Since these are presumably normatively positive outcomes we should *want* states to take the social relations that make them possible for granted, want states to treat them as natural, because that will make them harder to undermine. However, the

---

[31] *Social Theory of International Politics*, ch. 6.
[32] Cross, 'Explanation and the Theory of Questions', p. 245; emphasis in the original.

social relations constituting sovereign rights also have less satisfying consequences, like enabling states to repress their people, to keep out refugees, to wage war, and so on. If we want to eliminate these consequences by changing the terms of sovereign rights it does us little good to think about the shared understandings that constitute those rights as merely 'describing' them, as if they existed independent of what states think. That kind of reification is disempowering, and suggests that the only solution to the problems of sovereignty is to destroy the state, in the same way that the solution to AIDS is to destroy the AIDS virus. In contrast, if we can show that the negative effects of sovereignty are not independent of—are constituted by—what states think it should mean, then the possibility emerges of reforming sovereignty by getting states to change their minds about those meanings. Whether states should do so is of course another question, but if we come to see that sovereign rights are *explained* rather than merely described by certain shared understandings then we come to recognize our collective authorship and responsibility for the maintenance of those rights in their present form, and it becomes possible to have a more fully reflexive debate about whether that is what we want.

Conclusion

As a community, we in the academic study of international politics spend too much time worrying about the kind of issues addressed in this essay. The central point of IR scholarship is to increase our knowledge of how the world works, not to worry about how (or whether) we can know how the world works. What matters for IR is ontology, not epistemology. This doesn't mean that there are no interesting epistemological questions in IR, and even less does it mean that there are no important political or sociological aspects to those questions. Indeed there are, as I have suggested above, and as a discipline IR should have more awareness of these aspects. At the same time, however, these are questions best addressed by philosophers and sociologists of knowledge, not political scientists. Let's face it: most IR scholars, including this one, have little or no proper training in epistemology, and as such the attempt to solve epistemological problems anyway will inevitably lead to confusion (after all, after 2000 years, even the specialists are still having a hard time). Moreover, as long as we let our research be driven in an open-minded fashion by substantive questions and problems rather than by epistemologies and methods, there is little need to answer epistemological questions either. It is simply not the case that we have to undertake an epistemological analysis of how we can know something before we can know it, a fact amply attested to by the success of the natural sciences, whose practitioners are only rarely forced by the results of their inquiries to consider epistemological questions. In important respects we *do* know how international politics works, and it doesn't much matter how we came to that knowledge. In that light, going into the epistemology business will distract us from the real business of IR, which is international politics. Our great debates should be about first-order issues of substance, like the 'first debate' between Realists and Idealists, not second-order issues of method.

Unfortunately, it is no longer a simple matter for IR scholars to 'just say no' to epistemological discourse. The problem is that this discourse has already contaminated our thinking about international politics, helping to polarize the discipline into 'paradigm wars'. Although the resurgence of these wars in the 1980s and 90s is due in large part to the rise of post-positivism, its roots lie in the epistemological anxiety of positivists, who since the 1950s have been very concerned to establish the authority of their work as Science. This is an important goal, one that I share, but its implementation has been marred by an overly narrow conception of science as being concerned only with causal questions that can be answered using the methods of natural science. The effect has been to marginalize historical and interpretive work that does not fit this mould, and to encourage scholars interested in that kind of work to see themselves as somehow *not* engaged in science. One has to wonder whether the two sides should be happy with the result. Do positivists really mean to suggest that it is not part of science to ask questions about how things are constituted, questions which if those things happen to be made of ideas might only be answerable by interpretive methods? If so, then they seem to be saying that the double-helix model of DNA, and perhaps much of rational choice theory, is not science. And do post-positivists really mean to suggest that students of social life should not ask causal questions or attempt to test their claims against empirical evidence? If so, then it is not clear by what criteria their work should be judged, or how it differs from art or revelation. On both sides, in other words, the result of the Third Debate's sparring over epistemology is often one-sided, intolerant caricatures of science.

One of the important virtues of *Explaining and Understanding International Relations* and *Designing Social Inquiry* is that they both seek to get us out of this dead end and toward a more pluralistic and tolerant—because more confident— conception of our common endeavour, all too often forgotten, of making sense of international life. Despite my complaint about the baleful influence of epistemology talk on IR, if more such discourse can help purge its influence then it is all to the good. Yet in different ways both of these books frame the issues in ways that subtly help reinforce the very walls they seek to overcome. Hollis and Smith identify natural science with the outsider's perspective of causal theorizing, which suggests that natural scientists don't tell insider stories and therefore that social scientists who do tell them are not doing science and, by implication, can't be positivists. King, Keohane, and Verba assimilate Understanding to the positivist, scientific project, but see it as a form of descriptive inference and reduce Explanation to causal inference. Given the sociology of knowledge in our discipline that condemns Understanders to second-class status, and also obscures the role of ideas in producing the structures of international life, contributing to their reification and thus to a lack of perceived responsibility and control by the actors whose ideas constitute them.

In this article I advanced two arguments. First, against Hollis and Smith I argued that the difference between Explanation and Understanding should be seen as a difference between two kinds of question, causal and constitutive, which are routinely asked in both natural and social science. The data and methods appro- priate to answering these questions will differ in the two domains to the extent that natural and social kinds are made of different kinds of stuff, but this does not imply an epistemological difference. As King, Keohane, and Verba emphasize, in the two domains there are similar problems of theory construction, of inference to unobservables, and of adjudicating knowledge claims against publicly available evidence. This fact is not lost on most post-positivists, who in their empirical research are at least tacit positivists. As such, there seems little reason not to make this explicit and consider constitutive inquiries or Understanding as part of a positivist approach to social inquiry.

Second, against King, Keohane, and Verba I argued that the answers to constitutive questions are explanations rather than simply descriptions. Since these explanations are not causal this requires a broader conceptualization of 'explanation' than the one with which King, Keohane, and Verba operate, but this is fully in line with our ordinary, everyday understanding of what it means to 'explain'. That doesn't mean that there is no such thing as description, but rather that the description/explanation distinction cuts across the causal/constitutive distinction. Causal and constitutive theories alike both describe and explain. The effect of this argument is to elevate constitutive theory to an autonomous, co-equal status relative to causal theory, worth doing in its own right, rather than treating it as something we have to go beyond before we will really be doing science. And the argument also highlights the role of shared ideas in producing social kinds, which denaturalizes them and thereby expands the potential for progressive change.

Rather than engaging in gate-keeping against each other as the purveyors of false epistemological gods, positivists and post-positivists in IR would do better instead to adopt a rule of 'mutual recognition' toward each other's preferred questions, and focus on the respective logics, explanatory potentials, and truth conditions of those questions. A reflexive, critical science of international politics needs every kind of knowledge it can get.

A turn not taken:
Ethics in IR at the Millennium

MERVYN FROST

In everyday life we often engage in ethical argument about what ought to be done in international affairs; in a rough and ready fashion we engage in normative theory.[1] It is odd then to find that for most of its history, scholars in the discipline of International Relations (IR) have seldom explicitly engaged in this kind of theorizing. The reasons for their avoiding it are now well known.[2] Certain developments in the discipline over the past few decades, however, suggest that the discipline might now have taken the normative turn. But has it?

As a first step in seeking an answer to this question, I put forward a view, which I take to be the view of many ordinary men and women in everyday life, about what would be involved in thinking seriously about ethical issues in world politics. Turning to the discipline of IR I then briefly recapitulate the features of the discipline which blocked normative theory in the past, consider a range of recent developments in IR which appear to have opened up the possibility for the taking of the normative turn, and consider whether this possibility has indeed been realized. My conclusion is that this is a turn still not taken. In the main, IR theorists have yet to engage with normative theory properly so called. This conclusion does not imply that IR theorists do not have (and do not act upon) ethical stances on a whole range of issues. IR theorists, like everybody else, seek to advance certain policies in international relations as ethically superior to other possible policies. But for the most part their ethical stances are concealed under a disguise of scientific objectivity. Finally, I list a set of pressing issues which need the attention of scholars committed to taking normative theory seriously and I briefly suggest a way in which they might be tackled.

Ethics in everyday International Relations

In day-to-day world politics, a domain in which we all participate to some degree, we all hold and are guided by certain beliefs about what, from an ethical point of view, we think ought to be done. The 'we' I have in mind here includes Islamic people, anarchists, Christians, social democrats, liberals, Hindu people, Buddhists, nationalist groups, the members of liberation movements, radicals, Marxists, conservatives and

---

[1] In this paper I use the phrases 'ethics' and 'normative theory' interchangeably.
[2] For an extended discussion of these see my *Ethics in International Relations* (Cambridge: Cambridge University Press, 1996), chs. 1 and 2.

all the many other movements, groups, and social formations within which we live. Some of us, such as politicians, diplomats, church leaders, churchgoers, soldiers, freedom fighters, supporters of organizations (such as Amnesty International, Human Rights Watch and Hamas, to mention but three of many), are more directly active in pursuit of what we believe to be ethically right, than others who, although holding strong beliefs about what ought to be done, are not very active in support of their beliefs. Typical of the kinds of issues about which we hold ethical beliefs are the following: war (when is it justified?), terrorism (when, if ever, is it justified?), mass rape as a political tool, human rights (what rights do people have and who should do what to protect them?), the environment (who is responsible for it?), distributions of basic necessities such as food, water, housing, education, health care both at home and abroad (who ought to do what about these?), and the forms of political association which people ought to adopt as the basic framework within which they live their lives (authoritarian, socialist, communist, nationalist, democratic?).

On these issues many of us hold that from an ethical point of view peace is better than war, terrorism is generally wrong, mass rape as a weapon of war is ethically wrong, as is genocide, that we should seek to promote the cause of human rights (especially in those parts of the world where they are being systematically abused), that we have some duty to care for the environment and some duty to ensure a just global distribution of basic necessities, that democracy should be promoted and authoritarian forms of government opposed. Of course, it is not the case that we *all* agree about what actions are ethically right or wrong. There is a long history of argument about when, if ever, resort to warfare is ethically justified. Closely related to these are arguments between those who hold that the use of terrorist methods in pursuit of just goals is always wrong and those who consider that under some circumstances it is ethically acceptable. There is much argument about what 'natural' rights people have. These link up to arguments about what from an ethical point of view it would be right to do with regard to illegal migrants. There are arguments about what would be an appropriate ethical response to the problems of the environment.

It is crucial to notice that in everyday ethical discourse these are not arguments which we have within the confines of our discrete cultural, religious, ethnic, national, tribal or state-based groups. They are arguments which take place within common practices whose ambit stretches wider than the confines of such groups. They take place across the divides of the subordinate groupings which I have listed. Thus voices in Asia accuse the West of not taking Asian values seriously, voices in Africa make a case for the salience of African approaches to human rights, Islamic communities claim a right to pursue their traditional ways without interference from others, the Orientalist charge is made against Occidental understandings of Eastern ways. In all this what we are witness to are claims and counter-claims within a global conversation. That the conversation takes place at all is evidence of the existence of a global practice within which it takes place. In the absence of such a practice, no conversation, no argument, would be possible.[3]

In spite of the lack of agreement about the correct answer to the issues mentioned above, we do not believe that an appropriate way to settle such ethical disputes is by

---

[3] On the requirements of argumentation see Alain Perelman, *The New Rhetoric of the Humanities* (London: Reidel, 1979).

spinning a coin, or by deciding on a mere whim, desire or aesthetic fancy. We would not, in general, take seriously a suggestion that the question as to whether terror is ethically justifiable under certain circumstances may be decided on aesthetic grounds (would a bomb exploding in the market place look beautiful?) In like manner we would not accept as an ethical justification for opposing aid to the starving in Southern Sudan that we *simply prefer* having more for ourselves. The reader can easily imagine further examples, such as, would we accept as an ethical justification for the exploding of nuclear devices by India that it produced a pleasant sensation of power for India's leaders. In summary, then, although we differ about what is ethically right, we do not hold that our ethical judgements are arbitrary choices.[4]

The Palestinian who believes that his involvement in the *Intifada* was ethically justified, the runner who believes it ethically wrong to buy running shoes made by child labour, the lobby against the sale of arms to authoritarian regimes, the Saudi Arabian who defends the right of his country to impose capital punishment on convicted murderers, I take it that all of these people believe that their positions are not arbitrary, but can be justified; they believe that good reasons can be given in support of their stances on such matters. Were we to come across someone who decided her principles of conduct on this kind of matter according to the spin of a roulette wheel or the mood of the moment, it is to be doubted whether we would recognize the principles chosen in this way as her *ethical* principles at all.

When we disagree about what is to count as ethical conduct within world politics we do not typically regard such differences as merely attributable to differences in taste about which there can be no argument. Our stance is not the weary one of 'you like child labour, sex tourism, genocide, arms to tyrants, nuclear testing, *Jihads* and the like, whereas I don't'. Instead we hold that those who oppose us do not merely have different tastes to ours, but that they are wrong in what they believe. Typically we *argue* the merits of our case; we seek to *criticize* other people's attempts to attack our positions. We do this in any number of ways. Let me mention three. We might seek to rebut the suggestion that nuclear deterrence is ethically justified by showing that the claims of our opponents about the deterrence effect of nuclear arms are not proven. Here we might seek to show that certain factual claims made in defence of the opposing case are mistaken. A second example concerns the claim that sex tourism is ethically unjustified. An opponent of this view might argue that opposition to sex tourism appears to undercut his/her interlocutor's commitment to individual liberty, arguing that liberty includes the liberty to sell the use of one's body, if one so chooses. The argument here turns on an alleged incoherence between the claim being made and other values which the speaker professes to hold. A third example might be the Islamic believer who justifies a *Jihad* by referring to the relevant passage in the Koran which is taken to be the text of final authority.

In everyday life we confront a range of *different kinds* of ethical questions. Some are about how we, ourselves, ought to behave in a given context (do I have an ethical duty to provide aid to the victims of famine, AIDS, earthquakes, etc.?). Others involve the ethical evaluation of the conduct of other people either as individuals or as members of social institutions such as governments, churches, or international organizations. For example, do we, the British electorate, judge the government's

---

[4] It is crucial to note that the 'we' here is inclusive and does not refer narrowly to Europeans, Africans, liberals, or socialists (and so on).

foreign policy with regard to the sale of arms to foreign governments to be ethical or not? This might require of us that we weigh our government's duty to promote the domestic economy (in order to secure jobs for all citizens) against the government's duty to pursue a rights-based foreign policy which requires a refusal to sell arms to tyrannical regimes. A third kind of ethical question arises when we are called upon to make ethical evaluations of the basic institutional structures within which we live, structures such as families, churches, civil society, states and the system of states. Here I have in mind questions such as: Ought we to support the expansion of the WTO, an expansion based on free market principles, knowing that a practice based on these principles will erode the scope for sovereign states to pursue protectionist policies? Ought we to support the establishment of monetary union within the European Union knowing that it will curtail sovereignty, which many take to be a primary ethical value? What institutions would be ethically appropriate for the protection of the global environment?

It is important to note that the kinds of ethical decisions sketched above are not ones which arise only for a select group of ethical people (the righteous ones). They are questions which we all face, and they are questions which cannot be avoided *for we, as humans, are always confronted with the imperative of action.* In the hurly-burly of everyday life we have to act one way or another; in the face of these questions we have to decide what to do. This is as true of those in high places as it is for the rest of us. Ethical choices simply confront us and have to be answered one way or another. Even a decision not to do anything is a decision. In South Africa during the period of minority rule, many had to decide to help (or not to help) fugitives from South African *apartheid* law seeking to flee the country. British people have to decide whether to oppose or not to oppose the present British government's ethical foreign policy. We are called upon to decide where we stand with regard to proposed reforms of the UN system, the expansion of the EU, and the extension of the Lome Convention. Once the ethical issues have been raised for us, *we have to respond.* In short, then, in everyday life we cannot avoid taking international ethics seriously.

Speaking for myself as an ordinary citizen (and not as a scholar interested in international normative theory) in the last year I have had to think seriously about the following ethical issues (and this list is far from exhaustive): Where do I stand with regard to the deportation of the Gypsies who arrived illegally in the UK? (Do I think that the law as it stands is ethically justifiable or not; should I join a demonstration at the Dover docks to oppose their deportation or not?); should the international community intervene in the trial in Saudi Arabia of two British nurses accused of a murder there (besides the legality of the matter, what did I think of the justice of the non-intervention principle?); should I support the USA and British governments' attempt to launch a 'surgical strike' against Iraq for failing to obey the terms of a Security Council Resolution authorizing external inspection of sites where weapons of mass destruction were allegedly being made; what do I believe (and how should I act) with regard to the sale of British weapons to Sandlines, a private military company which helped topple a *coup* in Sierra Leone; and what response, on ethical grounds, should I support with regard to India and Pakistan's recent exploding of nuclear devices?

In summary, then, my contention is: first, that in everyday life most people encounter a whole series of ethical issues pertaining to their involvement in the international domain; second, that faced with the imperative of action people simply have to come to decisions on such matters; and third, that when they do so, they generally hold that their decisions are not based on a mere whim or fancy, but believe that they could defend their decisions with reasoned arguments.

The missing dimension: ethics in IR

If we now turn to the discipline of IR we find a strikingly different picture. Our everyday concern with ethical issues is not reflected in the discipline.[5] I need not dwell on the reasons for this. The two main ones are well known, and I need only mention them. First, there is the positivist bias in the discipline (which rests on a strong fact/value distinction) in terms of which the task of IR scholars is to *explain* events in world politics through the use of covering laws which are grounded, in the final instance, in observable factual data. Second, there is a general scepticism with regards to the epistemological status of value judgements which are generally pre-sented as being subjective, arbitrary, relative, and not based on anything approach-ing the firm foundation of observable data which underpin factual judgements.[6] Recently, textbooks in IR have begun to move towards admitting that normative theory (about what ought to be done in international relations) is important, but the majority still maintain a strong distinction between facts and values. In one such textbook, for example, we find this statement, 'Normative theory deals precisely with values and value preferences. Unlike empirical theory, however, propositions in normative theory are not subject to empirical test as a means of establishing their truth or falsehood. Normative theory deals not with what *is*, the domain of empirical theory. Rather, normative theory deals explicitly with what *ought* to be'.[7] The ontology of such positivist mainstream approaches to IR is an ontology of particulars. The particulars are taken 'to exist independently of theory and awaiting observation'.[8] This epistemology is 'as basic and simple version of empiricism as will warrant the governing precept that only perception and the testing of prediction can justify claims to knowledge of the world'.[9] For IR theorists who accept a rigid fact/value distinction in terms of which 'facts' are understood as statements referring to 'hard' intersubjectively observable data, it must hold that normative propositions are in some broad sense 'soft', since, in the end, they are not, as Viotti and Kauppi put it, 'subject to empirical test as a means of establishing their truth or falsity'.[10]

---

[5] In what follows I outline what I take to be the dominant position in IR. There are, of course, exceptions to the picture which I sketch of a discipline which does not take ethics seriously. The most notable exception is that body of scholars working in the field of human rights theory. This tradition has fed into the peace research programmes, integrationist studies and some feminist theories of IR.

[6] I have discussed the positivist bias in IR and the discipline's general scepticism towards normative theory in considerable detail in *Ethics in International Relations*. See also Chris Brown, *International Relations Theory: New Normative Approaches* (New York: Columbia University Press, 1992), and Mark Neufeld, *The Restructuring of International Relations Theory* (Cambridge: Cambridge University Press, 1995).

[7] Paul R. Viotti and Mark V. Kauppi, *International Relations Theory: Realism, Pluralism, Globalism* (New York: MacMillan, 1993), p. 5.

[8] Martin Hollis, *The Philosophy of Social Science* (Cambridge: Cambridge University Press,1996), p. 64.

[9] Martin Hollis, *The Philosophy of Social Science*, p. 64.

[10] *International Relations Theory*, p. 5.

A revival of normative theory? some false starts

Positivist openings to normative theory

Although the mainstream of IR still adheres to a tough-minded fact/value distinction, there have been a number of developments in recent years which at first glance would seem to open up the possibility for taking normative theory seriously and introducing it into the mainstream of IR.

The first of these is to be found within the mainstream tradition of IR within which several authors now argue that it is important to include norms in the explanations offered for international affairs. In this literature, norms are offered as important variables which should not be overlooked in explanations of world affairs. For a major review of this literature, see Gregory Raymond's 'Problems and Prospects in the Study of International Norms'.[11] Raymond discusses the ways in which norms have recently come to be included in the explanation of a number of topics in world politics.[12] He considers problems of definition and measurement which theorists face when seeking to include norms as significant variables in their explanations of international affairs. Beyond these, he considers the difficulties involved in specifying suitable data sources about norms and the difficulties encountered in creating typologies of norm types. *His focus throughout, though, is on norms as variables to be included in standard explanations of international affairs.* The authors whom he discusses have come to recognize that explanations which do not take into account the norms of the actors being studied will be deficient. They have also recognized that norms, being ideational, cannot be observed in any straightforward fashion, but have to be inferred indirectly by referring to 'surrogate indicators' such as public documents, legal treatises and behavioural events.[13]

Let me briefly consider an author mentioned by Raymond who asserts the importance of norms in the explanation of IR. Audie Klotz in *Norms in International Relations: The Struggle against Apartheid* uses the case of the international struggle against *apartheid* to argue that traditional methods of doing International Relations are not adequate to the task.[14] She makes the case that in explaining matters in international affairs, we ought to pay attention to the role of norms and she argues that the dominant approaches in IR at present do not do this. Both neorealism and neoliberalism explain international politics in terms of structures which compel actors to pursue their material interests. These approaches are inadequate, she argues, because they leave out of the account the salience of norms. As an example, she mentions the norm against racial inequality which guided the behaviour of the international community towards South Africa over a forty-year period. Klotz asserts that 'The increasing strength of a global norm of racial equality . . . provides a systematic though preliminary explanation of the adoption

---

[11] Gregory Raymond, 'Problems and Prospects in the Study of International Norms', in *Mershon International Studies Review*, 41,2 (1997), pp. 205–46. The article includes a very detailed 10 page bibliography.

[12] Raymond mentions the literatures on the war convention, the democratic peace, the long peace, alliance dynamics, and regime theory.

[13] Raymond, 'Problems and Prospects in the Study of International Norms', pp. 219–20.

[14] Audie Klotz, *Norms in International Relations: The Struggle against Apartheid* (Ithaca, NY: Cornell University Press, 1995).

of sanctions against South Africa by a broad and diverse range of international organizations and states'.[15] Her goal throughout the monograph is to determine 'when and why norms matter . . .'.[16] Let me drastically simplify her complex argument. Realists stress that the actors in world politics (the most important of which are states under conditions of anarchy) are compelled by the structure of global politics to maximize their own capabilities. Liberal theorists put the case that the key actors, which include states and many non state actors, such as multinational corporations, must seek to maximize their self-interest. In order to demonstrate the inadequacy of these approaches, Klotz shows how over a long period many key actors in the struggle against *apartheid* followed policies contrary to their material interests. She demonstrates how the norm of racial equality came, over time, to reshape what states and other actors took to be their material interests. Although there were, of course, significant differences between the policies pursued by Britain, the USA and the Front Line States, Klotz's key point is that in each case we can make no sense of the trajectory of policy development over this period if we do not pay attention to the influence of the norm of racial equality.

The inclusion of norms in the set of variables used to explain events in world politics is no doubt an advance on those approaches which fail to include such norms in the set of significant variables, but the inclusion of norms in explanations still falls short of a serious engagement with the normative questions outlined at the beginning of this article. The approaches discussed by Raymond call upon scholars to establish what norms hold amongst a given set of actors at a specified time, but importantly *they do not call upon the scholars to evaluate the norms in question* (such as the norm of racial equality mentioned by Klotz). They are not called upon to determine whether such a norm is worthy of support, to determine to whom it ought to be applied, how it ought to be understood in relation to other norms or to determine what action in support of the norm would be justified. The theorists discussed may be said to have moved from positivist social science (which places primacy on verification through reference to observable facts) to a philosophical realist position (which would include verification by reference to non-observables such as the ideas people hold). These latter ideational variables are acceptable because they can be inferred from observable behaviour. These approaches still maintain the primacy of positive explanation and maintain a sharp distinction between this kind of explanatory theory, on the one hand, and theories which tackle questions about how, from an ethical point of view, we ought to behave, on the other. For such approaches, and they are the mainstream approaches, normative theory is still marginal to the main business of IR theory.

Possibilities for normative theory in post-positivist IR theory

Far more promising for those looking for the possibility of the emergence of normative theory as a mainstream activity in IR are developments in what has come to be known as post-positivist IR theory. There are a number of subgroups involved

[15] Audie Klotz, *Norms in International Relations*, p. 7.
[16] Audie Klotz, *Norms in International Relations*, p. 3.

here. These include critical, feminist, post-structuralist, social constructivist and post-modern approaches amongst others. There are important differences and tensions between (and within) these groups. But it is the commonalities which interest me here, the first of which is the common insight that what social scientists study are human actions and interactions. The second (and which is related to the first point) stresses that the social wholes which are studied are the outcome of human choices. Consequently, and this is a third feature of such theories, our social world is a human construct and is not the outcome of some remorseless logic built-in to the social world as we know it. It is not the result of, for example, some inevitable modernizing force. 'The given' for social scientists, including IR theorists, is not natural, but constructed. This is particularly important when considering the international political and economic orders. We are to understand the global market as a human construct and not as a natural state of affairs. Fourth, these approaches stress that our self-understandings, which include our advanced theories about how our societies work, do not merely reflect the world but are themselves human constructs made for specific purposes and they play a role in the constitution of our world. IR theorists, in their theorizing activities, are themselves engaged in the constitution of the reality which they study. Thus, for example, their theories might contribute to maintaining the *status quo* within which some are advantaged at the cost of others. Fifth, our identities, who we take ourselves to be, are constructed within the social wholes within which we find ourselves. These social entities (societies) are themselves human constructs. There is a very real sense, then, in which we are self-made men and women. We constitute ourselves within social formations which themselves are constituted by us. Sixth, what we take to be 'reason' is itself a component of the social wholes which we have made for ourselves. Reason is not something outside of history and outside of the things which we make. It always makes sense with regard to any appeal to reason to ask 'Whose reason, when and where?' A seventh point is that these approaches all stress the key role of language in our self-constituting activities. Finally, eighth, the context of rules within which we act are understood to be both enabling and constraining. The set of rules which constitutes our interstate practice, for example, makes possible a whole menu of different kinds of actions for states but, conversely, it also rules out a whole range of possible actions as inappropriate for state actors.[17]

The important point for my present purposes is to note that these theories, let us call them 'constitutive theories', all acknowledge the role of norms in the construction of social reality. If our world is in some sense made by us, if it is the result of our choices, then it is certain that in the making of it, many of our choices will be guided by the values which we hold dear. The world we build will reflect our ethical beliefs. For example, it seems obvious that the market-based economic system which we currently have in place may be taken to embody the values of those who participate in it—values to do with individual liberty, the primacy of contract and the importance of private property. Similarly our system of sovereign states may be taken to embody certain values held dear by we who participate in it—such as the value of national autonomy and world order, to mention but two. For scholars who have taken the constitutive turn, ethical beliefs are not understood simply as

---

[17] The precise details of the commonalities which I have listed here may be disputed by adherents of some of the schools of thought which I have grouped together. However, as an approximation of what is common between these approaches I believe the list will do.

epiphenomena resulting from some deeper set of empirical causes, but are understood as being in part constitutive of that which is being analysed.

One example of constitutive theory is an approach which has become known as constructivism. One version of constructivism, that of Emanuel Adler, portrays it as presenting a middle way between the extremes of positivist social scientific approaches to IR (which include realist, neorealist, and liberal institutionalist accounts), on the one hand, with interpretivist approaches (which include post-structuralists, post-modernists and some feminist approaches to the IR) on the other.[18] Adler defines constructivism as 'the view that *the manner in which the material world shapes and is shaped by human action and interaction depends on dynamic normative and epistemic interpretations of the material world*'.[19] This is a 'middle way' in that it is based on a realist ontology which asserts the existence of the material world, but at the same time, it acknowledges that 'International Relations consist primarily of social facts, which are facts only by human agreement'.[20]

A crucial insight for constitutive theories is that the our current ways of constituting the world and ourselves within it create and privilege certain kinds of actors (identities, if you like) and denigrate others. Thus feminist IR theorists have pointed out how the system of sovereign states is a constituting form which has the effect of hiding women from view—of suggesting that women, as women, are insignificant for a proper understanding of world politics.[21] Similar points could be made about the other approaches to IR theory which have been grouped together here. A central task of constitutive theory is the bringing to light of what the current constitution of world politics (dominated by the system of sovereign states and by the global market) keeps hidden.

Here, then, in constitutive theory, it seems as if, at last, ethics might be reinstated as of central concern to IR. For the task of IR theory according to constitutive theorists is to reveal our global international social order to be a human construct within which are embedded certain values chosen by us and to show how this construct benefits some and oppresses others. This seems to be pre-eminently an exercise in ethical evaluation. It would seem to be self-evident that scholars (be they critical theorists, post-modern theorists, feminist IR scholars, constructivists, or structuration theorists) involved in such evaluative exercises must engage in serious ethical argument—argument about what is to count as oppression (as opposed to liberation), or about what is to count as an emancipatory practice (as opposed to an enslaving one), about what would be fair in international relations, what just, and so on. However, in practice, constitutive theorists have done very little of this kind of theorizing. They do not for the most part tackle the question 'What would it be ethical to do in the circumstances?'.

The hoped for move towards doing ethical theory has not materialized because, for the most part, constitutive theorists are still blocked from doing so by an ongoing commitment to the fact/value distinction and by a thoroughgoing descrip-

---

[18] Emanuel Adler, 'Seizing the Middle Ground: Constructivism in World Politics', in *European Journal of International Relations*, 3,3 (September 1997), pp. 319–64.

[19] Emanuel Adler, 'Seizing the Middle Ground', p. 322.

[20] Emanuel Adler, 'Seizing the Middle Ground', p. 323.

[21] See, for example, Cynthia Enloe, *Bananas, Beaches and Bases: Making Feminist Sense of International Politics* (London: Pandora Books, 1989).

tivism. Theirs is not the descriptivism of the positivists for whom bedrock data are empirically observable data. Instead theirs is a descriptivism based on an understanding of the practices (discourses, structures) being analysed. The approaches are descriptivist insofar as they aim to present the reader with something approaching a value-neutral reading of the way things are in the world being analysed. Social scientists of this ilk present themselves throughout, not as arguing with the people being theorized about as to how things ought to be arranged in the world, but as presenting to the reader an account of how things stand in the world under investigation. Thus we see constructivists pointing to the role which norms play in the constitution of international order;[22] we find feminists pointing to the silences in our global discourses (silences about the role played by gender in the constitution of international reality);[23] we find post-modern theorists pointing out to us how our state centric discourse upholds a certain kind of practice and precludes the articulation of alternative possible practices;[24] structuration theorists indicate to us how our discourses about war and peace structure gender relations;[25] and so on. In this literature we, the readers, are having practices described to us. Constructivists like Nicholus Onuf describe the complicated framework within which we do things with words. For example, making promises (the basis of all contract) requires an elaborate set of background conditions understood as binding by those making and those receiving the promises. One brand of constructivist, the communitarian kind, presents us with a picture of actors constructed within the context of single 'thick' national communities (Jews within the community of Jews, Afrikaaners within the community of Afrikaaners, Basques amongst the community of Basques, and so on) who are at the same time members of a 'thin' international community.[26] In an interesting permutation on this, post-modern theorists demonstrate how the community within which our identities are established are themselves assured of an identity only insofar as this communal identity is established over against rival communities (for example, Serbs against Croats, Greeks against Turks, and so on).[27]

The key difference between positivist IR and post-positivist IR concerns the criteria to be used in evaluating claims about how things are in the world. Positivists take bedrock data to be directly observable and measurable; post-positivists take it that the basic data of the social sciences require interpretation. They differ with regard to the appropriate means of aperception of the object under investigation.

---

[22] Audie Klotz, *Norms in International Relations: The Struggle against Apartheid*; Alexander Wendt, 'Anarchy is What States Make of It: The Social Construction of Power Politics', in *International Organization*, 46/2, (1992); Nicholus Onuf, *World of Our Making: Rules and Ruled in Social Theory and International Relations* (Columbia, SC: University of South Carolina Press, 1989); Friedrich Kratochwil, *Rules, Norms and Decisions: On the Conditions of Practical and Legal Reasoning in International Relations and Domestic Affairs* (Cambridge: Cambridge University Press, 1989).

[23] For example see Cynthia Enloe, *Bananas Beaches and Bases: Making Feminist Sense of International Politics*, ch. 1 and Christine Sylvester, *Feminist Theory and International Relations in a Postmodern Era* (Cambridge: Cambridge University Press, 1994), p. 164 and following pages.

[24] R.B.J. Walker, *Inside/Outside: International Relations as Political Theory* (Cambridge: Cambridge University Press, 1993), ch. 1.

[25] Vivienne Jabri, *Discourses on Violence* (Manchester: Manchester University Press, 1996).

[26] Michael Walzer, *Thick and Thin: Moral Argument at Home and Abroad* (Chicago: Notre Dame University Press, 1994).

[27] For an example of this style of argument, see David Campbell's discussion of the USA's post Cold War search for a hostile 'other' against which it could assert its identity in his 'Violent Performances: Identity, Sovereignty Responsibility', in Yosef Lapid and Friedrich Kratochwil (eds.), *The Return of Culture and Identity in IR Theory* (Boulder: Lynne Rienner, 1996).

All constitutive theorists present us with a picture of the wider set of rules (sometimes referred to as practices, or structures, or discourses) within which a certain set of actions must be understood. These practices are shown to privilege certain people, to be silent about certain actors, to construct certain sets of power relations, and so on. Throughout all this, we the readers are being given what might be broadly termed a sociological analysis in which the people being analysed are shown to hold a certain ontology (set of beliefs about what there is in the world), a certain epistemology (set of beliefs about the bases of knowledge), certain methodological beliefs (about how social inquiry should be conducted) and certain ethical beliefs (about how the world should be organized). Constitutive theorists themselves go to great lengths to show that they are super-aware of how their own ontologies, epistemologies, methodologies and ethical systems might influence their account of the subject matter under investigation.

The key turn made by constitutive theorists is to ask us to take seriously the possibility that the pictured state of affairs could be other than it is. They wish us to consider alternative possible worlds and ways of being. Thus, for example, identity-giving communities could be other than they are—for we know that the boundaries of identity-giving communities may and do shift during the course of history. A primary concern of such theorists is to demonstrate how the state (within the system of sovereign states) is nowadays a primary identity-conferring practice. Having been shown this we are then asked to consider the possibility of creating alternative non-state-centric identity-creating practices.

The post-positivists have given us rich accounts of the complex social structures within which we are constituted and within which we act. They have shown how these structures are not static but are in constant flux. They stress the important role which normative considerations play in the practices which we study and in our practices of scholarship themselves. But once again, following a long tradition of IR scholarship, they stop short of engaging in detailed normative theorizing about what ought to be done. In particular they fail to take on that most important normative question of all, which is: in what would a just world order consist?

What we are presented with by many such authors is a critical deconstruction of our conventional ways of thinking and acting in the international realm. The silences and the silencings are pointed out. The suggestion throughout is that better ways of arranging our affairs are available and ought to be pursued. But the answers given to the direct question 'What is to be done?' are suggestive, but vague. William Connolly suggests that we adopt an 'ethic of cultivation', which respects the ambiguities and indeterminacy of life.[28] David Campbell invites us to consider the question 'What modes of being and forms of life could we or should we adopt?'. He then indicates that we have considerable freedom to 'explore alternative possibilities'.[29] But what is missing is the detailed engagement with the classic questions of political ethics, what forms of political authority are just, what is freedom, what limits on it are justifiable, what (re)distributions are fair, what forms of participation will secure individual autonomy, what trade-offs between liberty and equality are ethically acceptable, and so on.

---

[28] William Connolly, *Identity/Difference: Democratic Negotiations of Political Paradox* (Ithaca: Cornell University Press, 1991), p. x.

[29] David Campbell, *Writing Security* (Manchester: Manchester University Press, 1992), p. 257.

Making the Turn

At the beginning of this article I mentioned a set of ethical problems which we all face in everyday international life. Problems to do with war, terrorism, human rights, the global environment, distributive justice, and so on. An ongoing problem concerns the tension which exists between sovereignty claims and human rights claims (these come sharply to the fore with regard to the issue of migrants and asylum seekers); another arises with regard to national self-determination (which 'selves' are entitled to it?); and finally there are those ethical problems which arise when considering the extraordinary power of the international market and the threat which it poses to people's rights to democratic government within their own state.

At the outset I made the point that these ethical arguments were not merely ones which we hold amongst ourselves about how to treat others (strangers) who are not, with us, members of certain practices in common.[30] Instead they must be understood as *intra-practice arguments* which we hold with those who are, with us, members of certain global practices, the key ones being the system of sovereign democratic and democratizing states, and global civil society. Indeed, we can only hold ethical arguments (or any other kind of argument, for that matter) with those who share certain practices with us. Ethical argument presupposes some points of departure held in common between the disputants. From these *topoi* we attempt to build coherent arguments and to point out incoherent ones. This is the tradition of rhetorical argument by which we seek to find guidance for the problems which confront us in daily life. This kind of argument is not foundational; it is not based on indubitable premises and thus its conclusions cannot themselves be beyond doubt. But in everyday life we do consider that we can distinguish those arguments which carry more weight from those which do not. This form of argumentation, which is the form which dominates in most spheres of our everyday life (except for those governed by the so-called 'hard sciences'), has a history harking back to Aristotle. It is to be found most explicitly in legal reasoning. The forms of this kind of argument and its history have been comprehensively discussed by Chaim Perelman and Olbrechts Tyteca in their classic *New Rhetoric.* An attempt to develop an approach to International Ethics within this tradition of argument is to be found in my *Ethics in International Relations.* In that work I started by listing a set of settled norms which hold in the two major practices of international life, the system of sovereign states and the international civil society, and then sought to determine whether they could be brought into coherence through the construction of a suitable background theory. Such a background theory, I maintained, would be useful in indicating solutions to those many 'hard cases' which arose in our fast-changing world.

[30] I use the 'practice' here as Ludwig Wittgenstein used it the following quotation: 'Where is the connexion effected between the sense of an expression "Let's play a game of chess" and all the rules of the game?—Well, in the list of rules of the game, in the teaching of it, in the day-to-day practice of playing.' Ludwig Wittgenstein, *Philosophical Investigations* (Oxford: Basil Blackwell, 1968), para.197. For our purposes we might ask 'Where is the sense of "Let's argue about how our political world should be organized" and all the rules of our political world? Well in the list of rules of our political world, in the teaching of these, in the day to day practice of world politics.' Just as making a move in the game of chess can only be understood within the wider practice of chess playing, so, too, making an argument about an ethical issue in world politics can only take place within the practice of world politics. The particular act presupposes the wider practice.

It is here that a great deal of work remains to be done. Those many different post-positivist approaches to IR which have indicated to us the salience of norms in international life, now need to move beyond this 'pointing out' phase. They need to engage in the process of constructing ethical theories which reveal the coherences and display the incoherences between the norms we hold in common in our international practice. By doing so they would help guide action towards a more ethical world.

Let me end this article with a list of some glaring incoherences which need to be confronted.

- All of us live in states and for the most part we hold it ethically important that our states are autonomous and do not become subject states of one kind or another.[31] This commitment clashes with another widespread settled norm asserting the importance of individual rights which may be claimed and enforced against all comers including states. There appears to be an incoherence between these two norms. It comes sharply into focus with regards to migrants, refugees, questions concerning non-intervention, and questions of national self-determination.

- There is an apparent incoherence between ethically valuing and participating in a global free market, on the one hand, and valuing a system of autonomous states, on the other.

- There are it seems tensions between attaching ethical importance to the nurturing of ethnic (and national and tribal) communities, on the one hand, and attaching such importance to democratic states, on the other.

- There is an apparent incoherence between asserting the ethical importance of state autonomy and asserting the ethical significance of a global commons.

- With regard to the so-called 'quasi-states' there may be a particularly acute ethical tension between respect for the sovereignty norm and respect for human rights. A thoroughgoing respect for the latter might involve undertaking major interventions in 'quasi-states.'

- Calls for humanitarian interventions in states beset by civil war bring to light acute tensions between the sovereignty norm, human rights norms, and norms asserting the rights of nations to self-determination.

- The control of nuclear weapons also brings to light ethical tensions between claims to the right to self-defence on the one hand and ethical claims made in the name of international peace and security on the other.

- There may be major tensions between values embedded in the system of sovereign states and the kind of system required for the flourishing of women free from the constraints of patriarchy.

---

[31] I say 'for the most part' because some people find themselves trapped in states from which they would prefer to secede. Consider the nationalists from East Timor, for example. However, it is important to note that they aspire to life in an independent *state* of East Timor.

Conclusion

My contention in this article has been that in spite of a range of post-positivist developments in IR, the discipline remains fixated on pointing out the crucial role norms play in our global practices and in our practices as social scientists. Scholars in IR are still hesitant to engage in the difficult business of providing answers to the question: What would it be ethically appropriate to do in these circumstances? The hesitancy no doubt arises from a desire to maintain IR's credentials as a social science committed to objective enquiry and value neutrality, from a belief that in world politics any attempt to prescribe what ought to be done might easily turn into an attempt to impose a pattern of conduct on others through the use of power, and from a belief that ethical questions are a matter for each individual (or people) to decide for himself, herself or itself. The hesitancy, though, is misplaced. For the very possibility of an objective and value-neutral social science has been subject to sustained and, in my opinion, very effective criticism. The other two reasons for hesitancy about tackling the ethical questions are themselves ethical positions. The first is based on the ethical notion that it is wrong to coerce people to follow a given ethical code and the second, is based on the ethical notion of autonomy. Both of these ought not to be accepted uncritically. It is to be doubted that coercion is always ethically wrong (is it wrong if used against slavery, apartheid, tyranny, genocide?). Similarly, is autonomy always to be respected (should racist elites be accorded autonomy)?

The imperative of action means that in multiple ways we all act in ways which entrench some values and erode others. IR theorists entrench ethical positions through the kinds of theorizing they do. It is time that they publicly defended the ethical choices they promote. As things presently stand for the most part ethical arguments about matters pertaining to the international realm are carried out by scholars outside of the discipline of IR in the disciplines of philosophy, political philosophy, politics, and sociology. Here scholars who have traditionally focussed on issues of justice, democracy, human rights, nationalism, equality, liberty (and so on) as they apply to matters within states are now beginning to consider these as they apply to world politics. Let me single out one such author who has moved from one discipline, in this case sociology, into the domain of IR to undertake exactly the kind of ethical theorizing so sorely missed in IR. David Held in *Democracy and the Global Order* takes on the big normative questions about the scope of political authority, about the functioning of democratic political orders in a globalized world, about the links and tensions between political authority and individual autonomy, and about the place of individual human rights in world politics.[32] The discipline of IR needs to learn the lesson it is being taught by colleagues in cognate fields. The discipline of IR needs to avoid falling behind in its own subject area.

---

[32] David Held, *Democracy and the Global Order* (Cambridge: Polity Press, 1996).

The eighty years' crisis, 1919–1999—power

PAUL HIRST

Power is one of the most commonly used concepts in the social sciences and in ordinary political discourse. It would seem to be central to the study of international relations. Before we consider the role of power in international relations in the short twentieth century, it is necessary to clear up some preliminaries about the concept in general. This is because power is a frustrating concept; its use seldom lives up to our expectations. To begin with there is a fundamental ambiguity; is power a phenomenon to be explained or an explanatory tool, a dependent or an independent variable? On closer inspection, the explanatory power of the concept of power is low. It is difficult to explain social relations and their outcomes, at either the national or the international level, in terms of power as it is normally conceived in the social sciences. Yet, however theoretically sophisticated we try to be, we are driven to use some such concept for want of an alternative.

The concept of power

The dominant concept of power in the social sciences has three main aspects. First, power is a factor in the relations between actors; typically it is conceived as that which enables one actor's will to prevail over another's, despite resistance, in a case where the actors' interests conflict. Secondly, power is considered as a simple quantitative capacity, one actor has more power than another and, therefore, prevails—whatever it is that enables actors to compel others to submit to their will is generalized into a single quantum. Thirdly, power is a zero-sum game: what one actor gains, the other loses, and thus an actor's capacities can be judged essentially by outcomes—who 'has' power is who prevails.[1] Thus Max Weber defines power in a classic and widely quoted way as follows:

---

[1] B. Russell, *Power: A New Social Analysis* (London: George Allen and Unwin, 1938—reprinted 1992 London: Routledge). Bertrand Russell defines power as follows: 'Power may be defined as the production of intended effects. It is thus a quantitative concept – given two men with similar desires, if one achieves all the desires that the other achieves, and also others, he has more power than the other' (p. 25). This strong dependence on intention may seem idiosyncratic, but Russell was no fool. He recognizes that this is the only way to measure effects in an actor-centred capacity-outcome view of power. To define power in terms of resources is ineffective: power does not exist unless it is used or put into contention and resources, however great, are of little value unless their use achieves the effects intended. Russell then remarks: 'There are no exact means of comparing the power of two men of whom one can achieve one group of desires, and another another . . . Nevertheless, it is easy to say, roughly, that A has more power than B, if A achieves many intended effects and B only a few'. Power thus has to be recognized as such *post hoc,* even if it is initially defined in terms of *intended* effects.

. . . we understand by 'power' the chance of a man or of a number of men to realise their own will in a communal action even against the resistance of others who are participating in the action.[2]

The concept of power has been exhaustively analysed by numerous authors in the period of the eighty years' crisis, but most penetratingly in recent years by Hindess, on whom this account is substantially dependent.[3]

Hindess[4] examines other dimensions of the concept than this simple capacity-outcome view of power. In particular he considers the concept, common in social theory since Hobbes, that power as capacity and as legitimate authority coincides in the rulers of a political community to whom the citizens have given consent. This notion of the self-governing political community, in which citizens' acceptance of political obligation gives the sovereign the power to govern within the national territory (limited only by the compact between rulers and ruled), has been central to the idea of the nation state as a distinct political actor.[5] That conception of state has been at the core of modern international relations thinking.

In the analysis of relations *between* states, however, the capacity-outcome conception of power prevails.[6] States are actors in a fundamentally anarchic international system; no ongoing compact or civil state of affairs exists between them. States interact externally. Power is thus whatever bears on the will of one state-actor in order to compel it to submit to the will of another. This view is central to the doctrine of realism, as is the belief that the dominant actors in the international system are states.

What is wrong with the capacity-outcome view that undermines its value as an explanatory device? Hindess cites two phenomena that make it difficult to conceive of power as a simple given quantity. First, power is an interaction and one in which the reciprocal action of the parties' means that each actor's moves conditions the actions of the other.[7] This notion has been clear since Clausewitz defined it as one of the fundamental properties of war and it long pre-dates game-theory-based accounts of strategic interactions. Nevertheless, the dominant concept of power finds it difficult to accommodate reciprocal action. Interactions and the means used in them are conditioned by skill, competence, and organization—factors difficult to

---

[2] M. Weber, 'Class, Status, Party', in H. Gerth and C. Wright Mills (eds.), *From Max Weber: Essays in Sociology* (London: Routledge and Kegan Paul, 1948), p. 180.

[3] B. Hindess, 'On Three Dimensional Power,' *Political Studies*, 24 (3) (1976), pp. 229–333. Of the substantial but generally unsatisfactory literature on the concept of power, the best examples are S. Lukes, *Power, a Radical View* (London: Macmillan, 1974), who serves as a foil to Hindess, and Wrong (New York: Transaction, 1979).

[4] B. Hindess,) *Discourses of Power: From Hobbes to Foucault* (Oxford: Blackwell, 1996).

[5] B. Hindess,) 'Imaginary presuppositions of Democracy', *Economy and Society*, 20 (2), pp. 173–95.

[6] This is not only true of classical realists, but also of their critics, who object to crude capacity-outcome views, but then fail to offer a coherent substitute. For an example of such criticism, see Robert O. Keohane 'Theory of World Politics: Structural Realism and Beyond' in Keohane, P. (ed. 1986) *Neo-Realism and its Critics* (New York: Columbia University Press, 1986). Susan Strange, whilst attempting to sweep away much of the theoretical furniture of conventional international relations theory, and particularly realism, retreats to the following definition of power: 'Power is simply the ability of a person or group of persons so to affect outcomes that their preferences take precedence over the preferences of others', S. Strange, *The Retreat of the State—The Diffusion of Power in the World Economy* (Cambridge: Cambridge University Press, 1996), p. 17. This is virtually a paraphrase of Weber.

[7] The best account of reciprocal action and its consequences for military strategy is E. Luttwak, *Strategy—The Logic of War and Peace* (Cambridge, MA: Belknap Press, Harvard, 1987).

reduce to simple quanta. Thus in war, both training and operational art may make a vast difference to the outcome—counteracting numbers of troops or machines. For example, in the Six Day War of 1967 between Israel and its Arab neighbours, the simple quanta of orders of battle had little relation to the outcome. Similar factors seem to apply in international economic negotiations. Why has the USA been so effective in promoting its positions on trade and investment within such forums as the Uruguay round of GATT? Is it the economic 'power' of the USA—an international debtor nation, the foreign trade of which is still a relatively modest percentage of GDP? Or is it that the dominant discourses in international trade are produced by US economists and commercial lawyers? The other 136 nations often have specific opposed interests, but these have to be presented as exceptions and self-interested against a hegemonic discourse of the generally beneficial results of trade openness.[8]

Secondly, the different means to exercise 'power' are seldom compatible. Hindess[9] gives the amusing example of two powers whose principal weapons are tanks and submarines trying to engage in combat. Thus considerable military or economic resources on one dimension may have no effect on those in another. Examples are obvious. In the Danish crisis of 1864, Bismarck threatened that if the British army interfered he would send the Prussian police to arrest it. Equally, of course, the trade and the colonies of the new German Empire after 1871 were wholly at the mercy of the Royal Navy. The spectacle of American supersonic jets bombing and failing to stop convoys of peasants pushing bicycles in Vietnam indicates that we have little *a priori* ability to rank quanta of power against one another—apparent weakness or backwardness can actually be a strength.

These examples are obvious, but they show how difficult it is to treat power as a quantum determined prior to the interaction, the outcome of which is to be explained by it. If that is so, the concept of power ceases to have a great deal of predictive value; rather, we have to describe the interaction *post hoc* or to try to model the possible moves of the actors, making various assumptions about rationality and motivation. Moreover, it is by no means clear that power has to be or is best considered as either exclusively a relationship between actors or a zero-sum game. There are other views of power—the most interesting of which for our purposes are those of Talcott Parsons and Michel Foucault.[10] Parsons considers power as a property of the social system; it is a medium for mobilizing resources much like money. Thus each actor depends on a social context for power resources, rather than possessing a quantum of power as an autonomous agent. Power enables

---

[8] See T.S. Biersteker, 'The "Triumph" of Neo-classical Economics in the Developing World: Policy Convergence and Bases of Governance in the International Economic Order', in Rosenau and Czempiel, *Governance without Government* (1992), pp. 102–31 for an attempt to explain the conversion of most of the developing world to neo-classical economics and R. Unger, 'A Really New Bretton Woods', in M. Uzan (ed.), *The Finaicial System under Stress. An Architecture for the New World Economy* (London: Routledge, 1996) for a serious attempt to advocate the necessity of alternative models of development in order to keep open options in economic evolution and maximize the potential for growth.

[9] B. Hindess,) *Discourses of Power: From Hobbes to Foucault* (Oxford: Blackwell, 1996).

[10] T. Parsons, 'On the Concept of Political Power', in T. Parsons (ed.), *Politics and Social Structure* (New York: The Free Press, 1969), pp. 352–404; M. Foucault, *Discipline and Punish* (London: Allen Lane, 1977); M. Foucault, *Power/Knowledge,* Colin Gordon (ed.) (New York: Pantheon Books, 1980); M. Foucault, 'Governmentality', in G. Burchell *et al.* (eds.), *The Foucault* Effect (London: Harvester Wheatsheaf, 1991).

things to be done within a system of collective action. It assigns capacities to actors that are legitimate in relation to collective goals and which enables them to be sanctioned or to sanction others if they fail to perform appropriately in relation to those goals. Thus power is not a zero-sum game. Actors may mutually benefit from increases of power within the social system as a whole, since this increases the total capacity for collective action and mobilization of resources.

Foucault also challenges the actor-centred view of power. For him, power is productive and not merely negative. It does not merely compel subjects to submit to the will of another; rather power is applied to transform both the nature of actors and their capacity for action. Most of his examples relate to power exercised within state societies, but, although he is concerned with examples such as psychiatry, public health and prisons, he shows that power is a widespread social phenomenon. It is not confined to the political sphere or to state officials.[11]

Both Parsons and Foucault are valuable in order to consider power relations at the international level in a new light. It we accept that today international relations can be described neither as dominated by external interactions between sovereign states that control all aspects of their internal affairs, nor as a new political community, in which states have been subordinated to new forms of supra-national governance, then we face new theoretical tasks. We must account for patterns of cooperation and conflict between states and also other bodies that are ongoing and without clear hierarchy. In these patterns, interaction is continuous and finite outcomes difficult to determine. We must also account for complex international forms of governance that are not state-like, that do not necessarily diminish the capacities of nation states but may actually enhance them by stabilizing certain key dimensions of their external environment. National and international governance interpenetrate. The problem is that we have no ready language in political theory for that interaction and governance which is between the interaction of externally related autonomous actors and that which takes place in political communities, in which actors are conditioned by legitimacy and obligation respectively. A world of governance beyond government, a politics of networks, and of quasi-polities requires a new account of its architecture before we can re-conceptualize the capacities for action, or power, if we prefer to call it so, that are created within it.

Power in 'The Twenty Years' Crisis'

We cannot, however, simply dismiss the capacity-outcome view of power, since it has been central in shaping our understanding of international relations. This brings us to E.H. Carr's classic. Power is one of the dominant concepts in his book, although it is never straightforwardly defined there. Carr takes his basic framework from Bertrand Russell's text.[12] Power is clearly seen by Carr, however, as the capacity to prevail over others and it is revealed in a conflict between opposed interests. In

[11] N. Rose, 'Government, Authority and Expertise in Advanced Liberalism', *Economy and Society,* 22, 3 (1993), pp. 283–99.

[12] B. Russell, *Power: A New Social Analysis* (London: George Allen and Unwin, 1938—reprinted 1992 London: Routledge).

Carr's period, 1919–39, the options of conceiving the international system were clear—realism and utopianism. For realists, states were the dominant actors in the international system and power determined the outcomes of their interactions. For the utopians, the international system was moving from anarchy to a civil order, the League of Nations was evolving toward a political community, and power politics were being replaced by peaceful means of resolving problems such as international administration, arbitration and international law. Carr savages the utopians, in essence for misdescribing the world and acting on the assumption that their errors are satisfactory states of affairs. He also condemns the pure realists, not for being wrong about states of affairs, but for having no goals other than those given by the existing situation.

Carr's book is valuable because it was written between two periods of liberal economic internationalization, the *belle époque* of 1870–1914 dominated by *laissez-faire* free trade doctrines and the *Pax Britannica*, and the post-1945 world, which can be subdivided into the period to 1973, characterized by managed multi-lateralism and the *Pax Americana*, and the period from the early 1980s onwards, which many regard as the era of economic globalization, the absence of a clear hegemon, and the return to a variant of *laissez-faire*.[13] Carr did not share the acceptance by the economic liberals of the Anglo-Saxon world that international economic openness was a natural state of affairs, disrupted by the selfish and self-defeating policies of some nations. He saw the international economy as structured by the interaction of inter-state politics and changing economic organization. Thus he could see the international regimes of monetary, trade and investment policy created by the liberal era as political and working to the advantage of certain states.

This perspective is still valuable, even if we discount Carr's peculiar combination of a flirtation with Marxism, particularly in the shape of Karl Mannheim,[14] and appeasement. Hindsight is easy. Carr was right to challenge the illusions of the more naïve proponents of the League. In doing so, however, he accepted a degree of legitimacy for the claims of the dissatisfied or have not nations, Germany, Italy and Japan. We can now see that their aspirations were neither legitimate nor appeaseable. Hitler was not just another aggressive nationalist politician. In the aftermath of 1939–45 we can sympathize more with Arnold Toynbee, whom Carr derides, when he said: 'International law and order were in the true interests of the whole of mankind . . . whereas the desire to perpetuate the region of violence in international relations was an anti-social desire which was not even in the ultimate interests of the handful of states that officially professed this benighted and anarchistic creed.'[15] The real problem with views like Toynbee's was not that they identified the interests of humankind with those of the 'have' states, but that the checking of those 'anti-social desires' could only be accomplished by force. The collective security measures of the League provided neither enough force nor the political will to use it. Indeed, the anti-political conception of international relations advanced by figures like Toynbee made such decisive action less legitimate, even if the liberal powers had been prepared to act.

---

[13] P. Hirst, 'The Global Economy—Myths and Realities', *International Affairs*, 73, 3 (1997), pp. 409–25.
[14] K. Mannheim, *Ideology and Utopia* (London: Routledge and Kegan Paul, 1954).
[15] E.H. Carr, *The Twenty Years' Crisis* (London: Macmillan, 1939), p. 83.

The changing capacities of the nation state 1919–1999

Carr's discussion of power is as good a perspective as any with which to survey the changing capacities of the nation state between the era of protectionism and competing nationalisms of the 1930s and the post-war period of international openness. Carr, following and adapting Russell, divided power in international politics into three dimensions—military power, economic power and power over opinion—and we may as well stick with these.[16]

A   Military power

In 1939 Stalin's question—'how many divisions has the Pope?'—still made sense, even if it was applied to an inappropriate political entity. Military power could be conceived as the possession of states and roughly assessable by orders of battle. From the mid-nineteenth to the late-twentieth century states acquired and then utilized a monopoly of the use of international violence from their territories. Earlier, from the mid-seventeenth to the mid-nineteenth century, states had to differing degrees and on different temporalities acquired a monopoly of the means of violence within their territories. As Janice E. Thomson[17] shows perceptively, the boundaries between state and non-state external violence were redrawn in the nineteenth century; the international state system acting to suppress piracy, privateering, mercenarism, and commercial companies' possession of military force. Without their complying with these international norms, states were increasingly neither recognized nor accepted as legitimate and, therefore, as sovereign powers—entities like the pirate state of Algiers or the English East India Company became less and less tolerable as armed actors.

Within this historically specific state monopoly of external violence, the classic Clausewitzian conception of war as the continuation of the states' external policy by other means could make sense.[18] War was a normal part of the intercourse between states and a means of settling fundamental differences of interest. States were at least minimally rational actors, and they monopolized the ability to make war. Even in the Clausewitzian era, differences in military competence and technology were radically altering the balance of power in war. The units of measure such as infantry divisions or battleships were always at best approximate.

By 1939, tactical skill, operational art and technical capabilities were almost as significant as numbers—for example, Richard Overy[19] argues against the view that the overwhelming industrial strength of the Allied Powers must have inevitably prevailed over the Axis. The Allies had to acquire military competence, and the Germans to make strategic errors. If anything, the Cold War reinforced the notion

---

[16] Thus Russell's category of Naked Power is redefined by Carr as military power, and such categories as Priestly Power, Kingly Power, Revolutionary Power, and Creeds as Sources of Power dropped. The reason is mainly, one supposes, because they do not fit in with the discussion of international relations.

[17] J.E. Thomson, *Mercenaries, Pirates and Sovereigns* (Princeton NJ: Princeton University Press, 1994).

[18] On Clausewitz and his concept of war in its political context see P. Paret, *Clausewitz and the State* (Princeton, NJ: Princeton University Press, 1985), especially ch. 11.

[19] R. Overy, *Why the Allies Won* (London: Cape, 1995).

of an order-of-battle world of competing states. States were organized in hier-archical blocs, and sponsored at best limited revolutionary or counter-revolutionary violence in the unstable zones at their margins. The Superpowers had to control such violence, lest it get out of hand. Clausewitzian war began to be impossible for the core states of these blocs with the development of an approximate balance of nuclear weapons between the USA and USSR in the 1960s.[20] Supposing minimal rationality, the use of nuclear weapons could only negate any possible policy pursued by both sides. Despite attempts at complex strategic and nuclear warfighting doctrines in the US, deterrence depended on a crude existential balance of terror that paralysed certain actions by state officials. Thus nuclear weapons had only one purpose in policy terms, as Bernard Brodie[21] perceptively understood at the very beginning of the new era, that is to negate their own use until a political solution to their existence could be found.[22]

Whether this solution has been achieved is moot. However, the end of the Cold War is a significant change, not because Russia is no longer a nuclear power but because it has ceased to be an internationally ideological one. War between the advanced states is unlikely, less because of the balance of nuclear power, than because external expansion or aggression no longer makes much sense to them either on ideological or on economic terms. There is no point in annexing territory if the result has little impact on productive resources. If modern economies depend on skill and knowledge rather than upon raw materials, then most of the key workers will flee on invasion or do little to cooperate. For example, Czechoslovakia had one of the highest GDPs per capita of the advanced nations in 1939, but by 1989 it had fallen to a level comparable with middle-income developing countries. The era of quantitative economic power, measured in tons of steel, cement, etc., ended just before Nikita Kruschshev threatened the West that 'we will bury you', in just such a crude contest of output. The microchip made this boast irrelevant. Moreover, the widespread acceptance of free trade has reduced the incentive to seize territory in order to gain access to markets.

War is still a possibility. Medium-range powers may still fight, as Britain did in the Falklands, or Greece and Turkey, for example, may in the Aegean. But such wars will be localized and will not rearrange the international system. War, in the sense of armed conflict, is increasingly a phenomenon that takes place *within* states rather than between them. Civil wars now predominate in the major world areas of conflict. The great powers either try to intervene, Congress of Berlin style, to impose solutions or as more limited peacekeeping and humanitarian forces. Equally, as Martin van Creveld points out in *Future On War*,[23] terrorism—either state-sponsored or by revolutionary sects—has become the central means of pursuing conflict between social interests in the lesser powers and the advanced states. War is thus ceasing to involve entities of the same type, where traditional balance-of-power considerations make sense. Conflict between stealth bombers and terrorist bases looks less like war than an expensive form of pest control. Military forces tend to merge in the uses to which they are put with police or with civil action, for example,

[20] B. Brodie, *Strategy in the Missile Age* (Princeton NJ: Princeton University Press, 1965).
[21] B. Brodie, *The Absolute Weapon* (New York: Harcourt Brace, 1947).
[22] The best account of nuclear strategic doctrines in their context is still L. Freedman, *The Evolution of Nuclear Strategy* (London: Macmillan, 1981).
[23] M. van Greveld, *On Future War* (London: Brassey's, 1991).

British troops arresting human-rights criminals or escorting relief convoys in Bosnia. Intelligence collecting becomes central in such conflicts; shifting state capacity toward the most developed technologies and the most advanced states, of which on this dimension of military power the USA has no equal.

The result, as van Creveld argues, is a complex non-Clausewitzian military system in which states no longer monopolize external violence, in which most advanced states no longer see war as a useful option in external policy, and in which military forces became less and less homogenous. This is neither a conflict-free world, nor one of greater humanity in conflict. It is, however, more multi-dimensional in its conflicts, the bodies entering into them, and the means utilized, from the mass genocide with such primitive weapons as pangas in Rwanda, to threats of American precision bombing by cruise missiles against Iraq. Seeing this in terms of 'power' is less and less sensible, since we lack common units of its measure. Seeing war as something that only states do, as part of international relations, is also less and less viable.

B   Economic Power

Carr saw that the doctrine of free trade rested on the assumption of the natural harmony of interests. His demonstration of the power-relations and asymmetrical interests lying behind the apparently neutral facts of market exchange was very perceptive: 'the mirage of the nineteen-twenties was . . . the belated reflexion of a century past beyond recall—the golden age of continuously expanding territories and markets, of a world policed by the self-assured and not too onerous British hegemony, of a coherent "Western" civilisation whose conflicts could be harmonised by progressive extension of the area of common development and exploitation, of the easy assumptions that what was good for one was good for all and that what was economically right could not be morally wrong'.[24] This passage is remarkable in that the dominant aim of most Western, and especially American, policy makers today is to maintain and reinforce a modern version of just such a world. Free trade is seen to be mutually beneficial—all are made richer by the gains from trade. Indeed, the more extreme globalization advocates, like Kenichi Ohmae,[25] seem to be promoting a new version of the liberal international utopia of Cobden and Bright; seeing the state as no longer a necessary evil but as an irrelevance, overstepped by world markets and transnational companies.

In such a new world, the nineteenth-century free traders' hopes for a dominance of commerce over the military mentality would be realized. Militancy would face the threat of a new and devastating 'Dollar diplomacy', in the form of collapsing exchange rates, equity and bond values, and exports in the face of a withdrawal of foreign confidence brought on by the prospect of military action or the attempt to interfere with the world free-trading system. Autarky is seen as no longer a viable policy, for in this view, the international division of labour is now so extended that

---

[24] E.H. Carr, *The Twenty Years' Crisis* (London: Macmillan, 1939), p. 83.
[25] K. Ohmae, *The Borderless World* (London: Collins, 1990); K. Ohmae, *The End of the Nation State* (London: HarperCollins, 1996).

no state can survive without foreign trade. Autarky could make sense when markets could be monopolized and when raw materials were still central to economic performance. Standardized mass production required a certain scale of output and, therefore, guaranteed markets of a certain size. The idea of a virtually self-contained industrial trading system was close to being realized in 1930s America, a tiny proportion of whose GDP was traded. This was the aim of the British turn to protectionism and Imperial Preference, and of the Greater East Asia Co-Prosperity Sphere of Japan, and of Germany's *Grossraumwirtschaft*. Carr saw this tendency toward closed economic blocs as an inevitable feature of economic modernity, as was the struggle between them to control markets.

It turns out that there are options between autarky and the ultra-globalizers' conception of the economic demise of the nation state and its subsumption in the global economy. The last modern attempts at autarky have clearly failed: strategies of revolutionary endogenous economic modernization in the developing countries, of import-substituting industrialization. Almost all developing countries seek foreign trade and foreign investment. Hence they are drawn into the world free-trading system on the terms of the advanced countries. Free trade is now the dominant economic doctrine. But this does not mean a liberal utopia in which the need for military force in the international system has disappeared. Recalcitrant states are the ones least likely to be deterred by the modern version of Dollar diplomacy, since they are either petrolic states, like Iraq, or states so absorbed in local nationalist projects that they are willing to suffer economic sanctions, like Serbia. Iraq needed to be defeated by a military coalition of almost all the advanced countries and their regional allies before it could be subjected to effective sanctions on its oil income. Serbia needed to be militarily defeated by Croatian and Bosnian troops before American pressure could force it to accept a negotiated solution. Thus economic constraints alone can seldom force the powers that most need to be constrained to the conference table.

Globalization has not occurred to the extent its most extreme advocates assert. The national economy and, therefore, the economic policy of the nation state continue to exist to a considerable degree.[26] In particular, transnational companies are less common than supposed. Most companies are multinational, trading internationally from an established national base (which accounts typically for about two-thirds of sales and three quarters of assets) through subsidiaries and affiliates abroad.[27] A crude sign of this continued lumpiness of the international economy is if we look at the composition of the G8 and compare it with the old Great Powers of 1914. What has changed? Simply that Canada has replaced the defunct Austria–Hungary.

There are, however, very real differences between the present international economy and that of the *laissez-faire* era before 1914. These are five. First, the state in the advanced countries spends a far higher proportion of GDP, typically in the range of 40–50% compared with 10% in 1914, and can, therefore, really affect the

---

[26] P. Hirst and G. Thompson, *Globalisation in Question* (Cambridge: Polity, 1996).

[27] P. Hirst and G. Thompson, *Globalisation in Question* (Cambridge: Polity, 1996); W. Ruigrok. and R. van Tulder, *The Logic of International Restructuring* (London: Routledge, 1995); L.W. Pauly. and S. Reich, 'National Structures and Multinational Corporate Behaviour: Enduring Differences in an Age of Globalisation', *International Organisation,* 51, 1 (1997), pp. 1–30.

economy in the way it behaves.[28] There is no significant tendency for such levels of public expenditure to fall or for them to converge. Secondly, new trading blocs have developed, chiefly the EU, NAFTA, APEC, and Mercosur. These are not aimed at promoting closure like the old autarkic blocs, but are regional constellations of economic governance within an open international economy.[29] Thirdly, advanced states regulate flows of migration far more tightly today than in the nineteenth century, which was the true age of mass migration. Passportism had replaced nationalism. Thus advanced states control their territories more tightly than in the liberal era, because they define citizenship (and access to welfare benefits) far more tightly. Fourthly, the international financial markets have changed in scale and character, although flows of capital are now not greater in proportion to GDP than they were in the principal capital-exporting countries before 1914.[30] The volume of short-term dealing has greatly increased since the 1970s, as has the degree of its divorce from financing trade (financial flows are now more than 40 times more than those needed to finance trade). This pool of liquid capital can produce volatility in short-term shifts between currencies and local equity markets—even so, most advanced countries still source about 90% of capital from domestic sources.[31] Lastly, there is now a far denser structure of international governance than in 1914—the international institutions of the post-1945 economic settlement like the IMF and World Bank continue in changed roles; they have been supplemented by new bodies like the WTO, and institutions of inter-state coordination between the advanced countries like the G7 and the Bank for International Settlements. The UN and its agencies are marginal in this governance, more so than the League and its bodies in Carr's period.

This open international economy is clearly structured by and for the benefit of the advanced countries, but the relation between less developed recipients of capital and the major investor nations has changed. In place of state-based dollar or sterling diplomacy, there is IMF tutelage. In the recent Mexican 1994–5 crisis and the current Asian crisis, Western investors have either exited or been protected by stabilization measures organized by the IMF and subsidized by OECD taxpayers. Domestic elites in the recipient countries are then required to enforce policy, if they can. Financial power is thus internationalized and quite different from nineteenth-century enforcement measures against defaulting states, such as the British protectorate in Egypt.

C Power over Opinion

In Carr's period, currents of opinion were dominated by nationalism and competing ideologies. To some extent Fascism and communism were international

---

[28] 'The Myth of the Powerless State', *Economist*, 7 October 1995.
[29] On the increasing tendency for trade to be concentrated within blocs and the domination of world trade by the big three blocs, APEC, EU and NAFTA, see P. Hirst, and G. Thompson, 'The Tyranny of Globalisation: Myth or Reality', Mimeo. Open University, 1998.
[30] P. Bairoch and R. Kozul-Wright, 'Globalisation Myths: Some Historical Reflections on Integration, Industrialisation and Growth in the World Economy', UNCTAS Discussion Paper No. 113 March 1996.
[31] D. Miles, 'Globalisation: the Facts Behind the Myth', *Independent*, 22 December, 1997.

ideologies. From this perspective, Spain between 1936 and 1939 could be seen as a battleground for a European civil war, in which the ideological states intervened on their respective sides. Yet both Nazism and Stalinism were essentially national doctrines. The roles other states or peoples could play were in walk-on parts as part of a supporting cast—as *volksgenossen* or supporters of Socialism in One Country.

The 1930s were the apogee of the nationalization of culture that had begun with the French Revolution. Nationalism aimed to make the population of a territorial state culturally homogenous; legitimating such policies by reference to a nation or people of which the state was supposed to be the expression. The propagation of national languages and the prescription of *patois* in mass education, the use of the conscript army as a 'school of the nation', the promotion of national symbols and ceremonies, and the nationalization of civil society through such bodies as diverse as folklore societies and the Boy Scouts were all means to make people culturally alike.[32] In a democracy, the notion that rulers and the ruled could be culturally unalike was unacceptable—hitherto it had been commonplace, and it still was in Europe's colonies.

Nationalism, therefore, inevitably led to propaganda. The Czechs, although a liberal state, were in this sense no less committed to moulding opinion than were the Nazis. Throughout Europe the new monopolized state broadcasting media were powerful tools of national ideologies.

This era of enforced national mass culture is over in the advanced countries. The internationalization of media, in many countries and cities, a plural society based on a multinational culture, and the rise of mass individualism, have radically undermined state attempts to control culture, belief and identity. Increasingly, individuals can choose from a wide range of sources of opinion, many of them originating outside the state territory. Digitalised media, satellite communications and the Internet make cultural prescription and censorship almost futile. These facts are obvious, but they illustrate the radical contrast between the two halves of the short twentieth century. It is not that opinion is free from constraint, that there is now no attempt to influence opinion, but that increasingly such attempts are not monopolized by the state—they are the projects of media barons or of fundamentalist religious sects or eco-warriors, and so on.

In *Nationalism and After* of 1945,[33] Carr deplored the tendency toward totalitarianism produced by competing militant nationalisms. He saw the ordinary sovereign nation state as finished. The world belonged either to competing autarkic blocs or to what he considered a better outcome: 'a balanced structure of international or multi-national groupings both for the maintenance of security and for the planned development of the economies of geographical areas or groups of nations'.[34] In a sense Carr was right; that is roughly what we did have in the system of blocs and security treaties like NATO. However, the international system now has larger elements of *laissez-faire* than he thought possible and more effective functionally specific international institutions.

---

[32] For a classic account of how such processes of national homogenisation were accomplished see E. Weber, *Peasants into Frenchmen* (London: Chatto & Windus, 1979), on France.
[33] E.H. Carr, *Nationalism and After* (London: Macmillan, 1945).
[34] Ibid., p. 70.

Power beyond the nation state

Until recently the classical concept of power could just about serve, provided one did not burden it with too many scientific expectations. It did not greatly harm the case Carr was making that it had fundamental theoretical limitations. The difference now is that the contest to theorize international relations is no longer primarily between realism and utopianism, but between different conceptualizations of a complex division of labour in governance. Concepts of power as a systemic capacity like those of Foucault or Parsons are more effective in explaining how governance resources are or could be mobilized in this system. Increasingly the nation state is but one node in a complex web of governance. It should be clear that there are no such things as 'states' as such, if there ever were. States are so unalike as to be qualitatively different. It is difficult to consider Sweden and Somalia as entities of the same type, whatever the formal theory of sovereignty may say.

States depend on the level of development of their economies for their degree of governance capacity, not least because in most countries the primary political goals today are economic. But all at least minimally developed states also rely on a structure of international economic governance through agencies which vary from the firefighting interventionism of the IMF to the quiet backroom regulatory work of the Bank for International Settlements, through international practices, like tariff reduction and market-opening measures, agreed by states in international treaties like GATT, through short-term stabilization measures like the Plaza and Louvre Accords agreed by the G7 in the 1980s, and though their increasing integration into trade blocs based on ongoing associations of states.

This should not be contrasted with the period before the oil price crises of the 1970s, as if nation states enjoyed domestic macro-economic autonomy then and have lost it now. The modalities of inter-relation between states and the international orders in which they operate have changed, but states never enjoyed a stand-alone autonomy. The architecture of international institutions and practices created by the Anglo-Saxon victors after 1945 certainly helped to promote trade and investment, and, therefore, growth. Trade grew at roughly twice the rate of growth in output between 1950 and 1973 (9.4% average as against 5.3%).[35] The managed multi-lateralism or 'embedded liberalism'[36] of this period certainly benefited from having the USA as a dominant economic power to underwrite it and to secure it militarily.[37] However, US hegemony, trade openness, and monetary stability served to provide the conditions for other states' national autonomy in macro-economic policy—that is, steady growth in world trade and the national control of capital movements. Thus

[35] P. Hirst and G. Thompson (1996) *Globalisation in Question* (Cambridge: Polity, 1996), table 2.4.

[36] J.G. Ruggie, 'International Regimes, Transactions and Change: Embedded Liberalism in the Post-war Economic Order', in S.D. Krasner (ed.), *International Regimes* (Ithaca, NY: Cornell University Press, 1983), pp. 195–231.

[37] Much of the discussion of US 'hegemony' in this period seems to miss the point, that the activities of the hegemon provided the conditions for greater rather than less autonomy by the member states of the system. See I. Clark, *Globalisation and Fragmentation—International Relations in the Twentieth Century* (Oxford: Oxford University Press, 1997), and B. Eichengreen and P.B. Kenen, 'Managing the World Economy under the Bretton Woods System: An Overview', in P.B. Kenen (ed.), *Managing the World Economy: Fifty Years After Bretton Woods* Washington DC: Institute for International Economics, 1994, for relatively uncontentious overviews of the institutions of this period of managed multi-lateralism and their effects.

state capacity came in large measure from the governance mechanisms of the international system. Power could neither be located in actors nor in their context, but through a complex interaction between the two. Such power, moreover, could not be considered as quantitative, but as qualitative; its exercise depended considerably on appropriate economic doctrines, analysis and policy measures.

A similar point could be made for the first of the major trading blocs, the Common Market. By stabilizing key external variables the predecessors of the EU helped to provide the conditions for effective governance at the national level. Alan Milward[38] has termed it, 'the European rescue of the nation state'. The first phase of European economic cooperation was designed to promote political goals: to secure political cooperation and, therefore, to undermine the possibility of conflict between France and W. Germany. But by doing so, it strengthened national governance by enabling W. European states safely to focus on economic and social issues. Medium-sized nation states like France gained from the integration of European economies, thus making macro-economic national planning and technology policies more effective. Capacity to govern does not come from isolation, but from integration.

However, whilst the post-1945 architecture of the international economy involved substantial benefits for national states, it also involved constraints. Those states that were full members of the Bretton Woods monetary system had to contain negative external balances if they were to maintain exchange rate parity.[39] Britain laboured under a severe balance of payments constraint, and the stop–go policies required to respond to it limited economic growth. Even the US eventually found that the system imposed constraints as substantial dollar balances builtup abroad. In the late 1960s US policy faced a choice between domestic economic policy and monetary stability. It chose to avoid austerity, fighting the Vietnam War and promoting social expenditures by deficit financing, and thus eventually was forced to suspend the convertibility of the dollar. Even a hegemon is bound by the rules of the system it underwrites.

The present international architecture is different from and looser than that of 1945–73, but it is no less elaborate. It has focussed on different goals. A new international monetary system to replace Bretton Woods has not been a priority, chiefly because of the structurally opposed interests of the USA and Japan about the respective values of the dollar and the yen. Where the US has had a clear objective and has been supported by a cohort of OECD nations, as with the second GATT treaty, then effective international agreements have resulted and an international agency created to police them. The record in environmental regulation is patchier, but the combination of a treaty regime and an international agency is equally possible, given the political will. In the case of international investment, it is possible that a combination of detailed international regulatory supervision and the international pressure for appropriate practices in recipient countries in the developing world will have some effect. The Asian crisis has changed elite perceptions of the inherent

---

[38] A. Milward, *The European Rescue of the Nation State* (London: Routledge, 1994).

[39] For a good account of the constraints of the Bretton Woods system and policy within it as capital flows built-up, see E. Helleiner, *States and the Re-emergence of Global Finance: From Bretton Woods to the 1990s* (Ithaca, NY: Cornell University Press, 1994).

wisdom of financial markets and has shifted discussion toward the need for their regulation.[40]

If international governance is vital for effective functioning of the national state, then so too is the right kind of subnational governance. Major world cities, economic regions, and industrial districts are the key sites of wealth production within advanced national economies—increasingly these function well only if they are appropriately governed at the relevant level.[41] National states are only effective if they give sufficient autonomy to such subsidiary governments.

The question is how can this series of levels of governance, from the city-region to the trade bloc and beyond, be held together and integrated? Some say that it cannot, and that we are drifting toward a world in which power and territory no longer coincide, in which the state no longer holds the two together.[42] The notion of a New Middle Ages seems superficially plausible, but the problem is that governance cannot function effectively today unless there is a minimally coherent architecture of institutions and a division of labour between them that avoids significant gaps in governance. Modern economies are too complex and too interdependent to allow significant inconsistency and incapacity in forms of regulation, for then power and economic activity will be lost in the gaps. How can the international agencies be held accountable and yet world cities given a chance to manage their affairs? Only if the nation state acts as the political lynchpin between the different levels, holding them together by its practices of scrutiny and constitutional ordering. The democratic nation state of the advanced countries is the body that is capable, at least in principle, of accomplishing this coordination of governance between levels. In essence this coordination will only work if enough states appropriately practice the art of distributing power 'downwards' and 'upwards'. Downwards, by practising the art of constitutional ordering, such that the central state delegates and distributes appropriate powers to subsidiary governments and then actively cooperates with them. Upwards, by states conferring powers on supra-national bodies and treaty regimes by appropriate international agreements.

The state is the only body capable both of sustaining such international bodies and agreements, and of attempting to ensure that they do not escape from their remits and thus appropriate excessive power to themselves. The nation state has the advantage that it is a territorial body and an exclusive one, thus can it speak internationally for a territory and the people settled on it. As a democratic body,

---

[40] See G. Soros, 'The Capitalist Threat', *Atlantic Monthly*, Feb., 1997, pp. 45–58, on the dangers of instability in the international financial system and G. Soros, 'Avoiding a Breakdown: Asia's Crisis Demands a Rethink of International Regulation, *Financial Times*, 31 December, 1997; J. Sachs, 'IMF Orthodoxy isn't what Southeast Asia Needs' *International Herald Tribune* Nov. 4, 1997; J. Sachs, 'The IMF and the Asian Flu,' *The American Prospect*, March–April, 1998, pp. 16–21; and J. Stigliz, 'Restoring the Asian Miracle', *The Wall Street Journal*, February 3rd, 1998, on the nature of the East Asian crises and new strategies of international economic governance.

[41] On the central role of major cities in the world economy see S. Sassen, *Cities in a World Economy* (Thousand Oaks, CA: Pine Forge Press, 1994); and on the centrality of regional economics and industrial districts; C. Sabel, 'Flexible Specialisation and the Re-emergence of Regional Economies' in P. Hirst and J. Zeitlin (eds.), *Reversing Industrial Decline* (Oxford: Berg,1989). P. Krugman, 'The Localisation of the World Economy' in Krugman (ed.), *Pop Internationalism* (Cambridge, MA: MIT Press, 1996) 'rediscovers' regional economies for himself, apparently blind to the vast amount of work on this topic in several countries. However, the fact that a mainstream economist has turned his attention to the issue shows how far it has become salient.

[42] P. Cerny, 'Globalisation, Fragmentation and the Governance Gap: Towards a New Medievalism in World Politics' mimeo, 1997; A. Minc, *Le Nouveau Moyen Age*, Paris: Gallimard, 1993.

obedient to the rule of law, it can creditably commit its people and successor governments to certain obligations. States, if they are stably democratic, can thus provide the fundamental legitimacy for the provisions of international agreements and for supra-national agencies. That is, such entities are underwritten by a substantial number of states that are themselves legitimate. Without this, such entities could neither function effectively nor be held to account at all. Control and accountability exercised by nation states at the international level are difficult, but that is the best political supervision we are likely to get, and it can be improved. Democracy, as it is understood in nation states, is not possible beyond them; international democratic control has to be indirect, through the actions of democratic states.[43]

Only states have the capacity to monitor international agencies, although they may be hassled to do it better by NGOs. Only if they are legitimated by many states can such agencies credibly monitor individual states and hold them to account. This mutual monitoring is still relatively underdeveloped, but it is becoming crucial as states and international agencies interact with increasing frequency in the process of governing a world that is neither fully globalized by autonomous international market forces nor capable of effective management at the national level alone. The IMF and the World Bank, for example, have mainly dealt with governments that are weakly legitimate and in economic trouble, like those in Sub-Saharan Africa. However, when the IMF interacts with new democracies with impressive records of industrialization, like South Korea, it will need to be credible, and, if it is not, and provokes a nationalist backlash, then the Western governments that underwrite it will find themselves discredited too. Again, when the WTO polices the domestic regulations in mature democracies to determine whether they are acting to restrain trade, it will need to get the politics right as well as the technocratic detail. Thus mutual legitimating and monitoring between states and supra-national agencies will have to evolve together. Legitimacy and governance capacity are related, even if the relationship is very far from that described in the classic notion of a political community. Power at the level of international governance is thus an emergent property of complex interactions, and is located neither exclusively in the actors nor exclusively in the context of their actions.

Increasingly, the new treaties and agreements are not like the old diplomacy of the Great Powers. Treaties like Maastricht or GATT 2 are compacts between states that establish ongoing relationships between them which redistribute power into new domains. The Treaty of Maastricht makes, for example, all citizens of member states common economic citizens of the European Union. The successful conclusion of the Uruguay Round of GATT means that the WTO has the power to receive petitions from those whose interests have been harmed by trade-restraining and trade-related measures and to enforce the terms of the Treaty and to constrain member states. Typically, the bodies thus established are quasi polities, that is, they

---

[43] Clearly this argument cuts across David Held's advocacy of 'cosmopolitan democracy', D. Held, *Democracy and the Global Order* (Cambridge: Polity, 1995). Whilst one may sympathize with his objectives, the scope for such measures is limited. If it is not channelled through the indirect agency of nation states, democracy has almost no purchase at the international level. Moreover, citizens continue to see states as the primary sources of loyalty and legitimation, even in such developed semi-polities as the EU. For a longer version of the account of the interaction of national and international governance advanced here, see Hirst and Thompson, *Globalisation in Question* (Cambridge: Polity, 1996), chs. 6–8.

are ongoing associations of states with collective decision procedures, but they are specific in scope and their powers are defined by treaty. They could not exist without the ongoing compliance on the part of and the legitimacy provided by states. Such quasi polities are halfway between the old international relations, external exchanges between states, and the notion of the state as a political community. These bodies vary from the strictly limited, like the International Whaling Commission, to the multi-dimensional, like the EU. But they could not work without the cooperation of states, and, they do not diminish the power of states, in the sense of their capacity for effective governance.

Power within the new emerging international system is thus closer to how Parsons conceived power, than as in the classic view, as an already given quantum of capacity that decides the outcomes of exchanges between agents. The powers that emerge in the system derive from, and are conditions for, ongoing relations between units in a system of collective action, that have some ability to maintain the relationship by monitoring and sanctioning one another. It is also capable of being productive in ways somewhat like those Foucault envisaged, boosting the total governance capacity available in the international system by mutual surveillance and the supervising of activities between states and supra-national bodies.

Lastly, the scope of international law has increased vastly since 1939. Strange[44] points out that companies have increasingly short-circuited national legal systems, and created a private international commercial law based on arbitration. Carr was right to deride the idea that it was possible to use international law to arbitrate inter-state differences in the conditions of bitter international rivalry of the 1930s. Changing values on the part of states in the international system and a growing number of states committed domestically to the rule of law means that the population of states that routinely obey international norms and are willing to settle disputes by arbitration has reached the point where such methods are increasingly effective. Of course, states often refuse courts' decisions and the states in question are often hardly marginal or of pariah states, for example, the case in the US refusal to accept the judgement of the International Court of Justice of liability for mining the sea off Nicaragua. But international law has come closer to the private law analogies with civil contracts that Lauterpacht[45] argued, much to Carr's scepticism. A large enough population of law-abiding states and a relatively stable international environment clearly change the terms of the relationship between force and law in the international arena.

Thus both the discourses and the phenomena of power have changed radically since Carr wrote *The Twenty Years' Crisis*. The international system, at least between the advanced countries and the most stable of the newly industrializing countries, is less committed to using force to settle disputes and has denser modalities of economic governance. The nation state has not declined or become functionless in the way that Carr feared and numerous commentators since have claimed. It has, however, changed its role radically and become a key part of a division of labour in governance. This change and the participation of states in quasi polities have changed the modalities and the meaning of power.

---

[44] S. Strange, *The Retreat of the State—The Diffusion of Power in the World Economy* (Cambridge: Cambridge University Press, 1996), p. 17.

[45] H. Lauterpacht, *Private Law Sources and Analogies of International Law* (London: Longmans Green and Co., 1927).

Nationalism and after

JAN JINDY PETTMAN

Until recently, International Relations (IR) paid remarkably little attention to identities, including its own. IR called up the nation-state, while displaying very little interest in either nation or state, or the meaning(s) of the hyphen in between. Assuming state-nations removed from view the contested politics of identity and boundary making within the state. This article seeks to make these politics visible. It considers, first, why IR might have missed nationalism, and then reviews different conceptions of nation. It analyses the gendered and global politics of nationalism, and concludes with the prospect and possibility of the nation in new transnational times.

It is surprising that nationalism has been so peripheral a concern to International Relations (IR). The discipline was founded in 1919 with an intellectual brief to seek understanding of the causes of war, in the shadow of World War 1 and in a time of validation and saliency of the principle of national self-determination, especially for Woodrow Wilson and to the League of Nations. The rise of virulent nationalisms through the 1930s, most dramatically nazism and fascism, reconfigured international relations and ushered in another extraordinarily violent world war. In the postwar decades, anticolonial movements came to power and the numbers of states multiplied. Modernization theories that analysed their attempts at nation-building were largely written out of IR, into comparative government or development studies.[1]

IR's lack of curiosity about different political identities, including nationalism, stems in part from the way the discipline constituted itself in relation to the in-between of states. The predominant identity story became that of sovereignty, assuming a coincidence of authority, territory, population and identity, and ascribing primary loyalty through citizenship to the state. It also grounded identity within bounded territorial limits, tying people to place. The territorializing logic and disciplinary power of the state[2] have also bounded IR as a discipline.

The construction of unitary and separate states was taken further by the tendency to represent states as actors, as purposive individuals, investing the state with an identity.[3] This enabled an apparently clear distinction between the inside and the outside of states, between 'domestic' and international politics, and between order

---

[1] There is a puzzle here about why IR so relentlessly evacuated dimensions and relations that seem essential to understanding world politics. Indeed, a number of recent papers and articles begin, as this one does, with 'until recently, IR ignored (race, culture, identity, ethnicity, migration, colonization, gender . . .).

[2] Chris Farrands 'Society, Modernity and Social Change: Approaches to Nationalism and Identity', in Jill Krause and Neil Renwick (eds.), *Identities in International Relations* (Basington: Macmillan, 1996).

[3] Jill Krause, 'Gendered Identities in International Relations', in Krause and Renwick, *Identities*.

within and anarchy beyond. Nationalism, on the other hand, can constitute a powerful force for disorder both within states and in inter-state relations.

IR's dominant practice of conflating nation and state homogenizes identities within states and sharply marks differences along state boundaries. In the process it obscures the politics of identity, including those which constitute 'the people' and endow the state with authority as their representative. So ways of interrogating nationalisms, for example by asking whose nation? whose state? and how do nation and state articulate in any particular case? are simply unavailable. As a result, nationalism studies remained largely the preserve of historians, sociologists and regional specialists.

Some IR scholars, including some called 'realist', have queried nationalism. Liberal IR, in its English manifestations,[4] paid some attention to civil society, and civic nationalism. E.H. Carr's review of nationalism written towards the end of World War 2 demarcated the history of international relations into phases, with reference to very different constructions of nation. The first identified the monarch and the nation. The second was ushered in by the French Revolution and the Congress of Vienna, in the form of liberal democracy, laissez-faire and free immigration. The third was shaping from 1870, through further democratization and the socialization of the nation, as 'the masses' expected their national governments to assume responsibility for their welfare. It 'climaxed' through 1914 to World War 2, and proved both the danger and the moral bankruptcy of nationalism. Carr speculated on postwar developments necessary to allow 'Europe and the world' to 'recover their balance in the *aftermath* of the age of nationalism'[5] (my emphasis). His focus on the US–European world failed to take account of anticolonial movements which would soon multiply the numbers and diversify the nature of states. But in the postwar years, the primary focus for International Relations became the titian confrontation between the West and the Soviet Union, and the nation-state attracted little attention in itself. IR could still be chided for its 'scant attention' to nationalism well into the 1990s.[6]

Griffiths and Sullivan observe that '[w]ith few exceptions, International Relations is the study of what happens *outside* states after they form'.[7] This might in part be explained by disciplinary ambivalence towards nationalism. It is a crucial concept in IR, authorizing state sovereignty and assisting the resolution of potential conflicts of obligation and affiliation by asserting the primacy of loyalty to the particular state rather than to human kind—especially important when the issue becomes that of violence against others. But there remains a fundamental contradiction between the Westphalian normalization of state sovereignty and the potentially explosive claims of national self-determination.[8]

Losing its national component by default, IR's state-centrism assumed that 'state=nation'.[9] In the process, the discipline disengaged from 'probably the most

---

[4] James Mayall, *Nationalism and International Relations* (Cambridge University Press, 1990); Martin Griffiths and Michael Sullivan, 'Nationalism and International Relations Theory', *Australian Journal of Politics and History*, 43 (1997), pp. 53–66.

[5] E.H. Carr, *Nationalism and After* (London: Macmillan, 1945), p. 73.

[6] James Mayall, 'Nationalism in the Study of International Relations', in A.J.R. Groom and Margot Light (eds.), *Contemporary International Relations: a Guide to Theory* (London: Pinter, 1994), p. 182.

[7] 'Nationalism', p. 54.

[8] Griffiths and Sullivan, 'Nationalism'.

[9] Roger Tooze, 'Prologue' in Krause and Renwick, p. xvii.

explosive force shaping domestic and global constitutional orders at the end of the twentieth century'.[10] It is this disengagement, and more broadly IR's lack of attention to political identifications, collective identities and 'culture', that contributed to the discipline's failure to predict, or comprehend, the end of the Cold War. Initially met with triumphantism, as the victory of the West, capitalism and democracy, the subsequent 'turbulence' and perceived upsurge of nationalism and other exclusivist identity movements and conflicts have unsettled this confidence.[11] In the process, they have forced questions of nation and identity into disciplinary view.

These developments have led to much disciplinary soul-searching, and prompted searches for more persuasive ways of engaging with the post-Cold War world. Calls for 'better accounts of the world' were propelled, too, by new critical challenges from within the discipline, and among those close by, including poststructuralists, postcolonialists and feminists (sometimes the same), whose approaches offered more productive ways of thinking about collective identifications and contemporary identity conflicts.[12] Nationalism has become more visible in IR, bringing with it, at times, other ways of writing the nation. *Millennium*'s 1991 special issue 'Reimagining the Nation' marked the first of a number of special issues on nationalism.[13] New scholarly interest in nationalism beyond IR included special issues in feminist journals,[14] and a spate of new journals, including *Nations and Nationalism* (1995), *Nationalism and Ethnic Politics* (1995), and on rather different intellectual terrain *Identities: Global Studies in Culture and Power* (1994) and *Social Identities* (1995).

Making the nation

Nationalism drives forms of political mobilization around the idea of and identification with 'the nation'. The nation is figured, often, as ancient, or at least as an unproblematic birth identity. Foundation myths tell of common origins or common sufferings, including resistance to colonization or other forms of domination.[15] Some conspicuously recent nationalisms, for example settler state nationalisms, drew initially on kin and histories from other places, but lately stress common

---

[10] Yosef Lapid and Friedrich Kratochwil, 'Revisiting the "National": Towards an Identity Agenda in Neorealism?', in Lapid and Kratochwil (eds.), *The Return of Culture and Identity in IR Theory* (Boulder: Lynne Rienner, 1996), p. 105.

[11] James Rosenau, *Turbulence in World Politics: a Theory of Change and Continuity* (Princeton: Princeton University Press, 1990). Note the frequency with which IR and other writings characterize contemporary nationalism in terms of 'upsurge'. Other popular descriptors include resurgent, elusive, paradox, surprising, pervasive . . . .

[12] Lapid and Kratochwil, *The Return*; Krause and Renwick, *Identities*; Geoff Eley and Ronald Grigor Suny (eds.), *Becoming National: A Reader* (New York: Oxford University Press, 1996); Phillip Darby (ed.), *On the Edge of International Relations: Postcolonialism, Gender & Dependency* (London: Pinter, 1997); and numerous articles within *Millennium* and *Alternatives* especially.

[13] *Millennium*, 20/3 (1991); see also *Millennium*, 22, 3 (1993), special issue on Culture and International Relations.

[14] For example, 'Nationalisms and National Identities', *Feminist Review*, 44 (1993); 'Gender, Nationalisms and National Identities', *Gender and History*, 5, 2 (1993).

[15] Recalling Renan's observation that 'Where national memories are concerned, griefs are of more value than triumphs, for they impose duties, and require a common effort', in Ely and Suny, *Becoming National*, p. 53.)

destiny and shared citizenship,[16] though not without challenge from those committed to more exclusivist notions of belonging.

Older forms of political identity are not necessarily eclipsed by nationalism, and
some of these are incorporated into national stories or as national markers. But
most scholars of nationalism agree that it is a modern political identity. In perhaps
nationalism's most famous text,[17] Benedict Anderson traces its emergence first
among creole (white) Americans resisting their unequal treatment by metropoles. It
spread in Europe from the French Revolution, in popular and in reactive state
'official' nationalisms. More recently, it has globalized through the independence of
states along the old colonial boundary lines. This stark outline is enough to suggest
that colonization, anti-colonialism and post-colonialism are crucial ingredients in
the study of nationalism, and indeed of international relations more generally.[18] So
too are the massive transformations associated with the rise of industrial capitalism
and new communications technologies; and the complex politics of state formation
and consolidation that tapped into or sought to contain nationalist passions. (It may
be no accident, then, that the current 'upsurge' of nationalist movements and
violence coincides with another series of dramatic transformations, including those
referred to in the short-hand globalization.)

One of the paradoxes of nationalism is that an identity frequently celebrated and
authenticated through reference to the past is judged in scholarship to be modern;
an identity naturalized and spoken of as inherited is judged invented, constructed,
imagined;[19] though nationalism does use cultural and memory resources to boost its
claims and normalize its affiliations. Materialists who point to uneven development
or to class articulations with nationalism focus, as well, on the materialization of
nationalism in representations and associations, in, for example, 'fictive ethnicity'.[20]
Some, while conceding that nationalism is a modern political identity, argue for
continuity or connections with pre-national forms. So Anthony Smith argues for a
much longer historical trajectory, and recalls 'ethnies' that inform nationalisms[21]
(though ethnies, too, were, presumably constructed, often in state or other authority
interventions and consolidations).

Prasenjit Duara argues that nationalism is not a new type of identity or mode of
consciousness. He usefully interrogates the relationship between nationalism and the
nation-state, and argues that '[w]hat was new was the global *institutional* revolution
. . . which produced its own extremely powerful representations of the nation-
state'.[22] What was new, and powerful, was the vocabulary and the world system of
nation-states, which legitimized state nationalisms, recognizing the state as primary

---

[16] Nira Yuval-Davis and Daiva Stasilius (eds.), *Unsettling Settler Societies* (London: Sage, 1995).
[17] Benedict Anderson, *Imagined Communities: Reflections on the Origin and Spread of Nationalism*
(London: Verso, 1991).
[18] Darby, *On the Edge*; the often-noted dominance of Anglo-North American centres and looking
positions in IR may be an explanation here. See Robert Crawford and Daryll Jarvis (eds.), *International
Relations: Still an American Social Science?* (New York: St Martin's Press, forthcoming).
[19] Ernest Gellner, *Nations and Nationalism* (Oxford: Basil Blackwell, 1983); Anderson, *Imagined
Communities*.
[20] Etienne Balibar, 'The Nation Form: History and Ideology', in Etienne Balibar and Immanuel
Wallerstein, *Race, Nation, Class: Ambiguous Identities* (London: Verso, 1991); see also Tom Nairn,
The Breakup of Britain (London: Verso, 1977).
[21] Anthony Smith, 'Gastronomy or Geology? The role of Nationalism in the Reconstruction of Nations',
Nations and Nationalism, 1 (1995), pp. 3–24.
[22] Prasenjit Duara, *Rescuing History from the Nation* (Chicago: University of Chicago Press, 1995), p. 9.

loyalty-claimant and identity-enforcer. This internationally sanctioned presumption of a coincidence of consent, authority and affiliation brings us back to sovereignty in its contemporary, nation-state form. Thus the system of states which IR has long taken as its field privileges and participates in the production of identity along territorially based and bounded state lines. In the process, the state comes to speak for, represent, and replace 'the people'. So the nation-state returns, but within a dynamic international context, and in such a way as to unsettle the hyphen between the nation and the state. This in turn draws our attention to the disciplinary power of the state and its implication, singly and within international concert, in the construction of its subject(s).

National stories

Nationalism, then, depends on history, but not in any innocent or predetermined way. Ernest Renan in his 1882 lecture 'What is a Nation?' observed that 'It is good for everyone to know how to forget'.[23] This theme is taken up in more recent writings on nationalism, tracing a politics of forgetting and remembering that help constitutes the national political subject. Duaru argues (with particular reference to China) that 'national history secures for the contested and contingent nation the false unity of a self-same, national subject evolving through time'.[24] Nationalism 'marks the site where different representations of the nation contest and negotiate with each other'.[25] History (capital H) produces the nation. Nationalism seeks to occupy a privileged position as the 'master identity', even as it competes with and interacts with both other identities, and other histories which suggest other readings of the nation. Sanjay Seth, writing of India, concurs: 'for most nationalisms "history" has been that space where national identity is formed and/or found'.[26]

States never succeed in completely eliminating or even silencing other nationalisms or more localized identities (though of course states are not singular either). Where they cannot defeat other imaginings, state and dominant nationalist elites seek to contain or deflect them. These moves might include more benign or inclusive constructions of the nation, like multiculturalism, recognizing difference even as it is depoliticized and culturalized. Struggles over history, about how and what to remember, are evident in contemporary 'culture wars', over history textbook writing, and so-called political correctness. They connect in fascinating ways with debates about collective identity and collective guilt, or responsibility.[27]

These contests over history and memory provide us with rich material for analysing the discursive construction of the nation, and its narration.[28] Making the nation entails 'hard ideological labour, careful propaganda, and a creative imagination'.[29]

---

[23] Quoted in Eley and Suny, *Becoming National*, p. 49.
[24] *Becoming National*, p. 4.
[25] *Becoming National*, p. 8.
[26] Sanjay Seth, 'Nationalism, National Identity and "History": Nehru's Search for India', *Thesis Eleven*, No. 32 (1992), p. 37.
[27] Note the current outbreak of apologies or demands for same.
[28] Homi Bhabha, 'DissemiNation: Time, Narrative and the Margins of the Modern Nation', in Homi Bhabha (ed.), *Nation and Narration* (London: Routledge, 1990).
[29] Eley and Suny, *Becoming National*, p. 7.

The complex politics of recognition and representation can be traced through the diverse cultural politics of disaffected or subordinated intellectuals, and the productive power of state identity practices. Cultural studies writers have traced the formation of national publics through literature, popular culture, mass education and communications, including through various state techniques of citizen manufacture, making the people.

Looking within the state, however, reveals not *the* people, but many people, many different political identities, none of which are ever finally or securely made. Nations, like states, are never complete—rather they are radically incomplete, plural, filled with tensions and conflicts. The nation is always in process, and in contest. Its articulation is not only 'imagined', but through imagining is materialized in contingent and contradictory ways.

Anderson gave impetus to understandings of the nation as imagined, asserting that nations 'are to be distinguished not by their falsity/genuineness, but by the style in which they are imagined'.[30] Gathering cultural studies, postcolonial and feminist writings within their collection 'On Becoming National', Eley and Suny direct attention towards 'how the nation is *represented*, how its aspirations are *authorized*, and how its origins and claims are *narrated*'.[31] Such de/constructions open up space to interrogate nationalisms over time and place. Exploring nationalism in various historical and particular contexts, we discover the diversity of nationalism*s*, of political projects which claim 'the nation'. It becomes clear that there is, indeed, 'no nationalism in general'.[32] We obverve that

nationalism is not a monolithic phenomenon to be deemed entirely good or entirely bad; nationalism is a contradictory discourse and its internal contradictions need to be unpacked in their historical specificity. The historical agency of nationalism has been sometimes hegemonic though often merely dominant, sometimes emancipatory though often repressive, sometimes progressive though often traditional and reactionary.[33]

The nation and its others

There is nothing fixed or inevitable in any one construction of the nation, in the boundaries drawn between those who belong and those outside, or in the consequences of inclusion or exclusion, in terms of privilege or penalty, safety or danger. There are, however, characteristics intrinsic to becoming national, some of which attach to the politics of identification more generally. Nationalism, like all political identities, is relational. It is about identity *and* difference; inclusion *and* exclusion. Its boundary making produces us *and* them; making 'the people' and simultaneously making the others, outsiders, strangers, immigrants . . . .[34] The nation-people are defined by their difference from those who do not belong, who are not part of the collective 'we'.

[30] *Imagined Communities*, p. 6.
[31] *Becoming National*, p. 24.
[32] Andrew Parker *et al.* (eds.), *Nationalism and Sexualities* (London: Routledge, 1992), p. 3.
[33] R. Radhakrishnan 'Nationalism, Gender and Narrative', in Parker (ed.), *Nationalism and Sexualities*, p. 82.
[34] Adam Lerner, 'Transcendence of the ImagiNation', International Studies Association conference paper, Vancouver, 1991.

Adam Lerner invites us to interrogate nationalism by asking who does the nation exclude?[35] Often in IR, it is assumed that the nation is defined against other nations. However, through earlier national times in Europe that definition was just as often one of the national people against those who were seen to be without nation, constituted as races, or natives for example.[36] Being English, or British, was constituted within an Empire frame. Contemporary European reactive nationalisms or reethnicizations now close against unwanted 'strangers within'. 'The immigrant' becomes code for black or Asian in the UK, for North African or Muslim in France, for Turk in Germany, for Asian in Australia; and so the nation is racialized as white. Even those born in the state and/or accorded formal citizenship occupy a kind of ambiguous nationality or suspect citizenship.[37] Similar processes of ethnic closure, often mobilising cultural–religious markers, are visible elsewhere, for example in BJP reconstructions of India as Hindu.[38]

Nationalist politics of belonging and boundary defence deploy complex politics of representation and difference. There is no automatic association of difference with danger, or inferiority, although there are examples aplenty of these associations currently, some with deadly effect. Ambivalence may abound, mixing pleasure and danger, fear and desire. Or difference may be a more constructive space, in which it is possible to begin to take account and to converse.[39]

But these days nationalism has a reputation as being dangerous. What makes nationalist politics and passions so powerful and potentially destructive is the way in which the boundaries of belonging can become the limits of the moral community, beyond which the use of organized violence can become thinkable, indeed do-able.[40] There is a fatal but by no means inevitable process here in the slide from multiple identities, including awareness of or identification with the nation, to a primary identification with the nation, to a readiness to use or condone violence in the name of the nation.

Nationalism enables the politics of identity making and boundary maintenance; the limits of the national community both needing and often fearing its others. This is an unstable mix, necessitating the hard ideological and imaginative work referred to earlier. It also associates nationalism with violence, and with the peculiar power of the nation as a 'community of life and death'.[41]

---

[35] Lerner, 'Transcendence'.

[36] Richard Handler and Daniel A. Segal, 'Nations, Colonies and Metropoles', *Social Analysis*, No. 33 (1993), p. 3. For articulations between nation and race, see Roxanne Lynne Doty, 'The Bounds of "Race" in International Relations', *Millennium*, 22 (1993), pp. 443–62; Avtar Brah, 'Re-framing Europe Engendering Racisms, Ethnicities and Nationalisms in Contemporary Western Europe', *Feminist Review*, No. 45 (1993), pp. 9–29; Kathryn Manzo, *Creative Boundaries: The Politics of Race and Nation* (Boulder: Lynne Reinner, 1996).

[37] Balibar, 'The Nation Form'; Roxanne Lynn Doty, 'Immigration and National Identity: Constructing the Nation', *Review of International Studies*, 22 (1996), pp. 235–55; Jan Jindy Pettman, 'Second Class Citizens? Nationalism, Identity and Difference in Australia', in Barbara Sullivan and Gillian Whitehouse (eds.), *Governing Gender: Sex, Politics and Citizenship in the 1990s* (Sydney: University of New South Wales, 1996).

[38] Shcheta Mazumdar, 'Women on the March: Right-wing Mobilization in Contemporary India', *Feminist Review*, No. 49 (1995), pp. 75–92; Javeed Alam, 'What Kind of Nation are We?', *Economic and Political Weekly*, June 22, 1996, pp. 1612–20.

[39] Hence the possibility of Australia as a 'multicultural nation'.

[40] I note 'organized' violence because the most common form of violence, within communities, is often 'domestic' violence, usually men against women with whom they are or have been living. This is ironic in view of men's construction as protectors of 'their' women, and of IR's representation of the inside as safe.

[41] Gopal Balakrishnan, 'The National Imagination', *New Left Review*, No. 211 (1995), p. 67.

De/constructivist explanations of nationalism leave us wondering why people might kill or die for a nation that is invented, or in Anderson's question 'why should so many be prepared to kill or die for a nation their grandparents had never heard of?'[42] IR's repertoire of political subjects seems an inadequate explanation. Sovereign man, political man and economic man is individual, abstract, competitive, calculating; free of the links and burdens of collectivity or care. Yet nationalism calls forth a different kind of man, and affective forms of political affiliation.

The close associations between nationalism and war makes IR's neglect of nationalism strange, for war is in a sense where the discipline began. Images of nationalism often cohere around a motif of sacrifice, and unquestioning obedience. 'My country right or wrong' removes the possibility of questioning the politics or ethics of foreign policy, and disguises the political investments of the state. The nation appears above politics, in the same way that it appears beyond history. The ultimate sacrifice is being prepared to lay down one's life for one's country, or its womenandchildren,[43] or one's mates. Images of blood, bond, love, and pain preside. Ross Poole finds in the language of nationalism and war, of care and self-sacrifice, 'not so much the construction of a new and virulent form of masculinity, as the recovery for masculine identity, of that relational form of identity constituted within the family. It is, in this sense, the return of the feminine'.[44] These emotional and affective relations are, however, contained within disciplining heterosexist militarism and backed by the coercive power of the prerogative state.

Such violence is powerfully endorsed through conceptions of sovereignty which grant to states the monopoly of the legitimate uses of violence, and the right to decide when such use is indeed justified. Bhikhu Parekh notes the 'strange process of mutation in which authority is *derived* from individuals . . . and *exercised* not just over them but over the territory'.[45] The state/community produces identity, constituting its members as citizens and as subjects 'in both of Foucault's senses of "subjection"—subject of and subjected to the nation'.[46] In this sense, foreign policy, too, constitutes the nation, its identity and its interest.[47] The binary identity: difference produces particular kinds of power relations, international relations, foreign policy, defence, and security.

State power and international norms around sovereignty authorize violence. This authority is all the more powerful when co-joined with the moral authority and appeal of the nation. Jean Elshtain suggests that 'Societies are, in some sense, the "sum total" of their war stories'.[48] These stories forge connections and evoke a language of blood, kin, home. They facilitate personal identification with the collective body and will. Some surmise in this men's search for meaning, intimacy and creativity; others, envy of women's birth-giving capacity.[49] Others return to Waltz's

[42] *Imagined Communities.*
[43] Cynthia Enloe, 'The Gulf Crisis: Making Feminist Sense of It', *Pacific Research*, November 1990, p. 3
[44] 'Gender and National Identity', *Intervention*, No. 19, 1985, p. 78; Jan Jindy Pettman, *Worlding Women: a Feminist International Politics* (London, Routledge, 1996), p. 50.
[45] Bhikhu Parekh, 'Ethnocentricity of the Nationalist Discourse', *Nations and Nationalism*, 1 (1995), p. 27.
[46] Stuart Hall, 'Culture, Community, Nation', *Cultural Studies*, 7, 3 (1993), p. 355.
[47] David Campbell, *Writing Security: United States' Foreign Policy and the Politics of Identity* (Manchester University Press, 1992).
[48] *Women and War* (New York: Basic Books, 1987), p. 166.
[49] Marilyn Lake, 'Mission Impossible: How Men Gave Birth to the Australian Nation', *Gender and History*, 4, 3 (1993), pp. 377–86.

first image, finding malignancy, irrational impulses, and blood lusts, in human nature or men's aggressive instincts. Still others seek more psychocultural understandings, for example deploying Lacanian psychoanalysis to processes underlying collective identifications and especially those fantasy structures that reward violence against others.[50]

The intensity of nationalism is forged in the struggle itself. Nationalism is the product as much as the cause of conflict, mobilization and terror. So the wars in the former Yugoslavia 'produced' new nationalist players and compulsory nationality. They also produced a logic of their own, whereby despite small and in recent decades largely tolerable differences between Serbs and Croats, these differences became worth dying for '*because* someone will kill you for them'.[51]

The nation can evoke commitment and emotion, love and hate, violence and sacrifice in 'ordinary' people, including those who would never consider using violence in their personal relations or home place. Naturalizing the call to violence in the name of the nation, then, requires an identification that transcends the everyday. For some, a possible explanation lies in Anderson's observation that nationalism is less an ideology, than something akin to religion.[52] But beyond such 'collective reenchantment' lies the family, and through family, ideas of overcoming death through continuity.[53] In family, too, are located the demands of kin and blood.

The language of nation assumes connectedness to the body politic, and to a collectivity which preceded and will survive any individual life. It is infused with domestic and family imagery, of emotion, intimacy, love and generosity. It both reproduces and reflects understandings of gender difference and gendered obligations and roles. Interrogating nationalism requires attention to the articulation between the gendered discourse of the nation, and gender relations.[54]

Gender and nation

The nation is usually imagined as female, the state as male, delivering particular, and gendered, expectations and demands upon the citizen-kin.

The nation as woman generates representations of the nation as under threat and sexual danger, and construes invasion or colonization as male heterosexual rape. In the national gender script, 'the rape of Kuwait' is typical—figuring a male perpetrator, a female or feminized victim, and a male hero. It also constitutes national

---

[50] Renata Salecl, *The Spirit of Freedom: Psychoanalysis and Feminism after the Fall of Socialism* (London: Routlegde, 1994); Alan Finlayson, 'Psychology, Psychoanalysis and theories of Nationalism', *Nations and Nationalism*, 4, 2 (1998), pp. 145–62.

[51] Michael Ignatieff, 'Nationalism and the Narcissism of Minor Differences', *Queen's Quarterly*, No. 102, 1996, p. 19; see also Slavenka Drakulic, *Balkan Express: Fragments from the Other Side of War* (London: Hutchinson, 1993).

[52] Adam Lerner, 'Transcendence of the Nation: National Identity and the Terrain of the Divine', *Millennium*, 20 (1991), pp. 407–27.

[53] 'National Imagination'.

[54] Nira Yuval-Davis, *Gender and Nation* (London: Sage, 1997), p. 39; see also 'Introduction', Kumkum Sangari and Sudesh Vaid (eds.), *Recasting Women in India: Essays in Colonial History* (New Brunswick: Rutgers University Press, 1990); Pettman, *Worlding Women*; Jill Steans, *Gender and International Relations* (Cambridge: Polity Press, 1998).

agency as masculine, so that 'women are the *symbol* of the nation, men its *agents*, regardless of the role women [and men] actually play in the nation'.[55]

There are now numerous studies on the gendered discourse of nationalism, and of the particular constructions of desirable masculinity and femininity required for the nation. Glenda Sluga, for example, remarks that in different historical contexts 'gendered forms of national identification and masculinist definitions of the body politic and the national citizen were mutually reinforcing'.[56] She traces the emergence of both the nation and the bourgeois public sphere through nineteenth century France, and explains the processes whereby citizenship is consolidated as masculine (including through women's legal exclusion until 1944). Analogies between nations and bodies made definitions of gender and sexual identity 'crucial to the imagining of national communities and national selves'.[57]

Gender relations constitute identities and are constituted through constructions of nation. The close association between masculinity, nationalism and militarism cohere around notions of honour, patriotism, and cowardice. The citizen soldier is (still usually seen to be) male.[58] The nation/military is a passionate brotherhood, a 'virile fraternity'.[59] Proving manhood and proving/defending nation are closely entwined. The birth of the nation is through the blooding of young men.

Men have particular national obligations, including as protectors of women, children, land and home. The nation's women have obligations too. There are complex moves which take us from the nation as woman, to the nation's women, to the familiar construction of women as mothers of the nation.[60] This last recognizes that the physical reproduction of the collectivity is women's business, but also requires determining which children can be recognised as belonging within the collectivity. National attention to women as reproducers might be an attempt to seek strength in numbers, or to utilize eugenic aspirations to 'improve the stock'. Especially in times of mobilized nationalism, there is pressure on women to have the right children, by the right men. Women's national obligations in reproducing the nation rest on their presumed, and often actual, responsibilities for children's upbringing and cultural transmission, as well as their care of the nation's men and households more generally.

Women also function as symbols of difference and markers of the boundaries of national and other political communities—hence the significance attached to women's clothing, and associations, especially their relations with 'other' men. Their symbolic significance and construction as national dependents or possessions can make them especially vulnerable to policing by in-group men, and to violence directed towards them as a means of 'getting at' their men. The systematic nature of

---

[55] *Feminist Review*, Editorial, No. 44, 1993, p. 1.
[56] Glenda Sluga, 'Identity, Gender, and the History of European Nations and Nationalism', *Nations and Nationalism*, 4 (1998), p. 87; see also Joane Nagel, 'Masculinity and Nationalism: Gender and Sexuality in the Making of Nations', *Ethnic and Racial Studies*, 21 (1998), pp. 242–69.
[57] Sluga, 'Identity, Gender', p. 101.
[58] Note the man it takes to be a good military man—not gay, and not a woman; Pettman, *Worlding Women*, ch. 5.
[59] Parker, *Nationalism and Sexualities*, p. 6.
[60] 'Nationalist wombs', Cynthia Enloe, *Bananas, Beaches and Bases: Making Feminist Sense of International Politics* (London: Pandora, 1990), p. 54; see also V. Spike Peterson, 'The Politics of Identity and Gendered Nationalism', in Laura Neack, Patrick J. Haney and Leanne AK Hey (eds.), *Foreign Policy Analysis: Continuity and Change in its Second-Generation* (Englewood Cliffs, NJ: Prentice Hall, 1995); Pettman, *Worlding Women*; Yuval-Davis, *Gender and Nation*.

mass war rape includes the objective of demonstrating enemy men's failure as protectors, as well as the violation of national women to disrupt the reproduction of the collectivity—hence the extraordinary identity of 'enemy babies'.[61]

Women are forever caught between the symbolic uses different national projects make of them, and the ways in which actual women experience, engage with or resist nationalism.[62] Women are implicated in their collectivity's use of violence, so often perpetrated in their name, or the collective womenandchildren that underlines their dependence and object status in the national project. But many women over place and time have supported nationalist movements and participated in wars and other forms of national violence. While some feminists and peace women may organize on the basis of a transnational identification with and as 'women', the national claim usually trumps gender (and class). It also makes organizing as feminists across national boundaries in times of more exclusivist and aggressive nationalisms extremely difficult.[63]

While feminists and nationalists may have difficult relations, they are not necessarily entirely opposed. Asian and Middle East anticolonial nationalisms grew through the nineteenth and early twentieth centuries, appropriating western political discourse around democracy and self-determination and reworking these through local traditions of political thought and to local political contingencies.[64] Their definition of nationalism against the West was located in difference, itself associated with the cultural or domestic sphere imagined beyond western control. In the process, women and gender relations became symbols of difference, and objects of nationalist concerns. Modernizing nationalist elites often supported women's education and improved status as part of national emancipation, though seeking a modern but not a western woman. More conservative nationalists deployed culture and tradition to defend women's difference, and their own national–cultural projects. 'Tradition' became the site on which both the nation and the rights of women were contested.[65]

Recently, many nationalist movements, both state seeking and state sanctioned, have taken more exclusivist turns, and enforced restrictive notions of woman in the name of nation.[66] Other mobilized identity movements deploying markers of religion, ethnicity or race also display a central concern with the rights and relations

---

[61] So the Pope appealed to raped women in the former Yugoslavia not to abort but to bear and love their 'enemy babies'.

[62] Deniz Kandiyoti, 'Identity and Its Discontents: Women and the Nation', *Millennium*, 20 (1991), pp. 429–43.

[63] Nationalism troubles feminism; but there are also inter-national feminist politics, and differences between women have become a primary issue amongst feminists. Pettman, *Worlding Women*; Pettman, 'Transcending National Identity: the Global Political Economy of Gender and Class', in Crawford and Jarvis, *Still an American Social Science*? See also Chandra Mohanty, Ann Russo and Lourdes Torres (eds.), *Third World Women and the Politics of Feminism* (Bloomington: Indiana University Press, 1991); Mary John, *Discrepant Dislocations: Feminism, Theory and Postcolonial Histories* (Berkeley: University of California Press, 1996).

[64] Partha Chatterjee, 'The Nationalist Resolution of the Women's Question', in Sangari and Vaid, *Recasting Women*; Parekh, *Ethnocentricity*, p. 47.

[65] Kumari Jayawardena, *Feminism and Nationalism in the Third World* (London: Zed Books, 1986); Lata Mani, 'Contentious Traditions: the Debate on Sati in Colonial India', in Sangari and Vaid, *Recasting Women*.

[66] Valentine Moghadam (ed.), *Identity Politics and Women: Cultural Reassertions and Feminisms in International Perspective* (Boulder: Westview Press, 1994); Yuval-Davis, *Gender and Nation*; Janet Agray, 'The War against Feminism in the Name of the Almighty', *New Left Review*, 224 (1997), pp. 89–110.

of women, imposing surveillance and control of in-group women's movements and sexual relations. These similarities in terms of gender dynamics and the uses of women to signify difference are indicative of the difficulties in making clear distinctions between nationalism and other kinds of collective political identities. These difficulties remind us of the necessity to locate processes of political identification within wider social relations, as power relations. They suggest, too, why thinking about nationalism *and after* becomes especially challenging.

After nationalism

Nationalism seems at present to be facing heavy competition from other forms of political identity, though this is especially so for official state nationalisms. Anti-state mobilizations move through different manifestations in identity cross-overs. A political collectivity might seek equality and participation within a state: failing this, its leaders might appeal for special status, or seek autonomy or separation, and so the language used changes along with the project. However, commentators also label any particular identity conflict in different ways. The wars in the former Yugoslavia are an example, where the boundaries were simultaneously described as ethnic, national, and religious divides. The multiple forms of identity mobilized in such political conflicts are often signalled by the label 'ethno-nationalist'. This suggests that nationalism shares key features with other collective political identities, though it can be distinguished in terms of the markers used to determine belonging or exclusion, or in terms of its particular political project, which might or might not include claiming a separate state.

Considering what might come after nationalism, then, seems premature, for the political configurations and passions associated with nationalism are far from over. However, we do face a difficult challenge regarding how we characterize the post-Cold War world, and what we now make of the nation-state and of nationalism.

We live in a time of conspicuous and often dangerous nationalisms;[67] though some question how new the 'new world disorder' is, and ask whether removing the spectacle of the Cold War has simply drawn our attention to other kinds of identity and difference. Following E.H. Carr's periodization of nationalism we may now be in its fifth phase, beginning in 1989. Its origins predate the end of the Cold War, and are located within the failures of nation and state building in many postcolonial and Soviet states, and especially within intensifying globalization processes which undermine state sovereignty and legitimacy more generally. But nationalist energies have also been released by the demise of the tacit global order patrols of the US and the former Soviet Union. They are fuelled by the dislocations and pain of economic restructuring, notably by structural adjustment programs enforced on third world states by international financial institutions and western governments, and by the economic liberalization accompanying the collapse of state socialism in Europe.[68]

[67] There are more benign forms of nationalism, for example contemporary forms of Welsh or Scottish nationalism.

[68] Isabella Bakker (ed.), *The Strategic Silence: Gender and Economic Policy* (London: Zed Books, 1994); Rae Blumberg, *et al.* (eds.), *EnGENDERing Wealth & Wellbeing* (Boulder: Westview Press, 1995).

Interestingly, some of these features resemble those which Carr was most anxious to evacuate from the national and international scene, in order to move beyond catastrophic nationalism. He advocated an internationalizing of concern for and institutions towards social justice, defined in terms of equal opportunity, freedom from want, and full employment. He specifically argued that there could be no return to the 'free' market economy of the nineteenth century, if nationalism were to be defused. Moving beyond nationalism would necessitate that the international 'become social'.[69] It is clear that contemporary globalization overrides both the social state and the possibility of a social international system.

A major preoccupation in IR currently is globalization and the consequent transformations of states, which in turn affect notions of place, space and identity. Nationalism, as usually understood, is a territorially located identity, in some relation with a state, its own or that which it mobilizes against. Now states seem under attack from above and below, and sovereignty is eroded by the dominance of the global market, and by communications and other technologies that bypass state borders.

Globalization reconfigures relations between states and markets, capital and labour, women and men, *and* states and nations. It is a multifaceted and contradictory process.[70] Its contemporary phase has dismantled the 'three ways' of state economic management that dominated the post-war world—welfare capitalism, state socialism and third world developmentalism.[71] It is marked by liberalization in trade and finance, transnational production and symbolic capital, and new communications technologies. These largely overflow or ignore state boundaries. They contribute to states' abandonment of many of the social and economic responsibilities forced upon them through previous political struggles. This shift impacts in particular ways on women, who as primary family managers and care providers must compensate for the withdrawal or reduction of 'unproductive' public expenditure. So, too, labour is disorganized, as the state which came to function as a site for class struggle and validation of labour or welfare victories vacates in favour of global and capital determinations.[72]

These transformations have contributed to state legitimacy crises, especially in postcolonial and post-Soviet states. Whilst nowhere is untouched by globalization, it is simplistic to represent these changes as equally affecting 'the world'. Their effects include growing disparities, within and between states. States are not innocent victims, but often complicit or enthusiastic agents of globalization.[73] They par-

---

[69] Carr, *Nationalism*, p. 70.

[70] V. Spike Peterson, 'Reframing the Politics of Identity: Democracy, Globalization and Gender', *Political Expressions*, 1 (1995), pp. 1–16. Jan Aart Scholte, 'The Geography of Collective Identities in a Globalizing World', *Review of International Political Economy*, 3 (1996), pp. 565–608; Roger Tooze, 'International Political Economy in the Age of Globalization', in John Baylis and Steve Smith (eds.), *The Globalization of World Politics* (Oxford: Oxford University Press, 1997); James Mittelman (ed.), *Globalization: Opportunities and Challenges* (Bouldner: Lynne Rienner, 1995); Eleanor Kofman and Gillian Youngs (eds.), *Globalization: Theory and Practice* (London, Pinter, 1996); *Review of International Political Economy*, 2, 1 (1995), special issue on The Power of Representation in International Political Economy.

[71] Samir Amin, 'The Challenge of Globalization', *Review of International Political Economy*, 3 (1996), pp. 216–59.

[72] 'The National Imagination'.

[73] Philip Cerny, 'What Next for the State?', in Kofman and Youngs, *Globalization*; Paul Hirst, 'The Global Economy—Myths and Realities', *International Affairs*, 73, 3 (1997), pp. 409–25; see also Held in this issue.

ticipate in a deepening contradiction between the official inter-state organization of sovereignty and the actual domination of 'the market'. That contradiction in turn undermines the nation-state, for the state has abrogated key components of its contract with its citizens, handing them over to transnational forces. So large segments of state populations withdraw their consent from, and their identification with, the state, and may attach to more localized or anti-state loyalties.

Globalization and economic nationalism are usually seen as oppositional. This might be too simple. George Crane pursues a different relation by viewing the intersection of state, nation and economy as a facet of national identity.[74] He develops the notion of 'imagined economy', and illustrates ways in which images of economic life, hard times and good, can be mobilized in relation to national identity. So, historically, Japanese industrialization and, more recently the 'East Asian miracle' were explained in terms of national character; though given the current crisis, 'Asian exceptionalism' has taken a beating. He goes further: 'The Asian currency fiasco is more than a financial problem, it is an identity crisis'.[75]

Crane notes E.H. Carr's designation of the period leading to the world wars as the 'socialization of the nation'. He asks how globalization affects the imagined national economy. Using China as his example, he demonstrates how 'globalization works from within the discourse of national identity as well as from outside the sovereign territory'.[76] Globalization challenges state managers, who must reimagine the nation, in part to attract global capital. The global redefines the national. Crane suggests that we are witnessing the 'globalization of the nation'.[77]

Another crucial component of globalization is migration.[78] Larger numbers than ever before are on the move, or resident in states other than that of their birth. Many of them are labour migrants, legally or illegally living beyond their state borders, with little likelihood of achieving full citizenship rights there. Increasing numbers of migrants are women, indicating the changing global division of labour in these globalizing times.[79] Migration stories tell of displacements, dislocations, and longing; though some also tell of escape, adventure and pleasure. Being away from home contributes to identity reconstitution. 'Routes' join 'roots' in 'the stories people tell themselves about who they are, where they live and how they got there'.[80]

---

[74] 'Imagining the Economic Nation: Chinese Responses to Globalization', ISA conference paper, Minneapolis, 1998, p. 1.

[75] Crane, 'The Economic Nation', p. 11; see also Jongwoo Han and Lily Ling, 'Authoritarianism in the Hypermasculinized State: Hybridity, Patriarchy and Capitalism in Korea', *International Studies Quarterly*, No. 42 (1998), 53–78, concerning recasting masculinities and femininities in the process of reconstituting national identity and political economy.

[76] Crane, 'The Economic Nation', p. 25.

[77] Crane, 'The Economic Nation', p. 30.

[78] Interestingly, Carr identified migration as a crucial dimension of nationalism, viewing freedom of migration as a vital feature of the comparatively benign second phase of nationalism, *Nationalism*, p. 12; and the closing of [European and United States] national frontiers to largescale immigration after 1919 as a 'fateful step' towards renewed nationalist conflagrations. He remarked, 'No single measure did more to render a renewal of the clash between nations inevitable', pp. 22–3.

[79] Jan Jindy Pettman, 'Women on the Move: Globalization and Labour Migration from South and Southeast Asian States', *Global Society*, 1998; see also Helene Pellerin, 'Global Restructuring and International Migration: Consequences for the Globalization of Politics', in Kofman and Youngs, *Globalization*.

[80] David Trend, 'Nationalities, Pedagogies and Media', *Cultural Studies*, 7 (1993), p. 89; see also Stuart Hall, in Jonathan Rutherford (ed.), *Identity: Community, Culture, Difference* (London: Lawrence and Wishart, 1990). There are questions here about what we now make of home? Can we have only one home? Can we presume, any more, that home means where we came from, or the state which officially identifies itself as 'ours'.

The presence of visible migrants appears to disrupt the sovereignty story, which usually links population, place, identity and citizenship. Significant numbers of the national people experience the migrant presence as a threat. Reactive nationalisms in migrant-receiving states reflect and produce resentment of the intrusion of difference. This can be articulated within classic state discourses, as threats to national identity and security—the enemy within. These can have the effect of reterritorializing identity, and ensure that many within the state are viewed as outside the nation. Borders are also enforced by state practices.[81] While liberalizing trade and finance, states tenaciously resist the freedom of movement of people, or labour. They claim as an aspect of their sovereignty the right to determine who will enter, stay, and have access to resources including citizenship in their state. In turn, experiences of discrimination or closure can activate new identities as, for example, a Turk, or Kurd, becomes 'ethnic' in Germany and a nationalist in her own view. She may become part of a diasporic national movement.

Migrants and racialized others negotiate their ways through multiple identities offered or denied to them. These negotiations bear the stamp of home, of the current place, and of global identity politics. Links and flows between them are facilitated by new communications technologies, including faxes, email and websites, which enable the emergence and growth of virtual national communities of affiliation and grievance. Through them, dispersed members become directly involved in nationalist causes at home.[82]

So, too, do diasporas reconfigure and replenish. Notions of home, and place, are often a part of a sense of identity.[83] But feelings of belonging need not depend on being there, or ever intending to return there permanently. At the same time, migration is no longer mainly from one state to another. Changes in state politics encourage returnees; family members maintain intimate connections and domestic economies across several or more states; women and men engage in multiple migrations or repeated border crossings, and routinely deal with agents and agencies of more than one state. Transnationalism becomes a part of millions of people's everyday lives and associations.[84]

These transformations not only affect people and nations. They recast states, too. Arjun Appadurai remarks on the difference between regarding the US as 'a land of immigrants', compared with its 'being one node in a postnational network of diasporas'. He argues that 'the nationalist genie, never perfectly contained in the bottle of the territorial state, is now itself diasporic', and adds 'no idiom has yet emerged to capture the collective interests of many groups in translocal solidarities, cross-border mobilizations, and postnational identities'.[85]

Nationalism is experiencing new times. To some extent, they do not seem so new—especially where exclusivist and violent nationalist politics exact horrific costs

[81] Roxanne Lynn Doty, 'Immigration and National Identity: Constructing the Nation', *Review of International Studies*, 22 (1996), 235–55; Thomas J. Biersteker and Cynthia Weber (eds.), *Constructions of State Sovereignty* (Cambridge: Cambridge University Press, 1996).

[82] Yuval-Davis, *Gender and Nation*.

[83] So is location, especially whether one lives within 'zones of peace' and 'zones of turmoil'; and in terms of nationality, for access to work and other rights, preferably in rich states.

[84] *Identities*, 4, 2 (1997), special issue 'Transnational Processes/Situated Identities'; Jose David Saldwar, *Border Matters: Remapping American Studies* (Berkeley: University of California Press, 1997); Masao Miyoshi, 'A Borderless World? From Colonialism to Transnationalism and the Decline of the Nation-State', *Critical Inquiry*, 19, 4 (1993), pp. 273–96; Appadurai, *Patriotism*.

[85] Appadurai, *Patriotism*, 423, 413, 418.

from those who are seen to be outside the nation, as they have done before. But emerging deterritorialized forms of power, identity and global flows are recasting nations, states and the international.

We may be living in post-nation-state times, though there was never a neat fit between nation and state. The nation often exceeds or displaces the state in many people's affection. But are we also witnessing post-national times? Or can the nation be reconfigured beyond its familiar territoriality and reference to the state, and within more multinational and multilocational reception? And can IR reconfigure itself in ways that enable productive engagement with contemporary international identity politics?

Condition(s) of Peace

EMANUEL ADLER

> 'Ladies and gentlemen, the time for peace has come.'
>
> The late Yitzhak Rabin, prime minister of Israel

Introduction

The conditions in which peace can exist are now just what they have always been (even if time and place make them appear different): a higher expected utility from peace than from war; a 'civic culture'; a commitment to the peaceful resolution of disputes; strong institutions; an ethical code; mutual legitimization; peacemakers (because peace is socially constructed); a social-communicative process; material and normative resources; social learning (to take us from here to there); shared trust; and, most important, a collective purpose and social identity. As I will explain below, these are not 'necessary' conditions in any formal sense. Nor are there really sufficient conditions of peace, other, perhaps, than lobotomy and the total elimination of weapons, including fingernails.

Like war, peace is a moving target. People in the Middle Ages probably understood peace very differently than did their descendants in the seventeenth century. Our understanding of peace, too, seems to be changing: if war may soon become the mutual infliction of disease, would peace mean a state of 'mutual inoculation'? And if, as I believe, future wars will be fought in and by computers, will peace exist only in cyberspace?

Again, is it not the case that peace has always been 'virtual', or nonexistent, from an epistemological or an ontological point of view? The notions of peace that realists of all colours and denominations have advanced since Classical Antiquity, under the rubric of 'the absence of war',[1] amount to nothing at all. The concept of 'negative peace'[2] may indeed represent a situation in the real world where organized

---

[1] See, for example, Thucydides, *History of the Peloponnesian War*, trans. Rex Warner (Baltimore: Penguin Books, 1972); Niccolo Machiavelli, *The Prince*, trans. Henry C. Mansfield, Jr. (Chicago: University of Chicago Press, 1985); Thomas Hobbes, *Leviathan*, ed. C. B. Mac Phearson (Hammondsworth, England: Penguin Books, 1954); Jean-Jacques Rousseau, 'Judgment on Perpetual Peace', in *A Project of Perpetual Peace*, trans. Edith M. Nuttall (London: Richard Cobden-Sanderson, 1927); Hans J. Morgenthau, *Politics among Nations: The Struggle for Power and Peace* (New York: Alfred A. Knopf, 1948); Robert Gilpin, *War and Change in World Politics* (Cambridge: Cambridge University Press, 1981).

[2] Johan Galtung, 'Violence, Peace, and Peace Research', *Journal of Peace Research*, 6 (1969), pp. 167–91; Johan Galtung, *Essays in Peace Research*, Vol. 1 (Copenhagen: Christian Ejlers, 1975); Kenneth E. Boulding, *Stable Peace* (Austin: University of Texas Press, 1978). See also Arie Kacowicz, *Zones of Peace in the Third World: South America and West Africa in Comparative Perspective* (Albany, NY: State University of New York Press, 1998).

violence between political units does not occur for a number of years. Epistemologically speaking, however, peace merely as the absence of war is an oxymoron; we
cannot positively define something as the opposite of something else.[3] In other
words, peace may exist but we cannot know it.

'Positive peace',[4] on the other hand, has no ontological existence at all; it is a goal
that can never be achieved in our times.[5] Idealists of all stripes have portrayed peace
as a utopia, incorporating the improvement of politics and human nature, social
justice, morality, international organization and law, and human progress.[6] Seen this
way, peace never existed, does not exist now, and probably never will. In other
words, although we may be able to imagine peace and understand what is required
to achieve it, peace really does not exist.

This is why, while inspired people, such as Immanuel Kant, may have been able to
imagine the necessary conditions for 'perpetual peace' among republics,[7] all that
contemporary scholars have been able to say about the 'democratic peace' (to stick
to Kant's theory) is that 'democracies *do not make war* on each other'.[8] Even
Kenneth Boulding, who was keenly aware of the ontological and epistemological

---

[3] During the 1960s and 1970s, Galtung and Boulding conducted a lively debate on the meaning of peace,
which centred in part on Galtung's notions of 'negative' and 'positive' peace. See Kenneth E. Boulding,
'Twelve Friendly Quarrels with Johan Galtung', *Journal of Peace Research*, 14 (1977), pp. 75–86.
Whereas Galtung defined 'negative peace' as the absence of physical violence, Boulding argued that the
concept of 'negative peace' is a 'complete misnomer', 'Peace . . . is not just "not-war" any more than
water is "not ice" ' (Boulding, 'Twelve Friendly Quarrels', p. 78). A year later, however, Boulding himself
referred to peace's 'negative side' as 'the absence of turmoil, tension, conflict, and war' (Boulding, *Stable
Peace*, p. 3). According to Herbert C. Kelman, the concept of negative peace is valuable because it
stresses the avoidance of violence and destruction', see Herbert C. Kelman, 'Reflections on the History
and Status of Peace Research', *Conflict Management and Peace Science*, 5 (Spring 1981), p. 105.

[4] Galtung is mostly in a category of his own when he defines 'positive peace' as the *absence* of something
else, i.e. 'structural [socio-economic] violence' (Galtung, 'Violence, Peace, and Peace Research', pp.
167–91; Galtung, *Essays in Peace Research*). See also Heikki Patomaki and Ole Waever, 'Introducing
Peaceful Changes', in Heikki Patomaki (ed.), 'Peaceful Changes in World Politics' (Research Report
No 71, Tampere Peace Research Institute, University of Tampere, 1995). Boulding, on the other hand,
correctly defined 'positive peace' in positive terms, i.e. as a 'condition of good management, orderly
resolution of conflict, harmony associated with mature relationships, gentleness, and love' (Boulding,
Stable Peace, p. 3).

[5] 'In this sense [positive peace] peace is one of the ultimate time's arrows in the evolutionary process, an
increasing product of human development and learning' (Boulding, *Stable Peace*, p. 3). According to
Kacowicz, positive peace 'includes also social and economic justice, and some kind of world order that
meets the needs and interests of the human population as a whole' (Kacowicz, *Zones of Peace in the
Third World*).

[6] See, for example, Isaiah 1:16–17, 2:2–4, 11:1–4,6,9, and 42:5–7; Matt. 5:3–11 ('The Beatitudes'); Dante
Alighieri, *Monarchy and Three Political Letters*, trans.. Donald Nicholl and Colin Hardie (London:
Weidenfeld & Nicolson, 1954); Emeric Cruce, *The New Cyneas*, trans. C. Frederick Farrell, Jr., Edith
Farrell (ed.) (New York: Garland, 1972); William Penn, *An Essay toward the Present and Future Peace of
Europe* (Washington, D.C.: American Peace Society, 1912); Abbé de Saint Pierre, *Ouvrages de Politique*,
16 vols. (Rotterdam, 1733–41); Antoine-Nicolas de Condorcet, *Sketch for a Historical Picture of the
Progress of the Human Mind*, trans. June Barraclough, introd. Stuart Hampshire (London: Weidenfeld
& Nicolson, 1955); Immanuel Kant, *Perpetual Peace and Other Essays*, trans. Ted Humphrey
(Indianapolis: Hacket, 1983); Jeremy Bentham, *Plan for a Universal and Perpetual Peace* (London:
Grotius Society, 1927); Norman Angell, *The Great Illusion* (London: Penguin Books, 1908); A
Zimmern, *The League of Nations and the Rule of Law* (London: Macmillan, 1939); Grenville Clark and
Louis Sohn, *World Peace Through World Law*, 3rd edn. (Cambridge, MA: Harvard University Press,
1973); Philip Noel-Baker, *The Arms Race: A Programme for World Disarmament* (London: Stevens and
Sons, 1958); Richard A. Falk, *A Study of Future Worlds* (New York: The Free Press, 1975).

[7] Kant, *Perpetual Peace*.

[8] Michael W. Doyle, 'Kant, Liberal Legacies, and Foreign Affairs, Part I', *Philosophy and Public Affairs*,
12 (Summer 1983), pp. 205–33; Bruce M. Russett, *Grasping the Democratic Peace: Principles for a Post-
Cold War World* (Princeton: Princeton University Press, 1993).

traps of characterizing peace in 'negative' and 'positive' ways, defined 'stable peace' merely as 'a situation in which the *probability of war* [my emphasis] is so small that it does not really enter into the calculations of any of the people involved'.[9]

And yet, at the end of the second millennium, peace, though still uncommon, does exist. It has a positive meaning, is ontologically real and epistemologically significant, and can be empirically described. The state of peace, as envisaged by E. H. Carr more than fifty years ago, given specific meaning by Karl Deutsch and Richard Van Wagenen more than forty years ago, and recently redefined by Emanuel Adler and Michael Barnett, is neither the antithesis of something else nor something that exists only in the future; rather, it is something very much like a *security community*.[10]

Deutsch and his associates defined a security community as 'a group of people which has become integrated'. This means 'the attainment, within a [transnational] territory, of a sense of community and of institutions and practices strong enough and widespread enough to assure, for a "long" time, dependable expectations of peaceful change'.[11] Thus peace is not some temporary absence of war or a phantom to be achieved in the future. The nature and quality of the relationships among states that share collective identities and trust one another can and have created transnational regions of people who maintain dependable expectations of peaceful change.

Because collective identities (and other collective understandings that are the marks of a security community) manifest themselves in and through practice, peace is, first and foremost, itself *a practice*.[12] Practices are real, not only because their physical and material manifestations can be empirically described, but also in the socio-ontological sense that they embody the collective meaning that people give to material reality. In other words, peace as it exists today can be traced back to the cognitive structures or collective understandings—mainly collective identities—that constitute the practices characteristic of security communities.[13]

Defining peace as a practice also endows the concept with a dynamic character. In this view, 'it is not possible to tame or freeze history for long';[14] that is, neither war

---

[9] Boulding, *Stable Peace*, p. 13.

[10] Karl W. Deutsch, Sidney A. Burrell, Robert A. Kann, Maurice Lee, Jr., Martin Lichterman, Raymond E. Lindgren, Francis L. Loewenheim, Richard W. Van Wagenen, *Political Community and the North Atlantic Area* (Princeton: Princeton University Press, 1957); Richard W. Van Wagenen, *Research in the International Organization Field: Some Notes on a Possible Focus* (Center for Research on World Political Institutions, Princeton University, 1952); Emanuel Adler and Michael Barnett (eds.), *Security Communities* (Cambridge: Cambridge University Press, 1998). See also E. H. Carr, *Conditions of Peace* (London: Macmillan, 1942). According to Kelman, 'positive peace does not imply an ideal, utopian situation, but merely a livable one' (Kelman, 'Reflections on the History and Status of Peace Research', p. 108).

[11] Deutsch *et al.*, *Political Community*, p. 5.

[12] 'If we can speak of violent practices, or of practices based on (threats) of violence . . . we can also speak of making practices more peaceful' (Patomaki and Waever, 'Introducing Peaceful Changes', p. 10).

[13] My approach follows a 'constructivist' line of reasoning. On constructivism, see Alexander Wendt, 'Anarchy is What States Make of It: The Social Construction of Power Politics', *International Organization*, 46 (1992), pp. 391–425; David Dessler, 'What is at Stake in the Agent–Structure Debate?', *International Organization*, 43 (1989), pp. 441–74; and Emanuel Adler, 'Seizing the Middle Ground: Constructivism in World Politics', *European Journal of International Relations*, 3 (1997), pp. 319–63. On the reality of 'social facts', such as practices, see John Searle, *The Construction of Social Reality* (New York: The Free Press, 1995).

[14] Patomaki and Waever, 'Introducing Peaceful Changes', p. 16.

nor peace is permanent and absolute or evolves according to some philosophically based teleology. Rather, they exist in time and space; which of the two dominates depends on whether, in dealing with their ever-changing reality, societies (not only of the anarchical type[15]) resolve their conflicts by violent means[16] or have learned to expect and implement peaceful change.

Defining peace as a practice also entails agency.[17] 'Peacemakers' (active or passive, individual or institutional) play a social and political role in endowing physical objects (including people and physical resources) with collective meanings, identities, and myths. Furthermore, the equation of peace with the practice of security community means that, like all practices, it can be arrived at through *learning*. Rather than existing as an a-historical fact, it owes its existence to the attachment of meaning to physical reality in particular historical, cultural and political contexts.[18] In other words, peace is socially constructed.

Finally, because meanings are not direct representations but interpretations of physical reality, which, in turn, depend on other meanings (for example, sovereignty and state), the social construction of shared meanings, and thus of security communities, depends on the sharing of experiences, narratives, symbols, and, more generally, historical, political, and cultural contexts. Whether states that enjoy an absence of war become a security community, then, depends not only on time (twenty, thirty, fifty years), but also on the particular contexts within which the social construction of shared meanings and identities takes place.

This means that, although we should look to constitutive conditions—such as collective identity, mutual trust, social processes of communication, and social learning—to explain the social construction of security communities, we should take account of facilitative conditions—including a higher expected utility from peace than from war or Great-Power commitment to the peaceful resolution of disputes—to explain the historical, political, and cultural contexts that permit the constitution of security communities. For example, a higher expected utility from peace than from war, in addition to bringing about the temporary absence of war, may also, and more importantly, help warring societies see each other with greater empathy and thereby promote the development of collective meanings and identities.

The state or *condition* of peace[19] is the practice of security community sustained by the attachment of collective meanings and purposes to physical reality. It can be concisely represented by the formula (borrowed from philosopher John Searle): 'X counts as Y in C'.[20] The paradigmatic case is: 'This paper counts as money in a given context'. In our case, X is the material aspect of living in peace in a security community (demilitarized borders, extensive trade, etc.); Y is the collective meanings

---

[15] Hedley Bull, *The Anarchical Society* (New York: Columbia University Press, 1977).

[16] Andrew B. Schmookler, *The Parable of the Tribes* (New York: Houghton Mifflin, 1984).

[17] There is a growing attention in the IR literature to the role played by agents in the constitution of international practices. One such type is known as 'moral entrepreneurs'. See, for example, Ethan Nadelmann, 'Global Prohibition Regimes: The Evolution of Norms in International Society', *International Organization*, 44 (1990), pp. 479–526.

[18] On learning, see Ernst B. Haas, *When Knowledge is Power* (Berkeley: University of California Press, 1990).

[19] Although I prefer the expression '*condition* of peace', to avoid confusion with the *conditions* of (for) peace I shall refer instead to the '*state* of peace',

[20] Searle, *The Construction of Social Reality*, pp. 43–51. See also the comments by Ian Hacking, Mary Midgley, Thomas Osborne, and John R. Searle in 'Review Symposium on John R. Searle', *History of the Human Sciences*, 10 (1997), pp. 83–110.

and purposes attached to physical reality, which are manifested in the practice of peaceful change ('we' democracies, '"we" who follow the Asian way', etc.); and *C* is the historical, cultural, and political contexts through and within which social reality acquires a particular meaning (the nuclear era, a global economy, American hegemony, etc.)

As used here, the *conditions* for peace—what Carr, in the title of his often-overlooked book, called the 'conditions of peace'—does not refer to its determinants in a positivist (if A then B) or a realist-scientific (A causes B) sense. Rather, I have in mind the material and ideological attributes that *enable* X to be constituted as Y in C—the propensities that, when actualized by the practices of peoples of states, enable them to de-emphasize national borders, stop imagining war among themselves as a real possibility, and feel instead that they can be safe within the cognitive borders of their community.

In this paper, I will define, describe, and explain the *condition* and the *conditions* for peace in the context of what, evoking E. H. Carr's *The Twenty Years' Crisis*,[21] this volume refers to as 'the eighty years' crisis'. I find it appropriate, therefore, to begin by pointing out that, more than fifty years ago, Carr believed that peace would take hold in the European continent only if and when the peoples of Europe came to understand that 'the national unit ha[d] become visibly too small' for controlling military and economic policy and were consequently 'induced to determine themselves into different units for different purposes' and build-up 'a wider form of international community'.[22] Moreover, according to Carr, Europeans might then discover that they had 'constructed something which mankind will come gradually to recognize as indispensable to its future well-being and which can some day be given both wider geographical extension and appropriate constitutional forms'.[23]

From the perspective of what Carr thought to be the resolution of the 'twenty years' crisis', the way out of the 'eighty years' crisis' becomes much more intelligible: the development of security communities and the diffusion of security-community practices and institutions around the world. Although, at the end of the second millennium, the crisis is far from being over (in fact, there is room to argue that it has gotten worse since the end of the Cold War), in some (overlapping) parts of the world—such as Scandinavia, Western Europe, the Euro-Atlantic space, the US and Canada, US and Mexico, the southern cone of Latin America, and, increasingly, the region encompassed by the Association of Southeast Asian States (ASEAN)—people who have learned to organize themselves into security communities now practice and experience peaceful change.

My arguments may sound profoundly idealistic; indeed they are, in the sense that ideational structures are both ontologically *real* and also help constitute reality. They are not idealistic (in the 'pie in the sky' sense), however, because they view power and socio-cognitive processes as two sides of the same coin. Otherwise, how can we explain that Carr, generally regarded as the 'father of realism', linked the development of a European international community to a collective transnational identity that arises from a shared moral purpose[24] In fact, Carr believed (as I do) that the

---

[21] E. H. Carr, *The Twenty Years' Crisis: 1919–1939* (New York: Harper, 1964).
[22] Carr, *Conditions of Peace*, pp. 123 and 274.
[23] Ibid., p 273.
[24] Ibid., pp. 102–25.

material world and power affect the world through the medium of purposeful and meaningful action;[25] consequently, history need not repeat itself endlessly and can evolve in directions made socially possible both by power relations and by the collective ideas of an age.

In the next section I shall continue to explore what Carr considered to be the reasons for the crisis of the twentieth century and its solutions, and compare his ideas about the development of shared purpose and loyalty with those of more recent scholars, especially Deutsch, Ernst Haas, and Charles Taylor. Section Three explains the concept of security communities and reflects on the processes by which domestic societies adopt new and broader transnational identities. Section Four analyses the conditions for peace and briefly describes some recently created war-prevention practices that enhance the propensity to the development of security communities. In Section Five, by way of example, I describe contemporary attempts to construct a 'Mediterranean Region' by imbuing leaders and civil societies with the practice of peaceful change. In the last section, I look around the corner of the year 2000, including the conditions of interstate, intrastate, and transnational violence, and reflect on courses of action that can protect and further promote the *state* and *conditions* for peace.

Common purpose, collective identity, and security community

Evoking the linkage between identity and understanding, Charles Taylor wittingly wrote that, in the human sciences, the valid response to 'I don't understand' is 'change yourself!'.[26] In this section, after a short review of Deutsch's notion of the security community I will draw on the work of Carr, Deutsch, Haas, and Taylor to advance the argument that peaceful change involves a change of identity, such that 'I' becomes 'we'.[27] In other words, a new and more encompassing social identity is developed, one that instils an enhanced sense of mutual trust and security in people's minds.

As already mentioned, Deutsch and his associates defined a *security community* as 'a group of people which has become integrated'. This means 'the attainment, within a [transnational] territory, of a sense of community and of institutions and practices strong enough and widespread enough to assure, for a "long" time, dependable expectations of peaceful change'.[28] Security communities may be either 'amalgamated' or 'pluralistic'. In an amalgamated community, two or more (sovereign) states formally merge into an expanded state. Deutsch cites the United States as an instance. A pluralistic security community preserves the legal independence of its component states but integrates them to the point that the units entertain 'dependable expectations of peaceful change'. A pluralistic security community develops when its members possess a compatibility of core values derived from

---

[25] Carr, *The Twenty Years' Crisis*, p. 92.
[26] Charles Taylor, 'Interpretation and the Sciences of Man', in Fred R. Dallmyr and Thomas A. McCarthy (eds.), *Understanding Social Inquiry* (South Bend: University of Notre Dame Press, 1977), p. 127.
[27] Ibid., p. 123.
[28] Deutsch *et al.*, *Political Community*, p. 5.

common institutions and mutual responsiveness—a matter of mutual identity and loyalty, a sense of 'we-ness', or a 'we-feeling' among states.[29]

Security communities, according to Deutsch, are different from more limited 'no-war communities'. Whereas the former are characterized by a communicative process that leads to integration at the level of 'we-feeling' or identity, thus making war 'unimaginable' among its members, the latter, which can best be exemplified by a successful balance-of-power system, is a community of nations enjoying a stable truce, where war is always possible and preparations for war among its members are always a distinct possibility.[30]

At first glance, associating Carr, 'the father of realism', and Deutsch, one of the main exponents of postwar 'idealism', as part of a common tradition may seem an aberration.[31] When it comes to the conditions for peace, however, it is not. According to Carr, peace is to be found only as a by-product of the search for something else.[32] Building peace, therefore, means creating positive conditions for an orderly and progressive development of human society;[33] these conditions in turn depend chiefly on the identification of a common moral purpose. Because modern military technology and economic life and organization demand the construction of transnational units that are larger than the modern state, however, a common moral purpose depends on the construction of new and broader transnational social identities.

When Carr applied these thoughts to the construction of a European trans-national unit (the 'New Europe') at the end of World War II, he realized that several conditions would have to be met: (1) There would have to be enlightened power,

---

[29] Deutsch *et al.*, p. 5; Emanuel Adler and Michael Barnett, 'Security Communities in Theoretical Perspective', in Adler and Barnett, *Security Communities*. To measure this 'sense of community', Deutsch and his associates quantified transaction flows, with particular emphasis on their volume, within and among nation-states. A relative growth in transaction flows between societies, as contrasted to flows within them, was thought to be a crucial test for determining whether new 'human communities' might be emerging. See, for example, Deutsch's essays in Philip E. Jacob and James V. Toscano (eds.), *The Integration of Political Communities* (Philadelphia: Lippincott, 1964): 'Communication Theory and Political Integration', pp. 46–74; 'Transaction Flows as Indicators of Political Cohesion', pp. 75–97; 'The Price of Integration', pp. 143–78; 'Integration and the Social System', pp. 179–208. For incisive analyses of Deutsch's contribution to integration theory, see Donald J. Puchala, 'Integration Theory and the Study of International Relations', and Arend Lijphart, 'Karl W. Deutsch and the New Paradigm in International Relations', both in Richard Merritt and Bruce M. Russett (eds.), *From National Development to Global Community* (London: George Allen & Unwin, 1981), pp. 145–64, 233–51.

[30] Karl W. Deutsch, *Political Community at the International Level: Problems of Definition and Measurement* (New York: Doubleday, 1954), p. 41.

[31] 'His [Carr's] readers, overwhelmingly realists, have pounced upon his attack on utopianism but generally have failed to note his . . . criticism of realism and his positive comments about utopianism' (Ken Booth, 'Security in Anarchy: Utopian Realism in Theory and Practice', *International Affairs*, 67 (1991), p. 531). There is a relatively large literature dealing with Carr's writings and ideas. On the realist side see, for example, Hans J. Morgenthau, 'The Political Science of E. H. Carr', *World Politics*, 1 (1948), pp. 127–34; William T. R. Fox, 'E. H. Carr and Political Realism: Vision and Revision', *Review of International Studies*, 11 (1985), pp. 1–16. On the Grotian side see, for example, Hedley Bull, 'The Twenty Years' Crisis Twenty Years On', *International Journal*, 24 (1969), pp. 625–638; Booth, 'Security in Anarchy'. For constructivist and critical theory critiques see, for example, Cecelia Lynch, 'E. H. Carr, International Relations Theory, and the Societal Origins of International Legal Norms', *Millennium*, 23 (1994), pp. 589–620; Paul Howe, 'The Utopian Realism of E. H. Carr', *Review of International Studies*, 20 (1994), pp. 277–97. For strong criticism of Carr's work, see Whittle Johnston, 'E. H. Carr's Theory of International Relations: A Critique', *Journal of Politics*, 29 (1967), pp. 861–84.

[32] Carr, *Conditions of Peace*, p. xxiii.

[33] Ibid.

because 'no durable peace can be made unless those who have the power have also the will . . . to take and enforce with vigor and impartiality the decisions which they think right'. Yet 'those who have the power should recognize the moral obligation which alone makes its exercise tolerable to others'.[34] (2) There would have to be a recognition that the right of nation-states to self-determination 'must carry with it a recognized responsibility to subordinate military and economic policy and resources to the needs of a wider community, not as a hypothetical engagement to meet some future contingency, but as a matter of the everyday conduct of affairs'.[35] (3) New institutions would be required that could 'be made effective only on the basis of new loyalties arising out of newly felt needs: yet to create the new loyalties new institutions are required'.[36] Finally, there would have to be (4) leadership and, above all, (5) a common moral purpose.[37]

Carr's analysis of the twentieth century's crises made perfectly clear that a common moral purpose was the most important condition. Beyond the crises of *liberal democracy* (which excluded the masses and thus failed to generate a feeling of mutual obligation),[38] *self-determination* (which equated self-determination with nationalism and led to the emergence of a large number of small states, whose survival was rendered problematic by advances in military technique),[39] and *laissez-faire economics* (which created unemployment and left war as the only way to generate employment),[40] there loomed the *moral crisis* of the breakdown of the ethical system that prevailed during the last part of the nineteenth century and the first half of the twentieth century: the 'harmony of interests' doctrine. The other three crises were only specific particular manifestations of the larger moral crisis.[41]

Solving the liberal-democratic, self-determination, and economic crises meant, therefore, that postwar Europe (C) would be compelled to develop a new common ethical purpose (Y) that would give meaning and direction to people's actions and their use of resources (X). This common moral purpose, however, was also needed in a more practical sense, that is, to enable the

---

[34] Ibid., p. 275.

[35] Ibid., p. 62.

[36] Ibid., p. 273.

[37] Ibid., pp. 117–25. On leadership, see p. 123.

[38] The failure to create modern mass democracy, Carr thought, had to do, first, with the 'failure to give adequate social and economic content to the concept of equality'; second, with the fact that political rights became 'a sham', because economic power exercised a predominant influence on political affairs; and third, with the removal of issues of great importance from popular control, because of the technocratic nature of the machinery of government (ibid., pp. 35–6).

[39] Ibid., p. 50. 'Shorn of its moral foundation . . . nationalism, as the history of the last twenty years has shown, could lead only to the doctrine of the morally purposeless super-nation or *Herrenvolk*. . . . The "good" nationalism of the nineteenth century . . . has been transformed into the "bad" nationalism of the twentieth century, the fertile breeding-ground of "economic nationalism", racial discrimination, and war' (ibid., pp. 106–7).

[40] Ibid., p. 101. 'Our most urgent economic problem is no longer to expand production, but to secure a more equitable distribution of consumption and a more regular and orderly utilization of our productive capacity.' Ibid., p. 80.

[41] 'Liberal democracy assumed that individual citizens would recognize the existence of a fundamental harmony of interest between them and would adjust apparent differences of interest on particular points by a process of give-and-take to their mutual advantage. . . . National self-determination was the sure basis for an international community because each nation, in pursuing its own highest interest, was pursuing the interest of the world as a whole, so that nationalism was the natural stepping-stone to internationalism. *Laissez-faire* economics assumed that by promoting their own interest individuals were doing all they could to promote that of the community' (ibid., p. 102).

establishment of a procedure of peaceful negotiation in disputes [which] presupposes, not merely an acute perception on both sides of the strength and weaknesses of their respective positions at any given time, but also a certain measure of *common feeling* as to what is just and reasonable in their mutual relations, a spirit of give-and-take and even of potential self-sacrifice, so that a basis, however imperfect, exists for discussing demands on grounds of justice recognized by both. It is this *common feeling* between nations, not the lack of a world legislature, and not the insistence of states on being judges in their own cause, which is the real obstacle in the way of an international procedure of peaceful change.[42]

Conceptually, then, Carr linked peaceful change to an effective bargaining mechanism that owes its existence to a collective identity. Historically, peaceful change was predicated on a resolution of the crises that dominated the twentieth century by means of the development of a European collective identity and a transnational unit, that, while satisfying the needs of modern military and economic organization, would at the same time respect 'the urge of human beings to form groups based on common tradition, language, and usage'.[43] This meant first creating the framework of international order and only then encouraging national independence to develop and maintain itself within the limitations of that framework.[44] Were Carr alive today, he would probably argue that it is a common moral purpose, on which a collective identity is based, that permits the emergence of a 'security community'.

Carr, echoing contemporary studies of security communities, also realized that a European collective identity would not evolve by itself but would have to be constructed by supranational institutions. This was the main rationale for his proposals to create a European Planning Authority (and Bank), a European Relief Commission, a European Transport Corporation, a European Reconstruction and Public Works Corporation, and an international military unit to keep the peace.[45] Fifty years later, Carr's vision was realized: Europe had become a highly institutionalized pluralistic security community.[46]

Although Carr found what he thought was the solution to the twentieth century's crises in the development of multiple identities and loyalties and the construction of something resembling a European security community, he nonetheless thought that to forecast the moral foundations and assumptions of the coming age would be ineffectual and presumptuous. He nevertheless insinuated that 'popular authority as much as popular liberty will be the keynote of the new faith'.[47]

Of the four theorists considered here, Carr was the only one who made a linkage between *moral* purpose, collective identity, and peace. Deutsch, Haas, and Taylor all saw community-building as chiefly a social–epistemological process that results from common meanings. Common meanings enable people to live in the same normative reference world. Deutsch argued that international community results mainly from communication, mutual responsiveness, and shared identity. Haas, on the other hand, linked the development of international community to a process of 'ration-

---

[42] Carr, *The Twenty Years' Crisis*, p. 220 (emphasis mine).
[43] Carr, *Conditions of Peace*, p. 63.
[44] Ibid., p. 272.
[45] Ibid., pp. 242–70.
[46] See Ole Waever, 'Insecurity, Security, and Asecurity in the West European Non-War Community', in Adler and Barnett, *Security Communities*, pp. 00.
[47] Carr, *Conditions of Peace*, pp. 117, 124.

alization' that accompanies the acceptance of liberal decision-making procedures, coupled with a growing inability of the classic state to satisfy people's economic and security aspirations.[48] All four agreed that common meanings and political community in general are socially constructed. In Taylor's words:

> Common meanings are the basis of community. Intersubjective meaning gives a people a common language to talk about social reality and a common understanding of certain norms, but only with common meanings does this common reference world contain significant common actions, celebrations, and feelings. These are objects in the world everybody shares. This is what makes community.[49]

Although Deutsch gave too little attention to the concept of collective identity, and his behaviourist methodology made it difficult for him to distinguish the growth of collective identity from mere instrumentally led interdependence, he nevertheless thought that the key constitutive factor of community was a 'we-feeling' or collective identity. By 'we-feeling', however, Deutsch did not mean a psychological, largely affective matter of feelings, emotions, and trust, but a socially constructed social-cognitive process.

The core of Deutsch's security community approach was the assumption that communication binds social groups in general and political communities in particular. 'Communication alone enables a group to think together, to see together, and to act together'.[50] Moreover, communication processes and transaction flows between peoples are not only 'facilities for attention' but also factories of shared identification. Through transactions such as trade, migration, tourism, cultural and educational exchanges, and the proliferation of communication facilities, a social fabric is woven among both the elites and the masses, instilling in them a sense of community, which becomes

> a matter of mutual sympathy and loyalties; of 'we feeling,' trust and mutual consideration; of partial identification in terms of self-images and interests; of mutually successful predictions of behavior . . . in short, a matter of perpetual dynamic process of mutual attention, communication, perception of needs, and responsiveness in the process of decision making.[51]

Communication, according to this view, is the social glue that enables peoples to share common meanings across national borders and, therefore, a common normative environment. Security communities can count on compliance with collective norms because some of them are not only regulative, designed to overcome the problems associated with interdependent choice, but also constitutive (Deutsch referred to them as 'main values', which 'can be determined from the internal politics of the participating units'),[52] a direct reflection of the actor's identity and self-understandings.[53]

---

[48] Deutsch *et al.*, *Political Community;* Ernst B. Haas, *Nationalism, Liberalism, and Progress: The Rise and Decline of Nationalism* (Ithaca: Cornell University Press, 1997); Taylor, 'Interpretation and the Sciences of Man'.

[49] Taylor, 'Interpretation and the Sciences of Man', p. 122.

[50] Norbert Wiener, cited by Karl W. Deutsch, *The Nerves of Government* (New York: The Free Press, 1966), p. 77.

[51] Deutsch, *Political Community*, p. 36. See also Adler and Barnett, 'Security Communities in Theoretical Perspective', p. 0.

[52] Deutsch, *Political Community*, p. 47.

[53] Emanuel Adler and Michael Barnett, 'A Framework for the Study of Security Communities', in Adler and Barnett, *Security Communities*.

Sense of community also requires particular habits of political behaviour, which are acquired through processes of social learning and socialization. People learn the new habits slowly, as background conditions change; they diffuse their 'lessons' and expectations to one another through various processes of communication. Security communities are thus communities with deeply entrenched habits for conflict resolution; they are a representation in the material world (X) of a collective identity (constituted by shared meanings through the medium of communication) (Y) in the context (C) of what Deutsch thought of as 'background conditions'—'main values', mutual responsiveness, and predictability of behaviour (so that people can 'perceive one another's sensitive spots or "vital interests", and . . . make prompt and adequate responses to each other's critical needs').[54]

Deutsch's notion that collective identities have a *history,* i.e. are *socially con-structed,* is evident from the fact that he thought that security communities may have humble and self-interested beginnings. All that is required initially, he thought, is a 'complementarity' of needs and resources.[55] With (a) increased communication; (b) a large number of transactions; (c) learning and socialization processes, which lead to the generation of a common normative framework and common behaviour patterns; (d) a 'core of power' that attracts weaker states; and under the guidance of (e) security-community–building institutions and (f) elites that use material and symbolic resources to empower a particular set of identity traits, to the detriment of others, the cultural affinities ('a way of life')[56] needed for a collective identity to exist would develop and become institutionalized.[57]

Like Deutsch, Haas rejects the idea that moral ideas are necessary for the construction of international community. Associating liberalism 'with a certain procedure for the making of collective decisions, not with a distinct moral sub-stance' that has universal connotations, he believes that attachment to a particular moral doctrine that must necessarily be less than universal would contradict the very notion of shared meanings that he advances.[58] Haas's mostly epistemic view of liberalism, however, is partly at odds with Deutsch's, who made the development of security communities contingent not only on expectations but also on (*de facto* liberal) values.

To be sure, Haas's analysis has much more to do with the rationalization of the nation-state and with progress—the improvement of every person's lot with respect to health, wealth, and peace[59]—than with the development of international community. Security communities have become important and a real possibility, however, because in some parts of the developed world rationalization processes are beginning to lead to the development of confederation-like transnational com-munities. The whole process is fuelled by common meanings.[60]

In short, Haas argues that states can effect outcomes that are first imagined by political actors and then projected onto the stage of history. Social visions, however, must have some coherence; in Haas's terms, they must be rationalized and consistent

---

[54] Deutsch, *Political Community*, ch. II; idem, *Political Community at the International Level*, p. 37.
[55] Deutsch, *Political Community*, p. 91.
[56] Ibid., p. 47.
[57] Ibid., chs. II and III.
[58] Haas, *Nationalism, Liberalism, and Progress*, pp. 19–20.
[59] Ibid., p. 323.
[60] Ibid., pp. 14–21, 59, 342, 351–2.

with a set of institutions. Nationalism, he claims, has provided this sense of rationalization to modernizing societies. But there are different types of nationalisms, each offering its own vision of coherence. Haas claims that liberal nationalism has been relatively successful in producing coherence in the North and in parts of the South because 'the overwhelming majority of the world's political elites wants to have the trappings of material-industrial civilization of the secular civilization of the West'.[61] Liberal nationalism, he continues, will eventually prevail in much of the Third World.

But, just as the Third World is beginning to enjoy the fruits of the 'rationalization' process, post-industrial states appear to be increasingly unable to govern and produce these same gains for their peoples. In response to these fundamental changes, and in an attempt to avoid jettisoning centuries of experience and progress, Western Europe is *learning*—questioning original shared meanings and replacing them with others—to create international community; in other words, it is inventing a new type of rationalization that, though depending less on an already ailing national myth, does not necessarily demand a pan-European national identity.[62] 'Only the kind of nationalism we call "liberal",' says Haas, 'is consistent with the progressive transnational sharing of meanings'.[63]

To sum up, Carr, Deutsch, and Haas agree that common meanings are the building blocks of the collective identities on which international or transnational communities are based. But whereas Carr believed that European states would have to develop a new common *moral* vision in order to overcome the twentieth century's crises and transform themselves into a peaceful transnational community, Deutsch and Haas understood the process of community formation as a social-cognitive rather than a moral process and as involving the social construction of shared understandings (Deutsch also introduced a normative dimension). Essentially, the three advanced a positive (temporally and spatially contextual) concept of peace, one that involves the progressive metamorphosis of nation-states into pluralistic security communities.

The state of peace: security communities

Peace, according to the positive definition put forward in Section One, refers to *pluralistic* rather than to amalgamated communities. States that have integrated to the point where they constitute a new enlarged nation-state do not fulfil the ontological and epistemological conditions for peace *among* sovereign states. Adler and Barnett have recently redefined pluralistic security communities as 'transnational regions comprised of sovereign states whose people maintain dependable expectations of peaceful change'; they distinguish 'loosely coupled' from 'tightly coupled' pluralistic security communities. Loosely coupled communities maintain the minimum properties of the foregoing definition. Tightly coupled communities, on the other hand, possess a political regime that lies somewhere between the sovereign state and centralized regional government. The latter kind of community is

[61] Ernst B. Haas, 'Nationalism: An Instrumental Social Construction', *Millennium*, 22 (1993), p. 541.
[62] Ibid., pp. 543–5.
[63] Haas, *Nationalism, Liberalism, and Progress*, p. 19.

something of a post-sovereign system, comprising common supranational, transnational, and national institutions, and some form of a collective security system.[64]

Empirical data indicate that pluralistic security communities can develop without a tightly coupled institutionalized environment; for example, in Scandinavia, the southern cone of Latin America, the Euro-Atlantic Community, and ASEAN (the last-mentioned is only in the process of becoming a pluralistic security community). Nor, as the cases of the United States and Canada and the United States and Mexico demonstrate, is such an environment required for security communities to remain stable over time. A tight institutional environment, therefore, is not a necessary condition for regional peace.[65] On the other hand, post-World War II conditions have increased the role of multilateral institutions in the social construction of pluralistic security communities; Western Europe has become a clear case of a tightly coupled pluralistic security community.

A tightly coupled security community lies between the anarchical arrangement of sovereign states and a system of rule characterized by either hierarchy (as within states) or heteronomy (as in the Middle Ages, when multiple layers of authority coexisted in the same territorial space). In these communities, mutual aid becomes a matter of habit, the institutional context for the exercise of power changes, and the right to use force is transferred from the units to the ensemble of states, which deems it legitimate only against external threats or against community members that revert to un-community ways.[66]

From the perspective of either loosely or tightly coupled pluralistic security communities, then, real positive peace does not require the transcendence of the nation-state or the elimination of existing cultural and ethnic loyalties and identities or full integration into a single state. It merely requires sovereign states to adopt a novel form of regional governance that, relying on collective identity and mutual trust for coordination and compliance with norms, sustains dependable expectations of peaceful change.

Dependable expectations of peaceful change are consequently driven by the development of trust and the formation of a collective identity. 'Trust and identity are reciprocal and reinforcing: the development of trust can strengthen mutual identification, and there is a general tendency to trust on the basis of mutual identification'.[67] Trust and collective identities are themselves prompted by the dynamic and positive relationship between structural variables—power and knowledge—and process variables—transactions, international institutions and organizations, and social learning.[68]

[64] Adler and Barnett, 'A Framework for the Study of Security Communities'.
[65] See, for example, Waever, 'Insecurity, Security, and Asecurity', and Guadalupe Gonzalez and Stephan Haggard, 'The United States and Mexico: A Pluralistic Security Community?' in Adler and Barnett, *Security Communities*.
[66] Adler and Barnett, 'A Framework for the Study of Security Communities'; Emanuel Adler, 'Imagined (Security) Communities: Cognitive Regions in International Relations', *Millennium*, 26 (1997), pp. 249–77.
[67] Adler and Barnett, 'A Framework for the Study of Security Communities'.
[68] Ibid. Trust is a social phenomenon that depends on the assessment that another actor will behave in ways that are consistent with normative expectations. Identities are 'images of individuality and distinctiveness ("selfhood") held and projected by an actor and formed (and modified over time) through relations with significant "others"' (Ronald L. Jepperson, Alexander Wendt, and Peter J. Katzenstein, 'Norms, Identity, and Culture in National Security', in Peter J. Katzenstein, *The Culture of National Security: Norms and Identity in World Politics* [New York: Columbia University Press, 1996], p. 59). Collective identities require people not only to identify (positively) with the destiny of other people but also to identify themselves and those others as a group in relation to other groups.

Structural variables make security communities possible. In this context, material and ideological resources are power, as is the authority to determine shared meaning and the 'magnetic' attraction that strong, secure, and materially successful states ('core of strength'[69]) exert over relatively weaker states. This attraction arises from weaker states' expectations of the security and economic benefits that can arise from belonging to a community that includes stronger states. Collective knowledge, mainly normative rules about proper behaviour in international *and domestic* affairs, makes possible the development of a regional governance system based on collective identity. Both—power and knowledge—may be considered to be collective resources that create the propensities for the development of security community practices.

Processes, on the other hand, translate material and social structural propensities into practice. To begin with, economic and social transactions are part of the interaction through which broader social identities are created and recreated. International institutions, on the other hand, not only provide monitoring capabilities and help states discover new areas of common interest; by helping establish, articulate, and transmit norms of acceptable and legitimate behaviour, they also encourage elites and people in general to consider themselves to be part of a region, thereby building a sense of community and shaping state practices. Finally, 'by promoting the development of shared definitions of security, proper domestic and international action, and regional boundaries, social learning encourages political leaders to see each other as trustworthy. And it also leads people to identify with those who were once on the other side of cognitive divides'.[70]

The idea that communication (even communication that is motivated by previous interests), such as debate and persuasion, can be the basis for new bonds and understandings is consistent not only with Deutsch's views of social communication but also with Jürgen Habermas's theory of 'communicative action'.[71] The main idea behind this theory is that social actors, rather than bargaining to achieve the utilities they expect, as in rational choice theory, engage in debate or discourse that helps demonstrate the validity of their arguments and thereby promote collective understanding.[72]

More specifically, according to Thomas Risse,

communicative behavior oriented toward argumentation, persuasion, and mutual understanding enables and changes social relations among actors. Such discursive processes can also establish a joint definition of the situation and, thus, define in the first place the situational structure and the nature of the collective action problem. Moreover, international negotiators may engage in a moral discourse challenging the validity claims entailed in each other's interests and preferences. Thus, the theory of communicative action abandons the

---

[69] Deutsch, *Political Community*, pp. 37–9, Adler and Barnett, 'A Framework for the Study of Security Communities'.

[70] Adler and Barnett, 'A Framework for the Study of Security Communities'.

[71] Jürgen Habermas, *The Theory of Communicative Action: Reason and the Rationalization of Society*, trans. T. McCarthy (Boston: Beacon Press, 1984); idem, *Between Facts and Norms: Contributions to a Discourse Theory of Law and Democracy*, trans. William Rehg (Cambridge, MA: The MIT Press, 1996).

[72] When we scratch the 'surface' of strategic rational choice, we realize that it is enabled and mediated by communicative action. For example, a closer look at Thomas Schelling's strategic and bargaining theory shows that its rational-choice assumptions can work only in the context of a process of social communication (Schelling's innovation was pointing out the tacit and implicit manifestations of such processes). See Thomas C. Schelling, *The Strategy of Conflict* (New York: Oxford University Press, 1960).

assumptions of 'common knowledge' and of fixed preferences in game theoretical approaches by showing that both are social constructs which can be established in the discursive process.[73]

Communicating and acting, in short, are two sides of the same coin. The key insight for the subject of security communities is that common meanings are necessary for communicative action and, when unavailable, must be socially constructed by institutional and individual agents.

Having identified the main variables that explain the development of security communities, I next turn to two questions that cut to the heart of the security community approach. First, how do people in domestic societies change their identities and preferences?[74] Second, do security communities, once constituted, recreate anarchy in their mutual relations?

With regard to the first question, a change in structural variables may bring domestic societies to learn new 'rules of the game', dealing mainly with how they should redefine themselves in order to achieve security and economic progress. Moreover, a structural change is likely to empower one set of domestic institutions and elites to the detriment of others. The empowered elites will be in a better position to persuade policy-makers that security and economic progress henceforth depend on the adoption of a new social identity and a set of related practices.

For example, Mikhail Gorbachev's decision to implement the momentous changes that led to the end of the Soviet empire and the Cold War was related to his understanding of the Soviet Union's domestic economic constraints as well as to his realization that the country could only gain from linking its fate to a transnational European identity and participating in the activities of multilateral institutions and practices. What prompted this understanding, however, was the continual strengthening of the Western alliance, not just from the military but also from the economic and technological perspective (to the point where the alliance became an indisputable 'core of strength') and new ideas about international reality (e.g., interdependence and 'cooperative security') that Soviet technocrats adopted and which Gorbachev expressed as part of his 'New Thinking'.[75]

Second, as the above example shows, even closed domestic societies need individual and organizational agents to drive home the implications of structural change. Through social-communicative processes, agents conceptually connect structural causes to what they consider to be desirable effects. Communicative processes involving debate and persuasion are the chief vehicle for constructing a collective transnational shared identity around material and cultural attributes. Moreover, collective understandings are diffused to domestic and societal settings around a would-be region through a dense web of economic and social exchange

---

[73] Thomas Risse, ' "Let's Talk!": Insight from the German Debate on Communicative Behavior and International Relations', paper presented to the annual convention of the American Political Science Association, Washington D.C., August 27–31, 1997, p. 8.

[74] Andrew Moravcsik, 'A Liberal Theory of International Politics', *International Organization*, 51 (1997), pp. 513–53.

[75] On Soviet ideas, technocrats, and the end of the Cold War, see Thomas Risse-Kappen, 'Ideas Do Not Float Freely: Transnational Coalitions, Domestic Structures, and the End of the Cold War', *International Organization*, 42 (1994), pp. 185–214. See also Jeffrey T. Checkel, *Ideas and International Political Change: Soviet/Russian Behavior and the End of the Cold War* (New Haven: Yale University Press, 1997).

and international and transnational organizations. Initially, domestic elites and societies in general may adopt collective meanings for instrumental reasons only. With the passage of time, however, and, especially with the rise to political power of individuals and groups that have internalized the new ideas (in fact, they probably came to power *because* they adopted these ideas), a new collective identity may become firmly established.

Third, with the intensification of exchange and under the prompting of security-community-building institutions, transnational subcommunities—of diplomats, business people, soldiers, academics, etc.—may form and add their input to the communicative processes referred above. Representing a variety of societal sectors and often intensely involved in state policy-making and implementation, these transnational subcommunities may become the carriers of a collective transnational identity. They also may play a major role in the internalization of new meanings by individuals and institutional routines and may thereby help frame the alternatives entertained by policy makers and the choices they make.[76]

Finally, when they interact, domestic institutions and elites from different countries come into direct sustained contact and may learn to 'know' each other as trustworthy and as belonging to the same region. As part of the process, they become involved in conceptual bargaining; that is, they bargain not only over the issues on the table but also about the concepts and norms that constitute their social reality. Sometimes they may learn to frame issues in totally new ways and make choices about the material and cultural attributes around which a collective transnational identity might be built.

I now return to the second question, namely, whether security communities can recreate anarchy in their mutual relations. To answer this question, it is essential to bear in mind that, when it comes to security communities, a state-centric logic is limited at best. It is true that (a) pluralistic security communities are composed of mostly sovereign states; (b) within security communities, (non-military) security dilemmas may still be common and the use of coercive power (other than war) may still occur; and (c) state elites are still the most important agents of security-community building.

On the other hand, security communities are neither military alliances nor collective security systems; nor are they state-like units, only larger. Rather, they are transnational non-territorial 'cognitive regions' where peaceful change is practised. Consequently, security communities cannot threaten one another, any more than peaceful interstate relations can be mutually threatening. Moreover, because security communities often have overlapping membership—for example, the Scandinavian countries constitute a security community that is in turn part of the wider Western European security community—it is hard to imagine that their relations could be similar to those of states in an anarchical system. It may help, then, to think of security communities, not as transnational aggregations of state power that are differentiated on spatial or functional lines and can therefore engender anarchy between security communities, but as transnational domains of peaceful practices

---

[76] I take these subcommunities to perform a role similar to that of epistemic communities. On epistemic communities, see 'Knowledge, Power and International Policy Coordination', special issue of *International Organization*, 46 (1992), ed. Peter M. Haas. On security issues, see Emanuel Adler, 'The Emergence of Cooperation: National Epistemic Communities and the International Evolution of the Idea of Nuclear Arms Control', ibid., pp. 100–145.

differentiated by their community meanings and consequently unlikely to engender intercommunity anarchy.

It follows, therefore, that whether security communities are also military alliances is less a function of intercommunity anarchy than of the 'neighbourhood' (the strategic environment) where the states organized into security communities happen to 'live'. It would be hard to imagine a Latin American security community—e.g. Argentina, Brazil, Paraguay, and Uruguay—forming a military alliance against the United States and Mexico, another security community.[77] Moreover, there is a military alliance in the Euro-Atlantic space today, not because a security community of Western European and North American states created NATO, but because, in response to the Soviet threat, these states created NATO and then gradually—and in part because of NATO—became a security community.[78]

The conditions for peace: contextual variables that promote the development of security communities

In the last section, I identified material and normative power, knowledge, communicative processes, institutions, and social learning as variables that contribute to the development of collective identities and mutual trust—which in turn drive dependable expectations of peaceful change. In this section, I will start by analysing conditions that, while not necessary for the development of security communities, may nevertheless play a facilitating role: (1) a higher expected utility from peace than from war; (2) a 'civic culture'; (3) Great-Power commitment to the peaceful resolution of disputes; (4) an ethical code; (5) mutual legitimization; and (6) peacemakers. Then I will consider multilateral war-preventing practices that may help avert war and create favourable conditions for the development of dependable expectations of peaceful change.

1. The development of security communities may be favoured where the expected utility of peace exceeds that of war, including victorious war. Technological change, economic development, and a perception of war as inefficient, unnecessary, and normatively unacceptable[79] may lead to what I have elsewhere called 'a peace trap', in which states, taking everything into consideration, choose peaceful rather than violent means of achieving their goals.[80] For example, nuclear weapons have had a strong influence on expectations of the outcome and efficacy of war and produced a recognition of the need to cooperate with adversaries (mainly through nuclear arms

---

[77] On the incipient security community in South America, see Andrew Hurrell, 'An Emerging Security Community in South America', in Adler and Barnett, *Security Communities*.

[78] On NATO as a security-community–building institution, see Emanuel Adler, 'Seeds of Peaceful Change: The OSCE's Security Community-building Model', in Adler and Barnett, *Security Communities*. See also Thomas Risse-Kappen, *Cooperation Among Democracies: The European Influence on U.S. Foreign Policy* (Princeton: Princeton University Press, 1995).

[79] John Mueller, *Retreat From Doomsday: The Obsolescence of Major War* (New York: Basic Books, 1989).

[80] Emanuel Adler, 'Seasons of Peace: Progress in Postwar International Security', in Emanuel Adler and Beverly Crawford (eds.), *Progress in Postwar International Relations* (New York: Columbia University Press, 1991), p. 128.

control).[81] To a large extent, these expectations help explain why the Cold War stayed and ended cold.

Also, consistent with liberal theory, since the end of World War II expectations of economic progress have done much to increase the disparity between the expected utilities of peace and war. Ole Waever, for example, has persuasively shown that one of the factors that encouraged Western Europe to become a tightly coupled security community was the evolution of a practice and discourse of international politics that gave greater prominence to economic than to security and defence issues.[82] Moreover, according to John Mueller, F. H. Hinsley, and Michael Howard, people attach a smaller social value to war than they did, for example, before World War I, when war was 'almost universally considered an acceptable, perhaps an inevitable, and for many people a desirable way of settling international differences'.[83]

The point is not that the ascription of a higher expected utility to peace than to war is a necessary or sufficient condition for the development of security communities. It may only explain the development of a 'non-war community'. But if people come to expect war only as an unwanted event that is caused by the predatory practices of a surviving minority of predatory states or breaks out only when all efforts to avert hostilities have failed, the higher expected utility of peace may be conducive to the promotion of social, economic, and cultural transactions, the legitimization and strengthening of multilateral institutional means of conflict prevention and resolution, and the development of a climate in which states redefine their understanding of international reality and their social identities and interests.

2. Peace among democratic states has become almost axiomatic, even though, as I argued above, when scholars refer to the 'democratic peace' they do not mean a *state* of peace, but only the absence of war among democracies.[84] Liberal democracy, however, may help create a favourable context for the evolution of security communities. To see this, we must take the liberal system of values that sustains democratic practices and institutions not as a deterministic variable, as 'democratic peace' scholars usually do, but as primarily the historical development and diffusion of a transnational '*civic culture*'[85] that, cutting across national borders, becomes an identity marker and indicator of reciprocal peaceful intentions.

A democratic civic culture encourages the creation of strong civil societies—and of transnational networks and processes—which promote community bonds and a common identity through the relatively free interpenetration of societies, particularly the movement and exchange of people, goods, and ideas. For example, strong civil societies greatly facilitate the spread of practices that promote human rights and environmental protection. These, in turn, help produce and reinforce a collective social identity and security-community bonds. Moreover, social networks constituted around liberal norms facilitate the transfer of democratic norms and practices to societies that lack them.[86]

[81] Robert Jervis, 'The Political Effect of Nuclear Weapons: A Comment', *International Security*, 13 (1988), pp. 80–90.

[82] Waever, 'Insecurity, Security, and Asecurity'.

[83] Michael Howard, 'The Causes of Wars', *Wilson Quarterly*, 8 (Summer 1984), p. 92. See also Mueller, *Retreat From Doomsday*, and F. H. Hinsley, 'Peace and War in Modern Times', in Raimo Vayrynen (ed.), *The Quest for Peace* (Beverly Hills, Ca.: Sage, 1987), pp. 77–8.

[84] See n. 8 above.

[85] Gabriel A. Almond and Sidney Verba, *The Civic Culture* (Boston: Little, Brown, 1963).

[86] Margaret Keck and Kathryn Sikkink, *Activists Beyond Borders: Advocacy Networks in International Politics* (Ithaca: Cornell University Press, 1997).

3. Security communities are more likely to develop and remain stable when 'outside' Great Powers (we already have seen that security communities tend to develop around 'cores of strength', which may include Great Powers) are committed to the peaceful resolution of conflicts.[87] Otherwise, their predatory practices may interfere with the proliferation of regional economic exchanges, the work of regional international institutions, and regional social learning processes; in the long run this can only endanger the development and stability of security communities. While it is possible that real or perceived outside military threats by Great Powers may trigger the development of security communities—for example, the Soviet Union vis-à-vis Western Europe and China vis-à-vis ASEAN—over the long term the threat and use of organized violence against some or all of the members of a security community may actually undermine its survival. To assess the future of ASEAN as a security community, therefore, we should keep an eye on China's behavior toward its members and on whether they manage to bind China to multilateral security practices and institutions.[88]

4. Despite all the horror stories of the twentieth century, Dorothy Jones maintains that what she calls the 'world of the warlord states' has increasingly been challenged by the development of a 'Code of Peace' or set of international standards of peaceful behaviour.[89] She claims (and I agree) that the August 1975 Helsinki Final Act—which spawned the continuing Conference on Security and Cooperation in Europe (CSCE)—did much to strengthen the 'Code of Peace'.[90] Although history has repeatedly shown that 'codes of peace' may prove insufficient to prevent war, they can nevertheless create favourable conditions for the development of security communities. Moreover, as in the case of the CSCE (which in 1995 became the Organization for Security and Cooperation in Europe [OSCE]), a 'code' may be merely a legal or political representation of the constitutive rules that make up a collective identity.

The Helsinki Final Act, which was signed by all European countries (except for Albania), the Soviet Union, the United States, and Canada, comprised ten principles of legitimate international behaviour (e.g. respect for territorial integrity and the political independence of states) and domestic political conduct (e.g. respect for human rights and fundamental freedoms). With the addition by the Charter of Paris (1990) and subsequent documents of important stipulations about democracy, the rule of law, and human rights, what began as a regional code of conduct turned into a constitutive normative structure for a security community expected to develop in the area between Vancouver and Vladivostok.[91]

The 'OSCE region' has not yet become a security community; I doubt that it will any time soon. In spite of the ethnic conflicts now raging in its domain, however, and despite the fact that two steps forward have sometimes been followed by one

---

[87] On the role of Great Powers in regional security, see Paul A. Papayoanou, 'Great Powers and Regional Orders: Possibilities and Prospects After the Cold War', in David A. Lake and Patrick M. Morgan (eds.), *Regional Orders: Building Security in a New World* (University Park, Pennsylvania: The Pennsylvania State University Press, 1997), pp. 125–39.

[88] On ASEAN as an emerging security community, see Amitav Acharya, 'Collective Identity and Conflict Resolution in Southeast Asia', in Adler and Barnett, *Security Communities*.

[89] Dorothy V. Jones, *Code of Peace: Ethics and Security in the World of the Warlord States* (Chicago: The University of Chicago Press, 1991).

[90] *Ibid.*, pp. 159–66; Adler, 'Seeds of Peaceful Change'; Adler, 'Imagined (Security) Communities', pp. 268–75.

[91] Adler, 'Imagined (Security) Communities', pp. 268–70.

step backward, OSCE injunctions have helped increase the interdependence of East and West and transactions between them, thereby laying the foundation for a liberal transnational collective understanding in the OSCE region. To a large extent, whether Eastern European states are accepted as members of the European Union (EU) and the North Atlantic Treaty Organization (NATO) will depend on the extent to which they internalize the OSCE 'code of peace', which now includes, for example, the innovative 'accountability norm' whereby OSCE states are accountable to one another and to the OSCE community for what they do to their own citizens.[92] Thomas Buergenthal captured the subtle but crucial essence of the OSCE 'Code of Peace' when he asserted that it can be compared to those national constitutions that, without being legally binding or enforceable in the courts, serve as the normative source of a country's public order.[93]

5. The development of a security community also requires states wishing to become part of it to see each other—and the future community—as legitimate. It is the community's legitimacy in the eyes of its members that, more than anything else, explains the workings of a regional governance system based on collective identity. At the same time, the conditions in which members of a security community view each other as part of a community and are given certain rights, obligations, and duties are contingent on their ability to abide by the community's constitutive principles.[94]

This explains why the EU and the Euro-Atlantic security community, as represented by NATO, have extended 'probationary' status to Eastern European states that wish to join them. The behaviour of the probationers is constantly scrutinized for indications that they can be legitimate members of these communities. The main purpose, for example, of NATO's Partnership for Peace is to transform (teach and socialize) some of the former Communist states of Eastern Europe into legitimate members of the Euro-Atlantic security community. As far as I know, nothing in realist theory says that states wishing to enter an alliance with other states must transform the prospective partners' domestic institutions and practices. NATO's enlargement, therefore, is not only the strengthening of an already strong military alliance, but also the expansion eastward of a veteran and generally stable security community.

6. Although particular individuals cannot be conceived as a necessary, let alone sufficient, condition for the development of security communities, I nevertheless include peacemakers in my list of the conditions for peace, because resourceful, powerful, and sometimes courageous and visionary leaders can create propitious circumstances for the development of security communities. In other words, it takes agency to create common purpose, collective identity, and mutual trust.[95] Moreover, it takes leaders who know they can be trusted to trust others as well.[96] More importantly, it takes peacemakers—whence my epigraph from Yitzhak Rabin—to start communicative processes in conditions of mistrust and adversity; in the long

---

[92] Ibid., p. 271. See also Marianne Hanson, 'Democratization and Norm Creation in Europe', *Adelphi Papers*, 284 (London: Brassey's for the International Institute for Strategic Studies [IISS], 1994), p. 34.

[93] Thomas Buergenthal, 'The CSCE Rights System', *George Washington Journal of International Law and Economics*, 25 (1992), pp. 380–1.

[94] Thomas M. Franck, *The Power of Legitimacy among Nations* (New York: Oxford University Press, 1990), p. 196.

[95] See n. 17 above.

[96] Robert Wuthnow, 'The Foundations of Trust', *Report from the Institute for Philosophy and Public Policy*, 18 (University of Maryland, 1998), p. 4. On trust, see also Barbara Mistzal, *Trust in Modern Societies* (Cambridge: Polity Press, 1996).

run, trust may spill over to the elites and the masses and thus be conducive to the construction of security communities.

Before ending this section, I would like to refer to war-preventing practices that help generate a propitious setting for the development of security communities. Nuclear arms control practices, for example, now widespread around the world, may help states and societies in conflict initiate communicative processes that create a common ground for evaluation and action. Elsewhere I have argued that the practice of nuclear arms control was beneficial not so much in limiting weapons, in a formal technical sense, but primarily because it engendered international cooperative processes that helped the superpowers develop a coordination game and discover the extent to which its symbolic contents suggested compromises, limits, and regulations.[97] To some extent, and beyond their specific functions—such as conflict prevention and resolution—multilateral diplomacy and UN global peacekeeping activities engage contending states in social communicative and exchange processes that augment the future possibility of peace.[98] Particularly noteworthy are the practices of 'cooperative security', such as confidence-building measures, which are being increasingly adopted in Europe, Southeast Asia, and Latin America. This demilitarized concept of security

has resulted in imbuing security with political and human dimensions, and in basing security on confidence and cooperation, the elaboration of peaceful means of dispute settlement between states, the consolidation of justice and democracy in civil society, and the advancement of human freedom and rights, including national minority rights.[99]

Thus, while arms control and cooperative security practices cannot, in and of themselves, help constitute a *state* of peace, they can do three things. First, they can promote communicative processes that help states discover their affinities and common interests. Second, they can help keep regional conflicts at bay and facilitate the development of transactions, institutions, and learning processes that are conducive to the development of security communities. Third, they can impede the spread of instability and predatory practices to regions that already enjoy a measure of dependable expectations of peaceful change. Thus, for example, in the absence of urgent and effective arms-control and confidence-building measures, the recent nuclear tests by India and Pakistan may not only bring disaster to these countries but may also unleash a proliferation chain reaction that would negatively affect existing security communities (such as the EU) and prevent the formation of new ones (in Asia and the Middle East, for example).

By way of example: constructing a Mediterranean region

There is no inevitable trend in world affairs toward security communities; as we have seen, people are enjoying a state of peace in only a few regions. In less 'fortunate'

---

[97] Adler, 'The Emergence of Cooperation'.

[98] John G. Ruggie (ed.), *Multilateralism Matters: The Theory and Praxis of an Institutional Form* (New York: Columbia University Press, 1993); Michael Barnett, 'The New UN Politics of Peace', *Global Governance*, 1 (1995), pp. 79–98.

[99] Janie Leatherman, 'Conflict Transformation in the CSCE: Learning and Institutionalization', *Cooperation and Conflict*, 28 (1993), p. 414.

parts of the world, such as Africa, South Asia, Central Asia, and North Asia, security communities are less likely to develop any time soon. And although Israel, the Palestinians, and Arab countries have recently flirted with ending their protracted conflict, the conditions for peace in the Middle East are weak or nonexistent and a state of peace may still be decades away.

On the other hand, the Euro-Atlantic community is expanding eastward, while the North and South American security communities may soon become a single Western Hemisphere security community. Moreover, in spite (or because) of internal and external sources of instability, ASEAN countries have been keeping on course toward becoming a security community. A weak but noticeable effort is under way to socially construct a Mediterranean regional identity that may in the long run be critical for what happens in the Middle East. Owing to the present and future importance of the Mediterranean area, I will focus on this case.

It is not implausible to suggest that the Mediterranean basin (Southern Europe, North Africa, and the Middle East) may soon become one of the world's most strategically important and contentious regions. Straddling two of the deepest divides of our era—that between the West and Islam, and that between the (prosperous) North and the (destitute) South—the Mediterranean basin harbours some of the most dangerous threats to contemporary international security, including proliferation of weapons of mass destruction, international terrorism, internal and external low-level warfare, interstate military conflict, and—no less serious—the drug trade, uncontrolled migration, and unsustainable development. As one of Samuel Huntington's critical areas, where the 'fault lines' of the 'Clash of Civilizations' are located,[100] the Mediterranean region provides a 'hard case' for assessing the conditions for and state of peace on the eve of the new millennium.

Thus it may be a sign of the times that, when Western states, especially the members of the EU, felt threatened by instability in the South, they chose, not to send in (or threaten to send in) the tanks, build a new system of alliances, or create a collective security system, but to extend the European area of stability southward and create a Mediterranean region and identity. To jump-start this process, European governments, EU institutions, the OSCE, the Western European Union (WEU), the Council of Europe (C of E), NATO (to some extent), and a large number of private non-governmental organizations began to promote: (a) increased economic and social interactions around the Mediterranean (for example, by means of free trade zones); (b) multilateral institutional dialogues, 'track-two diplomacy', and confidence-building measures; (c) a plethora of relations across civil societies between business, professional, and cultural groups; and (d) a long but nevertheless necessary social learning process.[101]

---

[100] Samuel Huntington, 'The Clash of Civilizations?', *Foreign Affairs*, 72 (1993), pp. 22–49; *The Clash of Civilizations and the Remaking of World Order* (New York: Simon & Schuster, 1996).

[101] On the construction of the Mediterranean region see, for example, Roberto Aliboni, George Joffé, and Tim Niblock, *Security Challenges in the Mediterranean Region* (London: Frank Cass, 1996); Alberto Bin (ed.), *Cooperation and Security in the Mediterranean: Prospects after Barcelona* (Malta: The Mediterranean Academy of Diplomatic Studies, University of Malta, 1996); Antonio Marquina and Hans Gunter Braude (eds.), 'Confidence Building and Partnership in the Western Mediterranean: Tasks for Preventive Diplomacy and Conflict Avoidance' (Madrid: UNISCI Papers no. 1, UNISCI, 1994); Fred Tanner, 'An Emerging Security Agenda for the Mediterranean', *Mediterranean Politics*, 1 (1996), pp. 279–94.

So far, however, this attempt has been impeded not only by violent conflict in the Middle East and Algeria, but also by Islamic states' suspicions that lurking behind the Mediterranean initiative are Western attempts to impose a hegemonic regional identity. Moreover, owing to the cleavages referred to above, the process of building a Mediterranean regional identity is likely to be much more difficult than any previous attempts of pluralistic regional integration such as the EU and ASEAN.[102] Thus, while the process of building a Mediterranean region is still in its infancy, the odds may already favour a 'clash of civilizations'. For this reason it is interesting to analyse the conditions for and state of peace in this area.

Past efforts to create a Mediterranean 'region' were severely limited or failed altogether. The first multilateral effort was launched in 1972 by the foreign ministers of Italy, Libya, Malta, and Tunisia.[103] They held a series of meetings aimed at establishing cooperative programmes in communications, tourism, fishing, and trade. The failure to attract other participants, however, kept such cooperation from materializing. In 1975, the predecessor of the OSCE, the CSCE, identified a Mediterranean component of its programme; throughout the 1970s and 1980s it convened regional experts in economics, science, culture, and the environment to explore cooperative efforts that would build mutual trust and contribute to regional stability.[104] The meetings accomplished little, however, and did not attract the attention of the United States, which focused primarily on the East–West conflict. The Euro-Arab Dialogue began in 1974, in the wake of the oil crisis, in order to institute cooperation between members of the European Community and members of the Arab League. These efforts, too, remained unproductive because of the Cold War, Iraq's invasion of Kuwait in 1991, and the Arab League's condition, rejected by the Europeans, that the Palestinian issue be included on the agenda. The Mediterranean Action Plan, formulated within the framework of the 1976 Barcelona Convention to combat pollution of the Mediterranean Sea, was indeed successful, but the focus of cooperation has remained limited to technical environmental issues, with no 'spillover' effects on other areas of concern.

In a post-war world dominated by East–West confrontation, the creation of a Mediterranean region of cooperation and stability was a low priority for the Great Powers. The end of the Cold War, however, promised to eliminate the obstacles to regional cooperation. Accordingly, the notion of a Conference on Security and Cooperation in the Mediterranean (CSCM) became popular. Like earlier efforts, the aim was to boost regional economic development and social conditions through cooperation and to increase regional trust and transparency.[105] The end of the Cold War created fertile ground for the OSCE, WEU, and C of E to become involved in regional activities to promote trust. In 1990–1, several southern European countries

---

[102] On Europe, see Weaver, 'Insecurity, Security, and Asecurity'; on ASEAN, see Acharya, 'Collective Identity and Conflict Resolution in Southeast Asia'.

[103] The following three paragraphs rely in part on Emanuel Adler and Beverly Crawford, 'Regional Security through Integration: Constructing the Mediterranean Region', draft proposal, December 1997; and on Emanuel Adler, 'The Cooperative Security Way to Stable Peace: Constructing Regional and Global Security Communities', paper commissioned by the Swedish Ministry of Foreign Affairs, August 1996.

[104] Victor-Yves Ghebali, 'Toward a Mediterranean Helsinki-type Process', *Mediterranean Quarterly*, 4 (1993), p. 92.

[105] Ibid., pp. 93–7.

proposed a plan for a Western Mediterranean CSCM; in 1994, NATO formulated a Mediterranean policy and promised to work with non-members to strengthen regional stability.

Encouraged by progress in the Arab–Israeli peace process, the EU became formally involved in the project to create regional stability with the establishment of the Euro-Med Partnership in 1994. In 1995, a Euro-Mediterranean Conference was convened in Barcelona to establish a framework for the region, with its population of 700 million people in 27 countries along the shores of the Mediterranean Sea. In addition to the 15 EU states, the Euro–Mediterranean Partnership (EMP) includes Algeria, Cyprus, Egypt, Israel, Jordan, Lebanon, Malta, Morocco, Syria, Tunisia, Turkey, and the Palestinian Authority. The political element of the Barcelona declaration includes a list of principles concerning respect for democracy and the rule of law, human rights, the right of self-determination, non-interference in the internal affairs of other states, and peaceful resolution of disputes. It also stipulates cooperation to combat terrorism. On the economic front, the Barcelona document provides for a regional partnership to promote economic development by means of a free trade zone to be created by the year 2010.[106] The objectives of the Barcelona Declaration were supposed to be confirmed by 27 Mediterranean countries in Malta in 1997. But the stalled Middle East peace process overshadowed that meeting and cast grave doubts on the success of the EMP.

The EMP and related efforts have in large part been about helping Mediterranean basin countries adapt to economic globalization and protecting European states from potential sources of regional instability and insecurity arising from the South.[107] Culture, nonetheless, permeates the entire initiative.[108] By culture, I mean neither what Huntington meant in 'the Clash of Civilizations' nor a romantic view of Mediterranean cultural attributes—olives, wine, sunshine, and gorgeous beaches. Rather, I have in mind the development of a relatively new type of preventive diplomatic practice that depends for its success on the political and social engineering of a Mediterranean 'we feeling' or collective social identity. Thus while it is true that the EMP is mainly driven by short-term incentives, such as material interests and a perceived mutual threat, the long-term interest behind the initiative is to catalyse conditions that may help bring about a future state of peace in the region.

Because few if any of the conditions mentioned in the previous section exist in the Mediterranean area, the challenge of the ongoing Mediterranean 'dialogue' is to *socially engineer* them. To do this successfully, however, greater efforts must be devoted to (a) providing economic incentives so that peace will have a higher expected utility than war; (b) seeking the support of the US (which seldom buys into the type of diplomacy associated with the EMP) and a commitment from that country and Russia to the peaceful resolution of disputes in the area; (c) developing

[106] *Barcelona Declaration Adopted at the Euro-Mediterranean Conference* (Barcelona, November 28, 1995).

[107] On economics, see George Joffé, 'The Economic Factor in Mediterranean Security', *The International Spectator*, 31 (1996), pp. 75–87. On regional security, see Aliboni *et al.*, *Security Challenges in the Mediterranean Region*.

[108] See, for example, Laura Guazzone, 'The Evolving Framework of Arab Security Perceptions: The Impact of Cultural Factors', *The International Spectator*, 31 (1996), pp. 63–74.

transnational and international social networks[109] to promote the emergence of a Mediterranean civic culture based on values that both Northern and Southern countries can live with, such as sustainable development and the rule of law (which allows for differences in political regimes); (d) investing resources and building strong multilateral institutions, in order to raise the regional political stakes to the point that it becomes imperative for political actors in the Middle East and North Africa to settle their differences; (e) instituting confidence-building measures to promote the development of mutual legitimacy and a consensual Mediterranean identity; and (f) agreeing on the basic normative or 'constitutional' principles—such as sovereignty, non-intervention, the rule of law, and sustainable development— around which shared practices can be constituted.

To sum up, behind the EMP and related efforts lies the haunting (some would say discouraging) idea that the most promising—perhaps only—way to achieve long-term security, economic welfare, political stability, and peace in the Mediterranean area is neither an elaborate system of alliances or collective security system, nor a functional scheme of economic integration, but the socio-cultural process of constructing a region. The challenges are immense; it will probably take decades to construct a Mediterranean region. Nevertheless, as long as other security practices are unavailable or impracticable there, the only alternative left for socially constructing the conditions for peace is Huntington's 'clash of civilizations'.

Beyond the eighty years' crisis

Since Carr referred to the twenty years' crisis, immense changes have occurred in international relations, notably the victory of liberal democracies over fascism and Communism, economic globalization, multilateralism, the widening gap between North and South, the development of nuclear weapons and other weapons of mass destruction, and the emergence of international human-rights and environmental regimes. These changes, however, have done little to overcome what Carr called the crisis of democracy, the crisis of self-determination, and the moral crisis. Many states have yet to become (liberal) democracies. The contradictions between self-determination and the sovereign integrity of states have worsened since the end of the Cold War. And, at the global level, we are very far from having found a common moral purpose around which to build 'the state of peace'. The 'twenty years' crisis' became 'the eighty years' crisis'. Moreover, the eighty years' crisis has probably become more intractable, because of (a) primordial primitivism; (b) technological and integration imperatives; (c) remnants of 'warlord' organization and doctrine; (d) economic inequality; and (e) unsustainable development.

It would go beyond the scope of this paper to analyse these threats to peace in depth; hence I will conclude with a few words about how they are endangering the state of and conditions for peace, supplemented by remarks about positive conditions that may help international society overcome these threats.

[109] See, for example, Roberto Aliboni, Abdel Monem Said Aly, and Alvaro Vasconcelos, *Joint Report of EuroMeSCo's Working Group on Political and Security Co-operation* (second draft), April 1997; Maria-Angels Roque, *Forum Civil Euromed: Towards a New Scenario of Partnership in the Euro-Mediterranean Area* (Barcelona: Institut Catala de la Mediterrania d'Estudis y Cooperacio, 1997).

By *primordial primitivism* I mean the return, mainly since the Cold War, of nationalist ideologies that glorify the restoration of an ostensible 'golden age', the triumph of the ethnic 'tribe' over other 'tribes', and the use of religion as a 'rational-izing' alternative to secular and modern nationalism. In some parts of the world, including Europe, primordial primitivism and the ethnic conflicts fuelled by it are threatening the state of and conditions for peace. Bosnia, Chechnya, Kosovo, and Hebron—all raise doubts about the ability of peacemakers and international institutions to promote the conditions for and state of peace and constitute warning signs for existing security communities.

Another dangerous threat to peace comes from what I call a *technological and integration imperative,* which is not unrelated to primordial primitivism. I mean the peril posed by the ultra-modern technologies in the hands of the leaders of some states that lack domestic integration and evince an inability and/or unwillingness to integrate into international society and a concomitant pattern of uninhibited bellicose behaviour.

Yet another threat to the state of and conditions for peace comes from the fact that practices of peaceful change, such as arms control and cooperative security, have not replaced what Dorothy Jones called 'warlord' organization practices and doctrines.[110] Even in the most stable security communities, military establishments and doctrines are changing much more slowly than regional economic and political behaviour and constitute a latent threat to dependable expectations of peaceful change.

The gravest threat of all, however, one that requires global cooperation to find adequate and equitable solutions, stems from the economic inequality between the North and South. In other words, the growing poverty, misery, hunger, and, most important, frustration of the less-developed countries that are home to a large fraction of the world's population interfere with social communicative processes and prevent the development of mutual trust both within underdeveloped regions and across the North–South divide. Moreover, unsustainable development, still prevalent in most of the world, coupled with unsustainable population growth, are ticking bombs that threaten to set off the wars of the next century.

To help overcome or at least manage some of these threats and facilitate the development of new security communities and strengthening of existing ones, we need to encourage: (a) the practice of establishing the rights and *obligations* of states and peoples by means of *politically* binding regional codes of conduct; (b) the principle of multiculturalism; and (c) managed globalization and sustainable development.

The promotion, negotiation, and establishment of *politically* binding codes of conduct, such as the Helsinki Final Act and related injunctions, may be crucial for alleviating the ongoing eighty years' crisis and creating favourable conditions for the development of security communities. These regional 'constitutions' or 'codes of peace' should not be seen as coming at the expense of the global constitutive norms, especially sovereignty, which constitute the identities of states *qua* states, but as complementary to them. Regional codes of conduct are constitutive only of privileged regional communities (privileged because they have developed a system of regional governance) and of the social identities of people living in them.

---

[110] Jones, *Code of Peace.*

To encourage the development of security communities, regional codes of conduct should include the 'accountability norm', make the rule of law a *sine qua non* principle of regional sociability, and—following Carr's suggestion of 55 years ago—consecrate not only the mutual *rights* of states (e.g. territorial integrity) and of peoples (e.g. human rights), but also the mutual *obligations* of states (e.g. protecting national minorities and preventing transboundary pollution) and peoples (e.g. respecting other peoples' right to self-determination).

The state of peace will also be enhanced by the promotion—through domestic (education) and international (multilateral diplomacy) means—of multicultural principles that encourage people to view nations not as 'real' but as 'imagined communities'.[111] 'One hundred and fifty years of civil peace in multicultural Switzerland make my point'.[112] In other words, taking national identities in a more plastic, if not socially constructed, sense should promote the idea that peoples of several cultures can self-determine and aspire to build up their shared state. Ernst Haas has shown that, while liberal decision-making procedures are better equipped than other types to accommodate multiculturalism, in practice liberal nation-states have still not learned to cope with it.[113]

Finally, to deal adequately with the pressures caused by economic globalization and unsustainable development, international society must develop a practice of preventing and managing global and regional economic crises. By managing economic crises, I do not necessarily mean interference with global and regional markets, but the development of improved routines of international cooperation that are better suited to foresee, prevent, and manage the undesirable effects of globalization on individual states and security communities. Concomitantly, the strengthening of the practice of sustainable development may not only help states and societies coordinate their development and environmental policies, but also, and more importantly, become an important resource for the social construction of transnational collective identities and thus of security communities.[114]

As we approach the new millennium, and in light of my analysis of the state of and conditions for peace, I find no better way to conclude this article than by referring to Carr's final statement in *The Conditions of Peace*, which is still relevant today, both morally and practically: 'The future lies with those who can resolutely turn their back on [the old world] and face the new world with understanding, courage and imagination'.[115]

---

[111] Benedict Anderson, *Imagined Communities: Reflections on the Origin and Spread of Nationalism* (London: Verso, 1983).

[112] Haas, *Nationalism, Liberalism, and Progress*, p. 40.

[113] Ibid., pp. 21 and 336.

[114] Philip Shabecoff, *A New Name for Peace: International Environmentalism, Sustainable Development, and Democracy* (Hanover: University Press of New England, 1996).

[115] Carr, *Conditions of Peace*, p. 275.

Politics, Norms and Peaceful Change

FRIEDRICH V. KRATOCHWIL

The best proof that E. H. Carr has written a true 'classic' is that *The Twenty Years' Crisis* provides much food for thought even now when some of its alleged foundational verities have become problematic. Rather than being limited to a 'realist' understanding of politics pure and simple, the reader encounters an analysis that is much more subtle though much less scientific than later realist interpretations would suggest. True, the first chapter is entitled 'The science of international politics' but the discussion about 'purpose', Carr's invocation of Marx, and the intellectual history he paints with a broad brush, make it clear that it is not a conception of natural science that informs his inquiry. Besides, as with every classic, different readings are possible.

One of the startling features for the contemporary student of international affairs is the much broader scope of the work when compared with the usual realist analysis of international politics. Carr not only writes a very explicit chapter about the limitations of the realist point of view, he also engages the topic of ethics and international politics, an issue which is nowadays at most addressed by some non-realist specialists, who 'do' ethics and international affairs. To that extent Carr bases his treatise implicitly on a substantive understanding of politics rather than on a method or some criteria derived from the philosophy of science, as has become the vogue ever since the 'second debate'.[1] For him, gaining a better understanding of international politics implies first and foremost coming to terms with the crisis into which our unreflected practices have led us, namely, constitution making and designing international organizations without much concern for their essential prerequisites. Gaining a better understanding also involves a critique of the prevailing ideology of liberalism which had given rise to such mistaken endeavours.

Carr's approach is, therefore, one of 'critical' rather than 'problem solving' theory in Cox's parlance.[2] It is perhaps not a theory at all, as all the trappings of a scientific theory are eschewed, and the mode of analysis develops out of the critical reflections of a student of history. The analytical tools are clearly those of an historiographer whose narrative emerges from the tensions engendered by the compositional principle of pairs of opposition. Thus 'utopia' and 'reality' become themes that serve as frames for further pairs of opposition that are supposed to illuminate political praxis. In this context the issue of determinism vs. free will, the opposition

---

[1] On the issue of the three debates that were constitutive of the 'discipline' see Steve Smith (ed.), 'The Self-Image of a Discipline: A Genealogy of International Relations Theory', in Ken Booth and Steve Smith (eds.), *International Relations Theory Today* (University Park, PA: Penn State Press, 1995), ch. 1.
[2] See Robert Cox, 'Social Forces, States, and World Orders', *Millennium*, 10 (Summer 1981), pp. 126–55.

between theory and praxis, between bureaucratic vs. intellectual modes of approaching political problems, between the 'Left' and the 'Right' make their appearance, as does the already mentioned opposition of ethics and politics.

Whether a mode of analysis that relies on a list of antinomies (in a way anticipating the binary oppositions which characterize the work of structuralists such as Levi Strauss) is sufficient is, of course, highly debatable. But it can be useful when one attempts to break out of the given conceptual schemes which are the reason for the observable crisis. Rather than starting with the state or the 'unit' in the system, Carr—as a student of history and in particular of the Russian revolution—is aware of the fundamentally different character of politics in the aftermath of World War I. Not only have the old elites shown their incompetence and bankruptcy, the new ideologies and their social manifestations showed the capacity of systematically subverting the measures by which traditional statecraft had attempted to create order.[3] A whole new dynamic was at work to which the traditional ideologies and their concomitant analyses had little to contribute. As Carr put it so aptly in his Preface to the first edition, which went to press in July 1939:

> Yet even while war is raging, there may be some practical importance in an attempt to analyze the underlying and significant, rather than the immediate and personal, cause of the disaster. If and when peace returns to the world, the lessons of the breakdown which has involved Europe in a second major war within twenty years and two months of the Versailles Treaty will need to be earnestly pondered. A settlement which, having destroyed the National Socialist Rulers of Germany, leaves untouched the conditions which made the phenomenon of National Socialism possible, will run the risk of being as short lived and as tragic as the settlement of 1919. . . . The next Peace Conference, if it is not to repeat the fiasco of the last, will have to concern itself with issues more fundamental than the drawing of frontiers.[4]

Here the importance of domestic structures for a durable peace is clearly recognized. Beyond that, Carr himself suggests in the 'Conclusion' of *The Twenty Years' Crisis* that one of the problematic areas for a science of international politics is the divergence between the state as a territorial form of organization and the 'economy'. Nevertheless, his suggestions remain within the traditional paradigm of socialist thought: While indicating that the best 'hope for progress towards international conciliation' lies 'along the path of economic reconstruction', his remedy involves, for us contemporaries somewhat curiously, 'the frank acceptance of the subordination of economic advantage to social ends'.[5] In this way, he concludes should 'the increasing elimination of the profit motive from the national economy' also 'facilitate . . . its partial elimination from foreign policy'.[6] As I shall argue below, this might be a utopian hope, but the organizational innovation which the decision makers hit upon at Bretton Woods provided some temporary stabilization of the relations between the economy and the (welfare)-state[7] that has been called into question again by the liberalizing pressures that threaten to once more 'disembed' the economy.

---

[3] See Carr's remark: 'The real international crisis of the modern world is in the final and irrevocable breakdown of the conditions which made the nineteenth century possible'. E.H. Carr, *The Twenty Years' Crisis* (New York: Harper, 1946), p. 237.

[4] Ibid., p. ix.

[5] Ibid., p. 238.

[6] Ibid., p. 239.

[7] See John Ruggie, 'International Regimes, Transactions and Change: Embedded Liberalism in the Post War Economic Order', in Stephen Krasner (ed.), *International Regimes* (Ithaca, NY: Cornell University Press, 1983), pp. 195–32.

It is here that the limitations of Carr's analysis become most visible. His inquiry is still informed by some conception of the national economy as a subordinate system of society. Both assumptions provide little guidance for analysing order problems in international relations, particularly when several processes of change converge in the processes of 'globalization' that we witness today. Deep-seated changes in the structure of production are paralleled by secular political changes, and both are linked and fed by the communications revolution that fundamentally transforms our way of thinking about global problems. It might be premature to conclude that the unit of international politics, the state, is on the decline but that it is affected and perhaps significantly altered by these converging streams of change can hardly be doubted. Already Carr had to admit in the Preface to the second edition that his analytical instruments were perhaps no longer adequate, that the main body of the book 'too readily and too complacently' accepted the nation state 'as the unit of international society'.[8]

With this admission, the challenge is squarely put to us to rethink and conceptualize anew the problematique of international politics at the century's end. This reflection has at a minimum to include a brief critique of the disciplinary understanding that developed in the aftermath of Carr's critique. Oddly enough, instead of a conception of politics which incorporates the tension between 'realism' and 'utopianism' which Carr advocated, the effect of the disciplinary emancipation of international politics from international law and history alike came at a heavy price: an implausible conception of politics was paralleled by an equally implausible conception of law, and the study of both was largely separated from that of history, a problem that the second debate correctly identified.

While I obviously cannot hope to untangle all the threads of the development of the discipline and its various internal criticisms,[9] I shall focus in this article on the role of international law and international organization in addressing one of Carr's main concerns: the issue of peaceful change. This in turn will involve me in a discussion of institution building in the international arena and the context in which such efforts take place. To that extent, the criticism of the disciplinary understanding has to be supplemented by a more constructive research agenda. Here I suggest that issues of legitimacy and the changing boundaries of the political are as important as technical knowledge or the problems of transparency. While the latter problem has received a great deal of attention in the realist and liberal perspective alike,[10] I want to suggest that a perspective focused on cheating and transaction costs is far too narrow. Notions of cost are crucially shaped by our normative understandings of legitimacy and by the available knowledge that provides for remedies but enters also into our definitions of problems that require international attention.

In other words, the article argues that if we accept Carr's challenge, we will have to engage in an inquiry into the possibilities and limitations of various organizational forms for resolving conflicts and for providing institutional grounding of cooperative endeavours. In this way, we neither submit to the error that the units of

---

[8] Ibid., p. viii.

[9] As Roger Epp shows in his contribution to this Special Issue, the persistence of the English school dedicated to the exploration of the historical genesis of state systems demonstrated at least that not all international relations theorists had submitted to the *fata morgana* of a transhistorically valid theory.

[10] See, e.g., the argument on cheating and transaction costs that inform most of the analyses on cooperation under anarchy. See, for example, the special issue edited by Kenneth Oye (ed.), 'Cooperation under Anarchy', *World Politics*, 38 (Oct. 1985).

the international system are simply given and to its corollary of structurally determined conflict,[11] nor are we led to believe that the templates of organizations we know from domestic society are necessarily the ones that could ensure peaceful change in the international arena. As civil wars and the 'crisis' of the state have shown, hierarchies and central governments are by themselves no insurance against political instability. Furthermore, the recent trends of increased reliance on decentralized forms of decision making, domestically as well as internationally, raise not only the issue of the fit between international and domestic institutions, but the even more important question of how this development shall be appraised.

After all, the description of the present sea change as liberalization suffers from the fact that certain of its consequences seem rather illiberal. There is an observable concentration of firms that results from deregulation in both the domestic and the international arenas. To that extent the economic side of liberalism, laissez-faire, seems increasingly at odds with the part of liberalism concerned with democratic theory. While the former part welcomes the growth of boundary-spanning networks, the latter has, at least traditionally, presupposed the existence of bounded communities which are now increasingly circumvented by such networks. Only by 'bounding' a number of 'subjects' a 'public' could be conceived which, in turn, provided the legitimizing basis of for binding decision, for ascribing rights and responsibilities, and for maintaining the community as a transgenerational concern. None of these presuppositions appears to be in place any longer and there seems to exist, therefore, a crisis in both political theory and political practice.

These are indeed troubling questions. While I obviously cannot hope to provide ready-made solutions, it is the task of this article to contribute to a better understanding of our predicament by engaging in an analysis of our disciplinary understandings and by subjecting some of the concepts that dominate the contemporary debate to further scrutiny. In order to make good on my claims, my presentation takes the following steps. In the next section I trace the development of the discipline of international politics. I show the oddly parasitic character that evolved between 'realism' and 'international law' as they lost their grounding in political praxis. By examining the respective disciplinary understandings of law and politics, their systematic blind spots as well as the parasitic character of the discourses—thus a legalistic and utopian understanding of law needs as its complement an equally unrealistic discourse of politics—we can critically reflect on the presuppositions of these two fields. We are also able to start afresh with a new set of substantive questions or puzzles, instead of relying on a methodology for defining a new approach to the study of international politics. In section three I take up organizational issues which resulted in two defining moments for institutionalizing peaceful change which David Kennedy has termed the 'move' to institutions at the end of World War 1. This section is devoted to the two episodes of the 'first move'. I suggest that this first move did not come to an end at Versailles, but that it had a second episode after World War Two. In the fourth section, I argue that we are in the midst of a *second move*. This move has less well defined historical benchmarks but is nevertheless as important as the first one for the analysis of

---

[11] For a discussion of this problem in the context of the end of the Cold War, see Reynold Koslowski, Friedrich Kratochwil, 'Understanding Change in International Politics: The Soviet Empire's Demise and the International System', in Ned Lebow and Thomas Risse-Kappen (eds.), *International Relations Theory and the End of the Cold War* (New York: Columbia University Press, 1995), ch. 6.

change in the international arena, since it draws attention to the impact of globalization on our domestic and international institutions.

The symbiosis of legalism and realism

If we begin our reflections with the two themes in Carr's work, i.e. utopia and realism, it is clear why the second quickly overwhelmed the first, when realism began to define the disciplinary understanding of the new field of international relations. There was not only the manifest challenge of fascist and communist ideologies which made appeasement as well as the resort to traditional means of diplomacy impossible, but the events and their purported lessons gave more weight to those voices which had become highly critical of the liberal project. To that extent, it is not surprising that a recovery of the concept of the 'political' from its ideological deformations was one of the characteristics of political theorists, most obviously in the émigré community in the United States. Whatever the suggested solutions were, virtually all voices agreed that the traditional focus of a theory of politics on constitutions and law was highly problematic. Arendt and Strauß attempted to arrest this 'decline' of theory by a historical recovery of its sources.[12] Adorno, Marcuse and Horkheimer pursued the project of a 'critical theory', and people like Carl Schmitt and Hans Morgenthau, the latter deeply influenced by Schmitt[13] and quite suspicious of the liberal constitutional state, concluded that neither the understandings nor the practices of the *ius publicum Europaeum* could provide any guidance for the contemporary world.

The crisis that liberalism had on the Continent also became a crisis of law. True, there remained some doubt as to what this attempt of founding a new discipline was supposed to be about, as various labels for designating the field of study indicate: international relations vs. international politics are indicative. But the focus on power rather than constitutions of formal political structures seemed to provide a way out of the dilemmas between an unfocused view on simple cross-boundary relations, and the problem of putting sovereignty and the state as the sole or main actor at the centre of the analysis. As Wiliam T.R. Fox, the first editor of *World Politics*—the journal that helped to define the discipline—once pointed out:

Pitting "power" rather than the "state" at the center of political science makes it easier to view international relations as one of the political sciences. So conceived, it is possible for some scholars to move effortlessly along the seamless web which connects world politics and the politics of such less inclusive units as the state..and to emphasize the political process, group behavior, . . . conflict resolution and decision making.[14]

---

[12] For a discussion of the influence of these ideas on the development of the 'discipline' political science, see John Gunnell, *Between Philosophy and Politics* (Amherst: University of Massachusetts Press, 1986), especially chs. 2 and 3.

[13] For the roots of Morgenthau's thought in Schmitt, see Marty Koskenniemi, ' Carl Schmitt and Hans Morgenthau', in Michael Byers (ed.), *The Role of Law in International Politics: Essays in International Relations and International Law* (Oxford: Oxford University Press, forthcoming).

[14] William T.R. Fox, *The American Study of International Relations* (Columbia, SC: Univ. of South Carolina Press, 1968), p. 20.

Power seemed, therefore, to avoid the problems more substantive conceptions of politics have, in terms of its association with a common good or a human *telos*. By its conceptual links to *process*, power also abated the dangers of conceiving politics in terms of largely static legal structures, as traditional institutionalism had suggested. It could therefore remain the linchpin of analysis long after most of the tenets of realism had been subjected to severe criticisms by the behaviouralists in the second great debate.[15]

Nevertheless, while power seemed to constitute the field, many of the old problems reappeared, as various conceptions of power coexisted uneasily with one another. There was the notion of 'power' as a medium, suggested by Morgenthau in his 'Six Principles of Political Realism',[16] largely conceived as a resource in an (unfortunately entirely) mistaken analogy to money. But there was also the conception of power, going back to Weber, which emphasizes the relational and interactive dimension. Finally, there was the Weberian legacy of linking force and legitimacy and of deriving the domestic political order from the monopoly of legitimate force. In this derivation, 'power' was no longer a simple medium of exchange that could be maximized analogous to the *homines oeconomici*, nor was it a type of influence exercised over another on the basis of various available resources. Rather, it was a certain form of force, i.e. legitimate compellence (*öffentliche Zwangsgewalt*), exercised by public authorities that now defined the political space.

With that last conceptual move the circle was closed, as power was now again intrinsically linked with institutional structures (rather than being simply some neutral medium). The often observable Freudian slip among later realists, i.e. of forgetting Weber's normative layer and deriving order from the monopoly of force, was the cause of serious distortions. It suggested first that there are no sources of legitimacy in the international arena, which is patently false. Thus, even Morgenthau has to admit that:

Power exercised in self defense or in the name of the United Nations has a better chance to succeed than equivalent power exercised by an "aggressor" nation or in violation of international law . . . . Political ideologies . . . serve the purpose of endowing foreign policies with the appearance of legitimacy.[17]

Second, such a conception asserts that questions surrounding the legitimacy of actions are settled rather than contestable, as long as they are made by the proper public authorities. The discursive gambit of Morgenthau to use the opposition of 'appearance' vs. 'reality' in order to imply the importance of normative factors in the domestic realm when compared to their rhetorical character in international politics, however, will not do. *Normatively* it is not clear why the legitimizing function of norms should be different in the two realms. If Morgenthau means that justifications are often self-serving then he is obviously right. But unless he also demonstrates that by some necessity they *have to be* self-serving in the international arena, while at

---

[15] See Hedley Bull, 'International Theory: The Case for a Classical Approach', *World Politics*, 18 (April 1966), pp. 361–77; Morton Kaplan, 'The New Great Debate: Traditionalism vs. Science in International Relations', *World Politics*, 19 (Oct. 1966), pp. 1–20.

[16] See Hans Morgenthau, *Politics Among Nations*, 4th edn. (New York: Knopf, 1967), ch. 1.

[17] *Politics among Nations*, 5th edn. (New York: Knopf, 1985), p. 34, as quoted by Helen Milner, 'The Assumption of Anarchy in International Relations Theory: A Critique', *Review of International Studies*, 17 (Jan. 1991), pp. 67–85, reprinted in David Baldwin (ed.), *Neorealism and Neoliberalism* (New York: Columbia University Press, 1993), ch. 6, quote at p. 150.

least sometimes they deserve to be taken seriously in domestic politics, the implication is obviously unwarranted. *Empirically* one has to wonder what phantasmagoric political reality is conjured up by such theoretical lenses when one remembers the massive resistance to discriminatory laws during the civil rights era and the protest against the 'illegality' of the war in Vietnam in the USA, as well as presently the continuous actions of environmental groups in the courts and in political arenas.

Nevertheless, the categorical distinction between internal and external politics, between 'anarchy' and 'order', became an intrinsic part of the disciplinary understanding.[18] Thus, in the writings of realists like Kenneth Waltz, a wholly unconvincing notion of politics emerges as the following passage intimates:

National politics is the realm of authority, of administration and of law. International politics is the realm of power, of struggle, and of accommodation. The international realm is preeminently a political one . . . . In politics force is said to be the ultima ratio. In international politics force serves, not only as the ultima ratio but as the first and constant one.[19]

This is an odd conception of politics indeed. Gone is not only the notion that political associations are based on common notions of the good and the just, as Aristotle suggested. Gone is the classical conception of a community as an association of people under a common law. Gone is also the notion that politics depends on bargaining and negotiation and nonviolent attitudes towards fellow-citizens (Aristotle's *peitho* and *philia* as political virtues). Gone is even the realism of the way in which we attempt to grasp social reality beyond the state, i.e. to understand international politics *via negativa* by means of the 'domestic analogy'. Now, we are held to a new standard, i.e. the criterion of *uniqueness,* which is to serve as the true foundation for our disciplinary understanding. Politics is not to be confused with all the epiphenomena, as real as they might appear to us. Its essence can be grasped only when we abstract from all that is familiar to us, when we cast radical doubt on all our practical experience and arrive, like Descartes, at the unshakable foundations that eliminate all further doubts.

In criticizing the attempts of some realists to establish such a disciplinary understanding, Judith Shklar points to the 'costs' that such a strategy entails for social analysis:

The rules of politics may never be confused (for realists) with those of morality or those of law. What the 'national interest' can be except an ideology is hard to say but one thing is clear to realists—it must never be conceived in terms of 'moral' or 'legalistic' values . . . .

The essential mark of politics is power. However taken as a formal concept, power is meaningless. Unless it is placed within a historical situation it is completely unimaginable. The only occasion in which it can be said to appear in 'pure' form, unconditioned by a host of circumstances, is in active combat. Here power means destroying an enemy physically or subordinating him to one will by the threat of destruction. This is why the only perfectly clear definition of politics as power is that of Carl Schmitt. The 'specific and self-evident distinguishing characteristic' of the 'realm of politics', analogous to the distinctions of good

---

[18] For a critical attempt to put this drawing of the 'inside' 'outside' distinction in perspective see R.B.J. Walker, *Inside/Outside: International Relations as Political Theory* (Cambridge: Cambridge University Press, 1993).

[19] Ibid., p. 113.

and evil in morality, and beautiful and ugly in aesthetics, he wrote, is 'the distinction of friend and enemy'. The terms 'friend', enemy and struggle obtain their real significance from their relation to the real possibility of physical killing'; that is, politics is active or potential physical violence.[20]

There are several corollaries to this argument. First, oddly enough, the focus on force and violence inhibits us from developing an adequate theory of power. After all, the analysis of power, whether it is conceived as a resource or as a relationship, always presupposes the specification of a 'contingency framework'.[21] Second, unless we believe that concepts somehow capture the essence of a subject matter, distilling the unique feature from some empirical material thereby also satisfying the criteria of relevance, such a procedure is rather problematic. We may end up with some trivial definition which might be true in a logical or taxonomic sense but might be entirely useless for directing the inquiry toward some interesting substantive problems. Thus, one could easily define man as a 'featherless biped' but such a definition would be useless as a foundation for a discipline as it does not locate the subject matter in a set of empirically and conceptually interesting puzzles (whereas the definition of language endowment does, although we no longer believe in the usefulness of essential definitions). Third, even if we were to insist on the importance of the uniqueness criterion, the discussion above showed that such an attempt fails on its own terms. Conceptions of law impact via sovereignty or legitimacy on the concept of politics and often supply, even if only implicitly, the necessary steps for the inferences which otherwise would be unfathomable.

Consequently, there exists a paradox in that attempts to separate these two disciplines as much as possible leads not only to similar conceptual difficulties but also uncovers a certain symbiotic relationship between these two foundationalist attempts. In other words, legalism (of which the theory of 'pure law' is only the most recent and best articulated version) needs realism not only as an opponent in regard to concrete issues, but also for its own self-understanding. Since this disciplinary understanding leads precisely to some misconceptions that Carr characterized as 'utopian' it might be useful to examine this problem in greater detail.

The first observation in regard to the paradox is that law (and in particular international law) as a discipline dealing with norms has to demarcate its domain *vis-à-vis* morals and politics alike. For the purposes of the former, it is significant that the symbiotic character of realism is clearly manifested in Kelsen's pure theory of law in that he understands law as a 'sanctioning' order. To this extent, all legal norms imply at least implicitly a sanction by the state (aside from being part of a system).[22] Again the subtle influence of a Weberian conception of the state and of enforcement is characteristic of this conception of law. Legal rules only secondarily inform the individual how to act (as this is also the function of rules of comity and morals) but they are primarily instructions to *public officials* to sanction non-conforming behaviour. Since in international relations no such sovereign exists, self-help has to substitute. For Kelsen, self-help is obviously not simply conceived as a

---

[20] Judith Shklar, *Legalism: Law, Morals, and Political Trials* (Cambridge, MA: Harvard University Press, 1986), pp. 124f.

[21] On this point, see the fundamental article by David Baldwin, 'Power Analysis and World Politics', *World Politics*, 31 (Jan. 1979), pp.161–94.

[22] See also Hans Kelsen. *Principles of International Law*, 2nd edn. by R. Tucker (New York: Holt, Rinehart and Winston, 1966).

result of anomic anarchy, but rather as a legal institution, i.e. a remedy, governed by certain rules that allow or empower state officials to take retaliatory measures in the defence of violated rights.

There is no need to rehearse here the criticism against a concept of law that seems over- as well as under-inclusive. A brief discussion is sufficient to show the problems. As to the over-inclusiveness: the violation of all types of rules might trigger sanctions. Consequently, this definition of law is determinate only if we implicitly place it in a modern statist framework. But conflating law with the state or with a particular organizational form is neither heuristically fruitful nor analytically clean. As to under-inclusiveness: many rules in a legal system are constitutive and enabling rather than regulatory in character. They instruct the actors how to proceed, when they want to attach legal consequences to their actions, such as signing a paper and thereby transferring property, or concluding a treaty of friendship and commerce. H.L.A. Hart[23] has made these points clearly and convincingly and proposed, therefore, a concept of law, that is conceived as a system of rules. To that extent the character tag of a legal rule does not consist in a sanction but rather in membership in a system or in the rule's 'pedigree'. A rule is part of the system if it has been created in accordance with higher-order norms which, as secondary rules, authorize the creation, abolition or modification of the lower-order norms (primary rules).

Thus according to the concept of law as a system of rules, law is truly a product of its own creation. It creates not only its own rules; it also establishes organizations by statute or treaty. Even the state is a product of the rules making up its constitution. No wonder then that there appears to be no limit (besides those set by law itself) to what can be done with legal rules. But somehow the idea that legal concepts operate in a self-referential fashion is more than strange as it seems to imply that the discourse lacks a common subject of conversation and, thus, is from its inception a 'conversation without content'.[24] Indeed, it is this very notion that is responsible for the illusion that to establish a peaceful international order we only need the progressive development of international law and some dispute-settling mechanisms.[25]

It is this conception of law that occasioned Carr's most critical remarks about utopianism. A moment's reflection shows why this criticism is not far off the mark, since the error results from a simple equivocation of the term 'create'. When we view law for analytical purposes as an autopoietic system, we do not refer to actual historical facts or the genesis of a rule but rather to the validity a rule has in virtue of its membership in a system.[26] Metaphysically we can picture a rule arising out of an authorization by a higher rule or norm. Such an issuance, however, has nothing to do with a rule being created historically. The latter cannot be discussed outside of particular historical circumstances and the action of the designated actors involved in such a process.

There is, however, also a second and equally strong objection to the notion of law as a system of rules disembodied from any social and political context: it is that such

---

[23] H.L.A. Hart, *The Concept of Law* (New York: Oxford University Press, 1961).

[24] David Kennedy, 'Theses about International Law Discourse', *German Yearbook of International Law*, 23 (1980), p. 376.

[25] See, for example, Sir Hersch Lauterpacht's proof, that all political questions are justiciable, in his *The Function of Law in the International Community* (Oxford: Clarendon, 1933).

[26] See, for example, a clear exposition of this position by Gunther Teubner, *Recht als Autopoetisches System* (Frankfurt: Suhrkamp, 1989).

a conception leaves out crucial aspects of the function of rules in shaping *praxis*. After all, no rule or norm can also contain all the facts and circumstances to which it will be applied. Consequently, the *interpretation* of rules and norms is not a peripheral matter that can be neglected in a theory of law. Representing law, therefore, as a disembodied system of rules misspecifies the legal problematique, and modern approaches to law have therefore increasingly accorded pride of place to 'judging', i.e. applying the rules to a case.[27] This not only involves the interpretation of legal concepts; it also entails choosing among competing narratives that transform the facts of a case into the relevant facts of legal ontology. In law, people just do not simply walk or punch or cross a river but they trespass, commit battery, or aggression. This legal ontology nearly always transcends observables (by including unobservable mental states like *mens rea*, or consent) and continuously intertwines objective and subjective elements of interpretation.

Given these characteristics of jural ontology it seems clear that we cannot be satisfied with a concept of law that limits it to a system of disembodied rules. After all, we invoke legal rules in order to ascertain that (1) certain events or actions occurred, which (2) exemplify some concept of the legal ontology, that (3) this concept is part of some institutional arrangement (diplomatic protection, anti-trust etc.), which, in case of violation, provide the wronged party with a remedy. Thus, contrary to what we might expect from the picture that Kelsen and Hart painted, a decision attains its validity not simply by being decided by a designated official, who simply subsumes the facts under some norms whose pedigree (s)he checks. Rather, rendering a legal decision is the result of quite different procedures: choosing the relevant facts and defining the issues, weighing up competing norms that might have a bearing on the case, evaluating actions and outcomes in terms of prevailing customary practices, thereby introducing prima facie extra legal standards into the decision-making process.[28]

In other words, the issue of judging can never be reduced to an exercise of formal authority by a public official, i.e. simply applying the rules of a legal system to some facts. To that extent the notion that the reasons provided by the official for the choices (s)he made in arriving at a decision need to be justified solely intra-systemically is open to serious challenge. These various points have been well made by the Critical Legal Studies Movement[29] as well as by adherents of the 'process approach' to international law, both of which view normativity not as a simple matter of rules, of their pedigree or membership, but largely as a matter of the pragmatic context.[30]

---

[27] See, for example, the various works of Ronald Dworkin, *Taking Rights Seriously* (Cambridge, MA: Harvard University Press, 1978); and Ronald Dworkin, *Law's Empire* (Cambridge, MA: Harvard University Press, 1986).

[28] On a further elaboration of this point, see my 'How do Norms Matter?', in Michael Byers (ed.), *The Role of Law in International Politics*.

[29] For a good overview of the main positions espoused by this movement, see Mark Kelman, *Critical Legal Studies* (Cambridge, MA: Harvard University Press, 1987).

[30] This was, of course, the point which the New Haven school under McDougal made. See Myres McDougal, 'Some Basic Concepts about International Law: A Policy Oriented Framework', reprinted in Richard Falk and Saul Mendlovitz (eds.), *The Strategy of World Order*, vol. 2, *International Law* (New York: World Law Fund, 1966), pp. 116–33: Myres McDougal and Harold Lasswell, 'The Identification and Appraisal of Divers Systems of Public Order', ibid., pp. 45–74. See also the writings of contemporary adherents to the process approach: Rosalyn Higgins, *Problems and Process: International Law and How We Use It* (Oxford: Clarendon, 1994); see also Harald Koh's review essay 'Why do Nations Obey International Law?', *The Yale Law Journal*, 106 (1997), pp. 2559–659.

It is here that the analogous conceptual cleansing that we observed in the case of politics also eliminates any form of realism from law. In defining justice as the purpose of law and giving it a legalist interpretation, i.e. constructing justice as strict adherence to rules, 'the law' is cleansed from all political distortions. Not only the notion of politics as violence is eschewed, but any notion of bargaining or unprincipled adjustment is similarly 'ruled out'. As Shklar put it aptly:

> The uncompromising character of justice . . . militates against any latitudinarian view of social morality. Instead legalism is apt to disparage every other type of social policy. All politics must be assimilated to the paradigm of just action—the judicial process. Direct bargaining, for instance, is often treated as a matter of disreputable expediency, a sort of ideological anarchy . . . Again, extreme legal formalism puts politics in brackets as rigidly, as it does morals, for here it is not logical deduction but pure chaos that reigns . . . . Thus to maintain the contrast between legal order and chaos and to preserve the former from any taint of the latter it is not just necessary to define law out of politics; an entirely extravagant image of politics as essentially a species of war has to be maintained.[31]

For international law these considerations might seem irrelevant, as obviously adjudication plays a rather modest role. But, as Ulrich Fastenrath has shown, similar problems arise when we try to identify the sources of law, or when the parties to a treaty argue about the proper interpretation of some rule or principle.[32] What impact legal norms have on actual decisions is, of course hotly contested. Aside from seeing in norms simply the reflection of power, realists accord to rules and regimes, at best, the role of an intervening variable. But even some international lawyers emphasize the defects of international law and see it hopelessly suspended between the antinomies of 'Apology and Utopia'.[33] The answer is, of course, more complicated, since it depends not only on our concept of law[34] but also on a variety of tricky theoretical and epistemological issues which cannot be settled by simply looking harder at the facts and seeing whether rules and norms matter.[35]

Thus, one thing seems rather uncontroversial, that the weakness of international law has several reasons, not the least of which is its insufficient institutional underpinnings. There is not only the problem that, given the absence of precedent and legislative action, it is often unclear what the law *is*. There is also the further problem that law can be an effective means of conflict resolution and peaceful change only when the *political process* is well institutionalized. To that extent the undeniable weakness of international law is as much the result of the weakness in the institutionalization of the political process, as it is ascribable to the flaws of the international legal system. In this perspective a rather different connection emerges than we found in the disciplinary understandings of realists and legalists, as the co-conditioning of law and politics is not only embraced but theorized. It neither

---

[31] Judith, Shklar, *Legalism*, p. 122.
[32] See Ulrich Fastenrath, 'Relative Normativity in International Law', *European Journal of International Law*, 4 (1993), pp. 305–40.
[33] See, for example, Martti Koskenniemi, *From Apology to Utopia: The Structure of Legal Arguments* (Helsinki: Finnish Lawyers Publishing Co., 1989).
[34] This point is forcefully made by Benedict Kingsbury, 'The Concept of Compliance as a Function of Competing Conceptions of International Law', *Michigan Journal of International Law*, 19 (Winter 1998), pp. 345–72.
[35] See my *Rules, Norms, and Decisions, On the Conditions of Practical and Legal Reasoning in International Relations and Domestic Affairs* (Cambridge: Cambridge University Press, 1989), particularly ch. 2.

makes one the servant of the other, nor does it engage in the denials and Freudian slips mentioned above. Rather, this perspective assesses 'law' and 'politics' from the perspective of a theory of social organization. It is in this context that some interesting puzzles arise for the analysis of peaceful change. The next section elaborates on this theme.

The first move to institutions: Versailles and the UN system

Whatever differences might exist among realists, idealists, peace-advocates or security specialists, there is a near universal consensus that World War I and the subsequent settlement represented a sharp break with the past. The new beginnings came in response to the changing external and internal conditions, as the Toquevillian vision of the USA and Russia determining the course of events loomed large on the horizon. Internally, the bankruptcy of the old political elites had been demonstrated not only in the case of the losers but also of the victors. The revolutionary stirrings, evidenced by the October Revolution and some uprisings in Germany (only to be ruthlessly suppressed by the proto-fascist 'free cops'), indicated the end of complacency and of the confidence in the inevitability and nearly automatic progress of civilization. All these events also suggested that a return to business as usual was not possible and that fundamentally new ways of organizing international and domestic politics would have to be considered.

There were, of course, some innovations attempting to address these changing conditions. The new concept of a 'collective security system', the idea of self-determination, and the recognition that the conditions of the working class were no longer simply only a matter of benign neglect or 'domestic politics' all belong here. Although of minor practical import, the founding of the ILO and the admission for the first time of non-state representatives into the inner sanctum of an inter-governmental organization indicated a fundamental change in thinking. While the 'new' and largely Wilsonian ideas were hotly contested among the European establishments and the various social movements who mobilized public opinion, there seemed to have been a sweeping feeling that the problems had to be addressed by new forms of organization. Somehow most of the official and social actors agreed that formal institutions were necessary in order to deal effectively with the contemporary challenges. To that extent the 'move to institutions' which David Kennedy has so painstakingly documented, appears to have transcended liberal, syndicalist and even radical feminist lines.

The belief in the effectiveness of formal organization seems to have been buttressed by two converging notions, i.e. that political problems could be solved by bringing to bear some technical know-how—an idea that had been gaining currency since St. Simon—and that formal organizations represented, because of their greater efficiency, the 'solution'. Bureaucracies would, as Weber suggested, sooner or later crowd out other forms of organizing. But the 'move to institutions' might actually have been much more subtle than the wholesale adoption of the technical-bureaucratic perspective attaining its full expression in functionalism. Liberal statesmen, even the 'idealist' Woodrow Wilson, like Kant before him, seem to have been less than enamoured with the prospects of some inchoate world governmental structure. Rather they hoped that the spread of democracy and the preponderance of the economic and military potential of democratic states in the aftermath of the war would make peace possible.[36]

It is, of course, the peace movements contesting the monopoly of the decision-making elites in negotiating the peace settlement and the belief in the efficacy of formal structures that Carr castigates as utopianism. In identifying these movements with the liberal tenets of the 'harmony of interest' and the bureaucratic mode of problem-solving, Carr not only suggested the inappropriateness of these efforts – quite puzzling in view of his socialist leanings and that ideology's privileging of the 'masses'—he also misconstrued the actual events, an error that prevents us from critically appraising the changing nature of organization in the international arena and from drawing the appropriate lessons.[37] As a matter of fact, some of the gravest shortcomings of the post-war settlement were not those identified by realists, but had to do with the insufficient attention given at Versailles to the management of the international economy.

It was only on their second try, after World War II at Bretton Woods, that the designers of institutions hit upon the felicitous solution of 'multilateralism'[38] as an organizational form. Only multilateralism was able to accommodate the new responsibility of states for full-employment while taking care of the externalities which the beggar-thy-neighbour policies had created when states had attempted to pursue full-employment policies. Similarly, today new externalities arise for states from 'liberalization', when point-of-entry barriers to trade have been virtually eliminated, when production has been globalized, and financial markets have been integrated. A new balance between positive and negative effects, creating new winners and losers, has to be struck. Otherwise the political consensus that sustained the 'first move to institutions', and which is essential for the functioning of new institutions, is in danger. True, a return to classical protectionism and the conflicts of yesteryear seem unlikely—not least because many of the protectionist measures which governments could formerly use have lost their bite[39]—but there is the possibility that conflicts might arise out of the growing disenchantment with some of the illiberal consequences of globalization. In a way, the increased liberalization of the economy might result in a serious incompatibility with another tenet of liberalism: democratic theory and the notion of positive rights. To that extent, the second move to institutions could not only undo much of the achievements of the first, but fundamentally alter once more the social bases on which domestic and international legal and political orders rest. To that extent Carr's mistrust in the liberal belief that all good things go together and that a natural harmony might eventually prevail is a useful reminder of the difficulties that lie ahead. A further discussion of the 'first' and the ' second' move to institutions seems in order.

[36] For a good discussion of these points see Andrew Moravcsik, 'A Liberal Theory of International Politics', *International Organization*, 51 (Autumn 1997), pp. 513–54.

[37] For a further discussion of the role of the various peace movements in the pre- and post-WWI era, see Cecilia Lynch, *Beyond Appeasement: Reinterpreting Interwar British and US Peace Movements* (Ithaca, NY: Cornell University Press, forthcoming).

[38] For a definition of this institutional form and its role in post WWII policy, see John Ruggie (ed.), *Multilateralism Matters: The Theory and Praxis of an Institutional Form* (New York: Columbia University Press, 1993); see also John Ruggie, *Winning the Peace: America and World Order in the New Era* (New York: Twentieth Century Fund, 1996).

[39] For a fundamental discussion of these points, see Richard Cooper, *Economic Policy in an Interdependent World* (Cambridge, MA: MIT Press, 1986).

Let us begin again with the first move. At the outset, we notice that the first move was reformist and perhaps far less radical than some of the contemporary movements and, with hindsight, also its realist critics had thought. Indeed, as David Kennedy suggests,[40] the ambiguous 'history' of the founders of the League and the inconsistencies in the narratives are important indicators for appraising the actual transformation. While originally the American peace movement was characterized by establishment figures such as Elihu Root, William Howard Taft, Andrew Carnegie and Theodore Marburg, the decade following the outbreak of the war saw a decisive shift towards radical feminist and progressive movements. These movements pushed the project from the institutionalization of legal settlement to international and social reform. However, as the war drew to a close, the initiative passed again to the more statist lawyers and officials who were engaged in post-war planning. Thus, the plans produced by Wilson's aids hardly mentioned judicial settlement. Instead they envisaged a political assembly for the resolution of international disputes and attempted to bring war into the framework of institutional sanctions and collective security. In other words, the institutionalization of the international *political* process, rather than radical social reform or pacifism, provided the main source of inspiration.

While it might be understandable that the actors in 1919 could have felt that they were riding the wave of the future, the many exclusions that occurred as well as the shifts in the positions of the participants themselves make such accounts highly problematic. A closer look reveals that many of the pre-war pragmatists became utopians at Versailles or after. For instance, the realist Smuts had, at times during the negotiations, utopian moments, as evidenced by his optimism when he saw the League as the heir to 'Europe's great estate'. Thus, most of the historical accounts maintain a narrative structure implying some system transforming progress within a continuity. While emphasizing reform, they were as distant from radical and allegedly irresponsible demands of social reform as they were from the calls for a return to the old order. As Kennedy points out:

> By mobilizing the rhetoric of war and peace, law and politics, or utopianism and realism, participants and historians have characterized the establishment of the international institutional regime as the crest of a progressive wave breaking forward from extremes which an institutionalized and redeemed international process must continually exclude. The architects of the new order both situated themselves at the cutting edge of a tradition and sought to continue and displace the work of earlier peace advocates. By contrast to wartime resisters and agitators, the institution builders styled their work a return to order from chaos and to reason from religious ideological passion. Sane hands were again at the helm. At the same time, these men represented the worldly embodiment of a human ideal. The torch of idealism had been passed to an institutionalized generation, inheriting, as it excluded the vision of women and wartime radicals.[41]

Nowhere does the ambiguity of the narrative that emphasizes the transformative character of the move become more visible than in the case of war. War, one of the traditional and accepted institutions of the state system, was now seen as a radical 'rupture' to be exorcised from inter-state relations. By identifying war with chaos, and peace with systematic organization, the 'move to institutions' created the topos

---

[40] David Kennedy, 'The Move to Institutions', *Cardozo Law Review*, 8 (April 1987), pp. 841–988.
[41] Ibid., pp. 897f.

that peace was synonymous with organization. Violence and disintegration were now thoroughly externalized from international relations and projected upon actors beyond the pale, such as terrorists or aggressors. The transformative effect of this narrative was that it not only imparted coherence to efforts at institutionalization in the past, but it sometimes suggested that the main achievement of this move was not so much the victory of law over politics, but rather that both violence and radical demands for systemic transformation had been cast aside in favour of crisis management. At the same time this move suggests that the repetition of history and its cycles of war and peace-making recognized by realists as the only means for ordering the international system[42] had been transcended.

To that extent the new understanding established a coherence between past and present. It legitimized an understanding in which different organizational forms were shown to be the 'forerunners' of the present organizational system, while not challenging the state system and its operation. Thus, the Concert is the forerunner of the Council, the former river commissions become antecedents to the functional agencies, and efforts at arbitration are the 'roots' for the Permanent (or International) Court of Justice. To that extent the establishment of the UN can be viewed just as the second part of this first move which attempted to incorporate the lessons learned from the failure of the League. These lessons made it necessary to have an organization with teeth instead of relying on the good will of its members. It placed universal responsibility for peace and security on the Great Powers thereby attempting to solve the collective action problem that is bound to arise when enforcement becomes an issue.

The story of the failure of the collective security arrangement, the emergence of alliances and blocs, and the substitution of peace-keeping for classical enforcement measures envisaged by Chapter 7 of the Charter have all been told many times. So has the story of human rights and the mandate system that facilitated decolonization by basing the justification of colonial rule increasingly on notions of 'trust' and a right to self-determination. The realization that the governmental authority of the colonial powers could no longer be justified by the classical international law principle of conquest or unequal treaties served, in turn, as a crystallization point for the local opposition and led finally to the rather smooth emancipation of the colonial world. It is in this context that political problems of legitimization and delegitimization rather than those of the management of force became one of the main contributions of the UN to peaceful change. In a way, though, the success of the world organization was also its bane. In the increasingly heated debates of the seventies where automatic majorities passed condemnation after condemnation, the instrument of censoring lost much of its bite. First the Great Powers and then increasingly also other industrial states refused to participate in these 'politicized' spectacles.

But the narrative of continuity and change on the basis of lessons learned hides some of the discontinuities and innovations that characterized this second episode of the first move. It also concerns the story of one 'lesson' whose organizational implementation had no forerunner or precedent, namely, 'multilateralism' as a new organizational form. These multilateral institutions proved surprisingly resilient in

---

[42] See, for example, Robert Gilpin, *War and Change in World Politics* (Cambridge: Cambridge University Press, 1981).

the post-war era, even though fundamental changes had undermined many of its foundations and the various *ad hoc* adjustments for meeting the emergencies seemed hardly promising. In short, this second episode of the first move concerns the institutionalization of the world economic system on the basis of shared understandings. John Ruggie has called this compromise between liberalism's laissez-faire prescriptions and the policy commitment to full employment, 'embedded liberalism'.

The multilateral institutions based on this compromise provided a solution for several problems which deep-seated changes in the nature politics, of economics and society, had thrust upon decision-makers in the inter-war period and for which the conventional wisdoms and ideologies had no answers. Accustomed to separating neatly politics and the economy and defining the role of the state as a guarantor for functioning markets, liberalism had in the Great Transformation[43] of the nineteenth century succeeded in dismantling most of the laws and privileges that stood in the way of an efficient allocation of resources. The establishment of a labour market, of arms-length free trade and of the 'private' gold standard set the parameters for economic activity. Even if not fully realized, the fundamental social and economic changes of this Great Transformation affected the architecture of both internal and external politics. Internally, social dislocations together with the slow but increasing emancipation of the working class created incentives to organize in to order counteract the deleterious effects of unrestrained laissez-faire. Externally, imperialism could be seen as a response to both economic crises and fears that the existing economic arrangements of free trade might be too fragile to ensure access (quite aside from the empirically dubious arguments of the higher returns on investment that Hilferding and Lenin invoked).

One point, however, was pretty clear to all decision-makers who were engaged in World War I. Because of the impossibility of adjusting the classical European balance by traditional means, the classical nostrums for reviving the European balance were no longer available. Territorial concessions were, if not directly unavailable, nevertheless costly. Because of nationalism no self-respecting government could conceive of the 'treason' of transferring part of its territory in the same way as the sovereigns of the *ancien regime* had done without many qualms. Furthermore, the fact that power increasingly depended more on industrial capacity than territory made the task of balancing even harder, since one had to control the *economic growth* and *innovative capacity* of one's competitors. Only under the condition that key economic areas were adjacent to one's own territory could one even consider territorial incorporation. Furthermore, it became clear to all chancelleries that a dynamic economy required far greater territorial units than even the largest European nation states provided. Finally, the tremendous costs of the war made the vision of a return to normalcy afterwards all the more unlikely the longer the hostilities continued. Consequently, when the war was not over as expected within a few weeks or months, most Foreign offices engaged in speculations on how this quandary could be resolved in a post-war settlement.

In Germany, the Chancellor, Bethman Hollweg, had already written on Sept. 9th 1914 a memorandum addressing this issue. The document has been quoted by Fritz

---

[43] For a comprehensive treatment of this issue, see Karl Polanyi, *The Great Transformation* (Boston: Beacon Press, 1957).

Fischer[44] as proof of the imperialist design of the German government and has been dubbed the '*Septemberprogramm*'. According to Fischer, Germany adhered to these war goals until the end of the war. Although the programme considered some territorial annexations in France and Belgium, newer historical research[45] has cast doubt on Fischer's main theses, i.e. that this programme represented a masterplan (it was rather an occasional piece that might have been written in order to preempt the Kaiser's enthusiasm for much larger annexations in Poland, Flanders, northern France and the Baltic region), and that Germany was determined to pursue these options throughout the war. Rather, historians such as Geoges Henri Soutou maintain that the actual aim of this document was the idea of a customs union which was to guarantee German economic recovery and strength after the war.[46]

In France, Etienne Clementel, the minister for industry and commerce, engaged in similar planning exercises in 1915. His proposal provided, aside from the return of Alsace-Lorraine to France, a regime of control over the Saar area and Luxembourg and a Customs Union with Belgium and Italy in order to cement France's economic hold on Western Europe. Encouraged by the Czar, who predicted the collapse and disintegration of the Reich,[47] the French position became increasingly punitive as the war went on.

In Britain, discussions about economic security took longer to shape up,[48] as here the conflicts between the goal of economic security through control and discrimination of Germany, and the aim of re-establishing British commercial and financial preponderance, became painfully obvious. After all, the latter goal depended on the revival of intra-European trade and the maintenance of a liberal economic order. Only the Inter-allied Conference on economic relations of June 1916 resolved this conflict in favour of economic security, since close economic cooperation among the Entente was linked to the continuation of discriminatory measures against Germany after the war. In April of 1917 the Imperial War Committee 'having due regard to the interest of our Allies' pleaded for the introduction of an imperial preference system and thus laid the foundation for transforming the Empire into an economic bloc.

When in 1918 London finally accepted that a revival of the British economy should be financed by reparations from Germany, the idea of a European economic reconstruction and the return to a liberal trading order were doomed. The rest of the story is well known. For a while, the informal recycling scheme let Germany pay its reparations with US loans, so that Great Britain and France could pay their debts to the US. But failure to pay reparations led to the occupation of the Rhineland, thereby creating new scores, as the pursuit of security had entirely subverted the liberal idea that the economy was a self-regulating system of private exchanges. Besides, the structural issue of how a general recovery could be achieved was never faced up to. On the one hand much depended on reparations extracted from the

---

[44] Fritz Fischer, *Griff nach der Weltmacht: Die Kriegszielpolitik des Kaiserlichen Deutschlands* 1914–1918 (Düsseldorf: Droste, 1961).

[45] See, for example, Georges Henri Soutou, *L'Or et le Sang, Les Buts de Guerre Economiques et la Permiere Guerre Mondiale* (Paris: Fayard, 1989).

[46] Georges Henri Soutou, Die Kriegsziele des Deutschen Reiches', in Wolfgang Michalka (ed.), *Der Erste Weltkrieg: Wirkung, Wahrnehmung, Analyse* (Munich: Piper, 1994), pp. 28–53.

[47] Horst Günther Linke, 'Rußlands Weg in den Ersten Weltkrieg' und seine Kriegsziele 1914–18', in Wolfgang Michalka (ed.), *Der Erste Weltkrieg*, pp. 54–94.

[48] See Matthias Peter, 'Britische Kriegsziele und Friedensvorstellungen', ibid., pp. 95–124.

vanquished, but economic security also made discrimination against that very country necessary, jeopardizing Germany's capacity to earn the sums necessary to meet the bill. The crash of 1929 ended all illusions. The radical delinking from the world economy and the erection of economic blocs were the result. The Schachtian system of bilateral economic relations based on barter and non-convertible currencies was one (exploitative) answer to the economic crisis, as was the Imperial Preference tariff. Beggar-thy-neighbour policies were designed to place the burdens of unemployment on others, as states scrambled to find solutions for the realization of the new state goal: full employment.

Only during the post-Second World War planning phase did the US decision-makers hit upon a solution that allowed for both the welfare state and a liberal international economic order. Through the organizational implements of 'multi-lateralism', structures were created that established not only the compatibility between international and domestic political structures,[49] but could also solve the problem of externalities which otherwise result from unilateral actions. International supervisory institutions like the IMF and GATT (after the demise of the plans for an international trade organization) were charged with providing and maintaining the non-discriminatory liberal regimes. Instead of blocs, convertible currencies and non-discrimination provided for the integration of losers and winners alike. Economies flowing from complementary endowments in resources were also utilized through the encouragement of the integration (rather than unilateral control) of entire sectors of the economy for which, e.g., the High Authority of the European Coal and Steel Community was given special powers. Loans and grants rather than reparations provided the initial capital for putting Europe back on the track of recovery. In an ironic twist 'security' was again identified with economic prosperity (until Korea, when notions of security again became militarized), although the measures adopted here were not those of control by a victor. In Kennan's original analysis and in the rationale of the Marshal Plan the threat to a peaceful world emanated less from the military threat of a Soviet invasion than from the likelihood of internal political disorder caused by the inability to initiate a rapid recovery. Consequently, economic rather than military means were considered the appropriate measure for meeting this threat.[50]

It is not possible to provide a comprehensive historical account of the 'peaceful change' that these organizations allowed and that led rather quickly to un-precedented prosperity. For our purposes it is sufficient to point out that the system functioned perhaps as much by fortuitous circumstance as by design. There was above all a structural problem in the world monetary system that could not be resolved. As the economist Triffin had already demonstrated in the 1950s, the dilemma consisted in the fact that sufficient liquidity was only provided when the US consistently ran deficits and engaged in expansionary monetary policies. But such a strategy eventually had to transmit inflationary pressures to the entire system thereby upsetting the balance of rights and duties among the members for structural

---

[49] On the link between the regulatory state structures emerging from the 'New Deal' and the organizations of the Bretton Woods system, see Ann Marie Burley, 'Regulating the World: Multilateralism, International Law and the Projection of the New Deal Regulatory State', in John Ruggie (ed.), *Multilateralism Matters*, ch. 4.

[50] On this point, see my 'The Embarrassment of Changes: Realism as a the "science" of *Reapolitik* without Politics', *Review of International Studies*, 19 (1993), pp. 1–18.

adjustment. The inability of creating a new consensus for this problem came to a head with the closing of the 'gold window'. The failure to re-establish a viable new regulatory regime ushered in not only the era of floating exchange rates, it also prepared the way for the integration of the world's financial markets. Capital controls—seen by Keynes as an absolute must in order to preserve free trade on the one hand but shelter the governments from the dangers of speculative flows on the other hand—no longer worked and were successively abandoned by virtually all states. To that extent the eroding consensus on the respective rights and duties of states for adjustment, the lack of effectiveness of the old policy prescriptions, the increasing disembeddedness of the world economy have engendered a crisis in our understanding and in designing new institutions that would facilitate peaceful change.

The 'second move' to institutions: liberalization

On the surface the dominant theme of the narrative of the demise of the Cold War is that of the success of liberalism in its philosophical, economic, and political dimensions. Not only has liberalism succeeded in making human rights a matter of universal concern, the United States has 'won' the Cold War, and even the former opponents are busy designing constitutions modelled on those of the Western liberal states. Internationally, the UN is no longer blocked from taking actions, and the defeat of aggressors as well as various peace-keeping operations promise, if not a new world order, at least a new vigour in the attempts by international institutions to prevent conflicts from escalating. Finally, the call for a New International Economic Order has ceased, and many of its former advocates are following the advice of monetarists by dismantling the structures credited with having inhibited economic growth in the past.

True, a few years after the 'end of history'[51] many of these claims seem somewhat hollow. The ugliness of civil war in Bosnia, the horrors of genocidal massacres in Rwanda, and the abject misery and poverty that have engulfed many states of the former Soviet empire provide sufficient doubt about the appropriateness of such a narrative. Nevertheless, doubts can be assuaged. Is the American economy not booming, contrary to all expectations? Is the expansion of NATO not a step in the direction of giving the notion of democratic peace some institutional under-pinnings? And could not the growth of human rights movements and the expansion of non-governmental organizational networks be ushering in a new, and for the first time, truly global civil society?

These are indeed important developments, but I have serious doubts whether all, or even most, of the conclusions follow. After all, an equally plausible counter narrative would draw attention to the following questions. What happened to the hopes for a new world order and future Great Power cooperation? Where is the optimism now about the prospects for Russia being able to redefine its role in a stable—has it foundered in the face of economic collapse and national humiliation? Are we not ruining NATO by expansion and are we not bringing about the very threat we allegedly want to deter by moving the defensive glacis farther East? Have

[51] See, for example, Francis Fukuyama, *The End of History and the Last Man* (London: Penguin, 1992).

the experiences of Rwanda and Bosnia not shown the limits of the old recipes of peace-keeping? Are the operations of peacemaking that require different techniques and potentially open-ended commitments politically and financially feasible, especially if such commitments further proliferate? Is the speculation of the emergence of a global civil society based on human rights committing a similar mistake to that of legalism after World War I, in that one is led to believe that laws and norms can create new structures by simply following the logic of the law? Is the success of the American economy bringing benefits to all, or will the impact of declining real wages and the increasing income gap ruin the middle class and thus one of the foundations for a liberal democratic order?

These are indeed troubling questions, and the fact that we cannot answer them in a straightforward fashion does not augur well for our grasp of the problems involved. There is indeed ample reason to move away from the original triumphalism and to focus first of all on the development of better analytical tools for assessing our predicament. Indeed, similar to the situation eighty years ago, we are again facing a crisis of momentous proportions. While I cannot, of course, provide ready-made solutions, I want to cast some doubts upon the generative themes of the narrative of 'liberalization'. It seems to misinterpret the events and provide faulty guidance for the design of the institutions in this second move. In particular, I want to call into question the proposition that the changes brought about by globalization are either insignificant and thus do not challenge our institutional structures, or of a 'liberal' nature and thus are necessarily compatible with, or even enhancing, our liberal *democratic* institutions. Furthermore, while I do not believe that these changes can be interpreted as the ascendancy of the 'market' over the state, the increasing disembeddedness of economic processes from its political and social moorings creates distinct dangers for our domestic and international order.

That increasing interdependencies can have significant impact on the state and its capacity to govern has been grist to the mill of international relations scholars, economists and futurologist alike. Thus one of the first questions concerns whether or not interdependence has increased or not. To that extent the view, whether propagated by Kenneth Waltz[52] or by Milton Friedman,[53] that levels of inter-dependence characteristic of today's economy were not unknown in previous eras, seems to suggest that there is nothing new under the sun; and that both the political system and the market can continue to work in the same way as before, only perhaps a bit more efficiently. The usual empirical support for such a proposition relies on comparing the size of the external sector of the economy as measured by the percentage of GNP. But such an analysis fails to take into account the changing structure of trade. While it was formerly arms-length trade in products, most of today's trade is intra-firm trade. The fundamental change in the structure of production makes it difficult to decide what an 'American' automobile is nowadays, as its component parts come from all corners of the world. But this observation also implies that trade occurs now in the form of exchanges among *administrative hierarchies* rather than external markets.

---

[52] See Kenneth Waltz, 'The Myth of National Interdependence', in Charles Kindleberger (ed.), *The International Corporation* (Cambridge, MA: MIT Press, 1970).

[53] Milton Friedman, 'The world is less internationalized in any immediate, relevant pertinent sense today than it was in 1913, or in 1929', in Milton Friedman, 'Internationalization of the US Economy', *Fraser Forum*, Feb. 1989, p. 8, as quoted in John Ruggie, *Winning the Peace*, p. 145.

It is already clear that historical analogies to previous periods of interdependence are rather problematic, and that increases in trade do not follow the liberal paradigm of decentralized exchange with all the virtues imputed to it. Indeed, the strongly ideological character of many policy prescriptions becomes visible when we realize that they are based on the notion that we are still dealing here with arms-length exchanges to be safeguarded from the interference of either national or international agencies. Here, legalism is experiencing a new revival. Unlike the advocates of the 'first' move who had learned from the failures of the inter-war period and attempted to supplement national regulatory agencies with strong international regimes and dispute-settling mechanisms, many proponents of privatization and liberalization today consider a policy only advisable if it rigorously eliminates restrictions to production and trade.[54] To that extent, shoring up the tottering regulatory state, or reproducing it on the international level through new international regimes, is like trying to drive a care whilst looking through the rear-view mirror. Whereas the 'first move' was animated by welfare concerns and the prophetic vision of 'forging swords into ploughshares' the 'second move' when viewed through the lenses of experts in trade law seems to be inspired by little more than the notion that ploughshares have to be forged into resumes, so that the service economy can be run properly by experts who will restore its competitiveness.

The above discussion should have driven home the fact that the reality of modern trade is no longer that of arms-length exchange or that of an exchange between countries with different factor endowments. The international division of labour and the benefits of trade that accrued originally to 'countries' are now internalized at the level of the firm. This observation has several corollaries. First, it suggests that purely national firms will experience a decrease in the margins of classical comparative advantage when compared to multinationally organized firms. Second, multinational firms, because of their organizational form, can move either through the actual transfer of production, or through bookkeeping operations, the location where value is added and taxes are assessed. Third, since the gains from trade no longer accrue to the country as such, especially not to the immobile factors of production such as labour (with the exception of highly skilled and mobile managers), firms become serious contenders in the international arena. Furthermore, these considerations explain: the boom of the stock market (as profits rise), the increasing concentration of industries and the formation of strategic alliances; the decline of real wages in most industrial countries; the growing wage differentials particularly in the upper brackets since there no meaningful market exists; finally it explains the lack of significant 'trickle down effects' of the boom, and the increasing difficulties of states to act as redistributive agencies and provide for social welfare.

From that it should also be clear that such a trend cannot be described as 'liberalization' in any meaningful way, since it leads inevitably to concentration (a situation which classical economic analysis considered detrimental to welfare). Even if newer models suggest that, contrary to classical analyses, competition might not cease even in oligopolistic markets and thus prices might actually decline when firms collaborate on research and product development, there remains a certain uneasiness with such arguments. It does not take much reflection to see that these developments

---

[54] For a general discussion of this point, see the critical review of some standard textbooks on international trade law by David Kennedy, 'International Style in Postwar Law and Policy', *Utah Law Review* (no volume) (1994), pp. 7–103.

are potentially dangerous, as fewer and fewer people benefit from both the boom and the lower prices. Therefore, visceral reactions from the great majority who feel that they are the losers of this globalization trend are rather likely. The dis-embedding of the economy puts economic market liberalism squarely at odds with another part of liberalism: democratic theory and its notions of distributive justice.

The predicament is not helped by the fact that this fundamental transformation cannot be understood simply as the ascendancy of the economy over the state and that the realization of the anarchist ideal of the possibilities of private ordering is around the corner. Consequently, one has to question the implication that politics will become less important, as networks will become the dominant organizational form in the future. It is certainly true that changes in production increasingly depend on access to capital and 'know-how', embodied in transnational networks. But the conclusion therefore that states as territorial organizations have ceased to be important does not follow for two interdependent reasons, one legal, the other political. The legal argument turns on the issue of property rights, which makes the image of a purely 'private ordering' rather problematic *ab initio*. As Peter Evans recently remarked:

If an economically stateless world could deliver in practice a global equilibrium that met the needs of TNCs, then eclipse (of the state) might indeed be in the offing. In fact, transnational investors trying to integrate operations across a shifting variety of national context need competent predictable public sector counterparts even more than do old-fashioned domestic investors who can concentrate their time and energy on building relations with a particular individual apparatus.[55]

Thus oddly enough the process of globalization requires the state, and a 'strong' state at that, and, by extension, also international regulatory regimes and dispute-settling mechanisms of considerable bite. The importance of secure property rights is even further enhanced by the emergence of a service economy where increasingly ideas and skills, not tangible products, are traded. Since the cost of production of ideas is practically zero, the 'franchising' of ideas is not subject to decreasing returns (other than fashions, or changes of taste) so that profits increase continuously with the size of the market. To that extent the limits result not from marginal costs in production but in the duration and scope of the patents, or the generally recognized intellectual property rights. Thus, the role of the state as guarantor of rights is more important than ever before. It is not the state *per se* that has not lost its rationale, rather its *functions* have been dramatically changed by the developments that we lump together under the heading of globalization.[56]

The picture of globalization as a process of homogenization, leading towards technocratic forms of rule in the economic as well as the political realm is rather superficial. First, as several studies have indicated, politics still matters and domestic institutions channel liberalization in quite different ways.[57] Even global

---

[55] Peter Evans, 'The Eclipse of the State? Reflections on Stateness in an Era of Globalization', *World Politics*, 50 (Oct. 1997), pp. 62–87.

[56] For a good discussion of this point, see Philip Cerny, 'Globalization and the Changing Logic of Collective Action', *International Organization*, 49 (Autumn 1995), pp. 595–626. See also his *The Changing Architecture of Politics* (London: Sage 1990).

[57] See, for example, Louis Pauly, *Opening Financial Markets: Banking Politics on the Pacific Rim* (Ithaca, NY: Cornell University Press, 1988).

firms differ significantly in their make-up,[58] as there does not seem to exist only one way of tackling problems. Thus, organizational structures which have been sedimented by past decisions continue to exert considerable influence. Second, quite different from the philosophical argument that we are part of just another episode of the relentless historical process leading to ever more inclusive forms of political organization, the spread of 'universalism' is strongly counteracted by the equally strong assertion of particularities. Precisely because the 'packed imagery of the visionary global culture is either trivial or shallow, a matter of mass commodity advertisement',[59] the norm of self-determination has served as a powerful tool for groups which seek to assert their independence in order to preserve their identity. To that extent we had better remember that the state as a political community is also a *membership organization* and the issue of belonging addresses more than some irrational needs.

Conceiving of a community as something which 'unites' all its citizens is important precisely because it provides the means of ascribing responsibilities and of indicating the levers for political action. Thus, persons who are excluded from influence, because they cannot participate in networks or markets owing to their lack of resources, are still part of the 'public' to which decision-makers and bureaucrats have to answer. In other words, the point is not so much that functioning markets and networks need regulators, although this is certainly a problem when national regulations can be avoided and equivalent international institutions are not in place, as the debt crisis showed. The point is rather to whom do these regulators have to answer? Is it only shareholders, inventors and marketing agencies which have acquired intellectual property, or is it the public at large? But which public, since networks are characterized by the disappearance of publics?

In short, what is missing in debates about strong vs. weak states, the ascendancy of the market over the state, and so on is *politics* plain and simple. By identifying it—different from realists who saw politics as potential violence—with government and governmental structures, the advocates of the strong state submit to the illusion of a neo-Weberian vision of bureaucratic efficiency and rationality. But, as we all know, politics is different: it is not only about dilemmas (rather than about simple administrative measures); it is also about representative choices and their legitimization; in modern times it is about gaining the consent of the governed. Precisely because the present transformations deeply affect our accustomed ways of dealing with problems, rules that affect our way of life need to be buttressed by a broad-based consensus. Administrative rationality is insufficient to deal with those problems, as has been demonstrated by Ulrich Beck.[60] Starting from the traditional notion of risk, Beck shows that such notions cannot guide us in dealing with modern risks. The uninsurability of an increasing number of problems suggests this much. Years ago, Habermas pointed to the legitimization crisis of the modern state[61] in which administrative procedures—a modern version of applied legalism, in which not judges but administrators play now the main role—overwhelm efforts at building political consensus. These pressures have increased and it is cold comfort to know

---

[58] Louis Pauly and Simon Reich 'Enduring MNC Differences Despite Globalization', *International Organization*, 51 (Winter 1997), pp. 1–30.

[59] Anthony Smith, *Nations and Nationalism in a Gobal Era* (Cambridge: Polity Press, 1995), p. 23.

[60] Ulrich Beck, *Risikogesellschaft: Auf dem Weg in eine andere Moderne* (Frankfurt: Suhrkamp, 1986).

[61] See Jürger Habermas, *Legitimationsprobleme im Spätkapitalismus* (Frankfurt: Suhrkamp 1973).

that networks and strong bureaucracies will continue to be part of our social reality as we face the 'second move'.

This argument certainly does not imply that nothing has changed in the international arena, or that the states with which we are familiar will persist. Rather it raises precisely the question of the basis of which criteria the 'units' of the system are going to be differentiated and what organizational forms between hierarchy and anarchy will develop and interact in the future. That politics will increasingly revolve around membership questions is suggested by the brief discussion above. To that extent we should perhaps ponder more carefully Benedict Andersons's astute observation, made long before the end of the Soviet Union, that there is in nearly every country a tomb of the unknown soldier, but none of the unknown Marxist.[62] The obliviousness of a discipline, which on the one hand calls itself 'international' relations or 'international' politics, but, on the other hand, fails to theorize the 'national' in its definition, is indeed more than surprising.[63] Such failures are not minor glitches but threaten the adequacy of our conceptual approaches. There is apparently some force to nationalist ideology that other ideologies have difficulty in matching, even though it might have nothing to do with primordialism, but might be a response to the changes of modernity. After the death of God—the traditional guarantor of order—'the people' remain the only source of legitimacy. By joining pre-modern ties and sentiments, characteristic of traditional ethnic communities, with modern ideas of popular sovereignty, nationalism provided a partial answer to the crisis of meaning engendered by modernity.

To that extent, notions of a world society and of the victory of universalism against the assertions of more particular identities seem rather anaemic, as are the strangely technocratic visions of 'private ordering', or of networks that displace the common space that a political order is able to create. Perhaps this is the warning that Carr tried to impart to us when he criticized utopian schemes while insisting that every conception of politics must have a utopian element. Since politics is about *projects* which are never complete and which constantly move between the is and the ought, its analysis cannot be reduced to the logic of law, to the structural constraints of the international system, to the economy of force, or to a historical trend. Those who had contributed to the institution-building of the 'first move' failed in a way because of their inadequate understanding. Their failure was costly, even though it made the success of the second episode of the 'first move' possible. But even those lessons seem of limited use to us who are now faced by the problems of a 'second move'.

Conclusion

This article had several purposes. Occasioned by an anniversary of the birth of the discipline, as seen through the prism of Carr's *The Twenty Years' Crisis*, it began by putting Carr's work into perspective. It did so by a fresh reading that was not

---

[62] Benedict Anderson, *Imagined Communities* (London: Verso, 1983), p. 10.
[63] See the critical discussion of this point by Yosef Lapid, Friedrich Kratochwil, 'Revisiting the "National": Toward an Identity Agenda in Neorealism', in Yosef Lapid and Friedrich Kratochwil (eds.), *The Return of Culture and Identity in IR Theory* (Boulder, Co.: Lynne Rienner, 1996), ch. 6.

encumbered by the 'realist' tradition which had tried to appropriate it. By focusing on the principles of construction that underlaid Carr's analysis I wanted to show that his work is much richer than subsequent interpretations suggested, and that it actually contradicts the dominant realist interpretation on several important dimensions.

A second task was to subject this analysis to criticism and show its possibilities and limitations for an understanding of our contemporary problems of order in the domestic as well as international arena. The disciplinary boundaries between 'politics' and 'law', as they emerged from the discussions generated by Carr, were examined in order to show not only the implausibility of their respective concepts of law and politics but also the mutual dependence on each other. The analysis of legalism, exemplified by the theories of law of Kelsen and Hart on the one hand, and of realism, rooted in a Schmittian conception of politics, on the other, were intended to bear out my contentions.

Finally, in order to assess the contribution of norms to the problem of peaceful change, one of the main themes in Carr's book, I examined the efforts of institutionalization during the last 80 years. For that purpose I utilized the notion of a 'move'. This analytical gambit was introduced by David Kennedy, who focused on the constitutive principles of our conventional narratives concerning the Versailles settlement and the creation of formal organizations. But where my analysis differs from Kennedy's is that I examined not only the legal narratives of the settlement but also that of the lessons learned in the inter-war period which served as the basis for the UN and the Bretton Woods System in the aftermath of World War II.

By showing the continuity (despite some decisive innovations) that made these two episodes part of one move, I then contrasted it with the crisis in our present understanding. This crisis is occasioned by the growing interdependencies that have since the late 70s called into question the appropriateness of most of our conceptual tools for the analysis of change in the international arena. By undermining the effectiveness of traditional international organizations that were designed for the abatement of the externalities flowing from the domestic order problems of the welfare state, the present situation is characterized by a crisis comparable to that which occasioned Carr's reflections. I argued that this problem can be described in terms of a 'second' move and utilized again the method of deconstructing the narratives of liberalization that has as its two underlying themes: the triumphalism of the 'end of history' and the argument about the inevitability of new forms of organizations that are going to overwhelm our traditional forms of organizing political life.

By showing the problematic character of both the 'end of history' argument and characterizing the secular change we are witnessing as moves towards liberalization, I brought to bear some of the insights of modern economic thought that takes the question of organization seriously. In this context I showed that the interpretation of the ascendancy of the market over the state is unconvincing, although such a reading does identify some important changes in the architecture of politics. Finally, having argued that the changes can remain peaceful if they are channelled by new strong domestic and international institutions, I nevertheless criticized the dominant strong state argument and its underlying neo-Weberian emphasis on administrative rationality. Instead, I argued that the problems of modern societies cannot be addressed by traditional modes of administrative decision making and that questions of consensus and legitimacy, as well as responsibility to a 'public', have not ceased to be political problems of the first order. I argued, therefore, that membership questions are going to regain new virulence, as the revival of nationalism also seems to indicate. Thus, the challenge of the 'second move' consists in building not only networks, but *political institutions* that can manage the present dislocations and channel them into avenues of peaceful change.

The End of the Old Order ?
Globalization and the Prospects
for World Order

DAVID HELD AND ANTHONY MCGREW

In reflecting upon the prospects for world order, in the concluding chapter of *The Twenty Years Crisis* , E. H. Carr advised that 'few things are permanent in history; and it would be rash to assume that the territorial unit of power is one of them'.[1] Based upon his observation that world order was being reshaped by the contradictory imperatives of progressive economic integration and a 'recrudescence of disintegrating tendencies', Carr concluded with a confident prediction that 'the concept of sovereignty is likely to become in the future even more blurred and indistinct than it is at present'.[2] Yet his devastating critique of inter-war idealism delivers a powerful rebuff to the hubris of those who seek to construct a new world order on the foundations of nineteenth-century liberal thought. Whilst Carr celebrated the importance of normative and utopian thinking in international relations, he grounded this in a sophisticated appreciation of the routines of power politics and the historical possibilities for international political change. Although a convinced sceptic of the Enlightenment vision of a universal human community and the inevitability of a 'harmony of interests', Carr nevertheless believed that 'it is unlikely that the future units of power will take much account of formal sovereignty'.[3] Indeed, he even went so far as to argue that 'any project of inter-national order which takes these formal units [sovereign states] as its basis seems likely to prove unreal'.[4] In surveying the prospects for world order at the end of the twentieth century, such observations appear remarkably prescient, especially in relation to the contemporary debate concerning globalization and the condition of the modern nation-state.

Any assessment of the prospects for world order must begin with some understanding of how the powerful historical forces of integration and disintegration, which Carr identified over sixty years ago, are articulated today and how they shape modern political life. It is in this context that the current discussion of globalization takes on a special importance. For at the core of this is an inquiry into whether globalization is transforming the nature of modern political community and thus reconstituting the foundations—empirical and normative—of world order. World order, in this context, is understood to embrace more than simply the ordering of relations between states and to include, as Bull conceived it, the ordering of relations

---

[1] E. H. Carr, *The Twenty Years' Crisis 1919–1939* (London, 1981), p. 229.
[2] Ibid., p. 230.
[3] Ibid., p. 231.
[4] Ibid.

between the world's peoples.[5] In the sections that follow, this paper will examine critically the globalization thesis, giving particular attention to what it reveals about the changing conditions of political community and the prospects for world order. This involves an examination of the existing organization, and the future possibilities, of political community as the fundamental building block of world order. The inquiry would be pursued within the spirit of Carr's dictum that 'mature thought combines purpose with observation and analysis'.[6]

Contemporary globalization: what's new?

Globalization refers to an historical process which transforms the spatial organization of social relations and transactions, generating transcontinental or inter-regional networks of interaction and the exercise of power.[7] It is possible to identify for analytical purposes different historical forms of globalization, from the epoch of world discovery in the early modern period to the present era of the neo-liberal global project. These can be characterized by distinctive spatio-temporal and organizational attributes. Thus to talk of globalization is to acknowledge that, over the *longue durée*, there have been distinctive historical forms of globalization which have been associated with quite different kinds of historical world order. Although contemporary globalization shares much in common with past phases it is nevertheless distinguished by unique spatio-temporal and organizational attributes; that is, by distinctive measures of the extensity, intensity, velocity and impact of global flows, alongside distinctive patterns of institutionalization, modes of contestation, stratification and reproduction. Moreover, since contemporary processes of globalization and regionalization articulate overlapping networks and constellations of power which cut across territorial and political boundaries, they present a unique challenge to a world order designed in accordance with the Westphalian principle of sovereign, exclusive rule over a bounded territory.

Of course, the character and significance of this challenge is hotly debated. For some, referred to here as the hyperglobalizers, these developments lead to the demise of sovereign statehood and undermine a world order constructed upon the basis of Westphalian norms.[8] Amongst those of a more sceptical mind, globalization is conceived as the great myth of our times; accordingly, the proposition that it prefigures the emergence of a new, less state-centric world order is dismissed.[9] By comparison, others argue that contemporary globalization is reconstituting or

---

[5] See H. Bull, *The Anarchical Society* (London, 1977), p. 22.

[6] Carr, *The Twenty Years' Crisis 1919–1939*, p. 20.

[7] For a more extended discussion of this definition, see the Introduction in Held and McGrew, *et al.*, *Global Transformations: Politics, Economics and Culture* (Cambridge, 1999).

[8] See, for instance, K. Ohmae, *The End of the Nation State* (New York, 1995); H. V. Perlmutter, 'On the Rocky Road to the First Global Civilzation', *Human Relations*, 44: 1 (1991), pp. 902–6; J. Gray, *False Dawn* (London, 1998).

[9] On the sceptical position see, for instance, C. Brown, 'International Political Theory and the Idea of World Community', in K. Booth and S. Smith (eds.), *International Relations Theory Today* (Cambridge, 1995), pp. 90–109; S. Krasner, 'Compromising Westphalia', *International Security*, 20: 3 (1995), pp. 115–151; P. Hirst and G. Thompson, *Globalization in Question,* (Cambridge, 1996); P. Hirst, 'The Global Economy—Myths and Realities', *International Affairs,* 73 (3 July, 1997), pp. 409–26.

transforming the power, functions and authority of the nation-state.[10] For these transformationalists, globalization is associated with the emergence of a post-Westphalian world order in which the institutions of sovereign statehood and political community are being reformed and reconstituted. In this post-Westphalian order, there is marked shift towards heterarchy—a divided authority system—in which states seek to share the tasks of governance with a complex array of institutions, public and private, local, regional, transnational and global, representing the emergence of 'overlapping communities of fate'.

This in not the place to review the claims, counter-claims and historical evidence relating to these competing accounts; that has been accomplished elsewhere.[11] Rather the central task is to examine the particular pattern of contemporary globalization in what Carr conceived as the key domains of power—the military, economic and the political.[12] This exercise is a prelude to assessing the central normative, institutional, and intellectual challenges which contemporary patterns of globalization present to the organizing principles of existing world order; namely, sovereign statehood and political community.[13] On the basis of such an assessment a taxonomy of the possible future shapes of world order will be developed.

Military globalization

Over the last century globalization in the military domain has been visible in, amongst other things, the geo-political rivalry and imperialism of the great powers (above all, from the scramble for Africa circa 1890s to the Cold War), the evolution of international alliance systems and international security structures (from the Concert of Europe to the North Atlantic Treaty Organization—NATO), the emergence of a world trade in arms together with the worldwide diffusion of military

[10] See, in particular, A. Giddens, *The Consequences of Modernity* (Cambridge, 1990); D. J. Elkins, *Beyond Sovereignty: Territory and Political Economy in the Twenty First Century* (Toronto, 1995); D. Held, *Democracy and Global Order* (Cambridge, 1995); R. O. Keohane and H. V. Milner (eds.), *Internationalization and Domestic Politics* (Cambridge, 1996); D. Goldblatt, D. Held, *et al.*, 'Economic Globalization and the Nation-state: Shifting Balances of Power', *Alternatives*, 22: 3 (1997), pp. 269–85; B. Jessop, 'Capitalism and its Future: Remarks on Regulation, Government and Governance', *Review of International Political Economy*, 4: 3 (1997), pp. 561–82; M. Mann, 'Has Globalization ended the Rise and Rise of the Nation-state?', *Review of International Political Economy*, 4: 3 (1997), pp. 472–96; J. Rosenau, *Along the Domestic–Foreign Frontier* (Cambridge, 1997).

[11] See Held and McGrew, *et al.*, *Global Transformations*.

[12] See Carr, *The Twenty Years' Crisis 1919–1939*, ch. 8.

[13] The concept of sovereignty lodges a distinctive claim to the rightful exercise of political power over a circumscribed realm. It seeks to specify the political authority within a community which has the right to determine the framework of rules, regulations and policies within a given territory and to govern accordingly. However, in thinking about the impact of globalization upon the modern nation-state, one needs to distinguish the claim to sovereignty—the entitlement to rule over a bounded territory—from state autonomy—the actual power the nation-state possesses to articulate and achieve policy goals independently. In effect, state autonomy refers to the capacity of state representatives, managers and agencies to articulate and pursue their policy preferences even though these may on occasion clash with the dictates of domestic and international social forces and conditions. Moreover, to the extent that modern nation-states are democratic, sovereignty and autonomy are assumed to be embedded within, and congruent with, the territorially organized framework of liberal democratic government: 'the rulers'—elected representatives—are accountable to 'the ruled'—the citizenry—within a delimited territory. There is, in effect, a 'national community of fate', whereby membership of the political community is defined in terms of the peoples within the territorial borders of the nation-state. See Held and McGrew, *et al.*, *Global Transformations*, the Introduction, for a fuller analysis of these terms.

technologies, and the institutionalization of global regimes with jurisdiction over military and security affairs, for example, the international nuclear non-proliferation regime. Indeed, it is possible to argue that all states are now enmeshed, albeit to varying degrees, in a world military order. This world military order is highly stratified, highly institutionalized, and shaped by a relatively autonomous arms dynamic. It is stratified in that there is broadly a first tier (with superpower status), second tier (middle-ranking powers) and third tier (developing military powers); and it is institutionalized in that military–diplomatic and multilateral arrangements define regularized patterns of interaction. Military globalization can be conceived initially as a process which embodies the growing extensity and intensity of military relations amongst the political units of the world system. Understood as such, it reflects both the expanding network of worldwide military ties and relations alongside the impact of key military technological innovations (e.g. steamships to reconnaissance satellites) which, over time, have reconstituted the world into an increasingly unified geo-strategic space. Historically, this process of time–space compression has brought centres of military power into closer proximity and potential conflict, as the capability to project enormous destructive power across vast distances has proliferated. Simultaneously, military decision and reaction times have shrunk with the consequence that permanent military machines, along with their permanent preparation for war, have become an integral feature of modern social life.

With the end of the Cold War the pattern of global military and security relations has been further transformed. In some respects, the structure of world military power at the end of the twentieth century reflects a return to a traditional pattern of multipolar power politics, but, in other respects, especially in relation to the sole military superpower status of the US, it is historically unique. As the Cold War has ended and the foreign military presence of the US and Russia has contracted (by quite spectacular proportions) the reassertion of regional and local patterns of inter-state rivalry has been intense. One consequence of this is the visible tendency towards 'the decentralization of the international security system'—the fragment-ation of the world into relatively discrete (but not entirely self-contained) regional security complexes.[14] This is evident, amongst other cases, in the resurgence of nationalist conflicts and tensions in Europe and the Balkans, in the Indo-Pakistan rivalry in South Asia, and in the rivalry over the South China seas in Southeast Asia. As the overlay of Cold War conflict has been removed, a significant external restraint upon regional conflicts (whose origins often predate even the age of the European empire) has disappeared. In some cases, such as South East Asia, the consequences to date have been relatively benign but in many regions rivalries and tensions have escalated. This 'regionalization' of international security represents an important distinguishing feature of the post-Cold War world military and security order.

One interpretation of this altering military landscape is that the global security and military order is undergoing a process of 'structural bifurcation'; that is, fragmentation into two largely separate systems, each with different standards, rules of conduct and inter-state behaviour.[15] The likely implications and costs of (conven-

---

[14] B. Buzan, *People, States and Fear* (Brighton, 1991), p. 208.
[15] J. M. Goldeier and M. McFail, 'A Tale of Two Worlds: Core and Periphery in the Post-Cold War Era', *International Organization*, 46: 2 (1992), pp. 467–91.

tional or nuclear) war among advanced industrial states, argues Mueller among others, are now so overwhelming that major war has become obsolete: it would be counterproductive either as a mechanism for resolving interstate conflict or as a mechanism for transforming the international status quo.[16] In contradistinction to this, states in the periphery (i.e. states in the developing world) operate within a system in which political instability, militarism and state expansion remain endemic, and in which there is no effective deterrent to war as a rational instrument of state policy. Accordingly, patterns of international military and security relations are diverging radically as the post-Cold War world order becomes increasingly bifurcated.

These processes of fragmentation and regionalization, however, can be counterposed to powerful centripetal forces reinforcing the unified character of the world military order. Four factors in particular deserve mention in this respect:

- First, in most global regions there is a gradual shift taking place towards cooperative defence or cooperative security arrangements. The desire to avoid inter-state conflict, the enormous costs, technological requirements and domestic burdens of defence are together contributing to the historic strengthening, rather than weakening, of multilateral and collective defence arrangements as well as international military cooperation and coordination. The end of the Cold War has not witnessed the demise of NATO, as many predicted in 1990, but rather its expanding role and significance. In many of the world's key regions, multilateral frameworks for security and defence cooperation are beginning to emerge alongside existing bilateral arrangements. These, like the ASEAN Regional Forum (ARF) in Asia–Pacific, may be at a very early stage of development and beset by all kinds of rivalries, but historically they represent a significant institutionalization of military and security relations. Moreover, many of these arrangements are becoming less regionally specific as the US has strengthened its global engagements (e.g. NATO and ARF). At the global level too, the peacekeeping activities of the UN and its more general collective security functions have become more visible, although not necessarily more effective. These developments reflect a realization that, with the end of the Cold War, and against the background of recent military technological change, 'the capacity of the state to defend territorial boundaries against armed attack' may have considerably weakened.[17] Certainly, many states now recognize that national security can no longer be achieved simply through unilateral actions alone.

- Second, the rising density of financial, trade and economic connections between states has expanded the potential vulnerability of most states to political or economic instability in distant parts of the globe. Accordingly, many states, not simply the world's major powers, remain acutely sensitive (if not vulnerable) to security and military developments in other regions. Such sensitivities may be highly selective, and certainly not all parts of the globe are perceived as of comparable strategic importance. Nevertheless, as the 1990 Gulf crisis demonstrated, military developments in strategically critical regions continue to be of global significance. Regionalization and globalization of military/security relations are by no means contradictory processes but may be mutually reinforcing.

- Third, threats to national security are becoming both more diffuse and no longer simply military in character.[18] The proliferation of weapons of mass destruction poses a potential threat to all states. But proliferation is in part a product of the diffusion of industrial and

---

[16] J. Mueller, *Retreat from Doomsday: The Obsolescence of Major War* (New York, 1989).

[17] J. A. Camilleri and J. Falk, *The End of Sovereignty: The Politics of a Shrinking and Fragmented World* (Brighton, 1992), p. 152.

[18] See B. Buzan, O. Waever, *et al.*, *Security: A New Framework for Analysis* (Boulder, CO, 1998).

technological knowledge as well as hardware. Preventing proliferation is thus a classic collective action problem in that it demands world wide action. Similarly, environmental, economic, narcotics, terrorist, cultural, criminal and other threats to national security cannot be resolved solely through either military or national means. Accordingly, there is a continuing demand for global mechanisms of co-ordination and co-operation to deal with the expanding penumbra of security threats.

- Fourth, in the global states system the military security of all nations is significantly influenced by systemic factors. Indeed, the structure of power and the actions of the great powers remain dominant influences upon the military postures of each other and of all other states. At one level this is simply because the great powers set the standards, be it in military technology or force levels, against which all other states ultimately calibrate their defence capability. Thus, US defence policy has more wide-ranging global effects than does that of Kiribati. How the great powers act or react affects the security of all the world's regions.

These points suggest that the contemporary geo-political order, far from simply fragmenting, remains beset by problems of global strategic interconnectedness. The lack of any serious global political and military rivalries of the kind represented by the Cold War, or the New Imperialism of the 1890s, should not be read as a process of military deglobalization. Despite the ending of Cold War rivalry there has not been a detectable return to earlier forms of national military autarky; nor has the world broken up into discrete regional security complexes. Globalization and regionalization in the military domain appear to be mutually reinforcing rather than mutually exclusive processes. Moreover, there are growing (financial, technological, industrial and political) pressures on states to engage in multilateral cooperative efforts to achieve the rationalization of their defence industrial base. This is contributing to the (admittedly slow) de-nationalization of defence industries in most advanced states, and to a globalization of defence production.[19]

The transnationalization of the defence industrial base represents a distinctive new stage in the organization of defence production and procurement akin to (but on a very different scale from) the global restructuring of industrial production.[20] It is also reinforced by the fact that many of the most critical defence technologies are produced in those very civil industrial sectors, such as electronics or optics, which have been subject to increasing globalization. These developments have quite profound, although not necessarily completely novel, implications for the orthodox approach to defence–industrial organization, which traditionally has privileged— alongside national strategies of defence and procurement—the national defence industrial base as the necessary underpinning to an 'autonomous' national defence capability. Both the regionalization and the globalization of the defence–industrial sector compromise such autonomy in a fairly direct way since they make the acquisition (and crucially the use) of arms and weapons systems (not to mention defence industrial policy) potentially subject to the decisions and actions of other authorities or corporations beyond the scope of national jurisdiction.

---

[19] See R. A. Bitzinger, 'The Globalization of the Arms Industry', *International Security*, 19: 2 (1994), pp. 170–98.

[20] See Bitzinger, ibid.; A. Moravcsik, 'The European Armaments Industry at the Crossroads', *Survival*, 33 (1991), pp. 65–85; H. Wulf and E. Skons, 'The Internationalization of the Arms Industry', *American Annals of Political and Social Science*, 535 (Sept., 1994), pp. 43–57.

In some contexts, however, such regionalization and globalization may be exploited to enhance defence industrial and military autonomy. Sweden, for instance, by engaging in collaborative and licensing arrangements with both American and European aerospace defence contractors, has been able to sustain a highly advanced defence industrial capability which it might otherwise have been unable to support. Japan, too, has reduced its military dependence on the US by exploiting an intensely competitive world market in military technology transfer and licensing. In the realm of defence production and procurement, globalization and regionalization by no means automatically prefigure the demise of a national defence industrial base, but they do alter the strategies and policies which governments have to pursue in order to sustain it as well as the patterns of industrial winners and losers. In the case of European states, the consolidation of 'national champions', through government-supported (but not necessarily initiated) mergers and acquisitions, has complemented the emergence of 'European champions' to compete in the global and regional arms market with their American rivals. Autonomy is, thus, sought through a changing mix of internationalization and nationalization. This in itself represents a significant departure from orthodox notions of military autonomy defined and pursued in essentially national terms.

In the contemporary era of declining defence procurement budgets, the internationalization of defence production provides one solution to the maintenance of a 'national' defence industrial capacity. Accordingly, this is not simply a process which is confined to Europe, or the trans-Atlantic region, where it is most evident, but is a part of a secular trend in defence industrial restructuring.[21] This is largely because, for many big defence companies, 'internationalization is one strategy of consolidation for long-term survival in the market'.[22] Restructuring of the national defence industrial base unfolds alongside a global restructuring of defence production. In varying degrees, all countries engaged in defence production are gradually being touched by these twin developments. As a consequence, in parallel to many political phenomena, the distinction between the 'foreign' and 'domestic' is breaking down. Indeed, the enormous complexity of cross-border intercorporate and production networks involves a 'shift away from traditional, single-country patterns of weapons production towards more transnational development and manufacture of arms'.[23] Global sourcing of defence production, as in the commercial sector, is a growing practice as cost containment becomes more critical. For industrializing states with an indigenous defence production capability, global sourcing remains essential to meeting defence interests.[24] But this is also supplemented by other forms of collaboration, sometimes with the governments of other developing countries or advanced states, in the development or production of 'indigenous' military systems. In the post-Cold War era, the global diffusion of military-technology and defence industrial capacity are becoming closely associated with a transnationalization of defence production.

---

[21] Ibid.

[22] E. Skons, 'Western Europe: Internationalization of the Arms Industry', in H. Wulf (ed.), *Arms Industry Limited* (Oxford 1993), p. 160.

[23] R. A. Bitzinger, *The Globalization of Arms Production: Defense Markets in Transition* (Washington DC, Defense Budget Project, 1993), p. 3.

[24] M. Brzoska and T. Ohlson, 'Arms Production in the Third World', in M. Brzoska and T. Ohlson (eds.), *Arms Production in the Third World* (Oxford, 1986), p. 285.

The spread of both defence industrial capability and military technology is facilitated by the increasingly central role acquired by commercial (civil) technologies (and civil technological innovation) in the development and manufacture of advanced weapons systems. The military technological revolution (MTR) of the late twentieth century is a product of the 'information age'. The same technologies which are revolutionizing aspects of everyday life, from the supermarket checkout to personal communications, are transforming the logistics of war and the modern battlefield which, as the 1991 Gulf War demonstrated, is now 'constructed' as 'a blizzard of electronic blips' rather than simply a 'storm of steel'.[25] Strategic technologies are today largely dual-use technologies. Dual-use technologies, by definition, are commercial technologies and the industries that produce them are considerably more globalized than the defence industrial sector. As a result, most dual-use technologies are intensively traded across the globe whilst the capability to produce them is actively dispersed through the operations of transnational corporations. According to Carus, the result is that an 'increasingly large number of countries have access to many of the technologies needed to exploit the military technological revolution'.[26] This in turn is transforming the stratification of military-technological power within the global system.

Military power has been fundamental to the evolution and the institutional form of the modern sovereign, territorial nation-state. The independent capacity to defend national territorial space by military means is at the heart of the modern conception of the institution of sovereign statehood. But, as discussed here, contemporary military globalization poses quite profound questions about the meaning and practice of state sovereignty and autonomy. For in the contemporary age, the traditionally presumed correspondence between the spatial organization of military power and the territorial nation-state appears to be changing.

The doctrine of national security remains one of the essential defining principles of modern statehood. The autonomous capacity of the modern state to defend the nation against external threats is a crucial (and to some the essential) ingredient of traditional conceptions of sovereignty. For if a state does not have the capacity to secure its territory and protect its people then its very *raison d'être* can be called into question. National security has, therefore, been understood traditionally in primarily military terms as the acquisition, deployment and use of military force to achieve national goals. Without such a capacity the very essence of the institution of modern statehood would be decidedly altered.

Of course, the ideology of modern statehood has not always been replicated in the political practices of states. But in the military domain, above all others, modern states have always sought to maintain their independence. However, in the contemporary era, military globalization and patterns of national enmeshment in the world military order have prompted a serious rethinking about the idea and the practice of national security. Although the discourse of national security dominates political and popular debate about military matters, it acts more as a simplified representation or legitimating device than a reflection of the actual behaviour of states. For many states the strategy for achieving 'national security' has become almost indistinguishable from an international security strategy. This is evident

[25] M. van Creveld, *Technology and War: From 2000 BC to the* Present (New York, 1989), p. 282.
[26] W. S. Carus, 'Military Technology and the Arms Trade', *AAPSS* 535 (Sept. 1994), pp. 163–74.

amongst Western states which collectively constitute a 'security community' within which military force plays no active role in the relations between member states.[27]

Within this 'security community' national defence and the exercise of military force are decided within an institutionalized alliance system (NATO) in which collective discussion and multilateral diplomacy complement existing national mechanisms of security policy. The development and pursuit of national security goals are, therefore, inseparable, in most key respects, from the development and pursuit of alliance security. National security and alliance security can be conceived as mutually constituted.[28] Even for states such as France, which has historically sought to pursue a highly autonomous defence posture, or Sweden, which retains a declared policy of neutrality, post-war national security policy effectively has always been shaped (and in the post-Cold War context increasingly so) by the functioning of this broader 'security community'.[29] Moreover, for the United States, membership of NATO represents an historic shift in national security posture away from autarky, isolationism, and the avoidance of external military commitments.[30] For the US, along with other members of the Western 'security community', the practice of cooperative security is redefining the traditional agenda of national security.

The widening agenda of security, combined with the institutionalization of cooperative defence (and security) and the global regulation of military power, through arms control and other regimes, has contributed to a broadening of defence and security politics. The notion that the politics of defence and security issues are coterminous with national political space is belied by such diverse phenomena as the existence of global campaigns to ban landmines or to establish an International Criminal Court for crimes against humanity, and defence contractors within NATO and Europe lobbying for changes in defence industrial policy or government regulations on both sides of the Atlantic or in the East. Political activity focused on 'national security' matters is no longer simply a domestic affair. Accordingly, there can be little doubt that contemporary military globalization has significant implications for the sovereignty, autonomy and politics of modern states. Although states are differentially enmeshed in the world military order and retain differential capacities to mediate military globalization, the institution of modern sovereign statehood is subject to powerful transformative forces. This thesis is also supported by a consideration of global economic processes.

Economic globalization

Today all countries are engaged in international trade and nearly all trade significant proportions of their national income. Around twenty per cent of world output is traded and a much larger proportion is potentially subject to international com-

---

[27] K. Deutsch and S. A. Burrell, *Political Community and the North Atlantic Area* (Princeton, 1957).

[28] See S. Weber, 'Shaping the Postwar Balance of Power: Multilateralism in NATO', in J. G. Ruggie (ed.), *Multilateralism Matters* (New York, 1993), pp. 233–92.

[29] See, in particular, R. H. Ullman, 'The Covert French Connection', *Foreign Policy* 75: 3 (1989), pp. 3–33; Commission on Neutrality Policy, *Had There Been a War—Preparations for the Reception of Military Assistance 1949–69* (Stockholm, Statens offenliga utredningar, 1994).

[30] This point is emphasized by Ruggie; see J. G. Ruggie, *Winning the Peace: America and World Order in the New Era* (New York, 1996), p. 43.

petition: trade has now reached unprecedented levels, both absolutely and in proportion to world output. If, in the past, trade sometimes formed an enclave largely isolated from the rest of the national economy, it is now an integral part of the structure of national production in all modern states.[31]

The historical evidence, at both the world and country levels, shows higher levels of trade today than ever before, including during the classical Gold Standard period. The post-war growth of trade, at rates above those previously recorded, has been related to a liberalization of international trade relations that is unprecedented in the modern epoch. The contemporary world trading system is defined by both an intensive network of trading relations embracing virtually all economies and evolving global markets for many goods and some services. This shift towards global markets has been facilitated by the existence of worldwide transport and communications infrastructures, the promotion of global trade liberalization through the institutionalization of a world trade system, and the internationalization of production. National markets are increasingly enmeshed with one another as intra-industry trade has expanded and global competition transcends national borders, impacting directly on local economies. In these respects individual firms are confronted by a potential global marketplace whilst they simultaneously face direct competition from foreign firms in their own domestic markets. The stratification of the global trading system also reflects these developments as a new international division of labour emerges associated with the evolution of global markets. To talk of North and South is to misrepresent contemporary patterns of stratification in respect of trade. For whilst a hierarchy of trading power remains, the North–South geographical divide has given way to a more complex structure of trade relations. Despite the historical concentration of trade amongst OECD states, global trade patterns have shifted during the contemporary era such that North and South, in this context, are becoming increasingly empty categories.[32] The composition of global trade is shifting too as trade in services becomes more intense. In all these respects, the world trading system is undergoing a profound transformation. An extensive and intensive network of trading relations operates, creating the conditions for functioning global markets, the domestic impacts of which extend well beyond the traded sector into the economy as a whole. While institutionalized trading arrangements have evolved, they have tended to reinforce the trend towards freer trade—as the evolution of the World Trade Organization (WTO) indicates.

From its inception the nation-state has used protection to raise revenues, manage balance of payments difficulties and promote domestic industry. By the late twentieth century institutional constraints, as well as economic costs, have severely limited the scope for national protectionism. Today, not only tariffs and quota restrictions, but also policies supporting domestic industry and even domestic laws with respect to business competition and safety standards, are subject to growing international scrutiny and regulation. In addition, the historical experience of achieving economic development through protection, though mixed, is now a much-diminished policy option, as the East Asian crisis of 1997–8 demonstrated.

---

[31] For more detailed statistical evidence on all aspects of economic globalization discussed here, see Held and McGrew, *et al*, *Global Transformations*, chs. 3–5. We would like to acknowledge our debt to our co-author, Jonathan Perraton, for helping clarify many of the points made in the section below.

[32] See A. Hoogvelt, *Globalisation and the Postcolonial World: The New Political Economy of Development* (London, 1997).

Autarchy, or 'delinking', too is off the political agenda. Recent enthusiasm for human capital policies—education and training—reflects not only academic and political interest in the potential of these measures for ameliorating some of the adverse consequences of global free trade, but also concerted pressures to foreclose other policy options. In these respects, the contemporary globalization of trade has transformed state autonomy and induced shifts in state policy. Furthermore, the global regulation of trade, by bodies such as the WTO, implies a significant renegotiation of the Westphalian notion of state sovereignty.

The explosive growth of global financial activity since the 1980s and the complexity of global financial markets has also transformed the management of national economies. Whilst global financial markets play a key role in the world-wide allocation of capital, they do so in a manner which has significant implications for national autonomy. Contemporary global finance is marked by both high intensity and relatively high volatility in exchange rates, interest rates and other financial asset prices. As a result, national macroeconomic policy is vulnerable to changes in global financial conditions. Speculative flows can have immediate and dramatic domestic economic consequences, as evident in the aftermath of the East Asian currency turmoil of 1997. Contemporary financial globalization has altered the costs and benefits associated with different national macroeconomic policy options, and has made some options—for example, pursuing expansionary demand management without due regard to exchange rate consequences—prohibitively expensive. These shifting costs and benefits, moreover, vary between countries and over time in a manner that is not entirely predictable. Besides these policy impacts, contemporary patterns of financial globalization also have significant institutional, distributional and structural consequences for nation-states.

Cross-border financial flows transform systemic risk in-so-far as financial difficulties faced by a single or several institutions in one country can have a major knock-on effect on the rest of the global financial sector. This was evident in the East Asian financial crisis of 1997 as the collapse of the Thai currency rippled through foreign exchange markets leading to precipitate falls in currency values across the region and affecting currency values in other emerging markets. Stock markets too were affected by the rush of short-term capital flows out of these economies. In a 'wired world' high levels of enmeshment between national markets mean that disturbances in one very rapidly spill over into others.

The existence of systemic risks produces contradictory imperatives. On the one hand, the desire on behalf of financial institutions, both public and private, to avoid a major international financial crisis produces a demand for more extensive and more intensive international regulation of world finance. Thus, in the wake of the 1997 East Asian financial crisis, the annual IMF/World Bank summit meeting in 1998 agreed to more effective international surveillance mechanisms and greater transparency in the release of financial information in an attempt to prevent such a crisis in the future. On the other hand, it is not in the interests of any state or financial institution to abide by more stringent regulatory standards than its potential competitors. The consequence is that regulatory instruments to manage systemic risks often fall far short of those necessary to deal with them effectively. The absence of any substantive attempts, following the East Asian crisis, to regulate short-term capital flows at an international level is indicative of this problem. Given the volatile nature of global financial markets, and the instantaneous diffusion of financial information between the world's major financial centres, systemic risks continue to pose a permanent threat to the functioning of the entire global financial system which no government by itself can either resolve or insulate its economy from.

The increased salience of systemic risk is, in addition, strongly associated with a structural shift in the balance of power between governments (and international agencies) and markets—more accurately, between public and private authority in the global financial system.[33] Although there is a tendency to exaggerate the power of global financial markets, ignoring the centrality of state power in sustaining their effective operation (especially in times of crisis), there is much compelling evidence to suggest that contemporary financial globalization is a market, rather than a state, driven phenomenon. Reinforced by financial liberalization, the shift towards markets and private financial institutions as the 'authoritative actors' in the global financial system poses serious questions about the nature of state power and economic sovereignty. As Germain observes, 'states have allowed private monetary agents, organized through markets, to dominate the decisions of who is granted access to credit (finance) and on what terms. The international organization of credit has been transformed . . . from a quasi-public to a nearly fully private one'.[34] In this new context the autonomy and even sovereignty of states become, in certain respects, problematic.

Compared with the era of the classical Gold Standard, or that of Bretton Woods, contemporary financial globalization has many distinctive attributes. Chief amongst these is the sheer magnitude, complexity and speed of financial transactions and flows. More currencies, more diverse and complex financial assets are traded more frequently, at greater speed, and in substantially greater volumes than in any previous historical epoch. The sheer magnitude of capital movements, relative to either global or national output and trade, is unique. All this relies upon a highly institutionalized infrastructure such that 24 hour real-time cross-border financial trading constitutes an evolving global financial market which generates significant systemic risks. Contemporary financial globalization represents a distinctive new stage in the organization and management of credit and money in the world economy; it is transforming the conditions under which the immediate and long-term prosperity of states and peoples across the globe is determined.

Aside from global finance, perhaps the commonest image of economic globalization is that of the multinational corporation (MNC): huge corporate empires which straddle the globe with annual turnovers matching the entire GNP of many nations. In 1996 there were 44,000 MNCs worldwide with 280,000 foreign subsidiaries and global sales of almost $7trillion.[35] Today, transnational production 'outweighs exports as the dominant mode of servicing foreign markets'.[36] A small number of MNCs dominate world markets for oil, minerals, foods and other agricultural products, whilst a hundred or so play a leading role in the globalization of manufacturing production and services. Together, the 100 largest MNCs control about 20

---

[33] See, for instance, A. Walters, *World Power and World Money* (Brighton, 1993); R. Germain, *The International Organization of Credit* (Cambridge, 1997); L. W. Pauly, *Who Elected the Bankers?* (New York, 1997).

[34] Germain, ibid., p. 163.

[35] UNCTAD, *1997 World Investment Report* (Geneva, 1997), p. 1.

[36] Ibid.

per cent of global foreign assets, employ 6 million workers worldwide, and account for almost 30 per cent of total world sales of all MNCs.[37] But the growth of MNCs does not tell the whole story about the globalization of production. Advances in communications technology and the infrastructural conditions which have facilitated the evolution of global financial markets and global trade have also contributed to an internationalization of production amongst small- and medium-sized enterprises (SMEs), at least within the most advanced economies in the world. SMEs are being integrated into production and distribution networks in which the manufacturing or distribution of goods and services is globalized.

By comparison with earlier epochs of business globalization, the contemporary phase is both more extensive and intensive as measured in terms of FDI, numbers and size of MNCs, subsidiaries, etc. Production capacity is now dispersed among an unprecedented number of countries across the globe. Whilst there has been a significant expansion of international production in the last three decades it has also become more institutionalized, as strategic alliances, sub-contracting, joint ventures and other forms of contractual arrangements regularize inter-firm networks and arrangements. Such arrangements have been facilitated by the liberalization of controls on FDI, capital movements and other restrictive measures on financial flows. In some respects, this is a return to the more 'open' investment climate of the turn of the century, although freed from the constraints of imperial priorities and policies. This freedom from imperial constraint is reflected in changing patterns of stratification as more FDI flows to NIEs and developing countries, in the organization of global production which is encouraging a new global division of labour, and in the internationalization of business within developing countries which is becoming a more visible feature of the global political economy.

MNCs are the linchpins of the contemporary world economy. Around 44,000 MNCs account for 25–33 per cent of world output and 70 per cent of world trade.[38] Despite regional concentrations of production, transnational business networks span the three core regions of the world economy, linking the fortunes of disparate communities and nations in complex webs of interconnectedness. MNCs are not simply 'national firms with international operations', nor are they 'footloose corporations', which wander the globe in search of maximum profits. Rather, MNCs play a much more central role in the operation of the world economy than in the past and they figure prominently in organizing extensive and intensive transnational networks of coordinated production and distribution that are historically unique. MNCs and global production networks are critical to the organization, location and distribution of productive power in the contemporary world economy.

Despite some obvious continuities with the past, such as the lasting traces of imperial ties on European FDI and MNCs, the contemporary globalization of business and production has transformed 'what goods and services are produced, how, where and by whom'.[39] Of course, multinational production still only accounts for a minority of total world production. Nevertheless, its growing significance has profound implications for the economic autonomy and sovereignty of nation-states,

---

[37] Ibid., p. 8.
[38] See S. Strange, *The Retreat of the State* (Cambridge, 1996); J. Perraton, *et al.*, 'The Globalization of Economic Activity', *New Political Economy*, 2: 2 (1997), pp. 257–77 and UNCTAD, ibid.
[39] Strange, ibid., p. 44.

although this is mediated by national patterns of enmeshment in global production networks.

Political globalization

Economic globalization has not occurred in a political vacuum, although it is too often interpreted as if it has. Alongside processes of global economic transformation there have been parallel but distinct political changes, referred to here as 'political globalization', by which we understand the shifting reach of political power, authority and forms of rule. The distinctive historical form of this in the contemporary period is captured by the notion of 'global politics'—the increasingly extensive or 'stretched' form of political relations and political activity. Political decisions and actions in one part of the world can rapidly acquire world-wide ramifications. Sites of political action and/or decision-making can become linked through rapid communications into complex networks of decision-making and political interaction. Associated with this 'stretching' is a frequent 'deepening' impact of global political processes such that, unlike in ancient or modern empires, 'action at a distance' permeates with greater intensity the social conditions and cognitive worlds of specific places or policy communities. As a consequence, developments at the global level—whether economic, social or environmental—can frequently acquire almost instantaneous local consequences and vice versa.

The idea of 'global politics' challenges the traditional distinctions between the domestic/international, inside/outside, territorial/non-territorial politics, as embedded in conventional conceptions of 'the political'.[40] It also highlights the richness and complexity of the interconnections which transcend states and societies in the global order. Although governments and states remain, of course, powerful actors, they now share the global arena with an array of other agencies and organizations.[41] The state is confronted by an enormous number of intergovernmental organizations (IGOs), international agencies and regimes which operate across different spatial reaches, and by quasi-supranational institutions, like the European Union. Non-state actors or transnational bodies, such as multinational corporations, transnational pressure groups, transnational professional associations, social movements and so on, also participate intensively in global politics. So too do many subnational actors and national pressure groups, whose activities often spill over into the international arena. Global politics today, moreover, is anchored not just in traditional geopolitical concerns, but also in a large diversity of economic, social and ecological questions. Pollution, drugs, human rights and terrorism are amongst an increasing number of transnational policy issues which cut across territorial jurisdictions and existing political alignments, and which require international co-operation for their effective resolution. Defence and security issues no longer dominate the global agenda or even the political agendas of many national govern-

[40] See R. B. J. Walker, *Inside/Outside* (Cambridge, 1994).
[41] For a detailed explication of this point, with supporting documentary evidence, see Held and McGrew, *et al.*, *Global Transformations*, chs. 1, 2, and 8.

ments. These developments, accordingly, challenge the conventional Westphalian (and realist) principles of world political order.

Nations, peoples and organizations are linked by many new forms of communication and media which range in and across borders. The revolution in microelectronics, in information technology and in computers has established virtually instantaneous world-wide links which, when combined with the technologies of the telephone, television, cable, satellite and jet transportation, have dramatically altered the nature of political communication. These new forms of communication enable individuals and groups to 'overcome' geographical boundaries which once might have prevented contact; and they create access to a range of social and political experiences with which the individual or group may never have had an opportunity to engage directly.[42] The intimate connection between 'physical setting', 'social situation' and politics which has distinguished most political associations from premodern to modern times has been ruptured; the new communication systems create new experiences, new modes of understanding and new frames of political reference independently of direct contact with particular peoples or issues. At the same time, unequal access to these new modes of communication has created novel patterns of political inclusion and exclusion in global politics.

The development of new communication systems generates a world in which the particularities of place and individuality are constantly represented and reinterpreted by regional and global communication networks. But the relevance of these systems goes far beyond this, for they are fundamental to the possibility of organizing political action and exercising political power across vast distances.[43] For example, the expansion of international and transnational organizations, the extension of international rules and legal mechanisms—their construction and monitoring—have all received an impetus from the new communication systems and all depend on them as a means to further their aims. The present era of global politics marks a shift towards a system of multilayered global and regional governance. Although it by no means replaces the sedimentation of political rule into state structures, this system is marked by the internationalization and transnationalization of politics, the development of regional and global organizations and institutions, and the emergence of regional and global law.

States are increasingly enmeshed in novel forms of international legal and juridical regimes. As Crawford and Marks remark, 'international law, with its enlarging normative scope, extending writ and growing institutionalization, exemplifies the phenomenon of globalization'.[44] Increasingly aspects of international law are acquiring a cosmopolitan form. By cosmopolitan law, or global law, or global humanitarian law, is meant here a domain of law different in kind from the law of states and the law made between one state and another for the mutual enhancement of their geopolitical interests. Cosmopolitan law refers to those elements of law—albeit created by states—which create powers and constraints, and rights and duties, which transcend the claims of nation-states and which have farreaching national consequences. Elements of such laws define and seek to protect

---

[42] See A. Giddens, *Modernity and Self-Identity* (Cambridge, 1991), pp. 84–5.

[43] See R. Deibert, *Parchment, Printing and Hypermedia* (New York, 1997).

[44] See J. Crawford and S. Marks, 'The Global Democracy Deficit. An Essay in International Law and its Limits', in D. Archibugi, D. Held and M. Köhler (eds.), *Re-imagining Political Community* (Cambridge, 1998), p. 82.

basic humanitarian values which can come into conflict, and sometimes contradiction, with national laws. These values set down basic standards or boundaries which no political agent, whether a representative of a government or state, should, in principle, be able to cross.[45]

Human rights regimes and human rights law, for example, sit uneasily with the idea of accepting state sovereignty alone as the sole principle for the organization of relations within and between political communities. They can be thought of as an element of an emerging cosmopolitan legal framework, along with the law of war, the law governing war crimes and environmental law (for example, the Convention on the Law of the Sea and elements of the Rio Declaration on Environment and Development). Together, these domains of law constitute a developing set of standards and constraints which bear upon and qualify the notion of an untrammelled principle of state sovereignty. While commitment to these standards often remains weak, they signal a change affecting the concept of legitimate state power. For the rules of war, laws governing crimes against humanity, the innovations in legal thinking concerning the use of resources and human rights regimes all mark out a shift in the direction of the subject and scope of international law. Opinion has shifted against the doctrine that international law must be a law 'between states only and exclusively'. At issue is the emergence of a vast body of rules, quasi-rules and legal changes which are beginning to alter the basis of coexistence and cooperation in the global order. The legal innovations referred to challenge the idea that the supreme normative principle of the political organization of humankind can and should remain simply that of sovereign statehood. Most recently, proposals put forward for the establishment of an International Criminal Court add further testimony to the gradual shift toward a 'universal constitutional order'.[46] The new legal frameworks aim to curtail and to delimit state sovereignty, and set basic standards and values for the treatment of all, during war and peace. Of course, this body of law is by no means subscribed to systematically; but it points to the development of a post-Westphalian order—setting down a new regulatory framework for the conduct of relations among political communities.

At the end of the second millennium, political communities and civilizations can no longer be characterized simply as 'discrete worlds'; they are enmeshed and entrenched in complex structures of overlapping forces, relations and movements. Clearly, these are often structured by inequality and hierarchy. But even the most powerful among them—including, the most powerful nation-states—do not remain unaffected by the changing conditions and processes of regional and global entrenchment. A few points can be emphasized to clarify further the changing relations between political globalization and modern nation-states. All indicate an increase in the extensiveness, intensity, velocity and impact of political globalization, and all suggest important questions about the evolving character of the democratic political community in particular.

---

[45] See Held, *Democracy and Global Order*, chs. 5–6.

[46] See J. Crawford, 'Prospects for an International Criminal Court', in M. D. A. Freeman and R. Halson (eds.), *Current Legal Problems 1995*, 48, pt. 2, collected papers (Oxford, 1995); J. Dugard, 'Obstacles in the way of an International Criminal Court', *Cambridge Law Journal*, 56 (1997); M. Weller, 'The Reality of the Emerging Universal Constitutional Order: Putting the Pieces Together', *Cambridge Review of International Affairs* (Winter/Spring, 1997).

Today the locus of effective political power can no longer be assumed to be national governments—effective power is shared and bartered by diverse forces and agencies at national, regional and international levels. Furthermore, the idea of a political community of fate—of a self-determining collectivity—can no longer meaningfully be located within the boundaries of a single nation-state alone. Some of the most fundamental forces and processes which determine the nature of life-chances within and across political communities are now beyond the reach of individual nation-states. The late twentieth century political world is marked by a significant series of new types of 'boundary problem'. In the past, of course, nation-states principally resolved their differences over boundary matters by pursuing reasons of state backed by diplomatic initiatives and, ultimately, by coercive means. But this power logic is singularly inadequate and inappropriate to resolve the many complex issues, from economic regulation to resource depletion and environmental degradation, which engender—at seemingly ever greater speeds –an intermeshing of 'national fortunes'. In a world where powerful states make decisions not just for their peoples but for others as well, and where transnational actors and forces cut across the boundaries of national communities in diverse ways, the questions of who should be accountable to whom, and on what basis, do not easily resolve themselves. Political space for the development and pursuit of effective government and the accountability of power is no longer coterminous with a delimited political territory. Contemporary forms of political globalization involve a complex deterritorialization and re-territorialization of political authority.[47]

Giving a shape to prospective world orders

Virtually all nation-states have gradually become enmeshed in and functionally part of a larger pattern of global transformations and global flows.[48] Transnational networks and relations have developed across virtually all areas of human activity. Goods, capital, people, knowledge, communications and weapons, as well as crime, pollutants, fashions and beliefs, rapidly move across territorial boundaries . Far from this being a world of 'discrete civilizations', or simply an international society of states, it has become a fundamentally interconnected global order, marked by intense patterns of interaction as well as by evident structures of power, hierarchy and unevenness.

Contemporary globalization is associated with a transformation of state power as the roles and functions of states are re-articulated, reconstituted and re-embedded at the intersection of globalizing and regionalizing networks and systems. The metaphors of the loss, diminution or erosion of state power can misrepresent this reconfiguration. Indeed, such a language involves a failure to conceptualize adequately the nature of power and its complex manifestations since it represents a crude zero-sum view of power. The latter conception is particularly unhelpful in attempting to understand the apparently contradictory position of states under conditions of contemporary globalization. For whilst globalization is engendering, for instance, a

---

[47] See, in particular, J. Rosenau, *Along the Domestic–Foreign Frontier* (Cambridge, 1997).
[48] T. Nierop, *Systems and Regions in Global Politics* (London, 1994), p. 171.

reconfiguration of state–market relations in the economic domain, states and international public authorities are deeply implicated in this very process. Economic globalization by no means necessarily translates into a diminution of state power; rather, it is transforming the conditions under which state power is exercised. In other domains, such as the military, states have adopted a more activist posture, whilst in the political domain they have been central to the explosive growth and institutionalization of regional and global governance. These are not developments which can be explained convincingly in the language of the decline, erosion or loss of state power *per se*. For such metaphors (mistakenly) presume that state power was much greater in previous epochs; and, as Mann reminds us, on almost every conceivable measure states, especially in the developed world, are far more powerful than their antecedents.[49] But so too are the demands placed upon them. The apparent simultaneous weakening and expansion of the power of states under conditions of contemporary globalization is symptomatic of an underlying structural transformation. This is nowhere so evident as in respect of state sovereignty and autonomy, which constitute the very ideological foundations of the modern state.

There are many good reasons for doubting the theoretical and empirical basis of claims that states are being eclipsed by contemporary patterns of globalization. The position taken in this article is critical both of hyperglobalizers and of sceptics. We would emphasize that while regional and global interaction networks are strengthening, they have multiple and variable impacts across diverse locales. Moreover, it is not part of our argument that national sovereignty today, even in regions with intensive overlapping and divided authority structures, has been wholly subverted— such a view would radically misstate our position. But it is part of our argument that there are significant areas and regions marked by criss-crossing loyalties, conflicting interpretations of human rights and duties, interconnected legal and authority structures, etc., which displace notions of sovereignty as an illimitable, indivisible and exclusive form of public power. Patterns of regional and global change are transforming the nature and context of political action, creating a system of multiple power centres and overlapping spheres of authority.

Neither the sovereignty nor the autonomy of states is simply diminished by such processes. Indeed, any assessment of the cumulative impacts of globalization must acknowledge their highly differentiated character since particular types of impact— whether decisional, institutional, distributional or structural—are not experienced uniformly by all states. Globalization is by no means an homogenizing force. The impact of globalization is mediated significantly by a state's position in global political, military and economic hierarchies; its domestic economic and political structures; the institutional pattern of domestic politics; and specific government as well as societal strategies for contesting, managing or ameliorating globalizing imperatives.[50] The ongoing transformation of the Westphalian regime of sovereignty and autonomy has differential consequences for different states.

Whilst for many hyperglobalizers contemporary globalization is associated with new limits to politics and the erosion of state power, the argument developed here is critical of such political fatalism. For contemporary globalization has not only

[49] See Mann, 'Has Globalization Ended the Rise and Rise of the Nation-state?'.

[50] See A. Hurrell and N. Woods, 'Globalization and Inequality', *Millennium*, 24:3 (1995), pp. 447–70; R. O. Keohane and H. V. Milner (eds.), *Internationalization and Domestic Politics* (Cambridge, 1996); Jessop, 'Capitalism and its Future'; Mann, 'Has Globalization Ended the Rise and Rise of the Nation-state?'.

triggered or reinforced the significant politicization of a growing array of issue-areas, it has also been accompanied by an extraordinary growth of institutionalized arenas and networks of political mobilization, surveillance, decision-making and regulatory activity which transcend national political jurisdictions. This has expanded enormously the capacity for, and scope of, political activity and the exercise of political authority. In this respect, globalization is not, nor has it ever been, beyond regulation and control. Globalization does not prefigure the 'end of politics' so much as its continuation by new means. Yet, this is not to overlook the profound intellectual, institutional and normative challenge which it presents to the existing organization of political communities.

At the heart of this lies a growth in transborder political issues and problems which erode clearcut distinctions between domestic and foreign affairs, internal political issues and external questions, the sovereign concerns of the nation-state and international considerations. In all major areas of government policy, the enmeshment of national political communities in regional and global processes involves them in intensive issues of transboundary coordination and control. Political space for the development and pursuit of effective government and the accountability of political power is no longer coterminous with a delimited national territory. The growth of transboundary problems creates what was earlier referred to as 'overlapping communities of fate'; that is, a state of affairs in which the fortune and prospects of individual political communities are increasingly bound together.[51] Political communities are locked into a diversity of processes and structures which range in and through them, linking and fragmenting them into complex constellations. Moreover, national communities themselves by no means make and determine decisions and policies exclusively for themselves when they decide on such issues as the regulation of sexuality, health and the environment; national governments by no means simply determine what is right or appropriate exclusively for their own citizens.

These issues are most apparent in Europe, where the development of the European Union has created intensive discussion about the future of sovereignty and autonomy within individual nation-states. But the issues are important not just for Europe and the West, but for countries in other parts of the world, for example, Japan and South Korea. These countries must recognize new emerging problems, for instance, problems concerning AIDS, migration and new challenges to peace, security and economic prosperity, which spill over the boundaries of nation-states. In addition, the communities of East Asia are developing within the context of growing interconnectedness across the world's major regions. This interconnectedness is marked in a whole range of areas from the environment, human rights, trade and finance, to issues of international crime. There are emerging overlapping communities of fate generating common problems within and across the East Asian region. In other words, East Asia, as recent developments have demonstrated, is necessarily part of a more global order and is locked into a diversity of sites of power which shape and determine its collective fortunes.

The idea of government or of the state, democratic or otherwise, can no longer be simply defended as an idea suitable to a particular closed political community or nation-state. The system of national political communities persists of course; but it

---

[51] See Held, *Democracy and the Global Order*; *Models of Democracy*, second edition (Cambridge, 1996); and Archibugi, Held and Köhler, *Re-imagining Political Community*.

is articulated and re-articulated today with complex economic, organizational, administrative, legal and cultural processes and structures which limit and check its efficacy. If these processes and structures are not acknowledged and brought into the political process they will tend to bypass or circumvent the traditional mechanisms of political accountability and regulation. In other words, we must recognize that political power is being repositioned, recontextualized and, to a degree, transformed by the growing importance of other less territorially based power systems. Political power is now sandwiched in more complex power systems which have become more salient over time relative to state power.

Accordingly, we are compelled to recognize that the extensity, intensity and impact of a broad range of issues (economic, political or environmental) raise questions about where those issues are most appropriately addressed. If the most powerful geo-political forces are not to settle many pressing matters simply in terms of their own objectives and by virtue of their power, then existing institutions and mechanisms of accountability need to be reconsidered. Such a reconsideration is an essential part of political inquiry, as Carr understood it. Political analysis, he wrote, 'must be based on a recognition of the interdependence of theory and practice, which can be attained only through a combination of utopia and reality'.[52] Thus, he always sought to link substantive inquiry into power with normative reflection on its desirable form. Pursuing this dual focus, we explore below recent approaches to the reconsideration of the proper nature and form of political power in the face of contemporary globalization. Indeed, it is possible to identify four leading schools of thought—the neo-liberal, liberal-reformist, radical and cosmopolitan—which together contribute a taxonomy of prospective world orders.

For the advocates of a neo-liberal world order, globalization today defines a new epoch in human history in which 'traditional nation-states have become unnatural, even impossible business units in a global economy'.[53] Such a view privileges an economic logic and affirms the emergence of a single global market alongside the principle of global competition as the harbingers of human progress. The neo-liberals celebrate the fact that economic globalization is bringing about a denationalization of economies through the establishment of transnational networks of production, trade and finance. In this 'borderless' economy, national governments are relegated to little more than transmission belts for global market forces. As Strange interprets this view, 'where states were once the masters of markets, now it is the market, which, on many critical issues, is the master over the governments of states... the declining authority of states is reflected in a growing diffusion of authority to other institutions and associations, and to local and regional bodies'.[54]

For the elites and 'knowledge workers' in this new global economy tacit transnational 'class' allegiances have evolved, cemented by an ideological attachment to a neo-liberal economic orthodoxy. Even amongst the marginalized and dispossessed the world-wide diffusion of a consumerist ideology also imposes a new sense of identity, displacing traditional cultures and ways of life. The global spread of Western liberal democracy further reinforces the sense of an emerging civilization defined by universal standards of economic and political organization. This civilization is replete with mechanisms of global governance, whether it be the IMF

[52] Carr, *The Twenty Years' Crisis*, p. 13. See also his remarks on realism and utopianism on p. 10.
[53] Ohmae, *The End of the Nation State*, p. 5.
[54] Strange, *The Retreat of the State*, p. 4.

or the disciplines of the world market, such that states and peoples are increasingly the subjects of a plurality of new public and private, global and regional, authorities. Accordingly, globalization is considered by many neo-liberals as the harbinger of the first truly 'global civilization'.[55] This represents a radically new world order; one which its advocates argue prefigures the demise of the nation-state and the liberation of peoples to pursue their interests unencumbered from the dictates of the stifling bureaucracy and the power politics of states. Economic power and political power, in this view, are becoming effectively denationalized and diffused such that nation-states are increasingly becoming 'a transitional mode of organization for managing economic affairs'.[56] For neo-liberals this is to be welcomed since it represents nothing less than the fundamental reconfiguration of world order to fit with the aspirations of peoples rather than states.

Rooted in what Carr referred to as the 'harmony of interests' between states—as opposed to a world shaped by global competition and global markets—liberal-reformism considers that political necessity will bring about a more cooperative world order. Avoiding global ecological crisis and managing the pervasive social, economic and political dislocation arising from contemporary processes of economic globalization 'will require the articulation of a collaborative ethos based upon the principles of consultation, transparency, and accountability. . . . There is no alternative to working together and using collective power to create a better world'.[57] In key respects, liberal-reformism is a normative theory which seeks to recast elements of world order. In essence, its contemporary advocates, such as the Commission on Global Governance, aim to construct a more democratic world in which states are more accountable to peoples. In late 1995 the Commission published its report, *Our Global Neighbourhood*.[58] The report recognizes the profound political impact of globalization: 'The shortening of distance, the multiplying of links, the deepening of interdependence: all these factors, and their interplay, have been transforming the world into a neighbourhood'.[59]

To achieve a more secure, just and democratic world order the report proposes a multifaceted strategy of international institutional reform and the nurturing of a new global civic ethic. Central to its proposals is a reformed United Nations system buttressed by the strengthening, or creation, of regional forms of international governance, such as the EU. Through the establishment of a Peoples' Assembly and a Forum of [Global] Civil Society, both associated with the UN General Assembly, the world's peoples are to be represented directly and indirectly in the institutions of global governance. Moreover, the Commission proposes that individuals and groups be given a right of petition to the UN through a Council of Petitions, which will recommend action to the appropriate agency. Combined with the deeper entrenchment of a common set of global rights and responsibilities the aim is to strengthen notions of global citizenship. An Economic Security Council is proposed to coordinate global economic governance, making it more open and accountable. Democratic forms of governance within states are to be nurtured and strengthened through international support mechanisms whilst the principles of sovereignty and

---

[55] See Perlmutter, 'On the Rocky Road to the First Global Civilization'.
[56] Ohmae, *The End of the Nation State*, p. 149.
[57] Commission of Global Governance, *Our Global Neighbourhood* (Oxford, 1995), pp. 2 and 5.
[58] Ibid.
[59] Ibid., p. 43.

non-intervention are to be adapted 'in ways that recognize the need to balance the rights of states with the rights of people, and the interests of nations with the interests of the global neighbourhood'.[60] Binding all these reforms together is a commitment to the nurturing of a new global civic ethic based upon 'core values that all humanity could uphold: respect for life, liberty, justice and equity, mutual respect, caring, and integrity',[61] central to this global civic ethic is the principle of participation in governance at all levels from the local to the global.

Richard Falk has referred to the Commission as the 'last of the great liberal commissions'.[62] Given their faith in progress and human rationality, liberal-reformists, since the last century, have argued that creating a peaceful and democratic world order is far from a utopian project but, on the contrary, a necessity in a world of growing interdependence. As a normative theory of world order, it is concerned with how to reform the system of states with the aim of abolishing power politics and war. In the twentieth century, liberal-reformist ideology has played a critical role in the design of international institutions, specifically under US hegemony, in the aftermath of both the First and Second world wars. The creation of the League of Nations, and a 'world safe for democracy', was effused with such ideology, as was the establishment of the UN system. In the context of the post-Cold War New World Order, liberal-reformist ideas have acquired renewed vitality but have been adapted to fit 'new times'. Whilst still remaining faithful to the liberal political ideal—'to subject the rule of arbitrary power . . . to the rule of law within global society'[63]—contemporary thinking, as reflected in the Commission's report, is decidedly reformist rather than radical. Reformist in this context refers to incremental adaptation of the institutions and practices of world order, as opposed to their reconstruction. As expressed by Keohane, this is a normative vision of 'voluntary pluralism under conditions of maximum transparency'—a harking back to Woodrow Wilson's notion of open covenants openly arrived at.[64] It is reformist also in the sense that it gives 'peoples' a voice in global governance whilst not challenging the primacy of states and the most powerful states at that. Thus, the accountability and legitimacy of institutions of global governance are ensured 'not only by chains of official responsibility but by the requirement of transparency. Official actions, negotiated amongst state representatives in international organizations, will be subject to scrutiny by transnational networks'.[65]

While liberal-reformism emphasizes the necessary adaptation of core organizations in the existing world order, contemporary advocates of the 'radical project' stress the creation of *alternative* mechanisms of governance based upon civic republican principles: that is, inclusive, deliberative and self-governing communities in which the public good is to the fore.[66] The 'radical republican project' is concerned to establish the necessary conditions which will empower people to take control of

---

[60] Ibid., p. 337.

[61] Ibid., p. 336.

[62] R. Falk, 'Liberalism at the Global Level: The Last of the Independent Commissions?', *Millennium*, 24: 3 (1995), pp. 563–78.

[63] Commission on Global Governance, *Our Global Neighboughood*, p. 5.

[64] R. Keohane, 'International Institutions: Can Interdependence Work?', *Foreign Policy* (Spring, 1998), pp. 82–96.

[65] Ibid.

[66] cf. Burnheim, *Is Democracy Possible?* (Cambridge, 1985); R. B. J. Walker, *One World, Many Worlds* (Boulder, CO., 1988); R. Falk, *On Humane Governance* (Cambridge, 1995).

their own lives and to create communities based upon ideas of equality, the common good, and harmony with the natural environment. For many radical republicans the agents of change are to be found in existing (critical) social movements, such as the environmental, women's and peace movements, which challenge the authority of states and international agencies as well as orthodox definitions of the 'political'. Through a politics of resistance and empowerment these new social movements are conceived as playing a crucial role in creating a new world order in a manner similar to the role of the (old) social movements, such as organized labour, in the struggle for national democracy. These new social movements are engaged in mobilizing transnational communities of resistance and solidarity against impending global ecological, economic and security crises. Underlying these projects is an attachment to the achievement of social and economic equality, the establishment of the necessary conditions for self-development, and the creation of self-governing political structures. Encouraging and developing in citizens a sense of simultaneous belonging to overlapping (local and global) communities is central to the politics of new social movements as well as to the search for new models and forms of social, political and economic organization consonant with the republican principle of self-government. The radical republican model is a 'bottom up' vision of civilizing world order. It represents a normative theory of 'humane governance' which is grounded in the existence of a multiplicity of 'communities of fate' and social movements, as opposed to the individualism and appeals to rational self-interest of neo-liberalism and liberal-reformism.

The cosmopolitan project, finally, attempts to specify the principles and the institutional arrangements for making accountable those sites and forms of power which presently operate beyond the scope of democratic control.[67] It argues that in the millennium ahead each citizen of a state will have to learn to become a 'cosmopolitan citizen' as well: that is, a person capable of mediating between national traditions, communities of fate and alternative forms of life. Citizenship in a democratic polity of the future, it is argued, is likely to involve a growing mediating role: a role which encompasses dialogue with the traditions and discourses of others with the aim of expanding the horizons of one's own framework of meaning and prejudice, and increasing the scope of mutual understanding. Political agents who can 'reason from the point-of-view of others' will be better equipped to resolve, and resolve fairly, the new and challenging transboundary issues and processes that create overlapping communities of fate. In addition, the cosmopolitan project contends that, if many contemporary forms of power are to become accountable and if many of the complex issues that effect us all—locally, nationally, regionally and globally—are to be democratically regulated, people will have to have access to, and membership in, *diverse* political communities. Put differently, a democratic political community for the new millennium necessarily describes a world where citizens enjoy multiple citizenships. Faced with overlapping communities of fate they need to be not only citizens of their own communities, but also of the wider regions in which they live, and of the wider global order. Institutions will certainly need to develop that reflect the multiple issues, questions and problems that link people together regardless of the particular nation-states in which they were born or brought up.

[67] See Held, *Democracy and the Global Order*; A. Linklater, *The Transformation of Political Community* (Cambridge, 1998); Archibugi, Held and Köhler, *Re-imagining Political Community*.

With this in mind, advocates of the cosmopolitan position maintain that the reform of world order needs to be rethought as a 'double-sided process'. By a double-sided process—or process of double democratization—is meant not just the deepening of democracy within a national community, involving the democratiz-ation of states and civil societies over time, but also the extension of democratic forms and processes across territorial borders. Democracy for the new millennium must allow cosmopolitan citizens to gain access to, mediate between, and render accountable, the social, economic and political processes and flows which cut across and transform their traditional community boundaries. The core of this project involves re-conceiving legitimate political activity in a manner which disconnects it from its traditional anchor in fixed borders and delimited territories and, instead, articulates it as an attribute of basic democratic arrangements or basic democratic law which can, in principle, be entrenched and drawn upon in diverse self-regulating associations—from cities and subnational regions, to nation-states, regions and wider global networks. It is clear that the process of disconnection has already begun as political authority and legitimate forms of governance are diffused 'below', 'above' and 'alongside' the nation-state. But the cosmopolitan project is in favour of a radical extension of this process so long as it is circumscribed and delimited by a commitment to a far-reaching cluster of democratic rights and duties. It proposes a series of short- and long-term measures in the conviction that, through a process of progressive, incremental change, geo-political forces will come to be socialized into democratic agencies and practices.[68]

Conclusion

It has been argued that the contemporary historical phase of globalization is transforming the very foundations of world order by reconstituting traditional forms of sovereign statehood, political community and international political relations. But these transformative processes are neither historically inevitable nor by any means fully secure. As a result, the contemporary world order is best understood as a highly complex, contested and interconnected order in which the interstate system is increasingly embedded within evolving regional and global political networks. The latter are the basis in and through which political authority and mechanisms of governance are being articulated and re-articulated. To refer to the contemporary world order as a complex, contested, interconnected order is to acknowledge the 'messy appearances' which define global politics at the turn of the new millennium. Globalization involves a shift away from a purely state-centric politics to a new more complex form of multilayered global governance. There are multiple, overlapping political processes at work at the present historical conjuncture.

In reflecting upon the inter-war years, Carr argued that the real lesson of this epoch of international crisis was 'the final and irrevocable breakdown of the conditions which made the nineteenth-century order possible'.[69] To seek to restore that order was, in Carr's judgement, a useless project. Yet, in certain respects, that

[68] See Held, ibid., pt. III.
[69] Carr, *The Twenty Years Crisis*, p. 237.

was precisely what many of the architects of the post-war order sought to achieve and in so doing unleashed a new, distinctive phase of globalization. At the close of the twentieth century there are strong reasons for believing that, under conditions of contemporary globalization, the old states order can never be fully restored or effectively realized. Paradoxically, the idealism of the contemporary epoch tends to be most in evidence amongst those strands of international political analysis which conceive of world order as an expression of eternal truths—whether couched in terms of power politics or of the market—but which have yet to come to terms with the transformative impacts of contemporary globalization. Today, in Carr's words, 'the old order cannot be restored, and a drastic change of outlook is unavoidable'.[70] Such changes of outlook are clearly delineated in the contest between neo-liberalism, liberal-reformism, radicalism and cosmopolitanism. Globalization is not, as some suggest, narrowing or foreclosing political discussion; on the contrary, it is reilluminating and reinvigorating the contemporary political terrain.

[70] Ibid.

Index